D0399170

DISCARD

DISCARD

TOBIAS SMOLLETT: THE CRITICAL HERITAGE

THE CRITICAL HERITAGE SERIES

GENERAL EDITOR: B. C. SOUTHAM, M.A., B. LITT. (OXON.)
Formerly Department of English, Westfield College, University of London

For a list of books in the series see the back endpaper

TOBIAS SMOLLETT

THE CRITICAL HERITAGE

Edited by
LIONEL KELLY
Lecturer in English
University of Reading

ROUTLEDGE & KEGAN PAUL
LONDON AND NEW YORK

First published in 1987 by
Routledge & Kegan Paul Ltd
11 New Fetter Lane, London EC4P 4EE

Published in the USA by
Routledge & Kegan Paul Inc.
in association with Methuen Inc.
29 West 35th Street, New York, NY 10001

Set in 10/12 pt Bembo
by Thomson Press (India) Ltd,
New Delhi
and printed in Great Britain
by T J Press (Padstow) Ltd
Padstow, Cornwall

Compilation, introduction, notes, bibliography and index
© Lionel Kelly 1987

No part of this book may be reproduced in any form without permission
from the publisher
except for the quotation of brief passages
in criticism

Library of Congress Cataloging in Publication Data

Tobias Smollett: the critical heritage.

(The Critical heritage series)
Bibliography: p.
Includes index.
1. Smollett, Tobias George, 1721–1771—Criticism and interpretation.
I. Smollett, Tobias George, 1721–1771.
II. Kelly, Lionel. III. Series.
PR3697.T64   1987   823'.6.   86–25977

British Library CIP Data also available

ISBN 0–7102–0905–3

General Editor's Preface

The reception given to a writer by his contemporaries and near-contemporaries is evidence of considerable value to the student of literature. On one side we learn a great deal about the state of criticism at large and in particular about the development of critical attitudes towards a single writer; at the same time, through private comments in letters, journals or marginalia, we gain an insight upon the tastes and literary thought of individual readers of the period. Evidence of this kind helps us to understand the writer's historical situation, the nature of his immediate reading-public, and his response to these pressures.

The separate volumes in the *Critical Heritage Series* present a record of this early criticism. Clearly, for many of the highly productive and lengthily reviewed nineteenth- and twentieth-century writers, there exists an enormous body of material; and in these cases the volume editors have made a selection of the most important views, significant for their intrinsic critical worth or for their representative quality—perhaps even registering incomprehension!

For earlier writers, notably pre-eighteenth century, the materials are much scarcer and the historical period has been extended, sometimes far beyond the writer's lifetime, in order to show the inception and growth of critical views which were initially slow to appear.

In each volume the documents are headed by an Introduction, discussing the material assembled and relating the early stages of the author's reception to what we have come to identify as the critical tradition. The volumes will make available much material which would otherwise be difficult of access and it is hoped that the modern reader will be thereby helped towards an informed understanding of the ways in which literature has been read and judged.

B.C.S.

224278

Contents

CONTENTS

On *Roderick Random*

On *Don Quixote* (1755)

Roderick Random in Germany (1755)

Roderick Random (1755)

The Reprisal (1757)

The Complete History (1757)

Smollett as Critic

The Complete History

Smollett as Critic

Roderick Random (1760)

Sir Launcelot Greaves (1760)

CONTENTS

Critics at War

55 Anonymous, from *The Battle of the Reviews*, 1760   162

Smollett as Historian

56 Unsigned review, *The Imperial Magazine*, October 1760   169
57 HORACE WALPOLE, from *Memoirs of King George the Second*, 1760   170
58 CHARLES CHURCHILL, from *The Apology*, May 1761   171

Sir Launcelot Greaves (1762)

59 Unsigned notice, *The Monthly Review*, May 1762   173
60 Unsigned review, *The Critical Review*, May 1762   173
61 Unsigned notice, *The Library*, May 1762   175
62 [WILLIAM RIDER], from *Living Authors of Great-Britain*, 1762   176
63 RICHARD SMITH, letter to Tobias Smollett, 26 February 1763   177
64 TOBIAS SMOLLETT, letter to Richard Smith, 8 May 1763   179
65 CHARLES CHURCHILL, from *The Author*, December 1763   179
66 GIUSEPPE BARETTI, from *Frustra Letteraria*, 20 January 1764   181

Travels Through France and Italy (1766)

67 [JOHN BERKENHOUT], *The Monthly Review*, June 1766   182
68 Unsigned notice, *The London Magazine*, 1766   184
69 Unsigned review, *The Royal Magazine*, May 1766   185

Smollett and Marivaux

70 Anonymous, *The British Magazine*, September 1766   185
71 'MERCURIUS SPUR' [CUTHBERT SHAW], from *The Race*, 1766   186

Travels Through France and Italy

72 PHILIP THICKNESSE, from *Observations on the French Nation*, 1766   187
73 MADAME RICCOBONI, from a letter to David Garrick, 14 November 1767   189

Smollett as Poet

74 OLIVER GOLDSMITH, from *The Beauties of English Poesy*, 1767   189

Travels Through France and Italy

75 LAURENCE STERNE, from *A Sentimental Journey*, 1768   190

x

Adventures of an Atom (1769)

Humphry Clinker (1771)

Humphry Clinker

Ode to Independence

Life and Works

Plays and Poems (1777)

CONTENTS

CONTENTS

CONTENTS

Scott on Smollett

Dickens on Smollett

Preface

Criticism of the novel in the eighteenth century is rarely an exercise of profound judgment. If it is a commonplace that the form itself was relatively new, it is also true that the most acute criticism of fiction comes from its practitioners, and the different practice of one novelist from another; as in the treatment of Richardson's *Pamela* by Fielding in *Shamela* and *Joseph Andrews*. Smollett's own contribution to this creative criticism lies in the energy of his application to a variety of possible forms—the picaresque, the Gothic, the Quixotic and the epistolary. The contemporary response to his novels often amounts to little more than generalized comments in terms of approbation for his understanding of life and manners, and his capacity for satirizing human weakness and folly in a vein of humour seen at once as abrasively vigorous and humanly just. There are numerous occasions when his critics go beyond these simple boundaries in brief illuminating moments. A public man of letters, Smollett was engaged in a variety of literary enterprizes, as a poet, dramatist, critic and historian. Much contemporary criticism of him is focused on these activities, rather than his novels. I have sought to give some examples of responses to his work in these spheres, but my main concern is to show what was reported and written about the novels, both in private and public documents. After 1756, Smollett's career, and his reputation, is intimately bound up with the development of the literary periodical as a new locus for public criticism of contemporary literature.

The effective cut-off date is 1821, with Sir Walter Scott's major critical account of Smollett; this text seems to me a proper conclusion, because it is the work not only of a fellow novelist, but also a fellow Scot. However, one later great English novelist could not be ignored: Charles Dickens. Dicken's personal enthusiasm for Smollett both affected his own work as a novelist, and encouraged a wider public audience for Smollett's novels.

Acknowledgments

Like all those who work on Smollett I am deeply indebted to Professor Lewis M. Knapp for his *Tobias Smollett: Doctor of Men and Manners*; for his exemplary edition of *The Letters of Tobias Smollett*; and for his personal encouragment. My work was greatly assisted by Fred W. Boege's *Smollett's Reputation as a Novelist*, and by all those who added to the bibliography of eighteenth- and nineteenth-century criticism of Smollett. In this connection I should like to record my gratitude to Professor Paul-Gabriel Boucé, who shared with me his unrivalled knowledge of Smollett criticism.

I should like to record my gratitude to the following libraries for their assistance, and permission to reprint material from their collections: the Bodleian Library, the British Library, Cambridge University Library, Dundee Public Library, the Library of Friends House, London, and Reading University Library. I am grateful to the Research Board of the University of Reading for grants to assist in the preparation of this work.

I am also grateful to Oxford University Press for permission to reprint material from the *Poetical Works of Charles Churchill* (1956) edited by Douglas Grant; the *Collected Works of Oliver Goldsmith* (1966) edited by Arthur Friedman; the *Complete Letters of Lady Mary Wortley Montagu* (1966) edited by Robert Halsband; the *Selected Letters of Samuel Richardson* (1964) edited by John Carroll; the *Letters of Richard Brinsley Sheridan* (1966) edited by Cecil Price; and the *Letters of Tobias Smollett* (1970) edited by Lewis M. Knapp. Thanks also to the William Andrews Clark Memorial Library, Los Angeles, for permission to reprint material from the Augustan Reprint Society's issue of Francis Coventry's *Essay on the New Species of Writing* (1962); and The Beinecke Rare Book and Manuscript Library, Yale University, for permission to quote from their copy of William Rider's *An Historical and Critical Account of the Lives and Writings of the Living Authors of Great Britain*.

I am grateful to many friends and colleagues who have generously helped me: to Dr Dinah Birch, Professor and Mrs W.F. Bolton, Dr Barrie Bullen, Faith Evans, Mrs Patricia Medhurst, Dr

John Pilling, Professor W. Redfern, Dr John Stokes, Dr Christopher Thacker, Professor A. Wardman, and Dr I. Williams. I owe a special debt of gratitude to my colleague Dr Nicola Bradbury for her help and her patience. I should like to give to Smollett himself the last words of these prefatory remarks, conscious that whatever is 'elegant' in this volume is due to his genius. I quote from *The Present State of All Nations*, London, 1768, vol. 2, pp. 224–5.

The task of collecting, collating and arranging old papers and records, is but ill suited to the impatience of the English disposition; but, this labour being in a great measure surmounted by those who had no other merit than industry, divers English authors have lately exhibited elegant, specimens of historical talents.

Introduction

Smollett's reputation has both benefited and suffered from his connection with more famous writers. In the Preface to his first novel, *Roderick Random*, he himself invoked the example of Cervantes and Le Sage. He translated Le Sage's picaresque novel *Gil Blas* in 1748 and Cervantes' *Don Quixote* in 1755. For a British novelist there were advantages and disadvantages to being a contemporary of Richardson and Fielding. *Roderick Random*, published anonymously in 1748, was thought by some to be by Fielding, while Smollett's inclusion in his second novel, *Peregrine Pickle*, of *The Memoirs of a Lady of Quality* attracted the censure of Richardson and his admirers. The savagery and comic bravura of his humour invoked comparison with Rabelais and Swift for many eighteenth-century critics, and distinction in tone from Sternian comic pathos. To later readers, he was associated with Sir Walter Scott by nationality, and later still was seen as a precursor to Dickens. Today the links with Fielding and Dickens seem most potent. Smollett's work as a comic novelist invites comparison with Fielding's; yet, if we think of the form of the novel his range is greater, though without Fielding's masterly control of plot. For Dickens, as for many other nineteenth-century writers, the pleasures of boyhood reading were intimately associated with Smollett, and for many of us the first encounter with Smollett's reputation comes early in the pages of *David Copperfield* where David is engaged to read aloud from *Peregrine Pickle* to Steerforth. Despite Dickens's partiality to Smollett, his critical reading of him is acute, and informs his incisively simple judgment that Smollett's way as a novelist was 'a way without tenderness'.[1]

For his contemporaries, Smollett was well known not only as a novelist but also as editor of one of the foremost journals of his day, *The Critical Review*. He had a considerable reputation too, as an historian, poet and playwright, though in this last he was least successful. As a qualified doctor, on intimate terms with the most distinguished medical men of his day, he took a lively interest in all the sciences, and often reviewed scientific books in *The Critical*

Review. His *Essay on the External Uses of Water*, 1752, argues the value of non-mineral water in cold and hot baths, and warns of the unhygenic conditions of the spa waters at Bath. The sense left by the most severely moralizing critics of the nineteenth century that Smollett was an uncouth man who wrote uncouth books is remote from the truth. He was a cultivated man of wide learning, experience and sensibility, who, like his contemporaries Johnson and Goldsmith, earned his living by his pen. He was a typical eighteenth-century man of letters, and if he was of Grub Street, he often rose above it.

I. BEGINNINGS; *RODERICK RANDOM*, 1748

Born in 1721 in Dumbartonshire, Scotland, Smollett went to Dumbarton Grammar School and later attended Glasgow University. In 1736 he was apprenticed to William Stirling and John Gordon, surgeons of Glasgow. If his late schooling prepared him for a medical career, his ambition was to write, and in 1739, at the age of eighteen, he left for London. Like Samuel Johnson before him, Smollett arrived in London with a tragedy in his pocket. It was a verse play on the story of James I of Scotland called *The Regicide*, a work he imagined would take the town by storm. He failed to get this performed, or printed until 1748, and the resultant animus he felt towards theatre managers, actors and noble patrons is told in fictional disguise in the sixty-second and sixty-third chapters of *Roderick Random*, in the inserted story of Melopoyn. A letter Smollett wrote to his Scots friend Alexander Carlyle in 1747 presents a neatly specific account of his difficulties with *The Regicide*:[2]

I am vain of your Approbation with regard to my Tragedy, which, as you imagine, suffered by the much lamented Death of Lord George Graham; tho', after the Assurances I had from many People of much greater Distinction and Influence than he, I little thought my Attempt to bring it on this Season could have been baffled by the Pitifull Intrigues of that little Rascal Garrick, who, at the time he gave me all the Incouragement I could desire, in assuring me he would contribute as much as in him lay, not only to bring it on, but also to act in it with all the ability he was master of, found means to prevail on Rich to reject it.[3]

Happily, his relations with Garrick improved in later years (No.

106) though Smollett was never a successful dramatist, as this comment in *The Critical Review* in 1757 shows: it occurs in a review of Smollett's comedy in two acts, *The Reprisal*, which was staged at the Drury Lane Theatre early that year:

The author does not seem to be so well acquainted with the *Jeu de théâtre* as some of his contemporaries: there is, however, throughout the performance a close imitation of nature, which will always please the judicious, though it may not set the galleries in a roar.[4]

Furthermore, when his plays were collected and published together with his poems in 1777, the reviews of that collection, whilst enthusiastic towards some of the poems, made little significant comment on the plays.

His beginnings as a poet were more successful. In the letter to Alexander Carlyle of 1747 he writes:

If I had an Opportunity, I would send you the New Play and Farce, Two Satires called Advice and Reproof which made some Noise here, and a Ballad set to Musick under the name of the Tears of Scotland, a Performance very well received at London.[5]

His two satires had been published in 1746 (*Advice*) and 1747 (*Reproof*), and they again invite comparison with Johnson. Indeed, it may well have been owing to the success of Johnson's imitation of Juvenal's third satire, *London*, of 1738, that Smollett tried his hand at satiric verse. *Advice* and *Reproof* present a dialogue between a poet and his friend on the injustices of the poet's present circumstances, a procedure Smollett might well have taken from the dialogue between Thales and his friend in Johnson's *London*; however, Smollett's poems are somewhat less than Johnsonian in quality, as this extract from the opening of *Advice* suggests:

> Enough, enough; all this we knew before;
> 'Tis infamous, I grant it, to be poor:
> And who so much to sense and glory lost,
> Will hug the curse that not one joy can boast!
> From the pale hag, O! could I once break loose;
> Divorc'd, all hell should not re-tie the noose!
> Not with more care shall H......avoid his wife,
> Not Cope flies Swifter lashing for his life:
> Than I to leave the meagre fiend behind.

Although these two satires, his early poem *The Tears of Scotland*

and the later *Ode to Independence* appeared in miscellaneous collections of poetry during his lifetime, the first collected edition of his poems is that of 1777.

His reputation rests principally on his achievement as a novelist, an achievement assured by the publication of *Roderick Random* in 1748. Published anonymously by J. Osborn in Paternoster Row, it excited considerable comment in polite society. There was no published criticism, however, because *Roderick Random* predates the practice of reviewing contemporary literature, which was initiated by Ralph Griffiths when he established *The Monthly Review* in May 1749. With Smollett's own later periodical, *The Critical Review*, which dates from March 1756, *The Monthly Review* was the foremost periodical of its kind, and the development of Smollett's reputation can be followed in these two journals throughout the course of his career.

Although *Roderick Random* was not reviewed immediately upon publication the response to it was enthusiastic, and it went into several editions in the next few years. With its success however there developed that persistent practice of reading the novel as disguised autobiography, which was encouraged by certain aspects of some of Smollett's later novels, such as his own appearance in *Humphry Clinker* when Jeremy Melford visits his Chelsea home. Alexander Carlyle's wry account of Smollett's meeting with the Scots historian William Robertson in 1758 recounts one example of such 'biographical' misinterpretation:

We passed a very pleasant and joyful evening. When we broke up, Robertson expressed great surprise at the polished and agreeable manners and the great urbanity of his conversation. He had imagined that a man's manners must bear a likeness to his books, and as Smollett had described so well the characters of ruffians and profligates, that he must, of course, resemble them. This was not the first instance we had of the rawness, in respect of the world, that still blunted our sagacious friend's observations.[6]

Given this mistaken assumption of coarseness in Smollett himself, it is interesting to note that the first reference to him in a periodical cites *Roderick Random* approvingly in an exhortation to morality (No. 6). In large part the critical response to *Roderick Random* is slight, and occurs in private documents such as letters. It may have been Smollett's own attempt to give the book new publicity that resulted in the laudatory anonymous *Remarks on*

Roderick Random inserted as a letter to the publisher in the 1755 Dublin edition, which claims to be the fourth edition (No. 42). The critical response to *Roderick Random* on the Continent was limited by two considerations: this, like his other novels, was badly translated, and his brand of humour was regarded by Continental critics as too English to travel well. In later years Smollett's reputation abroad was further adversely affected by the publication of his *Travels Through France and Italy*. Gotthold Lessing in a review of a German translation of *Roderick Random* in 1755 argues that it is unlikely to appeal to German 'readers of good taste' (No. 41). An extreme response to Smollett in France was voiced by Garrick's correspondent Mme Riccoboni, who, abjuring the *Travels Through France and Italy*, wrote that all Smollett's work was 'loathsome—I said loathsome' (No. 73). Yet, as we shall see from later discussion of the *Works*, *Roderick Random* remained a favourite with British commentators throughout the eighteenth century and beyond.

Roderick Random maintained its popularity on a number of counts. Though its structure is loosely episodic, it has a satisfying completeness of form. The plot charts several revolutions in Roderick's career: a prolonged series of adventures culminating in the restitution of family fortunes and his finding his rightful social place. Smollett gives the feel of actuality supported by particular reference to contemporary history in the shape of incident, scene and event, as in the chapters on the Voyage to Carthagena. Roderick himself is an engaging hero, tough, resourceful, passionate, gallant even, yet a man capable of refinement of feeling and expression. No less boyish than Tom Jones, he is sometimes coarser than his famous contemporary. In the sustained depiction of that camaraderie between Roderick and his companion Strap, Smollett has anglicized and familiarized the Don Quixote/Sancho Panza relationship from Cervantes. The use of the inset narrative is familiar from European picaresque, but in Smollett the interpolated stories of Miss Williams and the dramatist Melopoyn introduce elements of documentary realism into the fiction. He satisfies the demands of verisimilitude associated with the development of eighteenth-century fiction out of and away from the conventions of Romance. Smollett's great strength is in making characters. The figures in *Roderick Random* compose a gallery of portraits often distinguished by national or professional characteristics. This is a dominant feature of his work, whether the tone is scornful, neutral, or lovingly enthusiastic, and is particularly remarkable in Smollett's portrayal of doctors and naval men. Of this latter type an enduring favourite appears in *Roderick Random* in the figure of Lieutenant Bowling, who anticipates Trunnion, Hatchway and Pipes in *Peregrine Pickle*. Eighteenth- and nineteenth-century commentators on Smollett remark on each of these aspects of his work, but most frequently they recall individual characters.

The first published criticism of *Roderick Random* is in the remarks of 'an Oxford scholar' in an anonymous pamphlet (No. 5). It appears in a form closely associated with Smollett's reputation throughout the 1750s, when anonymous and pseudonymous pamphlets were spawned by the inclusion of Lady Vane's *Memoirs of a Lady of Quality* in *Peregrine Pickle*, and by Smollett's work as a reviewer in *The Critical Review*.

II. *PEREGRINE PICKLE* AND *THE MEMOIRS OF A LADY OF QUALITY*

Peregrine Pickle is, in design and structure, a repeat of the successful formula of *Roderick Random*, expanded in length and varied in incident. The history of Peregrine's boyhood is enriched by the invention of three naval characters—Commodore Trunnion, Lieutenant Hatchway and the bosun's mate Pipes—who become the favourites of later commentators on the book, and in one case the focus of an interesting attack on the authority of Smollett's naval portraits (No. 134). The novel contains what is now regarded as a sustained prose satire on the Grand Tour,[7] and features a series of portraits of Smollett's contemporaries, some satiric and some benign.[8] Like *Roderick Random*, it includes contemporary events and incidents, as in the representation of the Annesley Case.[9] But that part of the novel which attracted most contemporary attention is not Smollett's work.

Smollett's second novel did not repeat the commercial success of his first. It was not reprinted until 1757. The received view is that because Smollett retained copyright to the novel, the publishers did little to push it. Its reception was also complicated by the inclusion of Lady Frances Anne Vane's *Memoirs of a Lady of Quality* as chapter 88 of the first edition. Little is known about the relationship between Smollett and Lady Vane which might account for the use of her story in the novel. As far as it can be simply told, the story is as follows.

Lady Frances Vane was born Frances Anne Hawes in 1713. In 1732 at the age of nineteen she married William Hamilton, second son of the fourth Duke of Hamilton. Her husband, returned MP for Lanarkshire in 1734, died in that year. A year later she married the very wealthy and eccentric William Holles, Viscount Vane, cousin of the Duke of Newcastle. A great beauty in her late teens and early twenties, Lady Vane was reported to be unrecognizable by a correspondent who met her again when she was thirty-seven:

Lady Vane was there, with her Lord, and began several balls. She seems quite easy, though no woman of any rank took the least notice of her. In my whole life I never saw anybody altered to the degree she is. I have not seen her near since her days of innocence and beauty, and really should not have known her if I had not been told her name, as there is not the least remains of what she was.[10]

After decades of marital quarrels with Viscount Vane, and a series of much publicized affairs, she lived in comparative retirement in Hill Street, Berkeley Square, where she died at the age of 65 on 31 March 1778. A view of her at the zenith of her beauty is given by Lieutenant Colonel Charles Russell writing from Ghent on 9 June 1742, to his wife in London:

The greatest beauty we have here has followed us from England, which is Lady Vane, who arrived here last Monday night, and in reality has followed the brigade of Guards, which, as soon as she is tired with, intends to proceed to Brussels. She has no woman with her, and walks about each evening with an officer on each side of her.[11]

There is no record of comment from Lady Vane on the impact of her *Memoirs* in *Peregrine Pickle*. Nor is there evidence that Smollett was on terms of social intimacy with her. He refers to her once, neutrally, in a letter to John Moore of 1750.[12] There is no verification of the early story that Smollett was paid for including her *Memoirs* in his novel.[13] His reason for doing so remains a mystery. Lady Vane's motives for publishing her *Memoirs* are not known, but it is very likely that she was encouraged by the example of two earlier books which had achieved notoriety: Mrs Laetitia Pilkington's *Memoirs* (1748–54), and Mrs Theresa Constantia Phillips' *Apology* (1748) (No. 38). It is difficult to resist the view that Lady Vane sought to outdo her 'sister' memoirists.

The reception of *Peregrine Pickle* was further complicated by the intervention of Dr John Hill. Hill, the epitome of a Grub Street hack, was enjoying success in 1751 through his daily essay contributed to *The London Advertiser* from March 1751 to June 1753 under the title of the *Inspector*. Described as 'vain, impudent, facile, unprincipled, though not without some real abilities',[14] Hill involved himself in a rivalry with Smollett over the 'authenticity' of Lady Vane's *Memoirs*. It was good copy, and Hill was quick to seize the chance. In January 1751 notices appeared advertising the forthcoming publication of *Peregrine Pickle* including the *Memoirs of a Lady of Quality*. By 8 February Hill had written and published his own *History of a Woman of Quality: or the Adventures of Lady Frail*, which he claimed to be the 'true' account of Lady Vane's amours. *Peregrine Pickle* was then published on 25 February 1751. Three tracts relating to this appeared within the next few months, the most pertinent being *A Parallel between the Characters of Lady Frail, and the Lady of Quality in Peregrine Pickle* (No. 16). It may well be that Hill wrote all three tracts, and in addition, commented on the controversy ensuing in his Inspector papers from March 1751 to June 1753.[15] Hill's tracts, though of interest to the specialist, contribute little of substance to the lasting reputation of *Peregrine Pickle*.

The immediate response to *Peregrine Pickle* was mixed. Of Lady Vane's 'bluestocking' contemporaries, Lady Mary Wortley Montagu wrote sympathetically of the *Memoirs*, and praised the novel (No. 30), whereas Swift's friend Mary Delany thought the novel to be '*wretched stuff*; only Lady V's history is a curiosity. What a wretch!' (No. 31) Samuel Richardson wished his admirers would defend female morality against the novel, and wrote to his friend Sarah Chapone that he had sent her son 'that Part of a bad Book which contains the very bad Story of a wicked woman. I could be glad to see it animadverted upon by so admirable a Pen' (No. 10). Smollett and Richardson were on terms of reasonable professional intimacy later, since Richardson's printing house was involved in publishing the second or 'Modern Part' of a *Universal History* which appeared in forty-four volumes between 1759 and 1766, and of which Smollett was one of the compilers. In Smollett's extant letters to Richardson we see that he is scrupulous in expressing his high regard for Richardson's ability as a novelist and, dissociating himself from some denigratory remarks on Richardson in *The*

Critical Review, praises Richardson's work, even whilst admitting that 'I am not much addicted to Compliment.'[16] John Cleland, whose pornographic novel *Fanny Hill: or, Memoirs of a Woman of Pleasure*, appeared in 1748–9, paid Smollett the compliment of a long and judicious review of *Peregrine Pickle* in *The Monthly Review* of March 1751 (No. 13). He distinguished *Peregrine Pickle* from

that flood of novels, tales, romances, and other monsters of the imagination, which have been either wretchedly translated, or even more unhappily imitated, from the *French*, whose literary levity we have not been ashamed to adopt, and encourage the propagation of so depraved a taste.

Cleland's desire to differentiate between English and French taste leads us into the French response to *Peregrine Pickle*. Matthew Maty in the *Journal Britannique* commented that *Peregrine Pickle* offered a 'faithful picture of the customs of the century' (No. 20), yet the novel was not well received in France. Joliat reports that[17] the French were only interested in the *Memoirs* of Lady Vane, and this was probably the only section of the novel they read: comment was confined to this part of the novel. One curiosity emerged however: a French translation of the novel under the title of *Sir Williams Pickle*. In the *Avertissement* to the translation the bookseller wrote that he 'found in it some singularly original portraits, very finely sustained', yet confessed some anxiety: 'I feared at first that this would not suit the taste here but I reflected in the end that these pictures were not without merit; that they would at least serve to instruct us in English novels.' In a long review of this translation Elie Fréron drew attention to the originality of the novel, and was particularly struck by what he called the 'bizarrerie anglaise'. He concluded his review with these remarks:

The ingenious or pleasing qualities to be found in this work cannot compensate for the boredom induced by the reading of four long volumes. The translator acknowledges that the best English novel cannot stand comparison with ours. So what need is there for all these English productions.

According to Joliat we have to wait until the nineteenth century for a serious French critical response to Smollett's fiction, from Louis Mézières in his *Histoire critique de la littérature anglaise* of 1834.[18] Though Mézières recognizes the comic verve in Smollett, and admires the Lady Vane *Memoirs*, he nevertheless calls into question the now conventional placing of Smollett as one of the three greatest English novelists of the eighteenth century.

III. SMOLLETT, FIELDING AND THE 'PAPER WAR'

Meanwhile in London Smollett was engaged in a literary controversy. The London *General Advertiser* for 30 April 1751 announced the following publication: *A Vindication of the Name and Random Peregrinations of the Family of the Smallwits. In a letter to a Friend.* Printed for R. Griffith at the Dunciad in St Paul's Church-Yard. No copy of this pamphlet is known to exist but the impact on Smollett of this notice in the *General Advertiser* can be guessed at. Smollett may have suspected that Fielding instigated or wrote it: which would account for Smollett's satiric Portrait of Fielding in *Peregrine Pickle*, under the name of Mr Spondy, presented as a sychophant of Lord Lyttleton[19] who is lampooned in the novel as the poet 'Gosling Scrag Esq.' Lyttleton's Monody on the death of his wife is burlesqued by Smollett in chapter 102. Early in 1752 Fielding replied to this portrayal in his *Covent-Garden Journal*, using the pseudonym Alexander Drawcansir. He gives an account of the 'present war' and comically dismisses the eponymous figures of Pickle and Random (Peeragrin Puckle and Rodorick Random) (No. 24), who scatter at the 'first Report of the Approach of a younger Brother of General Thomas Jones.' Smollett replied to Fielding in the pseudonymous pamphlet *A Faithful Narrative* (No. 25) in which he makes Fielding confess, under the pseudonym Habbakkuk Hilding, that he had plagiarized Smollett's work in the making of *Tom Jones*:

Trunnion is the Man.—Spare me, spare me, good Commodore! I own I have wronged you, as well as your Nephew *Peregrine*, and his Cousin *Random*.—I have robb'd them both, and then raised a false Report against them.

There is no proof that Smollett wrote *A Faithful Narrative of Habbakkuk Hilding*, although it is always included in his bibliography. Whatever the truth of the matter, the pamphlet clearly supports his position in this less than serious rivalry with Fielding. This war of words continued through the publication of Fielding's

Amelia in 1752, the least successful of his novels. *Amelia* was itself the subject of satiric comment by Bonnell Thornton in *The Drury Lane Journal* (No. 26), and both Smollett and Fielding's work was guyed in other minor pamphlets of the day, such as William Kenrick's *Fun* (No. 28). In *Amelia*, Fielding, in pointed contrast to the self-advertisement of Lady Vane in her *Memoirs* in *Peregrine Pickle*, draws a decorous veil over human frailty in a famous bedroom scene. (No. 29)

The issue of decorum and morality in fiction was of continuing concern to commentators through the eighteenth and nineteenth century. The most serious contemporary contribution of this kind is that of Samuel Johnson's *Rambler* essay (No. 8), occasioned by the popularity of both *Tom Jones* and *Roderick Random*. Johnson's anxiety about the dangerous appeal to the young of 'immoral' heroes is echoed by subsequent readers of Smollett's novel (see, for example, No. 121).

IV. *FERDINAND COUNT FATHOM*

Smollett's third novel, published in 1753, was not a commercial success. It was not reprinted in his lifetime, and the seven-year gap between this and his next novel suggests perhaps a lapse in confidence due to the failure of *Ferdinand Count Fathom*. Modern critics have argued that it represents an endeavour to go beyond the conventions of the native picaresque form of *Roderick Random* and *Peregrine Pickle*, an endeavour not brought fully to success. Its most remarkable features are a criminal anti-hero, and the introduction of Gothic elements in Chapters 20 and 21. Defending his choice of protagonist Smollett wrote a 'Dedication' to the novel (No. 32), in which he argues that

the same principle by which we rejoice at the remuneration of merit, will teach us to relish the disgrace and discomfiture of vice, which is always an example of extensive use and influence, because it leaves a deep impression of terror upon the minds of those who were not confirmed in the pursuit of morality and virtue....

He calls upon the example of the drama in which he argues 'the chief personage is often the object of our detestation and abhorrence' and cites the examples of Shakespeare's *Richard III*, and

Maskwell from Congreve's *The Double Dealer*. This 'Dedication', largely ignored in the eighteenth century, has been thought by late nineteenth- and twentieth-century critics an inadequate defence of the novel.[20] E.A. Baker believes that

Smollett, in Ferdinand Count Fathom, falls between not two but a whole row of stools. First, he confounds the tale of picaresque adventure with the criminal biography, then he changes over to crude romance.... the only passages that cast any spell upon the modern reader are of yet another category—those in which Smollett plays upon our sense of terror and suspense and weaves an atmosphere of gloom which gives a foretaste of the Gothic novel.[21]

Modern critics have argued for and against the view that in this novel Smollett was borrowing the example of Fielding's *Jonathan Wild*, yet this connection was not made by Ralph Griffiths in his long review of the novel in *The Monthly Review* for 1753 (No. 34). He suggests that here Smollett has worked with a fund of ideas 'gleaned from *Gil Blas, Guzman de Alfarache, Lazarillo de Tormes*, the *English rogue*, etc. His Ferdinand Fathom is a compound of all that is detestable in the heroes of these ludicrous romances.' Griffiths is cautiously hostile to the novel, whilst finding things to praise in it. There are, he writes,

Some extravagant excursions of the author's fancy, with certain improbable stories... marvelous adventures, and little incongruities; all which seem to be indications of the performance being hastily, nay and carelessly composed.

On the bonus side he finds it shows the 'strong marks of genius in the author, and demonstrations of his great proficiency in the study of mankind.' Mary Delany, in three letters to her friend Mrs Dewes in 1753 comments from time to time on the experience of reading *Ferdinand Count Fathom*, and ends with the view that 'I think *Count Fathom* (though a bad, affected style) written with a better intention, and Melvin's character a good one, but then none of them are to be named in a day with our good friend Richardson' (No. 34). There is little other comment on *Ferdinand Count Fathom* in the 1750s. In 1762 William Rider (No. 62) in a pamphlet of biographical studies of contemporary writers suggests the superiority of *Ferdinand Count Fathom* over *Peregrine Pickle* on the grounds that *Ferdinand Count Fathom* is not a mere repetition of the design of *Roderick Random*, which *Peregrine Pickle* is. Thereafter, comments about *Ferdinand Count Fathom* usually arise in consideration of the ethical questions raised by Smollett's novels, and their impact on his readers. Richard Sheridan (No. 92) in confessing his love of Romances and hatred of novels, surely has both *Peregrine Pickle* and *Ferdinand Count Fathom* in mind when he writes that for him the great demerit of novels is in their fidelity to nature: 'Why should men have a satisfaction in viewing only the mean and distorted figures of Nature? tho', truly speaking not of Nature, but of Vicious and corrupt Society.' Similarly, in a debate between 'Nestor' and 'Caution' in *The Monthly Review* of 1773 (No. 94) 'Caution' argues that 'though he has painted vice in strong, and even glaring, colours, it does not seem to be done with a view to condemn it'. 'Caution' complains of the 'excessive profanity' of Smollett's language in his novels, and concludes them to be 'absolutely unfit for the perusal of youth, or even of mature age without the greatest caution.'

If such responses are largely matters of taste and ethical judgment, later writers in the eighteenth century did respond to the purely literary issues raised by *Ferdinand Count Fathom*. In the first substantial biographical /literary commentary on Smollett after his death, the writer of the *Westminster Magazine* article for 1775 (No. 97) argues that both *Ferdinand Count Fathom* and *Sir Launcelot Greaves* are much lesser creations than Smollett's other novels:

No doubt invention, character, composition, and contrivance, are to be found in both; but then situations are described which are hardly possible, and characters are painted, which, if not altogether unexampled, are at least incompatible with modern manners; and which ought not to be, as the scenes are laid in modern times.

Towards the end of the century Mrs Barbauld (No. 119) in an essay on the pleasure derived from objects of terror finds in *Ferdinand Count Fathom* the best 'conceived, and the most strongly worked-up scene of mere natural horror that I recollect... where the hero, entertained in a lone house in a forest, finds a corpse just slaughter-ed in the room where he is sent to sleep, and the door of which is locked upon him.' Similarly, Robert Anderson in the critical remarks prefaced to his edition of the *Miscellaneous Works* of Smollett of 1796 (No. 125) compares the Gothic chapters of *Ferdinand Count Fathom* favourably with the 'most terrible touches' in Horace Walpole's *The Castle of Otranto* (1765) and Ann Radcliffe's *The Mysteries of Udolpho*, (1794). In her introduction to Smollett's novels selected for the British Novelists series of 1810, Mrs Barbauld argues that what is different about *Ferdinand Count Fathom* from its predecessors is that Smollett here subjects his hero to the demands of poetic justice, and suggests that the intention behind the writing of *Ferdinand Count Fathom* was precisely to meet the objections to his earlier novels that he had allowed his characters to go unpunished for their moral and social misdemeanours. However, she complains of *Ferdinand Count Fathom* that 'the narration is far from pleasing; knavery is not dignified enough to interest us by its fall.' In an anticipation of Dickens's response to Smollett, she argues that 'Strong humour he possessed, but grace and delicacy were foreign to his pencil' and adds that he 'could not draw an interesting female character' (No. 135). (Narcissa and Emilia in *Roderick Random* and *Peregrine Pickle* are certainly no more than the stock image of the beautiful virtuous English girl, like Sophia in *Tom Jones*.) However, Mrs Barbauld found the images of Count Fathom's mother, a camp follower 'going about stripping the dying and the dead' impossible to contemplate 'without a thrill of horror.'

Sir Walter Scott (No. 157) has three sound points to make about *Ferdinand Count Fathom*. Like Mrs Barbauld he praises the Gothic chapters of the novel as 'a tale of natural terror which rises into the sublime; and, though often imitated, has never yet been surpassed, or perhaps equalled.' He remarks that in this novel Smollett makes the first attempt in fiction to do justice to 'a calumniated race' in the portrait of Joshua, the benevolent Jew. And in comparing *Ferdinand Count Fathom* with *Jonathan Wild*, Scott comes down firmly on Smollett's side, and argues that as a consequence of his powerfully expressive style and his strong inventiveness of character 'it becomes at once obvious that the detestable Fathom is a living and existing miscreant, at whom we shrink as from the presence of an incarnate fiend, while the villain of Fielding seems rather a cold personification of the abstract principle of evil' whose adventures Scott finds 'absolutely tiresome'.

V. TRANSLATOR, CRITIC AND HISTORIAN 1754–60

In a letter to Alexander Carlyle of 7 June 1748, Smollett wrote that he was contracted 'with two Booksellers to translate Don Quixote from the Spanish Language, which I have studied some time. This perhaps you will look upon as a very Desperate Undertaking, there being no fewer than four Translations of the same Book already extant, but I am fairly engaged and cannot recede.'[22] In his book *Smollett's Hoax: Don Quixote in English*, Carmine Linsalata seeks to demonstrate that Smollett's translation is a 'plagiarizing, paraphrasing, rewriting, and inverting' of Jervas's English translation of 1742, and that Smollett probably had little or no Spanish.[23] Smollett must have known his debt to Jervas and felt the slight on his command of Spanish in John Shebbeare's pamphlet (No. 46). He took ample revenge for this and other incivilities through his satiric portrait of Shebbeare as Ferret in *Sir Launcelot Greaves*. Smollett's version of Cervantes' novel appears to have been finished by 1751 but was not published until 1755. It aroused little public comment or formal criticism, except for Ralph Griffiths's review of it in *The Monthly Review* (No. 40). But it was a commercial success for the booksellers, went into several editions in Smollett's lifetime, and was frequently re-issued throughout the nineteenth century. Lady Mary Wortley Montagu (No. 39) regretted that Smollett wasted his time in translations.

Don Quixote is a difficult undertaking. I shall never desire to read any attempt to new dress him; tho' I am a meer pidler in the Spanish Language, I had rather take pains to understand him in the Original than sleep over a stupid Translation.

Ralph Griffiths reviews the translation by means of an extended comparison, line for line, with Charles Jervas's version of 1742, taking the episode in which Sancho Panza exposes the 'mistaken politeness of his master, in the affair of the table-precedency'. Griffiths feels that while Jervas's is the more exact version, Smollett's 'comes nearest the great original'. He concludes his review with a complaint about the absence of an index, a thing, he suggests, that 'men of genius, and imagination, seldom attend to; but nevertheless, *indexes* have their uses, and no book, of *considerable price* especially, ought to be without them.' Smollett expressed a nice sense of the relative value of his work on *Don Quixote* in a letter to his friend William Huggins:

I send my Spaniard to return the Compliment I have received by your Italian. Cervantes was a warm Admirer of Ariosto, and therefore Don Quixote cannot be disagreable to a Lover of Orlando furioso. Though I do not pretend to compare my Prose with your Poetry.[24]

In 1756 Smollett and three associates founded *The Critical Review*.[25] The first issue appeared on 1 March 1756, and contained seventeen articles on books published in January and February. One of his associates and friends, Dr John Armstrong, a medical doctor and a fellow Scot, wrote to the politician John Wilkes in January 1756 that:

Smollett imagines he and I may both make Fortunes by this project of his; I'm afraid he is too sanguine, but if it should turn out according to his hopes farewell Physick and all its Cares for me and welcome dear Transquility and Retirement.[26]

Samuel Johnson admired *The Critical Review* and thought it superior to *The Monthly Review*, but it did not make Smollett's fortune, and was often in financial difficulties throughout his association with it up to 1763, when he left England for two years for health reasons. Furthermore, *The Critical Review* involved Smollett in endless conflict with authors whose work received unfavourable reviews in its pages, and in one case embroiled him in a libel action which he lost, so that he was imprisoned in the King's Bench prison for three months. Amongst the many pamphlets and letters addressed to the editors of *The Critical Review* by enraged authors, I have selected extracts from those by John Shebbeare (No. 46), Dr James Grainger (No. 49), Joseph Reed (No. 50) and the anonymous pamphlet *The Battle of the Reviews* (No. 55), where the writers address themselves to Smollett's own creative writings. These documents speak for themselves, and are an index of the temper of eighteenth-century critical skirmishing in the environs of Grub Street. As the most prominent name associated with *The Critical Review* at its inception, it was inevitable that Smollett should be singled out for attack by disgruntled contemporaries. What he complains of in his letters of these years is being blamed for reviews he did not write. In this context it is worth recalling his letter to Samuel Richardson, cited earlier in this introduction, dissociating himself from adverse remarks on Richardson in *The Critical Review*; there were few other writers whose work he admired sufficiently to make this gesture.

Throughout the last five years of this decade Smollett was also deeply involved in his work as an historian. The record of his output from 1755 to 1761 is awesome evidence of his capacity for literary drudgery. In 1757–8 he published the first four volumes of his *Complete History of England*, the *Continuation* of which appeared in four volumes in 1760–1, with a fifth volume in 1765, bringing the *History* right up to date. In 1756 there appeared a seven-volume compilation of *Authentic and Interesting Voyages* of which he seems to have been the editor, and volume five of which he wrote himself. He was involved in the production of a forty-four-volume *Universal History* (1759–66), some of which he compiled himself as his business letters to Samuel Richardson and Richardson's son show. From 1761 he was editor of a thirty-eight-volume translation of the works of Voltaire. In addition to all this he was involved with the production of two other periodicals at this time, *The British Magazine* from January 1760 to December 1767, and *The Briton*, a political journal edited for Lord Bute from May 1762 to February 1763; a role which cost Smollett the friendship of John Wilkes. Small wonder that he expresses the fatigue of composition in several letters of this period. To William Huggins he writes on 20 June 1757: 'Cakes and Gingerbread to what I undergo. I have been groaning all day under the weight of Tindal, Ralph, Burnet, Feuquieres, Daniel, Voltaire, Burchet &c.,&.' and in letter to John Harvie of 10 December 1959 he writes:

If I go on writing as I have proceeded for some years, my hand will be paralytic, and my brain dried to a snuff. I would not wish my greatest enemy a greater curse than the occupation of an author, in which capacity I have toiled myself into habitual asthma, and been baited like a bear by all the hounds of Grub-street. Some people have flourished by imputed wit; I have suffered by imputed dullness. I have been abused, reviled, and calumniated for satires I never saw; I have been censured for absurdities of which I could not possibly be guilty.

As to his qualities as an historian, contemporary reviews were mostly concerned to dispute versions of relatively recent events. Reviewing his *Complete History of England* in *The Monthly Review* (No. 45) Oliver Goldsmith found nothing to complain of in Smollett's researches, and praised his style. A year later, criticizing volume IV of the *Complete History* in *The Monthly Review* (No. 47) Owen Ruffhead dismissed the work as history on the grounds that the 'Writer's merit is rather that of an ingenious novelist than of an accurate historian. His imagination overpowers his judgement.' The partisan nature of Smollett's political and religious attachments were attacked by Thomas Comber in his *Vindication of the Great Revolutions in England...as Misrepresented by the Author of the Complete History of England*. A long refutation of Comber's arguments appeared in *The Critical Review* for September 1758, but as this unsigned article bears the marks of Smollett's authorship it is not reprinted here.

What of the views of later professional historians? In the nineteenth century Thomas Carlyle mentions Smollett's *Complete History* in a number of letters of 1871 and 1882, Writing to Robert Mitchell in 1817 he refers to 'seven of Toby Smollett's eight chaotic volumes' and writes later to another correspondent that 'I fear Smollett is going to be a confused creature.' And in 1822 in a letter to John Carlyle, he writes: 'You might commence Smollett's *Continuation* of Hume, or any continuation of him—for a worse one can scarcely be imagined than Smollett's.'[27] Our survey concludes with Charles Lamb's comic and generous response to views like those of Thomas Carlyle when, pointing out how much the Scots dislike his admiration of their fellow countrymen, he writes (No. 156), 'Speak of Smollett as a great genius, and they will retort upon you Hume's History compared with *his* Continuation of it. What if the historian had continued *Humphry Clinker?*'

VI. *SIR LAUNCELOT GREAVES*, 1760–61

A number of particular circumstances attend the publication of *Sir Launcelot Greaves*, Smollett's fourth novel. First, some chapters of the novel were written whilst Smollett was in the King's Bench prison, serving his three months' sentence for the libel of Admiral Knowles. Second, *Sir Launcelot Greaves* is the first novel to make its initial appearance in serialized form in a British periodical. Third, it was illustrated, by Anthony Walker, and these are said to be the first magazine illustrations of a work of fiction.[28] The novel was published serially from January 1760 to December 1761 in *The British Magazine, or Monthly Repository for Gentlemen and Ladies*, and appeared in book form in March 1762. The critical response to it was slight, and of Smollett's five novels, this and *Ferdinand Count Fathom* have always been judged inferior to the others. Its subject matter and something of its form derives from Smollett's familiarity with *Don Quixote*, and it is part of that tradition of Quixotic fictions in English which includes Fielding's comedy *Don Quixote in England* (1734), Butler's *Hudibras*, Charlotte Lennox's *Female Quixote* (1752), and a Richard Graves's *Spiritual Quixote* (1772). Its titular hero is a knight-errant of means who travels the countryside rooting out injustice and folly. In Ferret it boast a Hobbesian misanthrope to counter-balance the chivalric energies of the hero; and in Captain Crowe there is another example of Smollett's fascination with naval characters.

Oliver Goldsmith publicized the novel in an essay in *The Public Ledger* for 16 February 1760 (No. 53) in a report of what he called a 'wow-wow' or gathering of country people to gossip and read the newspapers in the local public house. Goldsmith, a contributor to *The British Magazine*, sought to boost both the novel and the magazine: he has an Oxford scholar, led to the wow-wow by curiosity, read a serialized section of *Sir Launcelot Greaves* and announce that the piece is not only done in the very spirit and manner of Cervantes, but exhibits 'great knowledge of human nature, and evident marks of the master in almost every sentence' and he attributes it to the pen of the 'ingenious Dr——'. Everyone present at the wow-wow then gives orders for *The British Magazine*. Upon book publication *Sir Launcelot Greaves* was noticed in a back-handed compliment by *The Monthly Review* (No. 59) as 'Better than the common Novels, but unworthy the pen of Dr Smollett.' Smollett's journal *The Critical Review* dealt with it most favourably, arguing that it resembled *Don Quixote* without imitating it, and praised Captain Crowe as a successfully drawn naval character (No. 60). Of Crowe's exotically original seaman's language *The Critical Review* wrote:

It has been said that Shakespeare has drawn a natural character in Caliban, not to be found in nature. We may with equal reason affirm, that Crowe is a true seaman that never existed, who talks in tropes and figures borrowed from his profession, but never used before.

It was Captain Crowe who called forth the objections of a reviewer in *The Library* (No. 61) who, whilst admiring the novel in general terms, objected that Crowe appears too often in it, that his 'appearance is sometimes disgusting, and whose sea jargon is absolutely unintelligible to a land reader'. Some years later in his 'Essay on Laughter and Ludicrous Composition' (No. 99) James Beattie proposed that although Greaves is a kindred figure to Don Quixote, 'Smollet's design was, not to expose him to ridicule; but rather to recommend him to our pity and admiration. He has therefore given him youth, strength, and beauty, as well as courage, and dignity of mind. . . . Yet, that the history might have a comic air, he has been careful to contrast and connect Sir Launcelot with a squire and other associates of very dissimilar tempers and circumstances.' By the turn of the century, in general studies of Smollett's work, the acknowledgment of *Sir Launcelot Greaves*, like that of *Ferdinand Count Fathom*, is dutiful rather than enthusiastic.

VII. *TRAVELS THROUGH FRANCE AND ITALY* AND *THE ADVENTURES OF AN ATOM*

I give some evidence of the reception of the *Travels Through France and Italy*, though it lies outside my main concerns, and its critical reputation in England, France and Germany has been thoroughly described elsewhere.[29] Similarly, I give some of the reviews of the anonymously published *Adventures of an Atom* even though Smollett's authorship of it has never been proven; it is always listed in his bibliography.

The *Travels* was published on 8 May 1766, within a year of Smollett's return from the Continent where he had been living for two years in an attempt to improve his health, and to recover his broken spirits after the death in April 1763 of his only child, his daughter Elizabeth. The *Travels* consists of a series of letters to an unnamed correspondent, in which Smollett comments on life and manners in France and Italy. Smollett adopts the attitudes of a sturdy English moralist, passing judgment on foreign customs and manners, and his tone is often ill-tempered in the extreme. The *Travels* anticipates the mode of his last novel, the epistolary *Expedition of Humphry Clinker*, 1771, and there is a family resemblance between the persona of the letters and that of Matthew Bramble in *Humphry Clinker*. The *Travels* was well received on publication, and went to a second edition in the same year. There was, inevitably, a favourable review of it in *The Critical Review*, and an equally warm account in the rival *Monthly Review* (No. 67) where Dr John Berkenhout distinguishes between the 'insipid, tedious, and uninteresting... remarks of the generality of travellers' and Smollett's *Travels*. He writes that the author 'hath not travelled without a previous acquaintance with mankind; and his abilities, as a writer, are universally known.' He concludes with an expression of thanks 'for the entertainment we have received in the perusal of his travels; which, as they are the work of a man of genius and learning, cannot fail of being useful and instructive, particularly to those who intend to make the same tour.' Similarly approving short reviews appeared in *The London Magazine* (No. 68) and *The Royal Magazine* (No. 69). In France, inevitably, the *Travels* had a very hostile press[30] and the adverse reviews of the book there form the substance of Philip Thicknesse's comments on it in his *Observations on the Customs and Manners of the French Nation*, 1766 (No. 72). Garrick's French correspondent Madame Riccoboni wrote to him of the *Travels* that Smollett was 'a low knave who's no better acquainted with the *mores* of his own country than with those of France' (No. 73). Two years later the reputation of the *Travels* was irreparably damaged by Laurence Sterne in his *Sentimental Journey through France and Italy*, 1768. If Sterne's purpose in the *Sentimental Journey* was a general rebuke to the bad-tempered travel writer, his derisive portrait of Smollett as the 'learned SMELFUNGUS' (No. 75) effectively eclipsed the reputation of Smollett's book throughout the remainder of the eighteenth century and up to the early years of this century.

Smollett's political satire *The History and Adventures of an Atom* was published in 1769. A Dublin edition came out in the same year, but it was not otherwise reprinted in Smollett's lifetime. A satire of current affairs and public characters from 1754 onwards, it reflects Smollett's disgust at the intrigues of political life, with which he had become embroiled through his association with Lord Bute and his editing of *The Briton* from 1762–3. The device of the novel is that an atom moves from Japan to the brain of one Nathaniel Peacock, and dictates what he must write of the atom's 'Japonese' adventures: for Japan and the Japonese we are to read Britain and the British. The novel contains virulent attacks on statesmen, politicians, military and naval commanders, and the common people. Its principal theme is an exposure of the sycophancy of public life; its manner recalls Swift in the *Tale of a Tub* and *Gulliver's Travels*. Although Knapp seems anxious to question its ascription to Smollett, modern commentators confidently include it in discussions of his oeuvre.[31] Coming as it does at the end of Smollett's herculean labours as an historian, it is easy to see that he might have turned to this mode of writing to enact a form of private revenge on the public and political world he had been so closely bound up with throughout the preceding decade. It was reviewed in a number of periodicals of the day, one of which, *The London Chronicle* attributes it to 'the Author of *Roderick Random*' (No. 76). A long descriptive account of it in *The Gentleman's Magazine* (No. 77) concludes approvingly that 'The folly of the multitude, and the knavery of pretenders to patriotism, are ridiculed in this little work with great spirit and humour; but there is a mixture of indelicacy and indecency, which though it cannot gratify the loosest imagination, can scarce fail to disgust the coarsest.' *The Critical Review* (No. 78) found it to unite 'the happy extravagance of Rabelais to the splendid humour of Swift' and concluded that 'the man who does not love and relish this performance, has no wit in his own composition.' John Hawkesworth in *The Monthly Review* (No. 79) found in it 'much spirit, humour, and satire' but 'also much nastiness and obscenity: of that kind, however, which is disgusting, and consequently not pernicious.' The key identifying the fictional with the historical characters in the *Adventures of an Atom* is given in Appendix 2.

VIII. *THE EXPEDITION OF HUMPHRY CLINKER*

Humphry Clinker, Smollett's last and most enduring novel appeared in June 1771. A few months later, on 17 September he died in Leghorn, where he had been living since the autumn of 1768. He received notice of the interest which greeted his new novel in a letter written from London by John Gray, a minor writer on friendly terms with him. 'Shallow judges', wrote Gray, 'are not so well satisfied with the performance as the best judges, who are lavish in its praises. Your half-animated sots say they don't see the humour. Cleland gives it the stamp of excellence, with the enthusiastic emphasis of voice and fist; and puts it before anything you ever wrote' (No. 87). Gray's sense of a mixed response to the novel was accurate. It was extensively reviewed in the periodicals, but only *The Critical Review* gave it unstinting praise. *The London Magazine* (No. 82) wrote that the novel was not 'without imperfections' among which it singled out the impropriety of the novel's title in relation to the insignificant role played by Humphry in the book, and complained also of the paucity of action and incident in it, complaints reiterated by other reviewers. Some found in it an implied nationalism which promoted the virtues of Scotland and Edinburgh over those of England, London and Bath (cf. Mrs Barbauld's remarks in 1810 (No. 135)) and thought the presentation of these English cities unrecognizable. *The Monthly Review* (No. 88) was entirely hostile. The novel was seen as inferior to his first two novels and 'perhaps equal to the *Adventures of an Atom*', an appropriate conjunction in the light of the reviewer's attempt to place Smollett in the tradition of those 'nasty geniuses' who follow their great leader Swift, 'only in his obscene and dirty walks'. However, he admits that 'The present Writer, nevertheless, has humour and wit, as well as grossness and ill-nature.' *The Critical Review* (No. 89) praises Smollett's control of plot, incident and characterization, and reports that 'the same vigour of imagination that animates his other works, is conspicuous in the present, where we are entertained with a variety of scenes and characters almost unanticipated.' He goes on to praise the epistolary form of the novel, celebrating the variety that derives from the multiple narrative perspectives 'of the letters of the several correspondents'. He praises its realism, its inventiveness, and its capacity for releasing 'the understanding from prejudice', surely a hint of shared nationalist sympathies in support of Smollett's endeavour in *Humphry Clinker* to present Scotland and the Scots in a more favourable light than was often the case in the Metropolitan culture of England in the eighteenth century. It is one of the most informed and intelligent criticisms we shall find in all the contemporary reviews of Smollett's novels. *Humphry Clinker* went into many editions in the last quarter of the eighteenth century, and came to be recognized as Smollett's major work. Commenting on Smollett's power of characterization in it, William Mudford (No. 137) hesitates to compare him with Shakespeare, but nevertheless asserts than in *Humphry Clinker*, Smollett rises above description to real invention in an almost Shakespearian manner, demonstrating a 'power of intellect of much larger scope than in any of his preceding productions'. And Sir Walter Scott (No. 157) writes of Smollett's last months in Italy, 'where he prepared for the press the last, and, like music, "sweetest in the close," the most pleasing of his compositions, *The Expedition of Humphry Clinker.*'

IX. *PLAYS AND POEMS* (1777) AND *WORKS*

Smollett's *Plays and Poems* of 1777 gathers these texts together for the first time. The edition uses biographical and critical material on his life and work taken from *The Westminster Magazine* of 1775 (No. 97). Of the critical material in the introduction to *Plays and Poems*, I have extracted the writer's comments on Smollett's most famous poem, the *Ode to Independence* (No. 101). As Boucé points out[32] no new biographical material of substance appeared thereafter until Robert Anderson's edition of the *Works* in 1796, itself a revision of his earlier edition of the *Miscellaneous Works* published in Edinburgh in 1790. Anderson's 1796 edition (revised, amended and enlarged in several editions to 1820) was followed by Dr John Moore's edition of the *Works* in 1797, the introduction to which gave an account of the 'Progress of Romance' from which I have extracted material (No. 126). This criticism of Smollett which begins in 1775 in *The Westminster Magazine* and continues through Anderson and Moore to their successors, constitutes a sequence of heavily interdependent critical essays, which are however, extended from time to time with original contributions and fresh insights. My selection of this material avoids continual repetition of critical opinions, whilst attempting to convey what is new.

X. SCOTT, THE ROMANTICS AND DICKENS

Between the collections of Smollett's *Works* and Sir Walter Scott's *Life*, there appear two particularly interesting contributions to Smollett criticism. One of these is William Mudford's 'Critical Observations' on Smollett's novels in an edition of the British Novelists (No. 137). Mudford's work is striking because of his endeavour to write a genuinely independent and literary criticism. There is also Edward Mangin (No. 134) who in his *Essay on Light*

Reading of 1808 takes a dispassionate look at Smollett's naval characters.

Scott's critical assessment of Smollett in his *Lives of the Novelists*, 1821–4 (No. 157) is distinguished by its originality. It shows the mind of the novelist rather than the critic at work. Scott is vulnerable to the charge of nationalist partiality, yet in a sustained analysis of the relative merits of Fielding and Smollett, he ranks *Tom Jones* as the greatest of their novels; but he justly claims that *Roderick Random*, *Peregrine Pickle* and *Humphry Clinker* 'far excel *Joseph Andrews* or *Amelia*; and, to descend still lower, *Jonathan Wild*, or *The Journey to the Next World*, cannot be put into momentary comparison with *Sir Launcelot Greaves*, or *Ferdinand Count Fathom*.'

Amongst the early Romantics, Keats (No. 150) is the only one on record who positively discriminates against Smollett's novels. It is interesting that he compares Smollett and Scott; a pairing which was to dog the earlier writer throughout the nineteenth century, to his disadvantage. Lamb (No. 129), Leigh Hunt (No. 142), Hazlitt (No. 143), and Coleridge (No. 152) all respond enthusiastically to Smollett. Charles Lamb wrote to Wordsworth in praise of Smollett's 'beautiful bare narratives'; and the poet is reported to have distinguished Smollett from other 'Scotch historians' as one 'who wrote good pure English.' Leigh Hunt, despite an affection for Smollett deriving from boyhood reading, displays a rather ambivalent response to his vigour: 'His caricatures are always substantially true: it is only the complexional vehemence of his gusto that leads him to toss them up as he does, and tumble them on our plates.' Hazlitt picks out Smollett's eye for eccentricities. But Coleridge is, perhaps, critically more exact. In contrast to Mudford's generalized Romantic appeal to the genius of Shakespearian characterization, Coleridge goes back to Ben Jonson and the comedy of humours technique to account for what he calls: 'the congeniality of humour with pathos, so exquisite in Sterne and Smollett'.

Thomas Carlyle, despite his objections to Smollett as an historian, also enjoys his pathos, perhaps immoderately so: his judgment of *Humphry Clinker* is astonishing (No. 149).

Humphry Clinker is precious to me now as he was in those years. Nothing by Dante or any one else surpasses in pathos the scene where Humphry goes into the smithy made for him in the old house, and whilst he is heating the iron, the poor woman who has lost her husband, and is deranged, comes and talks to him as to her husband.

Grandiose comparisons are a feature of nineteeth-century criticism: Scott had concluded his *Life* of Smollett with a suggestion that 'Upon the whole, the genius of Smollett may be said to resemble that of Rubens.'

This is not the place to raise the issue of Dickens's literary debt to Smollett.[33] The complexity and power of their relationship may, however, be suggested by the masterly way in which Dickens filters into *David Copperfield*, between the boys, that particular novel by Smollett, *Peregrine Pickle*, which in its atmosphere of sexual impropriety anticipates the later development of David and Steerforth's relationship, and the seduction of Little Emily.

The criticism of Smollett from 1746 until Dickens displays intermittent warmth and animosity, but overall an increasing technical sophistication. Early commentators respond to Smollett as if he were a kind of prose Pope; a satirist of life and manners, sometimes excessively vulgar, whose interest is primarily moral rather than fictional. There is little sign of critical recognition of Smollett's formal experimenting with different kinds in the same fictional genre: from the English picaresque to proto-Gothic, and from extremes of emotion to varieties of technique culminating in the use of multiple perspectives in the epistolary *Humphry Clinker*. But the purity and energy of Smollett's prose style is often singled out for approbation. His stylistic virtues are evident to us also in the historical writing, his reviews, and, most brilliantly, in his letters.

NOTES

1 *The Letters of Charles Dickens* (1880), vol.I, p. 356.
2 For Alexander Carlyle, see No. 1.
3 *The Letters of Tobias Smollett*, ed. Lewis M. Knapp (Oxford, 1970), p. 4.
4 See No. 43.
5 Smollett, *Letters*, p. 5.
6 See No. 1. See also Paul-Gabriel Boucé, 'Eighteenth and Nineteenth Century Biographies of Smollett', *Tobias Smollett, Bicentennial Essays*, ed. G.S. Rousseau and P.G. Boucé (New York, 1971), pp. 201–30. Boucé refers to the complementary practice of 'inverted autobiography' in which Smollett's fiction is used to reconstruct the story of his life.

7 George M. Kahrl, *Tobias Smollett, Traveler-Novelist* (University of Chicago Press, 1945; repr. Octagon Books, 1968).

8 Akenside, Hogarth, Lyttleton, Fielding, and Garrick. In the 1757 edition of *Peregrine Pickle*, the attack on Garrick is turned to adulation, since by that time the relationship between Smollett and Garrick was on a friendly footing.

9 See Andrew Lang, *The Annesley Case* (English Notable Trials) (1912), pp. 1–79.

10 Lewis M. Knapp, *Tobias Smollett: Doctor of Men and Manners* (Princeton University Press, 1949), pp. 124–5: a letter from Lady Jane Coke, just returned to London from Tunbridge Wells, to Mrs Eyre at Derby, 21 August 1750.

11 Tobias Smollett, *The Adventures of Peregrine Pickle*, ed. James, L. Clifford (1964), p. 799, footnote to page 490.

12 Smollett, *Letters*, p. 14: a letter to John Moore, 28 September 1750: 'I have been favoured with two Letters from Mr Hunter of Burnsyde, the first of which was shewn to the Duke of Dorset by Lady Vane, who spoke of the Author as a Gentleman worthy of the Government's Clemency and Protection, and represented his Case and Character in such an advantageous Light that the Duke expressed an Inclination to befriend him, and advised Lord Vane to speak to his Cousin the Duke of Newcastle in his behalf.'

13 See, however, James R. Forster, 'Smollett's Pamphleteering Foe Shebbeare', *PMLA* LVII (1942), 1058.

14 See William Scott, 'Smollett, Dr John Hill, and the Failure of *Peregrine Pickle*', *Notes and Queries* CC (1955), 389–92.

15 The other two are: *A Letter to the Right Honourable the Lady V—ss V—, Occasioned by the Publication of her Memoirs in the Adventures of Peregrine Pickle* (London, for W. Owen, 16 March 1751, pp. (1) + 47). Then, on 9 July 1751, *An Apology for the Conduct of a Lady of Quality, lately traduc'd under the Name of Lady Frail* (London, for M. Cooper, pp. vii + 48).

16 Smollett, *Letters*, p. 48.

17 Eugène Joliat, *Smollett et la France* (Paris, 1935), p. 181.

18 Ibid., pp. 232–5.

19 'Candidates for literary fame appeared even in the higher sphere of life, embellished by the nervous style, superior sense, and extensive erudition of a Corke, by the delicate taste, the polished muse, and tender feelings of a Lyttleton': Tobias Smollett, *Continuation of the Complete History of England*, by Hume (new edn, 5 vols, 1822), vol. V, ch. XIV, section XXVIII, p. 408. Smollett adds on page 409, 'The genius of Cervantes was transfused into the novels of Fielding, who painted the characters, and ridiculed the follies of life, with equal strength, humour, and propriety.'

20 In Tobias Smollett, *The Adventures of Ferdinand Count Fathom*, ed. Damian Grant (1871), p. xvii, Damian Grant does not consider that 'Smollett fulfilled his formal intention, described in the Dedication.'

21 E.A. Baker, *History of the English Novel* (1930), vol. iv, p. 217, cited in Damian Baker's edition of *Ferdinand Count Fathom*, pp. xv-xvi.

22 Smollett, *Letters*, p. 8.

23 Carmine Linsalata, *Smollett's Hoax: Don Quixote in English* (1956).

24 Smollett, *Letters*, pp. 50-1.

25 These three appear to be Archibald Hamilton, Senior, Dr John Armstrong, author of *The Art of Preserving Health*, and the Rev. Thomas Francklin, Professor of Greek at Cambridge. See Knapp, op. cit., p. 174.

26 Ibid., p. 174.

27 *Early Letters of Thomas Carlyle*, ed. Charles Eliot Norton (Macmillan, 1886), vol. I, pp. 127, 133, vol. II, p. 28.

28 See Robert Mayo, *The English Novel in the Magazines* 1740–1815 (1962), frontispiece. See also *The Life and Adventures of Sir Launcelot Greaves*, ed. David Evans (1973), p. xxi. According to Evans, Anthony Walker (1726–65) was well known for his small book-illustrations executed from his own designs.

29 Tobias Smollett, *Travels Through France and Italy*, ed., Frank Felsenstein (1979), pp. xlviii-lxv.

30 Ibid., see pp. liii-lvii.

31 See Knapp, op. cit., pp. 280–3. For modern studies see Paul-Gabriel Boucé, *The Novels of Tobias Smollett* translated by Antonia White (1976), and Damian Grant, *Tobias Smollett: a Study in Style* (Manchester University Press, 1977), passim.

32 Paul-Gabriel Boucé, 'Eighteenth and Nineteenth Century Biographies of Smollett', passim.

33 John Stuart Mill in a letter of 18 July 1837 writes: 'Butler on the Pickwick business surprised me by speaking of Smollett; I fear that is loose speaking, but I have sent for the Pickwick on the faith of it, and will see.' This is a reference to Butler's review of *Pickwick Papers* in the *London Review* (1837). In a later, of 28 July 1837, Mill notes that he has read *Pickwick Papers*, and doesn't like it.

Note on the Text

Except for the occasional silent correction of some obvious typographical errors, the materials in this volume follow the original texts in spelling, conventions of punctuation, etc., in order that the reader may get some sense of the flavour of the originals. Many of the eighteenth-century reviews I have drawn upon contain material that summarizes the work under review, or describes it by extensive quotation. Omissions have been indicated in these extracts, and omitted material has been indicated by reference to the Shakespeare Head edition of Smollett's novels, 1925. Published in eleven volumes and including the five novels and the *Adventures of an Atom*, this represents the last complete edition of Smollett's novels to date. I have also consulted the Oxford English Novels editions of *Peregrine Pickle*, *Ferdinand Count Fathom*, *Sir Launcelot Greaves* and *Humphry Clinker*. In addition I have consulted the Oxford University Press edition of Smollett's *Travels Through France and Italy*, 1979, edited by Frank Felsenstein. I should like to record my indebtedness to the editors of these excellent editions. Readers may like to note that in the extracts that follow, Smollett's name is frequently misspelt. For commentary on *Roderick Random*, the translation of *Don Quixote*, and the various *Histories*, I have consulted eighteenth-century editions, and wherever possible, first editions.

The place of publication of all the entries is London, unless otherwise stated. Where the first edition of a text has not been cited, its date is given in brackets, and the date of the edition used is unbracketed.

1. Alexander Carlyle on Smollett

1746–58

From *The Autobiography of Dr Alexander Carlyle of Inveresk, 1722–1805*, ed. J.H. Burton, 1910 (1860).

Carlyle was an eminent Scottish minister who held a living at Inveresk, a suburb of Musselburgh near Edinburgh, for over fifty years. Smollett and Carlyle were good friends of long standing; Smollett visited him in Inveresk, and as can be seen from this and following extracts, Carlyle was frequently in Smollett's company on his visits to London. Extracts are given for the year recalled in the *Autobiography*, beginning pp. 197–200 for the year 1746.

John Blair had passed his trials as a preacher in Scotland, but having a few hundred pounds of patrimony, chose to pay a visit to London, where he loitered till he spent it all. After some time he thought of completing and publishing his Chronological Tables, the plan of which had been given him by Dr Hugh Blair, the celebrated preacher. He became acquainted with the Bishop of Lincoln, with whom he was soon a favourite, and having been ordained by him, was presented to the living of Burton Cogles, in his diocese. He was afterwards teacher of mathematics to the Duke of York, the King's brother, and was by his interest preferred to be a prebendary of Westminster. He was a lively agreeable fellow, and one of the most friendly men in the world. Smith had been abroad with the young Laird of MᶜLeod of that period, and was called home with his pupil when the Rebellion began. He had been ill rewarded, and was on his shifts in London. He was a man of superior understanding, and of a most gentlemanly address. With Smollett he was very intimate. We four, with one or two more, frequently resorted to a small tavern in the corner of Cockspur Street at the Golden Ball, where we had a frugal supper and a little punch, as the finances of none of the company were in very good order. But we had rich enough conversation on literary subjects, which was enlivened by Smollett's agreeable stories, which he told with peculiar grace.

Soon after our acquaintance, Smollett showed me his tragedy of *James I. of Scotland*, which he never could bring on the stage. For this the managers could not be blamed, though it soured him against them, and he appealed to the public by printing it; but the public seemed to take part with the managers.

I was in the coffeehouse with Smollett when the news of the battle of Culloden arrived, and when London all over was in a perfect uproar of joy. It was then that Jack Stuart, the son of the Provost,[a] behaved in the manner I before mentioned. About 9 o'clock I wished to go home to Lyon's, in New Bond Street, as I had promised to sup with him that night, it being the anniversary of his marriage night, or the birthday of one of his children. I asked Smollett if he was ready to go, as he lived at Mayfair; he said he was, and would conduct me. The mob were so riotous, and the squibs so numerous and incessant that we were glad to go into a narrow entry to put our wigs in our pockets, and to take our swords from our belts and walk with them in our hands, as everybody then wore swords; and, after cautioning me against speaking a word, lest the mob should discover my country and become insolent, 'for John Bull,' says he, 'is as haughty and valiant to-night as he was abject and cowardly on the Black Wednesday when the Highlanders were at Derby.' After we got to the head of the Haymarket through incessant fire, the Doctor led me by narrow lanes, where we met nobody but a few boys at a pitiful bonfire, who very civilly asked us for sixpence, which I gave them. I saw not Smollett again for some time after, when he showed Smith and me the manuscript of his *Tears of Scotland*, which was published not long after, and had such a run of approbation. Smollett, though a Tory, was not a Jacobite but he had the feelings of a Scotch gentleman on the reported cruelties that were said to be exercised after the battle of Culloden.

For the year 1753 (pp. 277–8):

It was also in one of those years that Smollett visited Scotland for the first time, after having left Glasgow immediately after his education was finished, and his engaging as a surgeon's mate on board a man-of-war, which gave him an opportunity of witnessing the siege of Carthagena, which he has so minutely described in his *Roderick Random*. He came out to Musselburgh and passed a day and a night with me, and went to church and heard me preach. I introduced him to Cardonnel the Commissioner, with whom he supped, and they were much pleased with each other. Smollett has reversed this in his *Humphrey Clinker*, where he makes the Commissioner his old acquaintance.[b] He went next to Glasgow and that neighbourhood to visit his friends, and returned again to Edinburgh in October, when I had frequent meetings with him—one in particular, in a tavern where there supped with him Commissioner Cardonnel, Mr Hepburn of Keith, John Home, and one or two more. Hepburn was so much pleased with Cardonnel, that he said that if he went into rebellion again, it should be for the grandson of the Duke of Monmouth. Cardonnel and I went with Smollett to Sir David Kinloch's and passed the day, when John Home and Logan and I conducted him to Dunbar where we stayed together all night.

Smollett was a man of very agreeable conversation and of much genuine humour; and, though not a profound scholar, possessed a philosophical mind, and was capable of making the soundest observations on human life, and of discerning the excellence or seeing the ridicule of every character he met with. Fielding only excelled him in giving a dramatic story to his novels, but, in my opinion, was inferior to him in the true comic vein. He was one of the many very pleasant men with whom it was my good fortune to be intimately acquainted.

For the year 1758 (pp. 355–6):

Robertson[1] had never seem Smollett, and was very desirous of his acquaintance. By this time the Doctor had retired to Chelsea, and came seldom to town. Home and I, however, found that he came once a-week to Forrest's Coffeehouse, and sometimes dined there; so we managed an appointment with him on his day, when he agreed to dine with us. He was now become a great man, and being much of a humorist, was not to be put out of his way. Home and Robertson and Smith and I met him there, when he had several of his minions about him, to whom he prescribed tasks of trans-lation, compilation, or abridgment, which, after he had seen, he re-commended to the booksellers. We dined together, and Smollett was very brilliant. Having to stay all night, that we might spend the evening together, he only begged leave to withdraw for an hour, that he might give audience to his myrmidons; we insisted that, if his business [permitted], it should be in the room where we sat. The Doctor agreed, and the authors were introduced, to the number of five, I think, most of whom were soon dismissed. He kept two, however, to supper, whispering to us that he believed they would amuse us, which they certainly did, for they were curious characters.

We passed a very pleasant and joyful evening. When we broke up, Robertson expressed great surprise at the polished and agreeable manners and the great urbanity of his conversation. He had imagined that a man's manners must bear a likeness to his books, and as Smollett had described so well the characters of ruffians and profligates, that he must, of course, resemble them. This was not the first instance we had of the rawness, in respect of the world that still blunted our sagacious friend's observations.

NOTES

a Lord Provost of Edinburgh when Prince Charlie took possession of the city.
b But on naming the far more distinguished men seen by him in the 'hotbed of genius,' Bramble says, 'These acquaintances I owe to the friendship of Dr Carlyle, who wants nothing but inclination to figure with the rest on paper.'—J.H.B. The reference here is to *Humphry Clinker*, Vol. II, p.61. Letter of M. Bramble, Edinburgh, 8 August. See vol. II, p. 38 for an earlier reference to Carlyle.
1 The reference here is to the famous Scottish historian William Robertson (1721–93), whose *Collected Works*, ed. by Dugald Stewart, appeared in 12. volumes in 1817.

2. Tobias Smollett, Preface to
The Adventures of Roderick Random

1748

Smollett's first novel was published on 21 January 1748, by
John Osborn of Paternoster Row. The Preface constitutes
Smollett's apologia for his novel and gives his ideas on the
nature of satire and Romance. He acknowledges a debt to
Spanish and French models, in particular to Cervantes and to
Le Sage.

Of all kinds of Satire, there is none so entertaining, and universally
improving, as that which is introduced, as it were, occasionally, in
the course of an interesting story, which brings every incident
home to life; and by representing familiar scenes in an uncommon
and amusing point of view, invests them with all the graces of
novelty, while nature is appealed to in every particular.

The reader gratifies his curiosity, in pursuing the adventures of a
person in whose favour he is prepossessed; he espouses his cause, he
sympathizes with him in distress, his indignation is heated against
the authors of his calamity; the humane passions are inflamed; the
contrast between dejected virtue, and insulting vice, appears with
greater aggravation, and every impression having a double force on
the imagination, the memory retains the circumstance, and the
heart improves by the example. The attention is not tired with a
bare Catalogue of characters, but agreeably diverted with all the
variety of invention; and the vicissitudes of life appear in their
peculiar circumstances, opening an ample field for wit and
humour.

Romance, no doubt, owes its origin to ignorance, vanity and
superstition. In the dark ages of the world, when a man had
rendered himself famous for wisdom or valour, his family and
adherents availed themselves of his superior qualities, magnified his
virtues, and represented his character and person as sacred and
supernatural. The vulgar easily swallowed the bait, implored his

protection, and yielded the tribute of homage and praise even to adoration; his exploits were handed down to posterity with a thousand exaggerations; they were repeated as incitements to virtue; divine honours were paid, and altars erected to his memory, for the encouragement of those who attempted to imitate his example; and hence arose the heathen mythology, which is no other than a collection of extravagant Romances.————As learning advanced, and genius received cultivation, these stories were embellished with the graces of poetry, that they might the better recommend themselves to the attention; they were sung in publick, at festivals, for the instruction and delight of the audience; and rehearsed before battle, as incentives to deeds of glory. Thus tragedy and the epic muse were born, and, in the progress of taste arrived at perfection.————It is no wonder, that the ancients could not relish a fable in prose, after they had seen so many remarkable events celebrated in verse, by their best poets; we therefore, find no romance among them, during the aera of their excellence, unless the Cyropaedia of Zenophon may be so called; and it was not till arts and sciences began to revive, after the irruption of the Barbarians into Europe, that any thing of this kind appeared. But when the minds of men were debauched by the imposition of priest-craft to the most absurd pitch of credulity; the authors of romance arose, and losing sight of probability, filled their performances with the most monstrous hyperboles. If they could not equal the ancient poets in point of genius, they were resolved to excel them in fiction, and apply to the wonder rather than the judgment of their readers. Accordingly they brought negromancy to their aid, and instead of supporting the character of their heroes, by dignity of sentiment and practice, distinguished them by their bodily strength, activity and extravagance of behaviour. Although nothing could be more ludicrous and unnatural than the figures they drew, they did not want patrons and admirers, and the world actually began to be infected with the spirit of knight-errantry, when Cervantes, by an inimitable piece of ridicule, reformed the taste of mankind, representing chivalry in the right point of view, and converting romance to purposes far more useful and entertaining, by making it assume the sock, and point out the follies of ordinary life.

The same method has been practised by other Spanish and French authors, and by none more successfully than by Monsieur

Le Sage, who in his adventures of Gil Blas, has described the knavery and foibles of life, with infinite humour and sagacity.— The following sheets I have modelled on his plan, taking the liberty, however, to differ from him in the execution, where I thought his particular situations were uncommon, extravagant, or peculiar to the country in which the scene is laid.——The disgraces of Gil Blas, are for the most part, such as rather excite mirth than compassion; he himself laughs at them; and his transitions from distress to happiness, or at least ease, are so sudden, that neither the reader has time to pity him, nor himself to be acquainted with affliction.—The conduct, in my opinion, not only deviates from probability, but prevents that generous indignation, which ought to animate the reader, against the sordid and vicious disposition of the world.

I have attempted to represent modest merit struggling with every difficulty to which a friendless orphan is exposed, from his own want of experience, as well as from the selfishness, envy, malice, and base indifference of mankind.—To secure a favourable prepossession, I have allowed him the advantages of birth and education, which in the series of his misfortunes, will I hope, engage the ingenuous more warmly in his behalf; and though I foresee, that some people will be offended at the mean scenes in which he is involved, I persuade myself the judicious will not only perceive the necessity of describing those situations to which he must of course be confined, in his low estate; but also find entertainment in viewing those parts of life, where the humours and passions are undisguised by affectation, ceremony, or education; and the whimsical peculiarities of disposition appear as nature has implanted them.—But I believe I need not trouble myself in vindicating a practice authorized by the best writers in this way, some of whom I have already named.

Every intelligent reader will, at first sight, perceive I have not deviated from nature, in the facts, which are all true in the main, although the circumstances are altered and disguised to avoid personal satire.

It now remains, to give my reasons for making the chief personage of this work a North-Briton; which are chiefly these: I could at a small expence bestow on him such educations as I thought the dignity of his birth and character required, which could not possibly be obtained in England, by such slender means as the nature of my plan would afford. In the next place, I could represent simplicity of manners in a remote part of the kingdom, with more propriety, than in any place near the capital; and lastly, the disposition of the Scots, addicted to travelling, justifies my conduct in driving an adventurer from that country.

That the delicate reader may not be offended at the unmeaning oaths which proceed from the mouths of some persons in these memoirs, I beg leave to premise, that I imagined nothing could more effectually expose the absurdity of such miserable expletives, than a natural and verbal representation of the discourse with which they are commonly interlarded.

3. Catherine Talbot, letter

15 February 1748

From a letter to Elizabeth Carter, *A Series of Letters between Mrs Elizabeth Carter and Miss Catherine Talbot*, 1809, Vol. I, p. 252.

Catherine Talbot (1721–70), educated by Thomas Secker, Archbishop of Canterbury, an author in her own right. Elizabeth Carter (1717–1806), miscellaneous writer, friend of Samuel Johnson.

Now I name acting, have you read that strange book Roderic Random! It is a very strange and a very low one, though not without some characters in it, and I believe some very just, though very wretched descriptions. Among others, there is the history of a poor tragedy author, ill used by actors and managers, that I think one cannot but be touched with, when one considers how many such kinds of scenes there are every day in real life. That wicked good-nature of the rich and great, that can see, and acknowledge merit in distress, speak it fair, promise high, raise expectations, and yet continue indolent, and do nothing to relieve it, is shewn in a striking manner; so is the cruelty of delaying people, and putting them off from day to day, and many other inhumanities unfelt by the doers; but not less blameable.

4. The Earl of Orrery on *Roderick Random*

12 March 1748

From John Boyle, Earl of Cork and Orrery (1707–62), in *The Orrery Papers*, ed. Emily Charlotte Boyle, Countess of Cork and Orrery, 2 vols, 1903, vol. II, p. 23. This extract, from a letter to Thomas Carew dated Caledon, 12 March 1748, is given as an index of fashionable interest in Smollett's first novel. Richardson's *Clarissa* appeared in seven volumes during 1747–8.

Clarissa kept us up till two in the morning. *Rhoderic* [*sic*] will keep us up all night, and he, I am told, is to be succeeded again by *Clarissa*, whom I left, adorable girl, at St Albans.

5. 'An Oxford Scholar' on *Roderick Random*

1748

From *The Parallel; or, Pilkington and Phillips Compared. Being Remarks upon the Memoirs of Those two celebrated Writers*, by an Oxford Scholar, 1748, pp. 7–8. This anonymous pamphlet, including a discussion of *Pamela*, *Joseph Andrews* and *Roderick Random*, is thought to be the first printed criticism of

Smollett's novel. As Martin C. Battestin points out in *Notes and Queries*, 213, 1968, 450–52 the writer's 'Judgement of the book is astute: the quality he finds most salient and disturbing is the starkness of Smollett's realism, the refusal to "represent Nature with a Veil"' (cf. No. 38).

Why then, Sir, *What think you of* Roderick Random? I think, said I, that it is very sprightly, very entertaining, and very full of poignant Satire. *In short, Sir, you think it excellent*; I did not say so, quoth I; a Book is excellent when it has no Faults, as well as an infinite Number of fine Things, but this has both Beauties and Blemishes, nay, what in one Sense are Beauties, are Blemishes in another. There are many free Strokes that please, because they are true and agreeable to Nature; but some Truths are not to be told, and the most skilful Painters represent Nature with a Veil. *Upon the whole, Sir*, says my Bookseller, by way of summing up, *we are, I find, of very different Opinions; I fancy you are fit for any Things, whereas you look upon yourself as good for nothing. Look ye, Sir, our Business is to distinguish Men's Talents, and take my Word for it, I have found out yours. You have a rare Head for* Criticism, *believe me. Why Doctor Quibus at Tom's, who is the great Censor of the present Age, pronounced the very same Judgment upon these Books that you have done.——There are your Materials; I must go to meet a Stationer at the* Temple Exchange, *I suppose you'll have done by* Tuesday, and so, Sir, speed the Plow; 'till then, I am your very humble Servant.

6. *The Gentleman's Magazine*

XIX, March 1749, 126

From a footnote to 'An Extract from a famed Sermon... by Edw. Cobden, D.D. Archdeacon of London, and Chaplain ordinary to his Majesty'.

The Gentleman's Magazine editor adds a footnote to Cobden's sermon, 'A Persuasive to Chastity', where Cobden describes the miseries following upon fornication.

This appears to be the first reference to Smollett in a periodical.

Of this wretched state, a most lively and striking picture is exhibited in *Roderick Random*, which we have here copied as a warning to one sex, and a remonstranse against t' other.

Miss Williams, who had been betray'd into a course of vice by the fraud and cruelty of a man of pleasure, is introduced relating the story of her own misfortunes:

[quotes from Miss Williams' story, *Roderick Random*, ch. 23, pp. 192–4]

7. [John Cleland], review of *The Regicide*
May 1749

In this unsigned notice in *The Monthly Review*, May 1749, i, 59–60, John Cleland, later notorious for his pornographic novel *Fanny Hill*, comments favourably on Smollett's tragedy. A fictional version of Smollett's endeavours to get *The Regicide* performed and published appeared as the inset story of the poet Melopoyn and his manuscript tragedy in chapters 62 and 63 of *Roderick Random*. There can be little doubt that *The Regicide* was finally published following the wave of Smollett's popularity after this novel.

This piece came out about the middle of May last, preceded by a preface, in which the author gives the public an account of the unworthy usage he met with from the managers of the two theatres, to whom he had tendered this play. This preface not only abounds in strokes of humour, and portraiture, peculiar to the author of *Roderick Random*, but is justly calculated for a warning to adventurers in writing for the stage.

8. Samuel Johnson in *The Rambler*

No. 4, 31 March 1750

This essay was occasioned by the popularity of *Roderick Random* and *Tom Jones* although neither Smollett nor Fielding is named by Johnson (see A. Chalmers, ed., *The Works of Samuel Johnson*, 1816, vol. iv, p. 24). It is taken here from *The Works of Samuel Johnson*, 9 vols, 1825, in the Oxford English Classics series, vol. 2, pp. 15–20.

Simul et jucunda et idonea dicere vita. Hor. A.P. 334.
And join both profit and delight in one. Creech.

The works of fiction, with which the present generation seems more particularly delighted, are such as exhibit life in its true state, diversified only by accidents that daily happen in the world, and influenced by passions and qualities which are really to be found in conversing with mankind.

This kind of writing may be termed not improperly the comedy of romance, and is to be conducted nearly by the rules of comick poetry. Its province is to bring about natural events by easy means, and to keep up curiosity without the help of wonder: it is therefore precluded from the machines and expedients of the heroic romance, and can neither employ giants to snatch away a lady from the nuptial rites, nor knights to bring her back from captivity; it can neither bewilder its personages in deserts, nor lodge them in imaginary castles.

I remember a remark made by Scaliger upon Pontanus, that all his writings are filled with the same images; and that if you take from him his lilies and his roses, his satyrs and his dryads, he will have nothing left that can be called poetry. In like manner almost all the fictions of the last age will vanish, if you deprive them of a hermit and a wood, a battle and a shipwreck.

Why this wild strain of imagination found reception so long in polite and learned ages, it is not easy to conceive; but we cannot wonder that while readers could be procured, the authors were

42

willing to continue it; for when a man had by practice gained some fluency of language, he had no further care than to retire to his closet, let loose his invention, and heat his mind with incredibilities; a book was thus produced without fear of criticism, without the toil of study, without knowledge of nature, or acquaintance with life.

The task of our present writers is very different; it requires, together with that learning which is to be gained from books, that experience which can never be attained by solitary diligence, but must arise from general converse and accurate observation of the living world. Their performances have, as Horace expresses it, *plus oneris quantum veniae minus,*[1] little indulgence, and therefore more difficulty. They are engaged in portraits of which every one knows the original, and can detect any deviation from exactness of resemblance. Other writings are safe, except from the malice of learning, but these are in danger from every common reader; as the slipper ill executed was censured by a shoemaker who happened to stop in his way at the Venus of Apelles.

But the fear of not being approved as just copiers of human manners, is not the most important concern that an author of this sort ought to have before him. These books are written chiefly to the young, the ignorant, and the idle, to whom they serve as lectures of conduct, and introductions into life. They are the entertainment of minds unfurnished with ideas, and therefore easily susceptible of impressions; not fixed by principles, and therefore easily following the current of fancy; not informed by experience, and consequently open to every false suggestion and partial account.

That the highest degree of reverence should be paid to youth, and that nothing indecent should be suffered to approach their eyes or ears, are precepts extorted by sense and virtue from an ancient writer, by no means eminent for chastity of thought. The same kind, though not the same degree, of caution, is required in every thing which is laid before them, to secure them from unjust prejudices, perverse opinions, and incongruous combinations of images.

In the romances formerly written, every transaction and sentiment was so remote from all that passes among men, that the reader was in very little danger of making any applications to himself; the virtues and crimes were equally beyond his sphere of activity; and he amused himself with heroes and with traitors, deliverers and persecutors, as with beings of another species, whose actions were regulated upon motives of their own, and who had neither faults nor excellencies in common with himself.

But when an adventurer is levelled with the rest of the world, and acts in such scenes of the universal drama, as may be the lot of any other man; young spectators fix their eyes upon him with closer attention, and hope, by observing his behaviour and success, to regulate their own practices, when they shall be engaged in the like part.

For this reason these familiar histories may perhaps be made of greater use than the solemnities of professed morality, and convey the knowledge of vice and virtue with more efficacy than axioms and definitions. But if the power of example is so great as to take possession of the memory by a kind of violence, and produce effects almost without the intervention of the will, care ought to be taken, that, when the choice is unrestrained, the best examples only should be exhibited; and that which is likely to operate so strongly, should not be mischievous or uncertain in its effects.

The chief advantage which these fictions have over real life is, that their authors are at liberty, though not to invent, yet to select objects, and to cull from the mass of mankind, those individuals upon which the attention ought most to be employed; as a diamond, though it cannot be made, may be polished by art, and placed in such a situation, as to display that lustre which before was buried among common stones.

It is justly considered as the greatest excellency of art, to imitate nature; but it is necessary to distinguish those parts of nature, which are most proper for imitation: greater care is still required in representing life, which is so often discoloured by passion, or deformed by wickedness. If the world be promiscuously described, I cannot see of what use it can be to read the account; or why it may not be as safe to turn the eye immediately upon mankind as upon a mirrour which shews all that presents itself without discrimination.

It is therefore not a sufficient vindication of a character, that it is drawn as it appears; for many characters ought never to be drawn: nor of a narrative, that the train of events is agreeable to observation and experience; for that observation which is called knowledge of the world, will be found much more frequently to make men cunning than good. The purpose of these writings is surely not only to shew mankind, but to provide that they may be seen hereafter with less hazard; to teach the means of avoiding the snares which are laid by Treachery for Innocence, without infusing any wish for that superiority with which the betrayer flatters his vanity; to give the power of counteracting fraud, without the temptation to practise it; to initiate youth by mock encounters in the art of necessary defence, and to increase prudence without impairing virtue.

Many writers, for the sake of following nature, so mingle good and bad qualities in their principal personages, that they are both equally conspicuous; and as we accompany them through their adventures with delight, and are led by degrees to interest ourselves in their favour, we lose the abhorrence of their faults, because they do not hinder our pleasure, or, perhaps, regard them with some kindness, for being united with so much merit.

There have been men indeed splendidly wicked, whose endowments threw a brightness on their crimes, and whom scarce any villany made perfectly detestable, because they never could be wholly divested of their excellencies; but such have been in all ages the great corrupters of the world, and their resemblance ought no more to be preserved, than the art of murdering without pain.

Some have advanced, without due attention to the consequences of this notion, that certain virtues have their correspondent faults, and therefore that to exhibit either apart is to deviate from probability. Thus men are observed by Swift to be 'grateful in the same degree as they are resentful.' This principle, with others of the same kind, supposes man to act from a brute impulse, and pursue a certain degree of inclination, without any choice of the object; for, otherwise, though it should be allowed that gratitude and resentment arise from the same constitution of the passions, it follows not that they will be equally indulged when reason is consulted; yet, unless that consequence be admitted, this sagacious maxim becomes an empty sound, without any relation to practice or to life.

Nor is it evident, that even the first motions to these effects are always in the same proportion. For pride, which produces quickness of resentment, will obstruct gratitude, by unwillingness to admit that inferiority which obligation implies; and it is very unlikely that he who cannot think he receives a favour, will acknowledge or repay it.

It is of the utmost importance to mankind, that positions of this tendency should be laid open and confuted; for while men consider good and evil as springing from the same root, they will spare the one for the sake of the other, and in judging, if not of others at least of themselves, will be apt to estimate their virtues by their vices. To this fatal errour all those will contribute, who confound the colours of right and wrong, and, instead of helping to settle their boundaries, mix them with so much art, that no common mind is able to disunite them.

In narratives where historical veracity has no place, I cannot discover why there should not be exhibited the most perfect idea of virtue; of virtue not angelical, nor above probability, for what we cannot credit, we shall never imitate, but the highest and purest that humanity can reach, which, exercised in such trials as the various revolutions of things shall bring upon it, may, by conquering some calamities, and enduring others, teach us what we may hope, and what we can perform. Vice, for vice is necessary to be shewn, should always disgust; nor should the graces of gaiety, or the dignity of courage, be so united with it, as to reconcile it to the mind. Wherever it appears, it should raise hatred by the malignity of its practices, and contempt by the meanness of its stratagems: for while it is supported by either parts or spirit, it will be seldom heartily abhorred. The Roman tyrant was content to be hated, if he was but feared; and there are thousands of the readers of romances willing to be thought wicked, if they may be allowed to be wits. It is therefore to be steadily inculcated, that virtue is the highest proof of understanding, and the only solid basis of greatness; and that vice is the natural consequence of narrow thoughts; that it begins in mistake, and ends in ignominy.

NOTE

1. Horace, *Epistles*, II.i.170. The translation is given in the text by Johnson, as 'little indulgence and therefore more difficulty'.

9. Samuel Richardson, letter

6 December 1750

From a letter to Sarah Chapone, Forster, MSS., XII, ii, f. 7: reprinted in *Selected Letters of Samuel Richardson*, ed. John Carroll, 1964, p. 173.

The reference here is in anticipation of the publication of Smollett's *Peregrine Pickle* (February 1751) which was to include Lady Jane Vane's *Memoirs of a Lady of Quality*: a cause célèbre in prospect.

I mentioned to Mr Chapone my Wishes, that the Lady who so admirably wrote to correct and instruct a very profligate Woman, should, from the same right Principles and Motives, undertake a Woman of Quality, whom I think, if possible, a worse Woman. If I can procure a Specimen Sheet of the Work, for it is not yet printed quite off, I will cause it, in Confidence, to be sent to that Lady: And I persuade myself, that she will, from that, see the Necessity of her severest Castigation for the public Good.

Mrs Pilkington, Constantia Phillips, Lady V. (who will soon appear, profaning the Word *Love*, and presuming to attempt to clear her *Heart*, and to find gentle Fault only with her *Head*, in the Perpetration of the highest Acts of Infidelity) what a Set of Wretches, wishing to perpetuate their Infamy, have we—to make the Behn's, the Manley's, and the Heywood's look white. From the same injured, disgraced, profaned Sex, let us be favoured with the Antidote to these Womens Poison!

10. Samuel Richardson, letter

11 January 1751

From a letter to Sarah Chapone, *Selected Letters of Samuel Richardson*, ed. John Carroll, 1964, p. 173. Forster MSS., XII, ii, ff. 11–12.

I send to your worthy son (I could not before) that Part of a bad Book which contains the very bad Story of a wicked woman. I could be glad to see it animadverted upon by so admirable a Pen. Ladies, as I have said, should antidote the Poison shed by the vile of their Sex....

11. [Francis Coventry], from *An Essay on the New Species of Writing*

1751

From *An Essay on the New Species of Writing founded by Mr Fielding: with a Word or Two upon the Modern State of Criticism* (1751), pp. 22–3.

Coventry was the author of *The History of Pompey the Little* (1751). This extract from *An Essay* is taken from Alan D. McKillop's fascimile edition (Augustan Reprint Society, Publication no. 95, 1962). An encomium on Fielding, he here criticizes Smollett for his excessively descriptive chapter headings in *Roderick Random*.

'Tis quite opposite to the Custom of the very best Writers in this Way, to give too full an Account of the Contents: it should be just hinted to the Reader something extraordinary is to happen in the seven or eight subsequent Pages, but what that is should be left for them to discover. Monsieur *Le Sage*, in his *Gil Blas*, (one of the best Books of the Kind extant) has always pursu'd this Method: He tells us *Gil Blas* is going to such or such a Place, but does not discover the least of his Adventures there; but he is more particularly cautious when any unexpected Event is to happen. The Title to one of his Chapters of that Kind is—*A Warning not to rely too much upon Prosperity*.—To another—*Chapter the fifth, being just as long as the preceding*: With many others which it is needless to enumerate. Note, 'Tis to be wish'd this Custom had been observ'd by the Author of *Roderick Random*, who tells us in his Preface, his Book is wrote in Imitation of the *Gil Blas* of Monsieur *Le Sage*. But with very little Success in my humble Opinion. As to the Titles of his Chapters, he is particularly tedious in them. This judicious Method of detaining the Reader in an agreeable Suspence, though it is right at all Times, is more particularly necessary when the History is near ended. No Writer has so strictly kept up to this as Mr *Fielding*, in his *Tom Jones*. We are too well assured of *Gil Blas*'s Prosperity a long Time beforehand, to be surpriz'd at it. But at the Beginning of the last Book of *Tom Jones*, the Reader is apt to think it an equal Chance whether he is to be hanged or married....

12. Unsigned review of Hill's *Lady Frail*

February 1751

From *The Monthly Review*, February 1751, iv, 307–8, reviewing Dr John Hill's anonymous *The History of a Woman of Quality: or, The Adventures of Lady Frail*. Hill's work appeared on 8 February 1751 two weeks before the publication of *Peregrine Pickle*, and sought to capitalize on the sensational aspects of Smollett's novel.

Whether these memoirs have *any* foundation in fact, we know not; nor who is the person designed to be understood under the name of

Lady *Frail*. The public, ever ready enough to be caught by such baits, have, on this occasion, agreed to mention the name of a lady, who is credibly reported to have given real memoirs of herself, to the author of a famous novel, entitled, The *adventures* of *Roderick Random*, to be inserted and made public in a new work of his. Accordingly, this author has signified by repeated advertisements, 'That no memoirs of that lady that may be obtruded upon the public, under any disguise whatever, are genuine, (*but an imposition*, &c.) except what are comprized in *his* work.' And we are inclined to believe him, not only from the regard due to his public declaration, but from our own persuasion, on a perusal of this history: in which there are many things too monstrous to be believed, especially on the credit of a nameless writer, whose chief design was, apparently, to make his advantage of the impatience of the public; and whose hasty crude performance seems, in every page, to put the reader in mind of the great hurry its author was in, *to come out first*. However, if the stories he relates could be depended on, as facts, his work would not be thought void of merit, in its way. The author has a lively, rapid, spirited manner, abounding with peculiar elegancies, and happy turns; but on the other hand, he makes so much haste to get to the end of his work, (probably for a very obvious reason) that his readers are thereby unhappily deprived of those moral inferences and observations which our first-rate *English* novels abound with, and which alone can make writings of any real use. Another talent, too, seems necessary to writers of this class, which our author wants, as well as the solid; and that is, *humour*. He has introduced no *Abraham Adams*, no Parson *Trullibers*, no *Thwackums*, *Westerns*, or *Straps*; so that the reader who takes up this book with any expectation of finding in it that fund of laughter and merry entertainment, that the works of *Fielding*, and the author of *Roderick Random*, afford, will find himself utterly disappointed.

13. Unsigned review of *Peregrine Pickle*
March 1751

The Monthly Review, March 1751, iv, 355–64. The review is by John Cleland.

Complaints are daily made, nor without reason, of the number of useless books, with which town and country are drenched and surfeited. How many productions do we see continually foisted upon the publick, under the sanction of deceitful title-pages, and against which we have more cause of complaint than merely from our being drawn in by *false tokens*, or on account of the loss of our money and time bestowed upon them: for to say nothing of those works which carry their own condemnation with them, (such as lewd or profane subjects, the pawn of indigence, of profligacy, or of both united) what are so many worthless frivolous pieces as we constantly see brought out, but the marks of that declension of wit and taste, which is perhaps more justly the reproach of the public than the authors who have been forced to consult, and conform to, its vitiated palate? Serious and useful works are scarce read, and hardly any thing of morality goes down, unless ticketed with the label of amusement. Thence the flood of novels, tales, romances, and other monsters of the imagination, which have been either wretchedly translated, or even more unhappily imitated, from the French, whose literary levity we have not been ashamed to adopt, and encourage the propagation of so depraved a taste. But this forced and unnatural transplantation could not long thrive in a country, of which the faculty of thinking, and thinking deeply, was once, and it is to be hoped, has not yet entirely ceased to be, the national characteristic.

The necessity then of borrowing from truth its colour at least, in favour of fiction, a point so justly recommended by *Horace*, and common sense, occurred, at length to some of our writers, who tried the experiment with success. To this new species of writing, the title of *biography*, humourously, and of course not improperly, assumed by the first ingenious author, has been however too lightly continued, since it certainly conveys a false idea. Pictures of fancy are not called portrait-painting, and no body who distinguishes terms will allow the title of *biographer*, which can only mean a writer of real lives, such as *Plutarch, Nepos,* &c. to be well applied to the authors of *Tom Jones, Roderick Random, David Simple,* &c. who may be more justly styled comic-romance writers. This piece of verbal criticism is the less insignificant, as it is owing to the mistake of a writer of great wit and humour, who likewise calls this is a *Life-writing age,* which may be true too, and yet not applicable to it, on most of the examples he quotes for the grounds of this epithet.

If this *epithet* too is used by way of ridiculing, or exploding this species of writing, (unless when too detestably employed in the service of lewdness and immorality, to deserve no more than being ridiculed) the censure does not seem intirely well warranted. There are perhaps no works of entertainment more susceptible of improvement or public utility, than such as are thus calculated to convey instruction, under the passport of amusement. How many readers may be taught to pursue good, and to avoid evil, to refine their morals, and to detest vice, who are profitably decoyed into the perusal of these writings by the pleasure they expect to be paid with for their attention, who would not care to be dragged through a dry, didactic system of morality; or who would, from a love of truth universally impressed on mankind, despise inventions which do not at least pay truth the homage of imitation. To judge then candidly and impartially of works of this sort, and to fix their standard, their mint may be tried by that short and excellent test, which *Horace,* perhaps the greatest, the wisest wit of any age, suggests to us in that so often quoted expression of *utile dulci.*

If we consider then in general, before we come to particular application, the true use of these writings, it is more to be lamented that we have so few of them, than that there are too many. For as the matter of them is chiefly taken from nature, from adventures, real or imaginary, but familiar, practical, and probable to be met with in the course of common life, they may serve as pilot's charts, or maps of those parts of the world, which every one may chance to travel through; and in this light they are public benefits. Whereas romances and novels which turn upon characters out of nature, monsters of perfection, feats of chivalry, fairy-enchantments, and the whole train of the marvellous-absurd, transport the reader unprofitably into the clouds, where he is sure to find no solid footing, or into those wilds of fancy, which go for ever out of the way of all human paths.

No comparison that affords such variety of just applications, as that of human life to a voyage, can ever disgust by its staleness, or repetition. And where is the traveller who would complain of the number of maps, or journals, designed to point him out his way through the number of different roads that choice or chance may engage him in? The objections that the number may bewilder, or the falsity, or insufficiency of them mislead him, are of little or no comparative avail, to the utility which may redound from them, since there is hardly a case occurs in these pieces, in which nature and probability have been consulted, but by its appositeness, or similarity, at least may afford respectively salutary hints, or instructions. And as to the last objection, it is easily refuted, by remarking, in pursuance of the same metaphor, that it would be vain and ridiculous to condemn the use of maps, or charts, because some are laid down by unskilful or treacherous artists. Something in all productions of this sort must be left to judgement: and if fools have not the gift, and are sometimes, in such reading, hurt by the want of it; such a consideration surely says but little against works, from benefiting by which, only fools are excluded, and even that is a misfortune to which nature has made them as insensible as they are incorrigible.

The author of the adventures of *Peregrine Pickle*, had before given, in those of *Roderick Random*, a specimen of his talents for this species of writing, which had been so well received by the public, as to encourage his entering on the present work.

The first volume is chiefly taken up with introductory accounts of the family of *Peregrine Pickle*, who is the hero of the piece, of incidents which preceded his birth—His boyish pranks—His mother's capricious aversion to him, which, after a fruitless appeal to his own father, who is too much wife-ridden to do his son natural justice, throws him into an intire dependence on his uncle—his falling in love with *Emilia*, the consequences of this passion, and several juvenile sallies, and adventures, till he arrives at a competent age for setting out on his travels to *France*.

In this volume, the author seems to have aimed more at proportioning his style to his subject, in imitation of *Lazarillo de Tormes, Guzman d'Alfarache, Gil Blas de Santillane,* and *Scarron's Comic Romance,* than he has respected the delicacy of those readers, who call every thing *Low* that is not taken from high-life, which is, however, rarely susceptible of that humour and drollery which occur in the more familiar walks of common life. But, to pronounce with an air of decision, that he has every where preserved propriety and nature, would sound more towards interested commendation than genuine criticism. Citations give the fairest play to all parties, and as this first volume lies the openest to the accusation of being *Low,* the following images, which are at least not selected from amongst the highest, may give a reasonable idea of the rest of the volume, however they may flatten to the reader by being thus detached from the body of the story.

[quotes: 'Among those who suffered by his craft and infidelity was Mr Jumble his own tutor...Peregrine answered with great resolution, that when...', vol. I, ch. 22, pp. 155–7. Then quotes: 'The first sample of their art...for having reduced them to such ridiculous distress', vol. I. ch. 13, pp. 89–91]

The second citation is placed here last, out of its order of time, to make way for an observation, that as low and ignoble as the adventure appears, from the nature of its subject, it has that objection to it in common with two of the most risible adventures in the famous *Comic Romance of Scarron,* not to mention that of one of the most humourous tales that was perhaps ever written, that of *Acajou* and *Zirphile,* by *Duclos,* author of the history of *Lewis* the eleventh, turns entirely upon the fate of one of these necessary utensils.

VOLUME *The Second.* The author rises in his stile, with his hero, whom he conducts to *Paris,* and from thence home by the way of *Flanders* and *Holland,* after a course of mixt adventures, in which are introduced, besides occasional gallantries and incidents of travelling two original characters.

The one a painter, under the name of *Pallet,* whose absurdities furnish *Pickle* with matter of entertainment.

The other a physician, whose character is rather overtouched, especially in the description of a feast given by him in the manner of the antients, for whom he is represented to have that sort of enthusiastic admiration, which is consequentially attended with a profound contempt for all modern merit whatever in arts and sciences. This extravagance, which like most literary pedantries, has its foundation in vanity, and the want of that just medium, in which true taste alone delights, is here too sarcastically exposed, for good nature not to complain, however poetical justice may smile at the execution.

Pickle returned to *England*, visits *Bath*, where, amongst sundry achievements, he contracts an acquaintance with another original, a misanthrope, who feigns himself deaf, that he may be more effectually a spy on the follies, and iniquities of mankind, which he sacrifices to his new friend *Pickle*, who being himself a character-hunter, makes his profit of this acquisition.

VOLUME *The Third* is principally remarkable for the memoirs of a woman of quality, episodically introduced.

As these memoirs are not only taken from a character in real life, but seem to be voluntarily furnished by the lady *V——* herself, who is the subject of them, they cannot but be interesting, both from the rarity, as well as the ingenuity of her confessions.

Thus begins the narrative:

[quotes: 'By the circumstances of the story... *because I loved, and was a woman*', vol. III, ch. 81, p. 63]

After this, she relates her first *happy* marriage, with lord *W—— H——*, in which every thing could not but be well ordered since love had the ordering it.

On the death, which she pathetically laments, of her first husband, succeeds the account of her marrying a second, her present lord, which she agreed, to get rid of the importunity of friends who consulted their views of conveniency, and an opulent establishment for her, more than they did her real happiness, and in determining her to which, they took the advantage of that careless insensibility, which is natural of a heart to sink into, when reduced, and worn down by exessive grief, to that state of quietism, which renders every thing, even life, or death, indifferent to those who are plunged in it.

As unhappily her husband wanted those qualifications which could render him amiable in her eyes; a heart so susceptible of the tender passions as her's was, could not long support the want of subjects to employ it on; and that sensibility, joined to the incessant persecutions of her lord, who was himself unfortunate enough to love, without the power of engaging a return, threw her into that course of irregularities and disorders, which, she is so far from making trophies of, that she every where occasionally laments the fatality of conjunctures, and her inability to resist the torrent that bore her away, against the opposition of her better reason.

$$\text{----------}Novi, \ meliora, \ proboque$$
$$Deteriora \ fequor\text{----------}^1$$

breathes through all her misconduct, and she expresses herself no where so pathetically as where she regrets her departure from the paths of honour and virtue.

[quotes: 'Love made up for all deficiencies to me, . . . as I have frankly owned my failings and misconduct', vol. III, ch. 81. p. 212]

This last corrective plainly shews, that she never meant, under the colour of being mismatched, which, at most, only mitigates her guilt, to insinuate that her conduct would, in strictness, bear a justification; casuistry so loose, so contrary to the universal reverence of all nations for the solemnity and obligations of the nuptial tie, would as little pass, as the attempt to pass it can, with any shadow of justice, be imputed to her ladyship, who every where mentions her errors, as her greatest and most deep felt misfortune.

In VOLUME *the fourth and last*, the author, instead of flagging, the usual consequence of exhausting a character, proceeds with increased importance and vivacity.

Peregrine is exhibited in various spheres of action; a rake, a candidate for a borough, an author, a prisoner for debt, an heir triumphant over all his misfortunes, and ultimately a happy bridegroom to the object of his first passion, the fair *Emilia*. And in all these vicissitudes, the author represents him with great uniformity of principle, unbending and fierce in adversity, nosing a prime minister, and refusing for wife a mistress whom he adores; but, tractable and supple in prosperity; a character, in short, too natural to be perfect, but in which the gentle shades serve only to raise the lights of the picture.

In this volume too are introduced several characters, which are said to be drawn from actual life, and are drawn so as cannot fail of giving offence to the supposed originals. It also contains the personal history of Mr *M——r*, the manager in the extraordinary cause between the claimant Mr *A——*, and the Earl of *A——*, defendant; in which the author seems to be much delighted with an occasion of paying respect to worth, or what he looks upon as such, tho' unseconded by success.

NOTE

1 Ovid, *Metamorphoses*, VII, 20: 'I knew the better course, and I approved it, but I followed the worse.'

14. Unsigned review of *Peregrine Pickle*

1751

The Royal Magazine, January, February, March 1751, II, 396–405.

The author of these adventures, is the same gentleman who some years since published, those of Roderick Random, and it is probably owing to the reception of that work met with from its readers, that the author has again appeared as a writer in the romantic biographical way, and now offer'd the adventures of Mr Pickle to the perusal of the public. In order that we may be fully appris'd of every circumstance which could possibly relate to the history and character of the hero of this romance, the author furnishes us with several minute particulars relating to his story, and particularly an account of the family of the Pickles, and several remarkable incidents preceding the birth of his hero.

Mr Gamaliel Pike, father of Peregrine, the hero of this romance, is represented as a phelgmatic indolent man, void of all refin'd sensations, a stranger to love, and actuated only by a spirit of covetousness, imbibed from his father, a merchant of London, who had acquired a large fortune, which on his death-bed he had enjoined his son to increase to a plum, and of which it at that time was not much deficient; Gamaliel endeavoured to fulfil the request of his father, but meeting with some disappointments and losses in trade, whereby his principal stock was diminished to 5000l. he in the 36th year of his age, relinquished trade, and retired into the country, in hopes by frugality to secure himself from want, and the dangers of a jail, of which he was under no small apprehensions. In this retirement he was accompany'd by his only sister Mrs Grizzle, who had managed his family since the death of his father, was now in the thirtieth year of her age, and had greatly encouraged his scheme of entring into rural life; being herself dissatify'd, that she had not hitherto made any conquests in town. This lady, whose person, was far from engaging, was a confirm'd prude, of a peevish rather than resigned piety, ill-natur'd and proud of her family; tho' in reality it was but an upstart one, and had never any thing remarkable happen'd in it, except that her father had been Lord-Mayor; a circumstance which she frequently took occasion of mentioning, as she dated all her observations from that important event.

Mr Gamaliel was no sooner settled in the country, than he determined to spend his evenings at a neighbouring alehouse, where he soon contract'd an acquaintance with commodore Trunnion and lieutenant Hatchway, who resided in the same parish, and made this alehouse their constant rendezvous. The commodore was an old morose rough tar, rich, but a great humourist, and a profess'd woman hater: though he had quitted the sea service, yet he could not entirely divest himself of all military appearance, he therefore surrounded his house with a ditch, called it the rison, and planted his court-yard with pateraroes, which he put under the direction of Mr Hatchway, a man of humour and a great joker, who had been his lieutenant, but being upon half-pay, lived with him; he was also attended by Tom Pipes, who was another favourite, had been his boatswain's mate, & now took upon him the superintendency of the servants, the male part whereof, every night, (after sending the maid-servants into an out-house, appointed for their apartment) turned out watch and watch, all the year round.

Mrs Grizzle, prompted by the ambition of preserving her family's name, soon propos'd a match between her brother, and the daughter of a gentleman who lived in the next parish, and though he possessed but a small fortune, was one of the best families in the county. This affair being soon concluded under the conduct of Mrs Grizzle, a day was fixed for the celebration of the nuptials, to which every body of fashion in the neighbourhood were invited; and among them the commodore and Mr Hatchway, neither of whom had been wanting in their endeavours to deter Mr Pickle from marrying, by throwing out invectives against that state.

Mrs Grizzle, who took upon her to be the principle figure at this festival, endeavoured to play off all her charms upon the single gentlemen, who were invited to the entertainment, and shewed an uncommon civility; while the commodore, who had not been us'd to female company, nor ever pronounced the word madam since he was born, found himself under very disagreeable restraints, from which he was not relieved till some of the company moved to adjourn into another apartment, where they might enjoy their bottles and pipes. It was not long after this marriage, before Mrs Pickle endeavoured to assume the government of her own family, which had hitherto been solely conducted by Mrs Grizzle, who now shewed great unwillingness to part from it; but Mrs Pickle insisting on her prerogative, & having gain'd an absolute ascendency over her husband, Mrs Grizzle found herself of so little importance in the family, that she determined to apply herself to no less difficult task, than that of making a conquest of the commodore's heart, in which design she engaged the assistance of lieutenant Hatchway. The extraordinary stratagems, difficulties and incidents which attended the execution of this plan, the obstinate refusals and perverseness of the commodore, the embarrassments this affair threw him into, are related, with some humour, together with an account of the several methods Mrs Grizzle took, the troubles she was involved in, tending & cherishing her sister during her pregnancy, and Mrs Pickle's being delivered of a son, who was christen'd by the name of Peregrine, and to whom the commodore stood godfather, are the subjects of several chapters. In these chapters the author, likewise relates some instances of Mrs Pickle's longings, and Mrs Grizzle's indefatigable pains to gratify them, which are extremely ridiculous, and do not carry the least air of probability.

Mrs Grizzle having at length to her great satisfaction teaz'd the obdurate commodore, to reconcile himself to wedlock, a day was fix'd for the nuptials, which however our author will not suffer to be celebrated, without their being interrupted by an accident, which befel the commodore in his way to the church, and delay'd till another day, the performance of the ceremony, he then gives us, the bill of fare of the wedding supper provided under Hatchway's management. An account of the alterations made by Mrs Trunnion in the economy of her house and family, and the methods whereby she asserted her prerogative, and attain'd an absolute sovereignity over the commodore. But these are not interesting enough to be mention'd here.

The commodore soon finding himself deprived of all hopes of propagating his own name, and his relations lying under the interdict of his hate, contracted a liking for Peregrine, who being then about 3 years old, had the appearance of a handsome healthy child, and shew'd some signs of archness, an inclination to mischief and unlucky pranks, which heightened the commodore's regard for him. Sometime after, Mrs Pickle found herself pretty far gone with another child, and receiving an intimation from the Pedagogue who had then the instruction of Peregrine, that he was the most obstinate and untower'd genius that ever had fallen under his care, began to abate her affections for the child, and was easily prevail'd upon by the commodore, to suffer him at his own charge, to place Perry at a boarding School near London.

Our author here fills several pages with a minute account of the many pranks play'd by Peregrine, till he arrived at the age of twelve years, the narration whereof can be no ways entertaining to those, who are older than Peregrine is said to have then been.

Mrs Pickle having increased her family by the birth of another son, who engross'd all the care for the present, and not having seen Perry for four years, was now perfectly wean'd of all maternal fondness for him; and on his going with the commodore to pay her a visit, she could not help throwing out some strong hints that her own child was dead, and this no other than an impostor to defraud her sorrow. This unaccountable passion of Mrs Pickle's was such a surprise to Trunnion, and threw him into so great a confusion that he immediately carried the boy back with him to garrison, and determin'd that he never should enter Mr Pickle's house again.

Trunnion having thus taken upon him the absolute care of Perry, adopted him as his own son, removed him from a private school in which he had hitherto been educated, and sent him under the inspection of Mr Jolter, whom he has appointed his private tutor, to Winchester school, and where he was also attended by Tom Pipes, in the capacity of a footman. Here Peregrine in a little time became not only distinguished for the acuteness of his apprehensions, but for the mischievous fertility of his fancy, instances whereof our author furnishes us with. And among many others, makes him the ring leader of a very riotous adventure, the particular circumstances of which he seems to take great pleasure in relating, and which from the fear of scholastic discipline ended in a revolt and secession of the greatest part of the scholars. This ignominious circumstance the author loads Winchester with, tho' it is well known, to have really happen'd at another public school, no longer ago than the last year.

Peregrine having passed the 14th year of his age, and made a great progress in his studies, our author thinks it necessary he should now assume the man of gallantry, and turn his thoughts on conquests over female hearts, in which he is so kind as to represent him extremely expert and successful, tho' he still continues him at school. Being at a ball given at the next Winchester races he fell a victim to the charms of his partner Aemilia, who our author does not fail to furnish, with all necessary qualifications of beauty and understanding.

She had it seems made so strong an impression on our young hero that he soon after elop'd from school, and paid her a visit at the house of her mamma; where he renewed his addresses, and met with such an agreeable reception, that he was not without some difficulties prevail'd upon to return to Winchester. Perry's ideas notwithstanding he was removed from the object of his wishes, being now totally engrossed by his mistress, he wrote the following lines which he inclosed in a letter, and ordered Pipes to carry and deliver into Aemilia's hands:

> Adieu ye streams that smoothly flow,
> Ye vernal airs that softly blow,
> Ye plains by blooming spring array'd,
> Ye birds that warble thro' the shade.
>
> Unhurt from you my soul could fly,
> Nor drop one tear nor heave one sigh
> But forc'd from Celia's charms to part,
> All joy desert my drooping heart.
>
> O fairer! than the rosy morn,
> When flowers the dewy fields adorn;
> Unsullied as the genial ray,

That warms the balmy breeze of May.

Thy charms divinely bright appear,
And add now splendor to the year;
Improve the day with fresh delight,
And gild with joy the dreary night.

Pipes proceeded on his errant, but had the misfortune of destroying the letter, before he arrived at the place of his destination, this threw him into a most terrible dilemma, nor could his genius suggest any better means of extricating himself from the difficulties he now laboured under, than by prevailing on the clerk of the parish to write a love letter in the most pathetic words he could invent, and sign it with Peregrine's name; the clerk who easily induced to perform this task, soon furnish'd him with a letter stuffed with the highest flights of bombast, and Pipes had no sooner received this curious piece than he hastened to Aemilia, and took care to deliver it into her own hands. The consequence whereof was, that Aemilia conceiving Peregrine had sent this letter with an intent to affront her, dismissed Pipes without any answer, to the great surprize of his young master, who could not account for this sudden alteration and coolness in Aemelia.

Peregrine being now in his 17th year was settled at Oxford with a very liberal allowance, and accompanied with the same attendants who lived with him at Winchester, but as he could not any longer confine himself to the prosecution of his studies, and look'd on the rules of the University as too severe, he soon contracted an acquaintance with the most profligate part of the University, who distinguish themselves by the name of *Bucks*, and is represented as guilty of such outrages, irregularities and indiscretions (some of which he acted against both his domestic and collegiate tutor) as tho' too frequently practiced by young gentlemen in the first outset from school, might have better been omitted in a work, which is likely to have the juvenile part of mankind, for the majority of its readers.

The remainder of the first volume is taken up with several other adventures of Peregrine, in which he breaks with the commodore but is again reconciled to him; pursues his overtures to Aemilia; fights a duel with her brother; takes a just revenge on his own brothers preceptor, who had without any provocation insulted him; is guilty of many irregularities in which the domestic peace of an innocent farmer is disturb'd and his wife debauched; and at length sent upon his travels into France. Peregrine was no sooner landed in France than he fell into company with a gentleman and lady lately arrived from England in their way to Paris, the gentleman was a man of a handsome estate; but having the misfortune to fall a sacrifice to the attractions of an oyster wench; who had decoy'd him into matrimony, had then brought her over to France, as well in order to give her instructions and education suitable to the person of his wife, as to avoid the compliments and congratulations which he expected from his friends and acquaintance, on so extraordinary a wedding. Peregrine no sooner saw this lady but he determined to enjoy her, which, after taking many extraordinary and unjustifiable steps to attain his ends, he at length effected. During his residence at Paris, we find his passions continually hurrying him into irregularities, as picking quarrels, fighting of duels, (intrigues, and amours which our author calls *gallantry*) and such other enormities as ended in his being sent prisoner to the Bastile, and from which he was not relieved, without great interest made by the English embassador, and even then only upon condition, that he should quit Paris in three days after his enlargement. While Peregrine was at Paris, he contracted an acquaintance with two Englishmen, one of whom is described by our author, as a young self conceited dr. of physic piping hot from his studies, enthusiastically fond of the antients, and possessed with a sovereign contempt for all modern merit in the arts and sciences, solemnly pedantic, and fond of introducing scraps of Latin and Greek in all his conversation. The other a painter of great levity and assurance, extreamly ignorant, in every house relating to skill, tho' affecting great his own profession, enamoured of the Flemish school, and preferring the works of the modern painters and statuaries to those of the antient artists. Peregrine greatly pleased with having commenced an acquaintance with these two extraordinary characters, makes them the companions of his tour, thro' France, Flanders and Holland. Here our author in his relation of what past in this journey, takes an opportunity of satyrizing very justly, the affected pedantry of those who can allow no merit to any but the antients, and have such a ridiculous ambition of being esteem'd men of learning, that they are at infinite pains in conning and getting by heart several detach'd pieces and expressions, from the Greek and Latin poets and philosophers, in order to retail them

63

in all companies, for the credit of their genius and knowledge. Neither does the infinite partiality which others frequently shew for the production of the moderns escape our author's censure, who judiciously and artfully shews that true taste consists only in observing a due medium between the one and the other, and in strictly giving commendations to real merit, whether it appears in the works of the moderns, or is found among those of the antients.

The great esteem and prejudices which some persons manifest for the laws, customs, policy manners, &c. of other countries, and in short for every thing that is foreign, is likewise here ridiculed, and the partial sovereign contempt which is shewn by others to whatever is not the production of their own native country, is fully exposed, and the folly of such ridiculous attachments and partiality represented in their true light. Great part of the 2d volume, is filled with an account of the little frolicks of Peregrine, calculated to tease the painter and physician; and a long succession of the hero's indiscretions, intrigues and amours, in most of which he meets with disappointments; and the little accidents which happened till his arrival in England, none of which are interesting enough to be inserted here. The Author's criticisms on the Tragedies, and Poetries of the Dutch, are very just, the absurdities of them are very properly exploded. The observations on the English stage made by a knight of Malta who had been long in England and frequented our theatres, and which are here related in a conversation at Lisle, between him & Pickle, may perhaps be agreeable to our readers.

[quotes: 'That you have good actors in England...even in those very circumstances wherein (as I have observed) they chiefly failed', vol. II, ch. 51, pp. 120–2]

Peregrine being arrived in England, visits his uncle, and the family at the garrison, by whom he is joyfully received, and soon after sets out for Bath, where he ruins a whole set of sharpers, acts the parts of a libertine, and cultivates an acquaintance with Cadwallader Crabtree, a misanthrope, who had run thro' a strange variety of scenes in life, and now feigned himself deaf in order to be a spy upon mankind without danger or interruption. Peregrine's stay at Bath being now determined by the death of his uncle the commodore who leaves him a large fortune, he sets out for London, waits upon his adored Aemelia, and makes a treacherous attempt upon her virtue, which meet with a deserved repulse, and occasions his being absolutely denied all further access to her. Our hero, disappointed in his design upon Aemelia, launches into the Beau Monde, and soon becomes acquainted with the celebrated lady——, who at his request (in a select party) gratifies his curiosity with the memoirs of her life, which take up the greatest part of the third volume.

She sets out with assuring him, that by circumstances of her story which she is going to relate, he will be convinced of her candour while she informs him of her indiscretion, and hopes he will be enabled to perceive, that however her head may have erred, her heart has always been uncorrupted, and that she has been unhappy, *because she loved and was a woman.* After this she says, that she was from her youth addicted to the love of pleasure, lively, and good natured, of an imagination apt to run riot, her heart liberal and disinterested, but so obstinately attached to her own opinions, that she could not brook contradiction, and in the whole of her disposition resembled that of Henry 5th, as described by Shakespeare. In the 13th year of her age, she felt the first emotions of Love; but not with any great violence, as they were occasioned by several different objects, that accidentally presented themselves; however, two years after she felt what love and beauty really were, and fell desperately in love with the second son of duke —— who felt an equal passion for her. His person, she says beggar'd all description, and his heart was fraught with sincerity and love, while truth and innocency prevail'd on her side. Not being able to gain her father's consent to the match with the lord W——, she elop'd from, and was privately married to my lord——, but in about three weeks after the marriage, she obtain'd the forgiveness and reconciliation of her father, was extremely well receiv'd by all lord W—'s relations, and had the honour to be introduced to the late queen, who, says she, expressed her approbation of my person in very particular terms, and observing the satisfaction which appeared in my countenance, with marks of admiration, desired the ladies to take notice, how little happiness depended upon wealth, since there was more joy in my face than in all her court beside. However the happiness she proposed to herself from this match was soon blasted by the death of lord W. who left her an unprovided widow, altogether dependant on the affections of her own family. During the ensuing winter, she receiv'd overtures for a match with the person who is her present husband, and who she says, she had always set down as the last man with whom she should chuse to wed, and was in every respect the very reverse of her late husband. However, the recommendation of her father and the solicitations and importunities both of her own friends and lord W——'s relations (who strongly represented to her the opportunity she now had of possessing a large fortune and being entirely independant,) together with the uneasiness she felt at home, and the indifference she had to all mankind, weighed so much with her, that she at last yielded to the addresses of the man she despised, and tho' with reluctance suffer'd the nuptial knot to be tied. The pusillanimous behaviour of her bridegroom, who the first night owned to her that he was ashamed to bed a woman whose hand he had scarce ever touched, no ways served to remove the prejudice she had imbibed against him, but help'd to further the addresses of Mr S—, who now endeavoured to cultivate her good graces with the utmost skill and assiduity. The artful solicitations of this gentleman were not rendered more unsuccessful by her lying whole nights by her husband whom she styles only a nominal one, and who teaz'd and tormented her for what neither she could give, nor he could take, so that he soon sapp'd the foundations of her conjugal faith; and at last obtain'd the completion of his wishes, though he did not find her virtue an easy conquest. Having now sacrificed her virtue to the indulgence of her passions, she insensibly fell into such gaieties, intrigues and indiscretions, as must naturally be attended with those of misery and distress, which are the subject of the remainder of her narrative, and in which she does not fail to relate several accounts of her husband's conduct and behaviour, which represents him in the most ridiculous and contemptible light, at the same time that they expose her own follies and vices. Throughout the whole of these memoirs, she is far from boasting of her irregularities that she continually laments the fatality of conjunctures, and her inability to resist the torrent that bore her away against the opposition of her better reason. Love, says she, makes up for all deficiencies to me, who think nothing else worth the living for; had I been blessed with a partner for life, who could have loved sincerely, and inspired me with a mutual flame, I would have asked no more of fate. Interest and ambition have no share in my composition. Love which is pleasure, or pleasure, which is love, makes up the whole. A heart so disposed, cannot be devoid of other good qualities; it must be subject to the impressions of humanity and good nature, and enemy to nothing but itself. This you will give me leave to affirm, in justice to myself, as I have frankly owned my failings and misconduct.

The lady having finished the narration of her memoirs, our author resumes the history of his hero, and attributes to him several adventures and frolicks which have not the least air of probability, and with which he ends his third volume.

Peregrine who has hitherto appeared in a successful condition of life, is now by the author represented in a variety of misfortunes and wretchedness, having contracted an acquiantance with a Newmarket nobleman, he is initiated so far into the mystery of horse-racing, as to become a dupe to the knowing ones of that place, thereby greatly injures his fortune, the ruin whereof is further effected by his lending part of the remainder on improper securities, and setting up for member of parliament, in which he is disappointed.

Peregrine puts himself under the protection of a noble lord, and in order to retrieve his affairs becomes dependant upon the minister, who gives him some assurance of his favour, but soon drops him upon the death of his noble patron. In these distresses our hero commences author, and becomes a member of a college of writers, of whose proceedings we have here a tedious description, in which is introduced a severe criticism upon the improprieties of the dress, speaking and gesticulation of one of our celebrated actors, in the characters of Pierre, Othello and Zanga. Peregrine being tolerably successful as an author in the poetic way produced among others the following piece wrote in praise of the lady whose memoirs we have taken notice of:

> While with fond rapture and amaze,
> On thy transcendent charms I gaze;
> My cautious soul essays in vain,
> Her peace and freedom to maintain:
> Yet let that blooming form divine,
> Where grace and harmony combine;
> Those eyes like genial orbs, that move,
> Dispensing gladness, joy and love,
> In all their pomp assail my view,
> Intent my bosom to subdue;
> My breast by weary maxims seel'd.

Not all those charms shall force to yield

But when invoked to beauty's aid,
I see the enlighten'd soul display'd;
That soul so sensibly sedate,
Amidst the storms of froward fate!
Thy genius active, strong and clear,
Thy wit sublime, tho' not severe;
The social ardour void of art,
That glows within thy candid heart;
My spirits sense and strength decay,
My resolution dies away;
And every faculty opprest,
Almighty love invades my breast.

Peregrine tho' successful in poetry was not quite so fortunate in his political lucubrations, for having wrote and printed in one of the papers, an essay upon the male administration of public affairs, he was arrested at the instigation of the minister, and thrown into the Fleet; deprived both of his liberty and his fortune, Peregrine amuses the melancholy of his confinement by conversing with the inhabitants of that unfortunate republic, the characters of most of whom he lays before the reader. Ultimately, Peregrine upon the death of his father succeeds to a large estate, triumphs over all his misfortunes, reforms his vicious courses and marries the object of his first passion, the fair Aemilia. In all these vicissitudes the author represents him with great uniformity of principle, unbending and fierce in adversity, nosing a prime minister, and refusing for wife, a mistress whom he adores, but tractable and supple in prosperity.

15. Thomas Gray, a letter to Horace Walpole on *Peregrine Pickle*

3 March 1751

From *Letters of Thomas Gray*, ed. Duncan C. Tovey (1900), vol. I, p. 212.

Gray, educated at Eton with Walpole, classical scholar, linguist, author of 'Elegy in a Country Churchyard', and other poems.

Has that miracle of *tenderness and sensibility* (as she calls it) *Lady Vane* given you any amusement? *Peregrine*, whom she uses as a vehicle, is very poor indeed, with a few exceptions. In the last volume is a character of Mr Lyttleton, under the name of 'Gosling Scrag,' and a parody of his Monody, under the notion of a Pastoral on the death of his grandmother.

16. [Dr John Hill], from *A Parallel between the Characters of Lady Frail, and the Lady of Quality in Peregrine Pickle*

March 1751

Published by R. Griffiths, 1751, pp. 1–47.

This anonymous pamphlet appeared shortly after the publication of *Peregrine Pickle*. Here Dr John Hill defends his own performance in the anonymously published *The History of a Woman of Quality: or, The Adventures of Lady Frail*, by means of a sustained comparison between this and Smollett's *Memoirs of a Lady of Quality* from *Peregrine Pickle*. These extracts are taken from the Bodleian Library copy of *A Parallel*, Vet. A5. e. 568.

The Subject these Authors have employed their Pens about is Woman in the most abandoned State of Prostitution. We would not pay so ill a Compliment to their Genius, or to human Nature, as to suppose that they either intended their Heroine's Character should pass for a real one, or that Nature could produce such a one; it is strangely lucky, however, that they have fallen into almost the same series of Adventures, by Means of which to express Prostitution incarnate, if we may be allowed the use of such a Term; and it is not a little to the Honour of the Cause in our Age, that tho' the Characters must appear to any body to have been drawn at random, and to be the mere Effect of Imagination; or at the nearest Approach to Truth, to be like the *Venus* of the old *Greek* Statuary, an Image formed from the several Vices of every unhappy Female of the Time, there has not been wanting a Lady who in a Manner lays Claim to the whole Merit of, at least, one of these two notable Performances. We are apt to believe, that if she chuses to continue her claim, the World will be ready to judge from this Parallel, that it can be only *Modesty* that prevents her declaring she has an equal Right to both.

Tho' the principal Facts in these several Performances are evidently the same, the Intent, as well as the Execution of the Works in which they are delivered, are evidently different.

The Prostitute in *Peregrine Pickle* sets herself up as a Model for Imitation to the rest of her Sex: She speaks every where in the first Person: She avows the having been criminal with Mr S——, with my Lord B——, and in short with People whose Names began with half the Letters of the Alphabet: She glories in the Success of these Amours: She speaks with Rapture of the Joys she felt with her dear Lovers, and declares there is no Part of it that she would not act over again.

The Character in Lady *Frail* is of the same Turn in every Particular, but it is exhibited in a very different Light; the Author tells the Story; and as he professedly tells us, hangs his Heroine up *in terrorem*, as a severe Example, and a dreadful Warning to every young Creature of the same Sex,

> *A fixed Figure for the Hand of scorn*
> *To point its slowly moving Finger at.*[1]

He goes so far as to assert, that Examples of superior Infamy like this are only permitted by Providence for this Purpose; and that he exhibits Lady *Frail* as the *Romans* used to do their drunken Slaves, to implant an Odium of the Vice that rendered them hateful, in the Minds of the rising Generation.

The Works are both far, very far from but the Appearance of Perfection. The Lady of Quality's Account of herself in *Pickle* is a cold, lifeless, spiritless, tedious, insipid and impertinent Recital of Facts, not one in fifty of which are of the least Importance; a repeated Detail of the Lady's running away, and of her Husband's following her. The History of Lady *Frail* is full of Spirit, full of Business, full of Variety, but it is written with a slovenly Carelessness, an utter Disregard of Ornament, and gives us the Lady not only without Paint and Patches, but with dirty Fingers.

The author of *Pickle* is deficient in his Plan; he only gives us the abandoned Wife: It is easy to conceive, that as the Woman who is a Wife, has been a Maid, and may be a Widow, the same Propensity to Vice must exhibit itself under very various Forms in these several States; and that the Picture is too limited, while it conveys Instruction only to the Adulteress. The Writer of Lady *Frail* has produced his Heroine on the Stage of Life unmarried, and has pictured Prostitution in this its first Period: He has married her after this, and given us the Figure of the Same Woman, actuated by the same Principles during that State; he has after this unmarried her, and shewn us the Widow of his original Virgin; and to leave nothing untouched, he has concluded his Picture with his Widow married again. It is singular, that two Authors, Strangers to one another, and who, in spite of all that can be pretended to the contrary, appear evidently to have been writing two mere Romances, and those by perfect Accident on the same Plan, should happen to fix upon the same kind of Female for their Model, and the same kind of Lords for her Husbands; and it is most Singular of all, that they should not only join in banishing the Terms *Colin*, *Strephon*, and the like, and using Letters of the Alphabet as Initials of the Names of Lovers, but that they should both have chosen the very same Intitials.

The Lady sets out in both upon the same great Principle, that *what is called Virtue in Woman, is not a Virtue*; and as a Secondary Maxim to this, that *Variety is Pleasure*. They both draw their Lady handsome and accomplish'd; they both take in a considerable Series of Years for the Time of the Action. The Author of Lady *Frail's* History gives her a proportionate Number of Admirers. But all the

World must laugh at the strait-lac'd Decency of the Lady in *Pickle*; who relating the Facts herself, hardly allows of more than Fifteen.

After these Preliminaries, we shall proceed to our intended Parallel, in which the gentle Reader will be amazed to find the Similarity of Facts, so far as the more circumscrib'd History goes; and from both which together, he will have before him a pretty full and fair View of what a Woman of Spirit may do on such an Occasion.

The Term *Genuine*, an odd Word ascrib'd to the Lady's Memoirs in *Peregrine Pickle*, and which we don't well know what to make of, shall prejudice us so far however in the favour of that Performance, that we shall give the Facts related in it as our Text, and employ those of Lady *Frail* only by way of Comment: the Reader we are apt to believe will join with us in allowing these are very happily calculated to explain and fill up the Lacunae and Deficiencies of the other.

Lady *Blank*, so we shall chuse to call the Lady in *Peregrine*, since she has not given herself any other Denotative in that Performance, than the Emblematic one of a long Line, produces herself to us at *Bath* a Virgin of Thirteen, courted by Multitudes, adored by every Body, but with no more of Courtship than mere innocent Civility; she finally tells us of a *Scotch* Captain who was rejected: and this closes the very important Scene of her Conduct and Adventures, at this gay Place.

Pages 20–1:

Thus have these two Writers led their Woman of Pleasure thro' the Several Stages of Dependence on a Father, Marriage with a Man she professes to have loved, Widowhood, and so much of a second Marriage as might very well reconcile the Husband to that's being at a Period to.

Pleasure is her sole View in both Histories, and Variety seems another Word expressing the same Thing: In the one she has a continued Series of new Objects; in the other, she who is too warm to be constant to a Husband, is cold enough to be faithful to a Lover. As both can certainly be no more than imaginary Characters, the Determination between them is easy; or, were they real ones, the Address of the one, and Indolence of the other, would very easily point out to us which of the two it is that has favoured us with that feeling System of Maxims under the Title of *The Oeconomy of Female Life*.

Pages 31–3:

Such, and so perfectly similar is the Conduct of the Story in these two remarkable Productions. The Intent is evidently the same in both, to draw a Woman formed by Nature to charm, qualified to give all the Happiness that Love in its most exalted Enthusiasm can bestow, and to receive as much; but who, mistaking Appetite for Sensibility, and Variety for Pleasure, finds, the only Way that such a Woman could have found to render herself despised.

A State of Neglect, not to say of utter Contempt, is the Period of her Gallantries in both: but tho' this falls in very well with the Intent of the Author of Lady *Frail*, who sets her up as a Warning to the rest of her sex, surely it but very ill coincides with the Plan of the other Writer, who introduces her as a Model for the rest of the Female World: Nor is her declaring herself not sorry for any thing she has done, but in a very good Humour to act it all over again, if she should be blest with Opportunities, at all of a Piece with the uncomfortable State in which she acknowledges herself to be at the Conclusion, and which could only be the Effect of these Actions. She declares her Dissatisfaction, as she tells us, a thousand Times, how willing, how desirous her Husband was to have her with him upon honourable and happy Terms, and that on her own Conditions.

Characters in considerable Numbers are necessary to be introduced for the carrying on such a History; but we who are to read it would wish to find Propriety and Variety in them. The Initials are in general the same in both Histories, and the same Set of Men perhaps as to Size, Stature and Complexion, are intended to be expressed by them; but in all other Respects they appear very different People in the Conduct of the Story.

Each of the Authors allows two Husbands to the Lady. Lady *Frail*, who is constant to herself, always in Character, and the same Creature from the first Sentence of her History to the last, is equally criminal during her Life with each; a Love of Pleasure, a Resolution of snatching at all Opportunities of getting at it, are the striking Parts of her Character through the whole; but the Lady of *Peregrine* is half a Dozen different People in the Course of the Work: She is chaste in her first Husband's Time, abandoned with the second, constant in her Attachment to one Lover; a Libertine in what she pretends to be an innocent Attachment with another.

As to the first Husband both Authors agree in his Character; but in regard to the second, the Author of *Peregrine* only seems to have thought it necessary to make him a bad one: The other seems to have imagined the Lady's Character would appear in a rather stronger Light on the making it a good one. Some little Impropriety there is, however, in the Attempt of the former; Since, while he tells us every where that he is a very ill one, and makes his Conduct the Excuse for the Lady's, the very Circumstances he brings in as Proofs of it tend rather the other Way; and as if there was something of Truth and Reality in the Case, that he must tell whether he would or no, he agrees in the main, tho' apparently against his Will with the other, who makes Lady *Frail's* Husband a generous, open-hearted, sensible, disinterested Man.

Page 47:

Upon the whole, the Characters in the two Books are extremely alike in all Things; but the Light they are represented in is very different: They seem two Portraits of the same Face, done by two Painters of different Genius and Qualifications. The Lady in *Pergrine Pickle* is a Picture of *W*——'s servilely close to the Course of a Vein, the Colour of a Knot, or the Number of Hairs in an Eye-lash: punctual in Circumstances of no Importance, but faint in the Expression of the striking Features: Lady *Frail* is a Portrait of *H*——, full of Fire, full of Spirit, full of Resemblance, but too carelessly finished not to disgust a judicious Eye; dawb'd, not coloured; and too crudely covered to be lasting.

FINIS.

NOTE

1 The reference is to *Othello*, IV, ii, 55–6. The quotation should read:

> The fixed figure for the time of scorn
> To point his slow unmoving finger at.

17. Anonymous verses on Lady Vane

March 1751

From *The London Magazine*, March 1751, XX, 135–6. James L. Clifford attributes these verses to Richard Graves (1715–1804), author of *The Spiritual Quixote*, 1773. See *The Adventures of Peregrine Pickle*, ed. James L. Clifford, Oxford English Novels, 1964, p. xviii.

The HEROINES: or, Modern Memoirs.

In ancient times, some hundred winters past,
When British dames for conscience-sake were chaste,
If some frail nymph, by youthful passion sway'd,
From virtue's paths incontinent had stray'd;
When banish'd reason re-assum'd her place,
The conscious wretch bewail'd her foul disgrace;
Fled from the world and pass'd her joyless years
In decent solitude and pious tears:
Veil'd in some convent made her peace with Heav'n,
And almost hop'd—by prudes to be forgiven.
  Not so of modern wh——s th'illustrious train,
Renown'd Constantia, Pilkington, and—,
Grown old in sin, and dead to am'rous joy,
No acts of penance their great souls employ;
Without a blush behold each nymph advance;
The luscious horoine[sic] of her own romance;
Each harlot triumphs in her loss of fame,
And boldly prints and publishes her shame.

18. Horace Walpole on Lady Vane

13 March 1751

From *The Letters of Horace Walpole*, ed. Mrs Paget Toynbee, 16 vol, Oxford 1904, vol. III, p. 37. From a letter to Horace Mann, later Sir Horace Mann, with whom Smollett was on friendly terms in his last months in Italy in 1770–1.

There have been two events, not political, equal to any absurdities or follies of former years. My Lady Vane has literally published the Memoirs of her own life, only suppressing part of her lovers, no part of the success of the others with her: a degree of profligacy not to be accounted for; she does not want money, none of her stallions will raise her credit; and the number, all she had to brag of, concealed! The other is a play....

19. Dr John Hill on Lady Vane and Smollett

19 April 1751

From Hill's *The Inspector*, 1751, No. 14, 74–75. Hill here impugns Lady Vane as a whore and lampoons Smollett as Mr Smallhead.

This Gentleman was succeeded by three smart Ladies, in the Autumn of their Beauty, who came to receive an Answer from the Court concerning the Apologies for their Lives, which they had left there last Month. *Genius* told them, that they had better repent than brag of Lives that it was a Shame to have lived; and their Books were accordingly put upon the Baker's Basket, and destined by the Court to share the same Fate with his Papers. What astonished me was, that this Mortification did not produce one Blush from either of the fair Authors. As they passed by me, my Companion told me, that the first of these Apologists was a Lady of Quality, the Second an *English*, and the third an *Irish* Prostitute of Note. These Ladies, who went away laughing, were succeeded by a grave Gentleman, who, with great Confidence of his Abilities, told the Court his Name was *Smallhead*, and that he came for the Answer of the Court concerning the Novel he left there last Month; upon which *Genius* told him, that, until he understood more of Human Nature, and could distinguish better between Satire and Scurrility, he could not have the Leave of the Court to print again. Upon this four Volumes were added to the Baker's Basket, to the no small Mortification of Mr *Smallhead*; who, turning on his Heel, threatened Vengeance on the Court. Here *Fame* placing her Trumpet to that Part which expresses Infamy, with harsh jarring Discords, played him out of Court. Here a very formidable Figure in a *Highland* Dress, with Durk and Pistol by his Side, who called himself Mr *Macduff*, bag'd Lave to acquent the Coort, that Mester *Smallheed* was not a *Scotsman*, notwithstanding he was thought so; nor did he ken of what Contry he was.

20. [Matthew Maty], review of *Peregrine Pickle*

April 1751

From *Journal Britannique*, La Haye, 1751, I, 429–31. Translated from Maty's French.

The adventures of Peregrine Pickle, which also include those of a lady of quality. The adventures of Roderick Random have already indicated the talent of our Author in this genre of writing. He undoubtedly has talent, and much of that vivacity which the English call humour. But his Portraits are loaded, and his settings are bawdy and licentious. Childish pranks, naval vulgarity, crude language and observations—these are the principal ingredients of this faithful picture of the customs of the century. A modern Julie[1] made the Author a present of the story of her intrigues, and since the piece had been announced in advance, it has contributed more than a little to the debut of the Work. However, I doubt whether, after having read it, one agrees with the Heroine that her heart had no part in the errors of her Spirit, and that all her unhappiness arose from having loved, and having been born a woman. I have read several satires of her Sex but to my mind this trait prevails over all others.

NOTE

1 The *Oxford Classical Dictionary* lists several 'Julias' noted for their intelligence and licentiousness.

21. Lady Henrietta Luxborough, letters

27 May 1751 and 25 August 1751

From two letters to William Shenstone, *Letters Written by the Late Right Honourable Lady Luxborough to William Shenstone, Esq.*, 1775, pp. 265–6 and 290–1.

Lady Luxborough was sister to Henry St John, Viscount Bolingbroke (1678–1751), statesman, political theorist, and addressee of Pope's *Essay on Man*.

Peregrine Pickle I do not admire: it is by the author of Roderick Random, who is a lawyer: but the thing which makes the book sell, is the History of Lady V——, which is introduced (in the last volume, I think) much to her Ladyship's dishonour; but published by her *own* order, from her *own* Memoirs, given to the author for that purpose; and by the approbation of her *own* hand. What was ever equal to this fact? and how can one account for it?

As to Peregrine Pickle, I hired it—and that merely for the sake of reading one of the volumes, wherein are inserted the Memoirs of Lady V——; which, as I was well acquainted with her, gave me curiosity. The rest of the book is, I think, ill wrote, and not interesting.

22. Anonymous verses on Lady Vane

1751

From *The Ladies' Magazine*, June 1751.

To Lady Vane
(Handed to her on her Leaving Bath)

As in your person without Fault,
　　So should your Conduct be;
For what avails a beauteous Form,
　　When stampt with Infamy.
If you'd not give up worldly Ease
　　For Titles, Wealth, and Fame:
Nor forfeit every Hope of Heav'n
　　To gain Contempt of Shame.
Hate Vice; let Virtue be your Guide,
　　For all her Paths are Peace;
And nobly toil to make your Mind
　　As beauteous as your Face.

23. Elizabeth Montague on *Peregrine Pickle*

1752

From *Elizabeth Montagu The Queen of the Blue Stockings*, ed. Emily J. Climenson, 2 vols, 1906, vol. II, p. 2. From a letter to her sister, Sarah Scott, early in 1752.

I recommend to your perusal *The Adventures of Peregrine Pickle*. Lady Vane's story is well told.

24. [Henry Fielding] in *The Covent-Garden Journal*

No. 2, 7 January 1752

Henry Fielding wrote this piece under the pseudonym Sir Alexander Drawcansir. This extract is from the section entitled *The* JOURNAL *of the present* WAR. Dated *January 6*, from the Head Quarters. This is Fielding's comic dismissal of Smollett in his account of the paper war of 1751–2. From *The Covent-Garden Journal*, ed. G.E. Jensen, New Haven, vol. I, 1964.

Having taken all Precautions, and given all the necessary Orders, on the 4th Instant, at Break of Day, we marched into Covent-Garden, and fixed our Head Quarters at the Universal Register Office opposite unto Cecil-Street in the Strand.

A little before our March, however, we sent a large Body of

Forces, under the Command of General A. Millar, to take Possession of the most eminent Printing-Houses. The great Part of these were garrisoned by Detachments from the Regiment of Grub-Street, who all retired at the Approach of our Forces. A small Body, indeed, under the Command of one Peeragrin Puckle, made a slight Show of Resistence; but his Hopes were soon found to be in *Vain*; and, at the first Report of the Approach of a younger Brother of General Thomas Jones, his whole Body immediately disappeared, and totally overthrew some of their own Friends, who were marching to their Assistance, under the Command of one Rodorick Random. This Rodorick, in a former Skirmish with the People called Critics, had owed some slight Success more to the Weakness of the Critics, than to any Merit of his own.

25. [Tobias Smollett], *Habbakkuk Hilding's Faithful Narrative*

15 January 1752

From *A Faithful Narrative of the Base and inhuman ARTS That were lately practised upon the BRAIN OF HABBAKKUK HILDING*, etc., by Drawcansir Alexander, 1752. Smollett, under this pseudonym, the inverse of Fielding's in *The Covent-Garden Journal* (see No. 24) contributes to the paper war. In this extract (from pp. 18–24) a troop of Fielding's fictional characters encounter some of Smollett's in a war of words.

Accordingly they proceeded down *Catherine-street* to the *Strand*, in a most tumultuous Manner, bellowing Defiance to all who should presume to oppose them ; their Commander leading the Van upon Assback, and his Brother bringing up the Rear, under the Guidance of one who called himself *Jones*, and pretended to be a Gentleman;

though he was in reality no other than a Player's Bastard, and had been formerly transported under another Name——. His Right-Hand Man was one *Partridge*, a notorious Felon and Imposter; and on his Left stalked a strange uncouth Figure with a long Beard, whom the said *Jones* stiled the Philosopher of the Hill; but, he afterwards proved to be a Sheep-stealer in Disguise—as for *Amelia* and her beloved *Booth*, they marched Hand in Hand immediately behind the General; the Wife brandishing a Broomstick, and the Husband weilding a Distaff, with a Glyster-pipe fixed to his Button-Holes——. He suffered a great many furious Looks from a termagant Oyster-Wench called *Matthews*, who walked at a little Distance from this fond Couple, and frequently flourished her Knife at them, with all the Marks of Jealousy and Despair.

In this Manner they continued their March without Opposition, to the Terror of his Majesty's peaceable Subjects; and made an Halt on the Banks of the Kennel that waters the *New Church* in the *Strand*—here they stopped with a View to send off Detachments to different Quarters of the Town, when all of a sudden the above-mentioned *Matthews*, seeing a decent Gentlewoman crossing the Street, ran up to *Habbakkuk* with violent Emotion, crying, 'D—n my Eyes! Justice, now is the Time to stand by me, for there's the B—ch Miss *Williams*, Waiting-Maid to Madam *Random*, coming for a Warrant to have me nabbed for nimming her Gown and Capuchin.'—At the same Instant, *Partridge* having descried a Journeyman Barber, with a remarkably long Chin, passing by *Somerset-House* in Conversation with another Man, roared out with uncommon Symptoms of Affright, 'Blood! We shall all be grabbed, don't you see the Dog *Strap*—the very Cull who hath a Warrant against me for[a] snabbling his Peeter and Queer *Joseph*—'tis Time to shabb off, d— my Liver.' With these Words he betook himself to his Heels, and fled with great Expedition, being followed by the *Pseudo Jones* and *Man of the Hill*, who though they did not rightly conceive his Meaning, knew themselves too well to hazard any Explanation with the Officers of Justice——This Defection produced an universal Pannick among the Soldiers and even Officers of the Second Line: insomuch that a general Rout ensued, and the blind Chieftain was overthrown by *Aristotle* in his Retreat.

Habbakkuk seeing this Disorder in his Troops, clapped Spurs to his Ass and pursued the Fugitives, cursing them for their

Cowardice, and exhorting them to return; but they soon vanished notwithstanding his Remonstrances, and when he wheeled about to encourage the rest to persevere in their Duty, the greatest Part of them were already dispersed, and his chief Friends and Favourites in the Custody of a Constable, who at my Solicitation had been detached by Justice *Le Gard*, to apprehend the Ring-leaders to such a Riot against the Laws of the Land, and the Peace of his Majesty's loyal Subjects.—This Event, instead of calming, rather inflamed the Delirium of the unfortunate *Hilding*, who uttered many frantic Imprecations against the Cowards who had betrayed, him, swore, in Imitation of his Predecessor and Namesake, that he would pursue his Conquests in his own Person, then couching his Mopstick, with a strange and ludicrous Distortion of Feature, applied his Heels to the Sides of the supposed *Bucephalus*, with Intent to charge his Opponents, whom, it seems, he mistook for one *Peregrine Pickle* and his Associates, in as much as he addressed himself to Mr Constable as to the said *Pickle*, exclaiming,

'I know thee well, a Blood thou art, Lord *Pickle*, So am I,'———With these Words he would have assaulted the Peace Officer had not myself and several of his Neighbours laid hold on him, and carried him to his own House, where by the Advice of an able Physician, he was immediately blooded, blistered and purged.

But his Frenzy still continues, and the Doctor seems to despair of his Recovery. For tho' by dint of the Evacuations he hath undergone, the Rage of his Frenzy is in some Measure abated, he still continues deprived of his Senses, and is between whiles, seized with shocking Fits of Horror and Despair, during which he is often heard to cry, 'Save me from that Ruffian *Pipes*! bind him over; he shakes his Cudgel at me.—What, no Evidence for Love or Money! Ha! *Polypheme* approaches, with his *Cyclopian* Eye! tie me under the Belly of a Ram.—I cry you Mercy, a *Misnomer*. *Trunnion* is the Man.—Spare me, spare me, good Commodore! I own I have wronged you, as well as your Nephew *Peregrine*, and his Cousin *Random*.—I have robb'd them both, and then raised a false Report against them.—But my poor Conscience suffers for all.—I have damned myself for the Sake of that miscreant *Scrag*. O that I could see him scragged in good Earnest!—Mercy! Mercy! I will find Bail.—Gentlemen, I plead guilty.—Don't pickle me.—I shan't quit Cost.—I am poor Carrion.—Don't you perceive, I stink of Mortality.' Such is the present Situation of this wretched Man. As for his Aiders and Abettors, they were forthwith committed to the House of Correction; and what is remarkable, *Amelia* and *Booth*, at the very first, performed the Operation of Milldolling, like Persons well skilled and long experienced in that salubrious Exercise.

This being a fair and impartial Account of the whole Transaction, I leave the World to judge whether I have been to blame in my Conduct towards the said *Hilding*, which was purely the Result of Humanity and Compassion; or whether the Wrath of God and Man will not, in all probability, pursue the infamous Authors of his Mishap, who not contented with the Misery they have already entailed upon him, have trumped up a false and scandalous Account of certain Victories which they pretend he obtained in the above narrated Expedition; tho' they took care to consult their own Safety, by keeping themselves without the Reach of that Tumult in which they had involv'd their innocent Friend: But, doubtless, their Design is to impose upon that vain Lunatick, with feignęd Reports of his own Prowess, that he may be incited to take the Field again, and become subservient to their sordid and unchristian Views of Interest and Revenge.

That the Father of Mercy would take Pity on his deplorable Condition, and deliver him, and all of us, from their perfidious Arts and infernal Snares, is the fervent Prayer of his unfeigned Wellwisher,

DRAWCANSIR ALEXANDER,
Fencing-Master and Philomath.

NOTE

a Snabbing his Peeter and Queer *Joseph*, in the Language of Thieves and Pick-pockets, signifies stealing his Knapsack and upper Garment.
Vide Dict. of Cant Works and Phrases.

26. [Bonnell Thornton], from *Have at You All: or The Drury-Lane Journal*

No. 1, 16 January 1752

Bonnell Thornton under the pseudonym Madam Roxana Termagant in his *Drury-Lane Journal, Addres'd to Sir Alexander Drawcansir, Author of the Covent-Garden Journal*. One of Thornton's parodies of Fielding in the 'paper war'.

A Journal of the Rout, Progress and Defeat of The Forces under Sir Alexander Drawcansir, engaged in the present Paper War.

Then, meeting with one PICKLE at the head of a troop of Novellists, (with whom he had before an encounter, in which he was slightly wounded by *Random* shot) he left him to dispute the field with his noseless Amazon *AMELIA*.

27. [Bonnell Thornton], from *Have at You All: or the Drury-Lane Journal*

No. 2, 23 January 1752

Discussing the identity of 'Mrs Roxana Termagant' (his pseudonym here), Thornton claims it is widely known who she is, and makes reference here to Lady Vane in *Peregrine Pickle*.

I have also had the honour to be mistaken for someone of those Female Apologists, who have admitted us into the privacy of their most secret (I might say, most scandalous) intrigues. The ladies of quality will have it, that no one but the Right Honourable Memoir-writer in *P. PICKLE'S* adventures could have attack'd the *loose* part of Sir *ALEXANDER'S* essays[1], as no woman, they are sure, could express herself so *feelingly* on those subjects as her Ladyship.—Nay, even the lower class of my female readers have employed their thoughts to the same purpose....

NOTE

1 Presumably Sir Alexander Drawcansir (i.e. Fielding). See above, No. 24.

28. [William Kenrick], from *Fun: a Parodi-tragi-comical Satire*

1752

From William Kenrick, *Fun: a Parodi-tragi-comical Satire, As it was to have been perform'd at the Castle-tavern, Pater-Noster-row, on Thursday, February 13, 1752, but suppress'd, by special order from the Lord-mayor and Court of Aldermen*, from Scene I, 4–5.

In this parody on *Macbeth* the Weird Sisters circle about their cauldron, casting in contemporary novels, periodicals, and pamphlets, including Smollett's *Roderick Random* and *Peregrine Pickle*.

All.   Around, around, around about,
    Dulness come running in, all *Wit* keep out.
1st Witch. Here a *Goose-quill.*
2d Witch.   Paper.
3d Witch.   Ink.

1st Witch. Brains that ne'er were known to
        think.
2nd Witch. Poet's Mark wherewith Men brand
        'em.
3d Witch. Shot in vain, thrown out at *Random.*
1st Witch. Valet.
2d Witch.   *Loveill.*
3d Witch.   And *Creole.*
All. Dead and damn'd without a Soul.
1st Witch. With Laughter that can never tickle.
Swell it up—Oh! here is *Pickle.*

29. Henry Fielding on authorial propriety

1752

From Henry Fielding, *Amelia*, 4 vols, published by A. Millar,
1752, vol. II, book IV, ch. 1. An oblique reference to
Smollett's publication of Lady Vane's *Memoirs* in *Peregrine
Pickle.*

The Governor then, having received his Fee, departed; and turning
the Key, left the Gentleman and the Lady to themselves.

In Imitation of him, we will lock up likewise a Scene which we
do not think proper to expose to the Eyes of the Public. If any over
curious Readers should be disappointed on this Occasion, we will
recommend such Readers to the Apologies with which certain gay
Ladies have lately been pleased to oblige the World, where they will
possibly find everything recorded, that past at this Interval.

But though we decline painting the Scene, it is not our intention
to conceal from the World the frailty of Mr Booth, or of his fair
partner, who certainly passed that evening in a manner inconsistent
with the strict rules of Virtue and Chastity.

30. Lady Mary Wortley Montagu, letter

16 February 1752

From a letter to the Countess of Bute, *The Complete Letters of Lady Mary Wortley Montagu*, ed. Robert Halsband, Oxford, 1966, vol. III, pp. 2–3.

Dear Child,

I receiv'd yesterday, Feb. 15 N.S., the case of Books you were so good to send to me. The entertainment they have allready given me has recompens'd me for the long time I expected them. I begun, by your direction, with Peregrine Pickle. I think Lady V[ane]'s memoirs contain more Truth and less malice than any I ever read in my Life. When she speaks of her own being disinterested, I am apt to beleive she really thinks her selfe so, as many highway men, after having no possibillity of retreiving the character of Honesty, please themselves with that of being Generous, because whatever they get on the road they allways spend at the next ale House, and are still as beggarly as ever. Her History, rightly consider'd, would be more instructive to young Women than any Sermon I know. They may see there what mortifications and variety of misery are the unavoidable consequences of Galant[r]ys. I think there is no rational Creature than [*sic*] would not prefer the life of the strictest Carmelite to the round of Hurry and misfortune she has gone through.

Her Style is clear and concise, with some strokes of Humour which appear to me so much above her I can't help being of opinion the whole has been modell'd by the Author of the Book in which it is inserted, who is some subaltern admirer of hers.[1] I may judge wrong, she being no Acquaintance of mine, thô she has marry'd two of my relations.

NOTE

1 March 1752, Lady Mary writes to the Countess of Bute, 'There is something Humourous in R. Random that makes me believe the Author is H. Fielding.' *Letters*, vol. III, p. 9.

31. Mary Granville Delany, letter

7 October 1752

From a letter to Mrs Dewes, in *The Autobiography and Correspondence of Mary Granville: Mrs Delany*, ed. Lady Llanover, 1861, vol. III, p. 162.

Mary Delany (1700–88) was a friend of Swift, and she introduced the novelist Fanny Burney to Court.

At candlelight D.D., and I read by turns, and what do *you think* has been part of our study?—why truly *Peregrine Pickle*! We never undertook it before, but *it is wretched stuff*; only Lady V's history is a curiosity. What a wretch! 'For sure at heart was never yet so great a wretch as Helen.'

32. Smollett's Dedication to *Ferdinand Count Fathom*

1753

From the Dedication, addressed 'TO DOCTOR ——, by Smollett. Opinion is that this Dedication is to Smollett himself, in what George Saintsbury called an 'autocritical' manner. The extract given below gives Smollett's views on the nature of the novel form in 1753.

A Novel is a large diffused picture, comprehending the characters of life, disposed in different groupes, and exhibited in various attitudes, for the purposes of an uniform plan, and general occurrence, to which every individual figure is subservient. But this plan cannot be executed with propriety, probability or success, without a principal personage to attract the attention, unite the incidents, unwind the clue of the labyrinth, and at last close the scene by virtue of his own importance.

Almost all the heroes of this kind, who have hitherto succeeded on the English stage, are characters of transcendent worth, conducted through the vicissitudes of fortune, to that goal of happiness, which ever ought to be the repose of extraordinary desert.—Yet the same principle by which we rejoice at the remuneration of merit, will teach us to relish the disgrace and discomfiture of vice, which is always an example of extensive use and influence, because it leaves a deep impression of terror upon the minds of those who were not confirmed in the pursuit of morality and virtue, and while the balance wavers, enables the right scale to preponderate.

In the Drama, which is a more limited field of invention, the chief personage is often the object of our detestation and abhorrence; and we are as well pleased to see the wicked schemes of a RICHARD blasted, and the perfidy of a MASKWELL exposed, as to behold a BEVIL happy, and an EDWARD victorious.[1]

The impulses of fear, which is the most violent and interesting of all the passions, remain longer than any other upon the memory; and for one that is allured to virtue, by the contemplation of that peace and happiness which it bestows, an hundred are deterred from the practice of vice, by that infamy and punishment to which it is liable, from the laws and regulations of mankind.

Let me not therefore be condemned for having chosen my principal character from the purlieus of treachery and fraud, when I declare my purpose is to set him up as a beacon for the benefit of the unexperienced and unwary, who from the perusal of these memoirs, may learn to avoid the manifold snares with which they are continually surrounded in the paths of life; while those who hesitate on the brink of iniquity, may be terrified from plunging into that irremeable gulph, the surveying the deplorable fate of FERDINAND Count FATHOM.

That the mind might not be fatigued, nor the imagination disgusted by a succession of vitious objects, I have endeavoured to refresh the attention with occasional incidents of a different nature; and raised up a virtuous character, in opposition to the adventurer, with a view to amuse the fancy, engage the affection, and form a striking contrast which might heighten the expression, and give a *Relief* to the moral of the whole.

If I have not succeeded in my endeavours to unfold the mysteries of fraud, to instruct the ignorant, and entertain the vacant; if I have failed in my attempts to subject folly to ridicule, and vice to indignation; to rouse the spirit of mirth, wake the soul of compassion, and touch the secret springs that move the heart; I have at least, adorned virtue with honour and applause; branded iniquity with reproach and scheme, and carefully avoided every hint or expression which could give umbrage to the most delicate reader: circumstances which (whatever may be my fate with the public) will with you always operate in favour of

Dear Sir
Your very affectionate
friend and servant,
The AUTHOR.

NOTE

1 The references are to Richard in Shakespeare's *Richard III*, Maskwell in Congreve's *The Double Dealer*, Bevil in Steele's *The Conscious Lovers*, and probably Edward the Black Prince in Shirley's play of that name acted at Drury Lane in 1750.

33. Unsigned review of *Ferdinand Count Fathom*

March 1753

From *The Monthly Review*, March 1753, viii, 203–14. Though unsigned, the reviewer is Ralph Griffiths, the editor.

As the public is already very well acquainted with the genius and talents of this writer, for works of imagination, there is little occasion for our saying much of his present performance.

He seems to have sat down to this work with a fund of ideas gleaned from *Gil Blas*, *Guzman de Alfarache*, *Lazarillo de Tormes*, the *English rogue*, &c. His *Ferdinand Fathom* is a compound of all that is detestable in the heroes of these ludicrous romances, with a larger portion of wickedness, and without any tincture of their comic humour; an article which our author has more sparingly used in this than in his former works of entertainment.

The character of *Fathom* is in truth that of the most execrable hypocrite (we will not say, that ever existed in real life, but) that the most inventive power of an author could possibly create, or the most fertile pen describe. His adventures are a series of such acts of treachery, fraud, ingratitude, and the most unparallel'd wickedness, that the recital becomes quite intolerable to the humane reader. The merit of other works of this kind has been, that the incidents they afforded gave the higher pleasure in the perusal, from the supposition of their reality; but here, we imagine, the reader's greatest satisfaction must spring from his continually bearing in mind the improbability that such a monster ever lived, or that such unnatural cruelties and and villanies were ever perpetrated.

That rogues of *Ferdinand's cast* may indeed have but too often appeared amongst mankind, cannot be denied; for every one that knows even but little of the world, must be convinced there are such: but tho' hypocrisy and ingratitude are perhaps the growth of every clime, yet we are persuaded, that it is not in nature to produce such a *master-piece* of diabolism as *Ferdinand* count *Fathom*.

The character of this hero, is that of an agreeable, soft, sober, specious, smiling hypocrite; who, under the mask of the most amiable deportment, and by the help of a very engaging person, passes for a miracle of goodness. Possessed of every exterior accomplishment, and wanting nothing but an honest heart, he imposes himself upon all his acquaintance, as the mirror of disinterested friendship, humanity, and benevolence; while these outward professions only serve to conceal the vilest schemes that an abandoned heart could possibly conceive: and all this from innate principles of wickedness; for *Ferdinand* was neither tutored in any school of vice, nor seduced by the contagion of evil example.

In the recital of such a wretch's exploits, can the reader be greatly interested? Or can any emotions be excited in his mind, but those of horror and disgust? And therefore of what use, it may be demanded, can such a recital prove? What tendency can it have towards the reader's instruction or advantage in any respect?—A point which writers in this way should ever keep in view, as well as meer amusement—Let our author answer for himself: hear his apology.

[quotes from *Fathom*: 'Almost all the heroes of this kind...the deplorable fate of Ferdinand Count Fathom', vol. I, p. 4, from the Dedication]

Whether this apology will effectually plead our author's excuse with his readers, we leave them to determine;—But he has still something farther to offer in his own behalf, by way of compensation for having introduced us into such unedifying company, and which we believe will have more weight than what he has already urged.

[quotes 'That the mind...to the moral of the whole', vol. I, p. 5, from the Dedication]

This part of our author's work is indeed, in our estimation, the most valuable, the most striking, and the most worthy his abilities. The story of *Melville* and *Monimia* affords as fine a lesson as we remember to have ever met with, against that criminal *credulity* by which the peace of many families hath been destroyed, and the ruin of many innocent and unsuspecting persons effected.

The episode of the *Spaniard's* history is well introduced, and executed in manner that warmly interests the reader in the fate of *Don Diego de Zelos*; whose character is a national one, admirably drawn, and sustained with great vigor and spirit throughout.

And tho' we are not greatly satisfied with following the infamous *Fathom* thro' the successful part of his villainous adventures, it must be acknowledged that the author makes us some recompence when he brings this hero to repentance. When accumulated vengeance bursts upon the guilty head of this wretch, his self-accusation, and retrospective view of his past conduct, is very pathetic, and adapted to answer the moral end which the author professes, as above, to have had in view.

[quotes 'To what purpose...to save me from the terrible abyss', vol. II, ch. 56, pp. 160–1]

On the whole, the history of count *Fathom* is a work of a mixed character, compounded of various and unequal parts. It abounds on the one hand with affecting incidents, with animated descriptions, and alternate scenes of melting grief, tenderness and joy; diversified with some few exhibitions of a humorous kind. On the other hand, (exclusive of the objections we have hinted at, with respect to the character of the principal personage) there are some extravagant excursions of the author's fancy, with certain improbable stories, (from which, indeed, none of the novels we have ever read are free) marvelous adventures, and little incongruities; all which seem to be indications of the performance being hastily, nay and carelessly composed. Yet, with whatever crudities it may be chargeable,— with all its imperfections, we may venture to pronounce that the work has still merit enough to compensate with the discerning reader for its defects: it carries with it strong marks of genius in the author, and demonstrations of his great proficiency in the study of mankind.

There is an admirable scene of humour in the first volume of this work, which, we doubt not, will very well entertain our readers.

Count *Fathom*, in the earlier part of his adventures, being at *Paris*, and a stranger in that city, unwarily contracts an intimacy with a set of gamesters, with whom the reader is made acquainted under the characters of a *French* abbé, a *Dutch* officer, a *Westphalian* count, and an *English* knight; whose designs upon him do not however immediately succeed; for being an adept in the same Mysteries, he foils them at their own weapons.

While he is exulting in his success, a very extraordinary personage falls in with the society, the consequence of whose arrival is related as follows.

[quotes 'He one day chanced... he would give him his revenge', vol. I, ch. 24, pp. 143–52]

Our author afterwards lets his readers into the mystery of this adventure; which was no other than a scheme laid by the party, to entrap, and revenge themselves on, the unsuspecting count *Fathom*.

34. Mary Granville Delany, letters

1753

Extracts from three letters to Mrs Dewes, in *The Autobiography and Correspondence of Mary Granville: Mrs Delany*, ed. Lady Llanover, 1861, Vol. III, pp. 216, 220 and 223.

24 March 1753:

We are reading *Count Fathom*, a very indifferent affair, as far as we have gone: they say it mends in the second volume, and so it had need.

7 April 1753:

Have you read *Count Fathom*? Though a great deal bad, there are some things very interesting, and the whole well intended.

21 April 1753:

I think *Count Fathom* (though a bad, affected style) written with a better intention, and Melvin's character a good one, but then none of them are to be named in a day with our good friend Richardson.

35. A French bookseller's view of *Peregrine Pickle*

1753

From the *Avertissement du Libraire* to *Histoire et Avantures de Sir Williams Pickle*, Amsterdam and Leipzig, 1753, pp. i–iv. Given here as a tendentious expression of French response to Smollett's novel in the mid-eighteenth century. An inaccurate translation in which the novel is mistitled *Sir Williams Pickle*.

As I do not know English, I addressed myself to someone who did, to engage him to translate the novel of *Williams Pickle:* and when it had been translated I found in it some singularly original portraits, very finely sustained; and some paintings from nature many of which, following English custom, had as subject-matter adventures in inns, public places and highways; many fights involving fists, feet and sticks, which our French people would find undignified because these blows do not kill so elegantly as sword-strokes. I feared at first that this would not suit the taste here but I reflected in the end that these pictures were not without merit; that they would at least serve to instruct us in English morals. Now it has everything that we ask for in Novels from London: because these characteristics are applicable to all nations, and to ours who paint man in general, or our morals in particular, we find them ingeniously sketched in many of our own novels, the best of which the English cannot yet approach; which is said without wishing to offend them, in as much as this is not an area of emulation on which they can pride themselves.

It has seemed to me in comparing the two texts that the translator has taken it upon himself to make curtailments, transpositions, and perhaps some changes; yet he was obliged to retain the essentials; for the work still has an English flavour, if one excludes the style, which seems to me as smooth as if it were the original; however I would not wish to maintain that there are not here and there several anglicisms. With the best will in the world, such things can escape one. When sifting the work, one does well to remove such things, but one does not perceive the things that remain; and it is for that very reason that they do remain.

If the English author should find his work a little disfigured as perhaps it is, I trust he will not be displeased; doubtless he knows that taste is a local thing and that such characteristics as could make his book's fortune in London would only discredit it in Paris. It remains to absolve the work from reproach. I divine that people will complain that there is not sufficient interest. But how in a novel such as this where the persons in themselves are already not sufficiently interesting, can one ask for a thing whose verisimilitude we could scarcely be interested in if it were there? At least I am permitted to offer my advice, which is no doubt that of many others, it matters little, it seems to me, that Sir Pickle or Miss Emily are vexed in their plans and in their love by a thousand complicated contingencies, and that subsequently by means of miraculous happenings the bobbin is unwound and they achieve their desires. It is not such doings as this, although they constitute the major interest, which remain in the mind and furnish food for the spirit; it is the paintings of detail. Here is the quintessence of a work, here is what nourishes that soul, even after one has forgotten it; as meat feeds the body a long time after digestion. I should certainly like to know what is the interest in *Don Quixote*, that Phoenix of novels: its entire merit is in its details. But your details, you will say to me, or those of your author, what are they worth? You can see for yourselves: I am involved in selling books and not in judging them, but I have always shown that one can produce a good novel without interest.

36. Élie Catherine Fréron on a French translation of *Peregrine Pickle*

1753

From *Lettres sur Quelques Écrits de ce Temps*, par M. Fréron, des Académies d'Angers, 1753. The review is of a translation called *Histoire et Avantures de Sir Williams Pickle*, Amsterdam and Leipzig, 1753. E. Joliat in his *Smollett et la France*, Paris, 1935, p. 181 regards this review as a just and accurate critique.

Inn scenes, public places, highways, numerous fights—with fists and with sticks—, details of an extremely base and uninteresting nature; these form, as a rule, the basis of English novels, and these are what you will find, sir, in the History and adventures of *Sir Williams Pickle,* in four volumes in duodecimo, which have just been published. It must, however, be admitted that it does contain some well-sustained characters, some of which are original.

Williams Pickle is a personable, witty, gallant, generous, proud, lively, scatter-brained, foppish, libertine young man, a courtier in High Society, a wit amongst Poets, frivolous in good company, silly and extravagant in taverns. The English Author goes into detail about all his hero's roguish tricks. I will only record the trick he played on the residents of Bath. He had observed that the only turnspits used in this part of the Country were turned by dogs, trained for this task. These animals are in the habit – or so claims the English Author—of making their way to the kitchen of an evening to fulfil their duties. Pickle took it into his head one day to steal all those dogs, and to shut them up under lock and key. At the hour when they normally put in the skewers, the Cooks appeared at their door, and whistled to their dogs; not one appeared. The whole Town was in an uproar. They had to resort to turning the skewers by hand; the captives were freed only when the meats had been cooked. The turnspit dogs of England must be better trained than ours; for in France these animals are careful to hide when they sense that the hour of work is at hand.

Williams had a great many adventures. He comes to Paris, and is put in the bastille for attacking a Prince. He returns to England where he ruins himself with mad expenditures. He is obliged to become a Writer in order to have enough to live on. He is admitted into a society of Scavans, where he comes across a clever Mechanic who had invented a fine machine for chopping up a large quantity of parsley in a short time. It is true that a Horse was required to set the machine in motion; which was not convenient in a kitchen. A famous Naturalist then read a dissertation in which he described a sure method of collecting fleas' eggs, preserving them and making them hatch, even in the depth of winter, by means of artificial heat.

The talent for writing Books could not preserve Williams from misfortune. His Creditors had him put in prison, where he remained until luck had changed. Adversity made him wiser. He married a young Lady whom he had always loved, although he had often been unfaithful to her: for Williams Pickle was nothing more than a sentimental lover.

I shall *not* review all the heroes who play a part in this novel. I shall content myself with drawing attention to those whose characters have something remarkable about them; I begin with Captain Trunnion. He is a Sailor, churlish, greatly given to swearing, who holds garrison at his house as if he were at war, whose Castle is surrounded by moats, and closed by a drawbridge. For fear of attack, he always has twenty rifles loaded and aimed in readiness. He bores everyone with tales of his expeditions at sea, and thinks of nothing but canons, bombs and swordthrusts. In all conversations he uses only nautical terminology. Strangely for a former Military Man, he believes in Ghosts. He has an insurmountable aversion of Attorneys and other officers of the Law. He is no fonder of women, and does not like even his servants to sleep in the house. However he married an old maid who would have inspired revulsion in the easiest-going libertine. Moreover, this man is both liberal and charitable.

Cadwallader is an original character of whom I can only give an indication by describing in detail his principal adventures. He was the youngest of a good family, and inherited from his father only his immoderate behaviour. At the age of eighteen he was recommended to a Peer who promised to advance Cadwallader, but failed to keep his word. His Host, to whom he owed money, had him put in prison where he remained for several months at the King's expense. On leaving this resting-place, he killed his creditor. His conduct often put him in a position to visit prisons again. In his youth no Provost dared arrest him without being accompanied by a dozen soldiers, and the Justices themselves trembled on their benches when Cadwallader was brought before them. He fought with a Carter, who maimed him; a Butcher cut off a part of his hip; he had an ear carried off by a pistol-shot. One day, having killed one of his enemies, he crossed to France where he took it into his head to talk irreverently of the King. He was put in the Bastille: he feigned madness in the hope that he would be set free; he was in fact released, but only to be sent to the Hulks. He found a means of escape. He made his way to Portugal, where he took it into his head to preach Protestantism; he was sent before the Inquisition. When he had got out of this, he crossed to Spain; arrived at Bologna, and there took up the profession of Doctor. Thus he traversed the greater part of Europe, at one time as a Pilgrim, at another as a Priest, as a Soldier, as a Labourer, as a Charlatan, etc.

After much suffering he came back to London, and lived in a garret there for some time. He sold drugs in the streets, haranguing people in bad English, and trying to pass for a German Doctor; by a lucky chance one of his parents died, and left him a considerable fortune. Cadwallader then reappeared in the world, not as a member of society, but as a spectator who came to take pleasure in seeing men exposed to ridicule. That he might better succeed in this object, he pretended to be deaf; by this means he became the depositary of a thousand little secrets that he would never have known but for his feigned deafness. He had access to the most glittering circles, and when people wanted to talk they were no more embarrased in front of him than in front of the household cat or dog. This old Misanthrope was informed of all the most scandalous anecdotes, and did not waste time in making them public.

Williams Pickle had gained the confidence of Cadwallader; the latter said to him one day:

[quotes *Peregrine Pickle* ch. LXXII, pp. 273–74. Reference is here given to the appropriate chapter in the Shakespeare Head edition, and not to the French translation]

Our Misanthrope could not have had a better accomplice than William Pickle.

There is one more Original in this Novel who deserves recognition. It is a young Doctor of Medicine, a great admirer of Antiquity, and a persistent critic of all modern customs. He invites several people to his house to eat, and in order to show them more consideration, has the meal prepared in the manner of the Antients. First of all he places three beds or couches around the table to represent the Triclinium. A boiled goose was served first, with a rich sauce of pepper, coriander, mint, rue, anchovy and oil. At each end of the table were pies of the Roman type; one was filled with a superb broth made of poppy-syrup; the other with ham rissoles cooked in honey and garnished with parsley, parsnips, cheese and chicken livers. There was also a loin of veal boiled with fennel and chervil, swimming in a sauce composed of honey and flour, a strange hachis of the lights, the livers and blood of the hare. Next a pluck of pork was brought on, filled with the flesh of the same animal chopped very tiny with eggs, cloves, garlic, aniseed, rue, ginger, oil and pepper. The roast meat course consisted of several chickens stuffed with a mixture of pepper and assafoetida, with a sauce of wine and vinegar in which herrings had been marinaded. As a side dish there was a fricasee of snails cooked in milk, and fritters of pumpkins oregano and oil. The dessert appeared, and one saw with pleasure a great bowl of olives, side-by-side with another containing a very special jelly. Of all that was served at this ridiculous meal hardly anything was touched but the olives. The guests thought that they would be poisoned by the other dishes, except for the Amphytrion of the feast who found everything excellent. Much Burgundy wine was drunk, because there was no Falernian.

In imitation of Homer and Virgil, who described everything that was engraved on the shields of some of their heroes, the English author gives us a description of a chamber-pot:

[quotes: probably a reference to the chamber-pot 'waggish enterprise' in *Peregrine Pickle*, ch. XIII, pp. 89 ff., but see ch. XIV of Clifford's Oxford English Novels edition, pp. 65ff.)

The ingenious or pleasing qualities to be found in this work cannot compensate for the boredom induced by the reading of four long volumes. The translator acknowledges that the best English novel cannot stand comparison with ours. So what need is there for all these English productions.

37. Lady Mary Wortley Montagu, letter

23 July 1754

From a letter to the Countess of Bute, *The Complete Letters of Lady Mary Wortley Montagu*, ed. Robert Halsband, Oxford, 1966, vol. III, pp. 66–8.

Fielding has realy a fund of true Humour, and was to be pity'd at his first entrance into the World, having no choice (as he said himselfe) but to be a Hackney Writer or a Hackney Coachman. His Genius deserv'd a better Fate, but I cannot help blaming that continu'd Indiscretion (to give it the softest name) that has run through his Life, and I am afraid still remains. I guess'd R. Random to be his, thô without his Name. I cannot think Fadom wrote by the same hand; it is every way so much below it....

Since I was born, no original has appear'd excepting Congreve, and Fielding, who would I beleive have approach'd nearer to his excellencies if not forc'd by necessity to publish without correction, and throw many production into the World he would have thrown into the Fire if meat could have been got without money, or money without Scribbling. The Greatest Virtue, Justice, and the most distinguishing prerogative of Mankind, writeing, when duly executed do Honor to Human nature, but when degenerated into Trades are the most contemptible ways of getting Bread. I am sorry not to see any more of P[eregine] Pickle's performances; I wish you would tell me his name.

38. Mrs Laetitia Pilkington on *Roderick Random*

1754

From *Memoirs of Mrs Laetitia Pilkington 1712–1750. Written by Herself* (1748–50), English Library edn., ed. J. Isaacs, with an Introduction by Iris Barry, 1928, p. 350.

These *Memoirs*, along with Mrs Theresa Constantia Phillips' *Apology* (1748) provided a 'model' for Lady Vane in her *Memoirs of a Lady of Quality* inserted in *Peregrine Pickle*.

Dr Matthew Pilkington and Laetitia were friends of Swift in Dublin. He described them in 1730 as 'a little young poetical parson, who has a littler young poetical wife'.

> Stand apart now, ye Roderick Randoms,
> Foundlings, bastard sons of wit,
> Hence ye profane, be far away,
> All ye that bow to idol lusts, and altars raise,
> Or to false heroes give fantastic praise.

39. Lady Mary Wortley Montagu, letter

1 January 1755

From a letter to the Countess of Bute, *The Complete Letters of Lady Mary Wortley Montagu*, ed. Robert Halsband, Oxford, 1966, vol. III, p. 78. The reference here is to Smollett's translation of *Don Quixote* which appeared in 1755.

I am sorry my Friend Smollet[1] [*sic*] loses his time in Translations. He has certainly a Talent for Invention, tho' I think it flags a little in his last work. *Don Quixote* is a difficult undertaking. I shall never desire to read any attempt to new dress him; tho' I am a meer pidler in the Spanish Language, I had rather take pains to understand him in the Original than sleep over a stupid Translation.

NOTE

1 As Halsband notes, in calling Smollett her friend, Lady Mary refers only to her fondness for his writing: they had never met.

40. Unsigned review of Smollett's translation of *Don Quixote*

September 1755

From *The Monthly Review*, September 1755, xiii, 196–202. The reviewer is Ralph Griffiths, and he makes a sustained comparison between Smollett's translation and that of Charles Jervas, whose translation appeared in 1742.

Dr *Smollet* undertook this translation in dependence upon the encouragement of a subscription; in which we have not heard what success he met with, nor is there any list of subscribers names; however, the books are delivered from the press in a genteel and elegant manner, in respect both to the paper, type, and engravings.

The ingenious translator informs us, in a short advertisement, that his aim in this undertaking, was to maintain that ludicrous solemnity, and self-importance, by which the inimitable *Cervantes* has distinguished the character of *Don Quixote*, without raising him to the insipid rank of a dry philosopher, or debasing him to the melancholy circumstances, and unentertaining, caprice of the ordinary madman; and to preserve the native humour of *Sancho Panza* from degenerating into mere proverbial phlegm, or affected buffoonry;—that he has endeavoured to retain the spirit and ideas, without servilely adhering to the literal expression, of the original; from which, however, he has not so far deviated, as to destroy that formality of idiom so peculiar to the *Spaniards*, and so essential to the character of the work;—that the satire and propriety of many allusions, which had been lost in the change of customs, and lapse of time, is restored in explanatory notes; and the whole conducted with that care and circumspection, which ought to be exerted by every author, who, in attempting to improve upon a task already performed, subjects himself to the most invidious comparison.

How far the doctor has succeeded in the above mentioned respects, it may not become us hastily to determine. *Don Quixote* is perhaps the most difficult book in the world to translate; and for this plain reason, that it is the most difficult to be understood. Few, very few, of even the *Spaniards*, of the present day understand all its beauties, or can explain the obscurities which the lapse of time, as Dr *Smollet* says, hath occasioned: how then can it be expected that *Englishmen* should be perfect masters of this author? It is true, we may be able to read him in the orginal, and that with great delight; but to transfuse all his spirit, his fine humour, and the beauty of his numerous allusions, into a foreign language in these remote times too, and the nation likewise so remote, is a task which a genius equal to that of *Cervantes* himself could not perform, without the same knowledge of the country, and of the times in which this excellent author lived: including also the most extensive acquaintance with the language, idioms, customs, humorous expressions, provincial phrases, and proverbial sayings, of the people for whom the translation is intended.

But as all these advantages must be considered as unattainable; as the best translation we can look for must be expected from the hand of a person chiefly qualified by books; we fancy a better than Dr *Smollet's*, upon the whole, will not speedily appear. *Jarvis's* may, in some respects, be thought a more exact version; but in our opinion, the doctor's genius (notwithstanding some things that appear to be rather inaccuracies than defects in judgment) comes nearest the great original.—With regard to those translations from translations, published by *Matteux*, and others, they deserve no farther mention; except to express our wonder, that under the burlesque veil, and farcical disguise, in which they have enveloped the author, they have not been able totally to divest him of his native dignity: yet,—after all, we doubt not but many readers, who take up an *English Don Quixote*, merely to be *diverted*, will pronounce *Matteux's* the best book.[1]

A small specimen will shew the difference between the translation of Dr *Smollet*, and of his predecessor, Mr *Jarvis*. We shall take from each the notable story told by *Sancho*, to expose the mistaken politeness of his master, in the affair of table-precedency: those who are possessed of this work in the original, may, perhaps, have the curiosity to compare both with the *Spanish*.[2]

From Dr Smollet.	*From Mr* Jarvis.

The duke and dutchess came to the door to receive him. [*Don Quixote*] attended by one of those grave ecclesiastics who govern the families of noblemen; who, being of no birth themselves, know not how to direct those who are; who seek to measure the grandeur of the great by the narrowness of their own souls, and in attempting to make their pupils economists, convert them into downright misers: such, I say, was the

The duke and dutchess came to the half-door to receive him, and with them a grave ecclesiastic: one of those who govern great mens houses; one of those, who, not being princes born, know not how to instruct those that are how to demean themselves as such; one of those who would have the magnificence of the great measured by the narrowness of their own minds; one of those who, pretending to teach those they govern to be

From Dr Smollet. *From Mr* Jarvis.

grave clergyman who came out to receive *Don Quixote*, with the duke and dutchess. After a thousand courteous compliments, they walked on each side of him to the table, where the duke complimented him with the upper end; and tho' he refused that honour, they importuned him so much that he was obliged to comply; the clergyman sitting opposite to him, and the duke and dutchess taking their places at the sides.

Sancho, who was present at all this ceremony, being confounded and astonished at the honours which were paid to his master, and perceiving the formality and intreaties that passed between his grace and *Don Quixote*, about sitting at the head of the table intruded himself, as usual, into the discourse, saying, 'With your honour's leave, I'll tell you a story of what happened in our village with respect to the upper hand in sitting.'

Scarce had he pronounced these words, when the knight began to tremble with apprehension, that he was going to utter some absurdity; but the 'Squire seeing and understanding the cause of his master's trepidation, 'Signor,' said he, 'your worship needs not be

frugal, teach them to be misers. One of this sort, I say, was the grave ecclesiastic, who came out with the duke to receive *Don Quixote*. A thousand polite compliments passed upon the occasion; and taking *Don Quixote* between them, they went and sat down to table. The duke offered *Don Quixote* the upper end, and, tho' he would have declined it, the importunities of the duke prevailed upon him to accept it. The ecclesiastic seated himself over against him, and the duke and dutchess on each side. *Sancho* was present all the while, surprised and astonished to see the honour those princes did his master, and, perceiving the many intreaties and ceremonies, which passed between the duke and *Don Quixote*, to make him sit down at the head of the table, he said, 'If your honours will give me leave, I will tell you a story of a passage that happened in our town, concerning places.' Scarce had *Sancho* said this, when *Don Quixote* began to tremble, believing, without doubt, he was going to say some foolish thing. *Sancho* observed, and understood him, and said, 'Be not afraid, Sir, of my breaking loose, or of my saying any thing that is not pat

From Dr Smollet.   *From Mr* Jarvis.

afraid that I shall misbehave, or say something that is not to the matter in hand; for, I have not forgot the advice I just now received from your worship, about speaking a little, or a great deal, to the purpose, and not to the purpose.' 'I know nothing at all of the matter,' answered the knight, 'say what thou wilt, so thou say'st it quickly.' 'Well then,' replied *Sancho*, 'what I am going to say is so true, that my master, *Don Quixote*, here present, would not suffer to me to tell a lie.' 'As for me,' said *Don Quixote*, 'you may lie as much as you please, without let or molestation: but I advise you to consider well what you are about to say.' 'I have it so well considered, and reconsidered, that I am as safe as he that has the repique in hand, as will appear in the performance.' 'Your graces will do well,' said *Don Quixote*, 'to order the servants to turn out this madman, who will commit a thousand blunders.' 'By the life of the duke!' cried the dutchess, 'I will not part with my good friend, *Sancho*, for whom I have a very great respect, because I know him to be a person of wit and pleasantry.' 'Pleasant may all the days of your holiness be, for your good

to the purpose: I have not forgotten the advice your worship gave me a little while ago, about talking much or little, well or ill.' 'I remember nothing, *Sancho*,' answered *Don Quixote*, 'say what you will, so you say it quickly.' 'What I would say,' quoth *Sancho*, 'is very true, and should it be otherwise, my master, *Don Quixote*, who is present, will not suffer me to lie.' 'Lie as much as you will for me, *Sancho*,' replied *Don Quixote*, 'I will not be your hindrance; but take heed what you are going to say.' 'I have so heeded, and reheeded it,' quoth *Sancho*, 'that all is as safe as the repique[a] in hand, as you will see by the operation.' 'It will be convenient,' said *Don Quixote*, 'that your honours order this blockhead to be turned out of doors; for he will be making a thousand foolish blunders.' 'By the life of the duke,' quoth the dutchess, '*Sancho* shall not stir a jot from me: I love him much, for I know he is mighty discreet.' 'Many such years,' quoth *Sancho*, 'may your holiness live, for the good opinion you have of me, tho' it is not in me: but the tale I would tell is this.

A certain gentleman of our town, very rich, and of a good family—for he was descended

From Dr Smollet.　　　　*From Mr* Jarvis.

opinion of my deserts,' said the 'squire, 'tho' God knows, they are but slender enough: however, my story is this:

There was an invitation given by a gentleman of our town, who was both rich and well born, as being come of the *Alamos* of *Medina del Campo*, and married to *Donna Mencia de Quinones*, daughter of *Don Alonzo de Maranon*, knight of the order of St *Jago*, who was drowned in the *Heradura*, and occasioned a quarrel some years ago in our village; in which, if I am not mistaken, my master, *Don Quixote*, was concerned; but this I know, mad *Tom*, the son of old *Balvastro* the blacksmith, was hurt on that occasion; now, Sir Master of mine, is not this God's truth; speak upon your worship's honour, that these noble persons may not look upon me as a chattering liar.' 'Hitherto,' said the clergyman,' 'I take you to be a chatterer rather than a liar; but I know not what I shall take you for in the sequel.' 'Thou hast produced, so many witnesses and tokens,' replied the knight, 'that I cannot but say the story looks like truth; proceed, however, and shorten thy tale; for thou art in the way of lengthening it out for the space

from the *Alamas* of *Medina del Campo*, and married *Donna Mencia de Quinnones*, who was daughter of *Don Alonzo de Marannon*, knight of the order of St *James*, who was drowned in the *Herradura*; about whom there happened that quarrel in our town, some years ago, in which, as I take it, my master *Don Quixote*, was concerned, and *Tommy*, the madcap son of *Balvastro* the smith, was hurt— Pray, good master of mine, is not all this true? Speak by your life, that these gentlemen may not take me for some lying prating fellow.' 'Hitherto,' said the ecclesiastic, 'I take you rather for a prater than for a liar: but henceforward I know not what I shall you take for.' 'You produce so many evidences, and so many tokens, that I cannot but say,' quoth *Don Quixote*, 'it is likely you tell the truth; go on, and shorten the story; for you take the way not to have done in two days.' 'He shall shorten nothing,' quoth the dutchess, 'and to please me, he shall tell it his own way, tho' he have not done in six days; and should it take up so many, they would be to me the most agreeable of any I ever spent in my life.'

'I say then, Sirs, proceeded

From Dr Smollet.	*From Mr* Jarvis.

of two whole days.' 'He shall not shorten it,' said the dutchess, 'if he consults my entertainment; but, on the contrary, tell it in his own way, tho' it should not be finished in six days; for should it hold out so long, they will be some of the pleasantest I ever passed.'

'Well then, my masters,' proceeded *Sancho*, that same gentleman, whom I know as well as I know these two hands, for it is not above bow-shot from his house to mine, invited a farmer, who, tho' not rich, was a very honest man.' 'Dispatch, brother,' cried the priest, interposing, 'for at this rate your story will reach to the other world.' 'It will hardly go half as far, an it please God,' answered the squire, who thus proceeded. 'So as I was saying, the farmer going to the house of the gentleman-inviter, who is now dead, God rest his soul! by the same token, they say he died like an angel; for my own part, I was not present at his death, having gone a reaping to *Tembleque*.' 'As you hope to live, son,' cried the ecclesiastic, 'return quickly from *Tembleque*, and finish your story, without staying to inter the gentleman, unless you have a mind to bury us all.' 'Well, to come to the

Sancho, that this same gentleman, whom I know as well as I do my right hand from my left, (for it is not a bow-shot from my house to his) invited a farmer, who was poor, but honest, to dinner.' 'Proceed, friend,' said the ecclesiastic, 'at this period: for you are going the way with your tale, not to stop till you come to the other world.' 'I shall stop before we get half-way thither, if it pleases God,' answered *Sancho*, 'and so I proceed. This same farmer coming to the said gentleman-inviter's house,—God rest his soul, for he is dead and gone, by the same token it is reported he died like an angel; for I was not by, being at that time gone a reaping to *Tembleque*.' 'Prithee, son,' said the ecclesiastic, 'come back quickly from *Tembleque*, and, without burying the gentleman, (unless you have a mind to make more burials) make an end of your tale.' 'The business then,' quoth *Sancho*, 'was this, that they being ready to sit down to table—methinks I see them now more than ever.' The duke and dutchess took great pleasure in seeing the displeasure the good ecclesiastic suffered by the length and pauses of *Sancho's* tale; but *Don Quixote* was quite angry and vexed. I

From Dr Smollet.

From Mr Jarvis.

point,' replied *Sancho*, 'when the two came to be seated at table. Methinks I see them now more than ever.' The duke and dutchess were infinitely pleased with the disgust which the reverent ecclesiastic expressed at the tedious and circumstantial manner in which the 'squire related his story; while *Don Quixote* was almost consumed by shame and indignation. 'I say, moreover,' resumed *Sancho*, 'that the two, as I have already observed, coming to sit down at the table, the farmer obstinately refused to take the upper end, according to the desire of the entertainer; while the gentleman, on the other hand, as obstinately insisted upon his compliance, alleging that he ought to be master in his own house; but the farmer, who piqued himself upon his politeness and good breeding, still persisted in his refusal; until the gentleman growing angry, took him by the shoulders and thrust him into the seat, saying, "Know, Mr *Chaffthresher*, that wheresoever I sit, I shall always be at the head of the table." Now this is my tale, and I really believe it was brought in pretty pat to the purpose.'

say then,' quoth *Sancho*, 'that they, both standing, as I have said, and just ready to sit down, the farmer disputed obstinately with the gentleman to take the upper end of the table, and the gentleman, with as much positiveness, pressed the farmer to take it, saying, he ought to command in his own house. But the countryman, piquing himself upon his civility and good breeding, would by no means sit down, till the gentleman, in a fret, laying both his hands upon the farmer's shoulders, made him sit down by main force; saying, Sit thee down, chaff-threshing churl; for, let me sit where I will, that is the upper end to thee. This is my tale, and truly I believe it was brought in here pretty much to the purpose.'

We shall here take leave of Dr *Smollet's* performance, with just mentioning one small circumstance of omission in his book, that might easily have been supplied, viz. the want of a table of contents to the adventures of *Don Quoxite*; which *Jarvis* has given. Without such assistance, readers may be often very much at a loss to turn to particular parts of a work, as occasion may require.—We hope it will not be thought we intend the mention of such a matter as this, to pass for a *criticism*: these are things that men of genius, and imagination, seldom attend to; but nevertheless, *indexes* have their uses, and no book, of *considerable price* especially, ought to be with out them.

NOTES

a *Alluding to the game of picquet, in which the repique may be safe against the greatest cards in appearance.*
1 See Peter Anthony Motteux (1663–1718), *The History of the Renown'd Don Quixote*, 4 vols, 1700–3.
2 See Smollett's *Don Quixote* (1775), 1793, 4 vols, vol. III, pp. 289ff. The passage considered comes from part II, book II, ch. 14, 'Which treats of manifold important subjects'.

41. Gotthold Lessing on a German translation of *Roderick Random*

1755

From G. E. Lessing, *Sämtliche Schriften*, Stuttgart, 1890, ed. Karl Lachman, vol. V, pp. 442–3. Lessing reviews a translation of the third English edition of *Roderick Random*, part I only, published in Hamburg in 1755.

It would be too generous for one to want to attribute to these adventures the same preference which English novels have in their favour. The writer is neither a Richardson nor a Fielding; he is an author such as one comes across in great numbers among the Germans and the French. He admits that he chose in particular Mr Le Sage as his paragon, whose *Gil Blas* will always remain a masterpiece of humorous novel-writing. But, how far beneath him he has remained! It would certainly be a surprise if German readers of good taste were to find as much pleasure in the school pranks, in the anecdotes about brothels, in the brawls and the adventures on board a ship, as the English populace, which has already gone through three editions of the book. At the end of this section the hero is found in a precarious position, and in his despair, resolves to die. One need not worry overmuch about this since he still wrote the second part, which it is hoped, will soon be available in German. The translation seems to have been done in rather a hurry.

42. Anonymous, 'Remarks on *Roderick Random*'

1755

From the fourth edition of *The Adventures of Roderick Random*, Dublin, 1755. 'Remarks on *Roderick Random* in a Letter from a Gentleman at TWICKENHAM, to his Friend in LONDON', pp. i–iv. These remarks on imagination, truth, and the representation of virtue and vice in fiction suggest the anonymous author is Smollett himself.

Dear Sir,

As I have long held all Novel and Romance to be no other than the *Centaurs* and *Chimeras* of an extravagant Imagination; I was scarce persuaded to cast an Eye on your darling *Roderick Random:* However, your Importunity at last prevailed, and favoured by an idle Hour, conducted me through several Scenes of human Life, all delightfully natural, interesting, and entertaining.

Where the Sentiment is founded in Truth, I am by no Means an

Enemy to Fable; which then serves as an agreeable *Medium*, to convey the *Light* of Nature to the Soul.

Through the ordinary Occurrences of Life, we seldom meet with any Thing that affects, or surprizes; and even on these rare Occasions there are few who reflect with Delicacy, or permit the due Impression to dwell on their Minds.

Here then the Author may agreeably interpose, and Supply what is deficient in the Object or the Observer. He may imagine or collect a Number of choice Incidents, that may at any Time have happened through the infinite Variety of human Affairs; these he may connect and dispose to an easy and natural Order. He may thereupon form due Inferences and instructive Reflections; and by uniting the whole in a few personated Characters, may convey, to every separate Reader, the Improvement and Experience of several Ages.

It is thus alone, that, whatever is dark or disgustful in mere Precept, acquires a pleasing Light and Influence; Morality approaches as a Friend, that is embodied and animated to our Senses; and we not only hear, but see and feel the Truth of Things.

This Method hath been authorized from the earliest Times, in the Example of the famed *Aesop*, and a few Others: But its best Precedent and Sanction is derived from the several Parables, divinely affecting, throughout the old and new Testament.

To compass any Thing considerable in this Way, it is not sufficient to have a Brain, like the Mud of *Nile*, productive of monstrous Births, and half formed Conceptions: Your Knights-adventurer at the Pen, are ever Knight-errant from Reason and common Sense. A fancy that takes Judgment by the Hand, an extensive Experience of Men, Manners and Misfortunes, a Humour native and peculiar, a clear Head, are requisite; and above all a feeling Heart, that comprehends the full Sense of that Line of *Virgil*, inexpressible by any other Language——*Sunt Lachrymae Rerum et Mentem Mortalia tangunt.*[1]

The Criticks, who framed Laws for the Drama and Epic Poem, derived those very Laws from the Excellencies of the Writers who had been eminent in that Way; and it is thus I acknowledge myself particularly indebted to your favourite Author, for this Detail of Talents that are requisite for Fable.

We further learn from this Author, that Characters of Vice may be made the most conducive to the Promotion of Virtue. For though Virtue is in herself absolutely amiable and attractive, when placed in a proper Light, and remarked with due Attention; yet Vice can assume her graces with so cunning a Mimickry, that the Detection must come from Eyes of uncommon Discernment.

It is in this material Distinction that your Author is happy. He strips Vice of all that served to adorn or disguise. He lifts her to the Light. He exposes her native Deformity. He gives her Affectations to Ridicule, and her Allurements to Detestation. He places her in Opposition to her Adversary; and, by a contrast so evident, demonstrates, that nothing is beneficent, that nothing is desirable but Virtue.

The Heads of most Writers, in forming their Characters, teem an Offspring little different from *fortem Gyam fortemque Cloanthum*,[2] a Group of Figures altogether twinned, and only distinguishable by subscribing the Name. But this Author is peculiarly skilful at featuring his Progeny, at one Glance we know each from the other; and *Bowling, Strap*, and *Morgan*, though of equal Integrity, are as well noted as a Courtier from an honest Countryman.

But what is truly most admirable in this Genius, is that Variety in which he dishes up Virtue to the Appetite. Where he once sows the Principle of Goodness in the Heart, the Fruit is correspondent through an Infinity of different Productions. He renders it equally fashionable under all Manners, and equally eloquent in all Dialects. Hear it from the Mouth of his *Tar!* and let Philosophy listen and learn——(Says *Bowling* in his greatest Distress) *Life is a Voyage in which we must expect to meet with all Weathers; sometimes it is calm, sometimes rough; a fair Gale often succeeds a Storm; the Wind does not always sit one Way, and Despair signifies nothing; but Resolution and Skill are better than a stout Vessel: For why? because they require no Carpenter, and grow stronger the more Labour they undergo.*

I shall conclude with remarking the Master-stroak of this Author in his Character of *Strap*, whom he purposely divests of every Talent and Accomplishment, to shew how amiable Virtue is independent of all Addition. This indeed was a singular Achievement, whereby he feelingly inculcates this greatest of Morals——*That the Heart is infinitely more estimable than the Head, that one Drachm of Goodness outweighs a thousand Pounds of Understanding.*

I am, Sir &c.

NOTES

1 Virgil, *Aeneid*, I, 455: 'These are matters for tears, and thoughts of mortality touch the mind.'
2 Virgil, *Aeneid*, I, 222: literally, 'strong Gyam and strong Cloanthes'.

43. Unsigned review of *The Reprisal*
February 1757

From *The Critical Review*, III, February 1757, 159–60.

Smollett's play *The Reprisal*, a comedy in two acts, was published in January 1757 and staged at the Theatre Royal in Drury Lane in January and February.

Impartial judges, and those who have real taste, allow the author of this piece to be not only a master of genius and invention; but happily just at drawing characters.

Could this piece have been so planned as to have furnished a few more incidents; could the scenes have been shorter, and sometimes changed, the whole would have been more entertaining. The author does not seem to be so well acquainted with the *jeu de théâtre* as some of his contemporaries: there is, however, throughout the performance a close imitation of nature, which will always please the judicious, though it may not set the galleries in a roar.

44. Unsigned review of *The Reprisal*

February 1757

From *The Monthly Review*, February 1757, xvi, 179.

Calculated for the Meridian of Bartholomew-Fair; but, by some unnatural accident, (as jarring elements are sometimes made to unite) exhibited eight nights at the Theatre-Royal in Drury-lane.

45. [Oliver Goldsmith] on the *Complete History*

June 1757

From *The Monthly Review*, June 1757, xvi, 530–6. Goldsmith here reviews the first three volumes of Smollett's *The Complete History of England*; volume four of the *History* appeared in 1758, and was then reviewed in *The Monthly Review* by Owen Ruffhead, see No. 47.

When the Historian relates events far removed from the age in which he writes, when evidence is become scarce, and authorities are rendered doubtful, from the obscurities which time has thrown upon them, he ought, above all things, to be careful that his narration be as amply authenticated as the nature of his researches will allow. Strictly speaking, the eye-witness alone should take upon him to transmit facts to posterity; and as for the Historians, the Copyists, the Annotators, who may follow him, if possessed of no new and genuine materials, instead of strengthening, they will only diminish the authority of their guide: for, in proportion as

History removes from the first witnesses, it may recede also from truth,—as, by passing thro' the prejudices, or the mistakes of subsequent Compilers, it will be apt to imbibe what tincture they may chance to give it. The *later* Historian's only way, therefore, to prevent the ill effects of that decrease of evidence which the lapse of years necessarily brings with it, must be, by punctually referring to the spring head from whence the stream of his narration flows; which at once will cut off all appearance of partiality, or misrepresentation. As in law, the rectitude of a person's character is not alone sufficient to establish the truth of a fact, so in history, not merely the Writer's testimony, be our opinion of his veracity ever so great, but collateral evidence also is required, to determine every thing of a questionable nature. The fundamental materials for the general history of any country are the public records, ancient monuments, and original Historians of that country; and in proportion as they are slighted by the *Compiler*, these venerable Originals themselves may fall into neglect, and, possibly, in the end, even into irretrievable oblivion:—and when *they* are gone, in vain may we look for an enlightening ray to guide us thro' the darkness of antiquity: we must then be content with the uncertain gleam with which an erroneous or partial leader is pleased to conduct us.

There were of old, and still are, indolent Readers, who turn to an Author with the design rather of killing than improving their time; and who, scared at the serious face of instruction, are rather attracted by the lively, florid stile of a Florus, than the more substantial disquisitions of a Polybius. With such Readers, every step an Historian takes towards determining the weight of evidence, or the degrees of credibility, is an excursion into the regions of dulness; but while the Writer proceeds in his narrative, without reflection, they continue to read without reflecting: and his history enlightens then just as much as a romance would have done: for they are equally unconcerned about truth in either.

Truth should be the main object of the Historian's pursuit; *Elegance* is its only ornament: if, therefore, we see a Writer of this class plume himself upon his excelling in the last, and at the same time slighting the evidences that ought to ascertain and support the first, suspicion will naturally arise, and the Author's credit will sink in proportion.

With respect to the History now before us, the Compiler does not pretend to have discovered any hidden records, or authentic materials, that have escaped the notice of former Writers; or to have thrown such lights upon contested events, or disputed characters, as may serve to rectify any mistaken opinions mankind may have entertained, with respect to either. His care is rather to disburthen former Histories of those tedious vouchers, and proofs of authenticity, which, in his opinion, only serve to swell the page, and exercise the Reader's patience. He seldom quotes authorities in support of his representations; and if he now and then condescends to cite the testimony of former Writers, he never points to the page, but leaves the sceptical Reader to supply any defect of this kind, by an exertion of that industry which the Author disdains: and thus, on the veracity of the Relator are we to rest our conviction, and accept his own word for it, that he has no intention to deceive or mislead us.

That this Author, however, has no such design, may be fairly presumed from his declining all attempts to bias us by any remarks of his own. Determined to avoid all *useless disquisition*, as his plan professes, he steers wide indeed of the danger, and avoids all *disquisition as useless*. A brief recital of facts is chiefly what the public is to expect from this performance. But, with submission, we think the ingenious Author might have afforded us something more. He has undoubted ability; and he well knows, that a moderate interspersion of manly and sensible observations, must have greatly enlivened his work, and would hardly have been deemed superfluous by such Readers as have any turn for reflection.

With respect to the stile of this Historian, it is, in general clear, nervous, and flowing; and we think it impossible for a Reader of taste not to be pleased with the perspicuity, and elegance of his manner. But what he seems principally to value himself upon, and what his Patronizers chiefly mention in praise of this performance, are the characters he has summed up, at the close of every reign. Here, however, we cannot entirely fall in with the ingenious Doctor's admirers:—But we forbear to enlarge, and shall therefore proceed to enable our Readers, in some measure, to judge for themselves, by a few specimens taken from such parts of the History as, we apprehend, the Author's friends will think we do him no injustice in selecting.

[quotes from the *History*: characters of James I, Charles I, Oliver Cromwell, Charles II]

We shall conclude with the following summary of the qualifications required in an historian. His learning, says Bayle, should be greater than his genius, and his judgment stronger than his imagination. In private life, he should have the character of being free from Party, and his former writings ought always to have shewn the sincerest attachment to truth. I ask several questions, says the same Author, who the Historian is? of what country? of what principles? for it is impossible but that his private opinions will almost involuntarily work themselves into his public performances. His stile also should be clear, elegant, and nervous. And lastly, to give him a just boldness of sentiment and expression, he should have a consciousness of these his superior abilities.—As to the first requisites, how far our Author is possessed of them, his former productions will abundantly demonstrate; but in the last he seems to have fallen short of none of his predecessors.

46. Dr John Shebbeare on Smollett

1757

From *The Occasional Critic, or the Decrees of the Scotch Tribunal in the Critical Review Rejudged: etc.*, 1757, pp. 9 ff. Shebbeare (1709–88) wrote this pamphlet in response to a review in the *Critical Review* of his *Third Letter to the People of England*, and returned to the attack in *An Appendix to the Occasional Critic* of December 1757. Shebbeare, it is believed, advised Lady Vane on the writing of her *Memoirs*, and was caricatured by Smollett in the figure of Ferret in Smollett's *Sir Launcelot Greaves*. A Westcountryman of dubious medical qualifications, Shebbeare was a hack political writer and author of two novels, *The Marriage Act* (1754) and *Lydia* (1755).

Then, like a true *Champion*, the Knight of *La Mancha*, you arrive to rescue the Charms of Literature from the avaritious Hands of the hireling Necromancers in the *Monthly Review*. What an Advantage it is in a Critic to have transcribed Don Quixote, tho' it may prove a great *Loss* to the Bookseller who *hired* him.

From a footnote to p.61:

A Millar,[1] soliciting Subscriptions to the Editor of Don *Quixote*, when it was objected by one of his own Countrymen; that the Translator did not understand *Spanish*, assured him that the Author had been full six Weeks to study that Language amongst the native *Spaniards*, at *Brussels*.

From p. 63, on *The Regicide*:

A Tragedy, written by one of the Gentleman Annalists, never played, sometime published, totally forgotten, which, before its being printed by Subscription, raised a great Clamor against the Patentees, who rejected it, and on being published, justified their Refusal.

From p. 127:

... Your hero, whose Wit seems to consist in placing two Words beginning with the same letter, to succeed each other, as *Roderick Random*, *Peregrine Pickle*, *Ferdinand Fathom*, *Pillory Politician*. Nothing so easily imitated, and though I am ashamed of the Thing, lest you should imagine me deficient in that way of being witty, I will show you with what Facility it is to be obtained. For Example, *Codsheaded Critics*, *asinine Annalists*, *rascally Reviewers*, *scabby Scotchmen*, all which are as applicable to you, as *Pillory Politician* is to the author of The Fourth Letter.

NOTE

1 One of the publishers of Smollett's *Don Quixote*.

47. [Owen Ruffhead], review of Smollett's *Complete History*, vol. IV

April 1758

From *The Monthly Review*, April 1758, xviii, 289–305. The concluding part of the review complains of Smollett's Toryism, and argues that his virtues are those of the novelist, rather than those of the 'accurate historian.'

As many able pens have been employed in expatiating on the use of History, and ascertaining the requisite qualifications of an Historian, it will be needless to enlarge on those general heads, which have been already so amply discussed.

But, though the general accomplishments of an Historian have been frequently enumerated and explained, yet we are of opinion, that some particular requisites have not been sufficiently recommended and enforced. Learning, knowledge, discernment, solidity, and discretion, are previous endowments without which no man should assume the office of an Historical Writer. But to these constituent qualifications he should unite the requisite *duties* of an Historian, and exercise his talents with care, accuracy, and impartiality.

Of our later Historians some have been little better than laborious Compilers; others no more than random Essayists. A History which is only a circumstantial narrative of facts, without reflections upon them, may be only regardable as a file of Newspapers: and one that abounds with reflections, without due attention to facts, differs little from a romance or a novel.

An Historian should be careful to omit no incident of moment. Yet he ought not, therefore, to content himself with a meer relation of events; but wherever they appear to be generally interesting, he should offer his observations upon them, apply his discernment to trace the causes which produced them, and exhibit the consequences which flowed from them.

He should particularly exert this faculty in his account of any remarkable alteration in the laws of the country he treats of. It behoves him to state what the law was at the time of the change, and to shew the effects produced by the variation. He ought not, however, to indulge a fondness for expatiating too far, lest it should insensibly withdraw his mind from a due attention to the chain of historical facts. It is necessary, therefore, that his judgment should be greater than his imagination; otherwise he will be tempted to employ his powers in the vain glow of colouring, and will be more studious to dazzle the imagination with a gaudy display of splendid sentiments, and pompous phraseology, than to engage the understanding by just reasoning, and solid reflections. He ought to remember, that in History, Ornament should be but a secondary consideration; and that the first and principal requisite, is Utility.

A History should not be calculated, like a novel, only to entertain us in the perusal, and then to be thrown aside, or consigned to oblivion; but ought rather to be a faithful repository of interesting events, to be occasionally referred to for the purposes of information and instruction. An Historian, therefore, should be more solicitous to say what is just and authentic, than what is brilliant and striking.

He ought, above all things, to avoid haste. Hurry is the worst excuse which any Writer can make to atone for his defects: but in an Historian it is more especially inexcusable. A History is not to be wrote *Stans pede in uno:* and if we should see one start up within a compass of time too short for a diligent Collator even to compare the various authorities referred to, we may then conclude that the Writer has taken his matter upon credit.

It should be the first office of an Historian, attentively to read the several authorities from whence he intends to extract his materials. But yet it is not sufficient that he produces authority for what he advances; he should exert his sagacity to determine the degree of credibility due to the Writers from whom he draws his extract: he should make himself acquainted with their country, their principles, and the age they lived in. The knowledge of these particulars, may enable him to reconcile their contradictory evidence, and to develop truth from the clouds of national and party prejudice.

Having formed his judgment of the authenticity of their several relations, his next care should be accurately to digest and arrange the various matter he has collected. For want of this caution, Histories are frequently rendered obscure: for it often happens, that different Writers relate the same circumstances under different periods of time; by which means the Compiler, who turns from one to the other, without comparing them together, and digesting his extracts, is frequently led into perplexing obscurities, idle repetitions, and inexcusable anachronisms.

An Historian, above all other Writers, should think for himself. He should, as far as possible, banish from his mind all prejudices imbibed by education, or received from reading or discourse. It is not sufficient that he is of no party; he should write as if he was of no country. He ought to be careful to draw no inferences but what are warranted by the premises he has related; and should ground no conclusuons on the foundation of public report.

It has been an usual failing in many Historians to be more particularly minute and circumstantial in their detail of military, than of civil transaction. They will acquaint us how an army was marshalled, and relate every particular evolution, as if their History was calculated only for the perusal of Generals, and Drill-Serjeants; But in their accounts of civil proceeding, they frequently hasten to the event, without taking notice of any intermediate circumstances. They think it sufficient to tell us, that such or such a treaty was made, without specifying any of the material articles it contained, shewing how it contributed to strengthen or diminish the interest of the contracting Parties, or making any mention of the intrigues which were used to promote or impede the conclusion of it. This is an inexcusable error: for the civil concerns of past times, are more generally interesting than the military operations.

In the same manner they often hurry over important trials, and debates, contenting themselves with barely stating the decision; which can give little satisfaction to reflecting Readers, who will be curious to learn the reasons and arguments that were offered to warrant the determination. Some, who state the arguments, often represent them partially, and repeat those only which were urged on one side of the question: which manifestly shews, that they are guided by the blind zeal of prejudice, instead of being governed by the sincere love of truth.

The portraying of Characters, is a task on which Historians generally lavish all their powers. Common Readers are more curious about persons, than things; and Writers who are more solicitous to gain the applause of the multitude, than the approbation of the judicious, endeavour to adapt their writings to the standard of popular taste. In describing characters, they give way to an implicit faith, and unbounded fancy. They do not scruple to sum up every quality, which idle report, partial attachment, or prejudiced malice, has imputed to the personage they are delineating; which they seldom fail to embellish with all the decorations that their own imagination can supply. They generally fall into a fondness for Antithesis, and, in the end, make their general account give the lie to the particulars they have related in the course of their History. Their motley characters may, with little alteration, be adapted to any persons whatsoever; or be distributed into lots, and drawn at random. But a careful and judicious Historian will make no inferences, nor confer any qualities, which are not warranted by the particular circumstances premised. He will draw from the original before him, and not from his own imagination.

In short, Truth should be the object of the Historian's enquiry; Discernment should guide his researches; Judgment warrant his conclusion; Candour direct his reflections; and Elegance of Stile adorn his composition.

Let us now examine how far the Historian before us is endowed with the requisite qualifications, and with what degree of diligence he has performed the duties incumbent upon him. If he shall appear to have been deficient, his defects will be the more unpardonable, as he seems to be master of natural abilities, which, with a proper share of application, would have enabled him to have acquited himself with credit: and however men may pride themselves upon their genius, there is certainly more merit in a single grain of *acquired* knowledge, than in the largest portion of *native* talents. For the latter, we are indebted to nature, but what we gain by our industry, we may challenge as our own.

In a former Review, we have given an account of the three preceding volumes of this work; which contained little more than a brief narrative of facts, in which the Author affected to avoid all *disquisitions* as *useless*. In the volume before us, however, he appears to have altered his mind, and is very liberal of his observations, which makes it necessary for us to be more particular in our examination.

This fourth volume opens with an enumeration of omissions[a] at the time of the revolution, in which, according to his practice throughout, he confounds his own reflections with those he has adopted from authority. 'The maxim,' he says, 'of hereditary

indefeasible right, was *at length* renounced by a free Parliament.'
From this expression we are led to conclude, that this was the first
instance of any public renunciation of that doctrine; but, if we are
not mistaken, this maxim, however avowed by a few slavish
individuals, was never adopted by a free Parliament; on the
contrary, it has always been opposed by Parliament, and has been
frequently renounced in the most solemn manner. If we recur to
the form of the Coronation of King John, and many of our former
Kings, we shall there find express stipulations against the claim of
Hereditary Right.[b]

In his account of the trials of Sir John Friend and Sir William
Perkins, for treason, in conspiring against King William's life, this
Writer does not appear to have observed the strictest impartiality.
He says, that 'Lord-chief-justice Holt declared, that although a bare
conspiracy or design to levy war, was not treason within the statute
of Edward III. yet, if the design or conspiracy be to kill, or depose,
or imprison the King, by the means of levying war, then the
consultation and conspiracy to levy war becomes high-treason,
though no war be actually levied.' *The same inference*, our Historian
observes, *might have been drawn against the authors and instruments of
the Revolution.*

In his reflections of these trials, which he has borrowed, almost
verbatim, from Mr Ralph, he has copied that Writer's severe
animadversions on Lord-chief-justice Holt, without doing the
same previous justice to his character: and he has added, that *the
judge acted as Counsel for the Crown.* Yet notwithstanding these harsh
imputations, that worthy Judge does not appear to have exceeded,
or violated, the duty of his office. As to his Declaration, it was
consonant with the opinion of able Judges, his predecessors.
History will inform us, that a consultation to levy war, with intent
to kill, depose, or imprison the King, had been deemed high
treason long before his time; and that delinquents had been found
guilty of high-treason, within the Act of Parliament, for words
which indicated their treasonable intent.

It does not follow, as our Historian asserts, after Mr Ralph,
that—, the same inference might have been drawn against the
'authors and instruments of the Revolution.' The case at
the Revolution was widely different. The King had stretched the
Prerogative, violated his coronation-oath, and openly invaded the
rights of his subjects. Under these circumstances, it was lawful to

resist him as a tyrant; but no such pretences could be urged in favour of the conspirators against King William. There is undoubtedly a very material difference between a Rebellion and a Civil War. The first is properly where subjects take up arms against lawful Governors, lawfully governing: but where a Prince violates the established laws of the kingdom, and persists in his violation, then resistance, in vindication of the Liberties of the nation, cannot be called Rebellion: and, as Sydney justly observes, there can be no such thing in the world as the Rebellion of a *Nation* against its own Magistrates.

Had our Historian shewn himself as forward to praise as ready to censure, he might have found a theme for panegyric, in the conduct of Chief-Justice Holt, in regard to the contested election for Ailesbury. But though he is so ready to reflect on the Chief-Justice's opinion in the former instance, yet he takes no notice of his spirited declaration in the case of Ashby and White.

In his account of Sir John Fenwick's case, he gives an abstract of all the arguments of the Counsel in behalf of the prisoner, and then contents himself with saying—'Their arguments were answered by the King's Counsel.' But he makes no mention whatever, of the purport of those arguments. His state of the facts likewise is somewhat imperfect. He has, in particular, omitted the contents of the letter which Sir John Fenwick wrote to his Lady; without which it is difficult to have a clear comprehension of the subsequent matter.

It must be observed, likewise, that his reflections, in many instances, are highly exceptionable. Speaking of the proposals of peace which Lewis the XIVth sent to the Allies, he makes the following observation on their demands.

Their demands were so insolent, that Lewis would not have suffered them to be mentioned in his hearing had he not been reduced to the last degree of distress. One can hardly read them without feeling a sentiment of compassion for that Monarch, who had once given law to Europe, and been so long accustomed to victory and conquest. Notwithstanding the discouraging dispatches he had received from the President Rouillé, after his first conferences with the Deputies, he could not believe that the Dutch would be so blind to their own interest, as to reject the advantages in commerce, and the barrier which he had offered. He could not conceive, that they would chuse to bear the burthen of excessive taxes, in prosecuting a war, the events of which would always be uncertain, rather than enjoy the blessings of peace, security, and advantageous commerce: he flattered himself, that the allies would not so far deviate from their proposed aim of establishing a balance of power, as to throw such an enormous weight into the scale of the House of Austria, which cherished all the dangerous ambition and arbitrary principles, without the *liberality and sentiment peculiar to the House of Bourbon.*

What! did Lewis the XIVth deserve compassion because he had once given law to Europe, and been accustomed to victory and conquest? Is a tyrant entitled to compassion, because he is spoiled of the fruits of successful tyranny? Did not Lewis XIV. engage in war from the motives of rapacious pride, and the instatiate thirst of arbitrary sway? Had he a right to give law to Europe? and does he deserve pity, because he was humbled to a state of incapacity, which prevented him from plundering his neighbours, and extending an illegal despotism over the European Powers? A distressed Prince, is no more an object of pity than an afflicted Peasant. It is not the *person* who suffers, but the *cause* of his suffering, which justifies our compassion. What is there in the distresses of a *King* to move our pity, unless the *man* deserves it? A king, who becomes a Tyrant, sinks in worth beneath the lowest of his subjects: and it would be a weakness to commiserate the calamity he merits—Where has this Historian discovered the liberality and sentiment *peculiar* to the house of Bourbon? We are not fond of national reflections, but we cannot forbear remarking, that the perfidy and chicanery which the Bourbons have displayed, in all their political measures, bear no very favourable testimony of their *liberality or sentiment.*

His reflections on the Duke of Ormond are not less liable to objection. 'A man of candor,' he says, 'cannot, without an emotion of grief and indignation, reflect upon the ruin of the noble family of Ormond, in the person of a brave, generous, and humane Nobleman; to whom no crime was imputed, but that of having obeyed the commands of his Sovereign.' And he afterwards takes notice, that 'the Duke and Lord Bolingbroke, who had retired to France, finding themselves condemned *unheard,* and attainted, engaged in the service of the Chevalier, and corresponded with the Tories in England.' But the Duke of Ormond's fate was undoubtedly merited. His conduct at the head of the army was certainly base and scandalous; and even the commands of the Sovereign cannot justify a General, in acting to the prejudice or dishonour of his country. Besides, to say, 'that no crime was imputed to him, but that of having obeyed the commands of his Sovereign;' is neither talking like an historian or a politician. It is well known, that he was one of the principal leaders of that faction, which gave such pernicious council to their Sovereign, and then sought to shelter themselves under the sanction of those very commands, which they in fact had dictated themselves. If Sovereign commands were sufficient to authorize the servants of the Crown in the execution of orders, however illegal, then the crown would in fact be arbitrary, and, as the King can do no wrong, no one would remain answerable for the abuse of the executive power. Even Sovereign orders could not justify the Duke of Ormond in his secret, we may say, traiterous correspondence with the French General. As to his being condemned *unheard*, it is a ridiculous observation, with regard to a delinquent, who betakes himself to flight, and does not stay to make his Defence.—And how it was agreeable to the character of a *brave, generous*, and *humane* Nobleman, to enter into the service of the Chevalier, and foment a horrid rebellion in his native land, out of personal pique to the Ministry, we own ourselves at a loss to determine.

The same impropriety appears in his remarks on the opposition to Sir Robert Walpole. 'It must be acknowledged,' says he, 'they were by this time irritated into such *personal animosity* against the Minister, that they resolved to oppose *all* his measures, whether they *might or might not* be *necessary for the safety* and advantage of the kingdom. Nor, indeed, were they altogether *blameable* for acting on this maxim, if their sole aim was to remove from the confidence and councils of their Sovereign, a man whose conduct they thought prejudicial to the interest and liberty of their country.

Amazing! Were they not blameable for opposing the Minister in *all* his measures, even in such as might be *necessary* for the *safety* of the kingdom? Could any motive, whatever, justify such treason against their country? Besides, was it a probable method to remove the Minister from the confidence of his Sovereign, to oppose *all* his measures, *right or wrong*? Would not such an unjust opposition rather increase that confidence which they laboured to destroy? Was it not the way to convince their Sovereign and the world, that they acted from personal animosity; and that their dislike was to the Minister, and not to his measures? It would be wasting time to take further notice of such inconsiderate reflections.

Our Author has taken great pains to place the peace of Utrecht in a favourable light; and has retailed all the exploded arguments used in vindication of that treaty; without stating, as an Historian ought to have done, what was urged in opposition to it. He makes the very worst apology for the conduct of the Ministry, when he says, 'that they saw no hope of safety, except in renouncing their principles, and submitting to their adversaries, or else in taking such measures as would hasten the pacification; and with which view they set on foot a *private* negotiation with Lewis.' But whatever gloss party-colouring may put on this treaty, the advantages obtained by it were not only inadequate to what we might *reasonably* have expected and *demanded*, and greatly inferior to the terms which Lewis had before humbly offered, nay almost implored us to accept,—but the manner of concluding it was dishonourable to the nation. When a confederacy is formed against a common enemy, no party in it ought to treat *privately*, or separately. Indeed any one is at liberty to detach himself, if the rest are so obstinate as to refuse *reasonable* propositions; but he should first endeavour to persuade them to an acceptance of the terms offered, and give them notice, that in case of their refusal, he will conclude a separate peace. This duty is obligatory, even where the confederate powers have *not* fixed on any particular points to be gained by the war. But this obligation is much stronger where they have stipulated not to lay down their arms till they have obtained such and such particular ends. In this case, no one is at liberty to detach himself, till those proposed advantages are acquired. If in the course of the war, the acquisition of them should be thought impracticable, yet *not one*, but the *whole confederate body* must judge of the impracticability. The allies in the war of 1712, agreed not to suffer Spain and the Indies to remain in the House of Bourbon. This was the express end of the war; and till that end was accomplished, or given up by the *Confederates* as impracticable, no one in particular had a right to conclude a separate peace. Besides it was an express article in the treaty, 'that no party should treat of peace, truce, &c. but jointly with the rest.'

It in vain for our Historian to adopt the stale pretence made use of by the advocates of this peace—'that the liberties of Europe would be exposed to much greater danger from an actual union of the Imperial and Spanish crowns in one head of the House of Austria, than from a bare possibility of Spain's being united with

France, in one branch of the House of Bourbon.' This might have been a good argument against our entering into any express stipulations to prevent the crown of Spain's being enjoyed by the House of Bourbon, but could not justify our withdrawing ourselves from the terms of the alliance, against the consent of the Confederates, after we had engaged. If solemn treaties among nations are to be explained away, and made subservient to the particular interests of a faction, there is an end of all national faith; and we cannot complain, that our allies prove faithless in their turns, and desert us when it suits their convenience. Besides, if there was reason to think, that the Emperor Charles VI. would become too powerful by the accession of Spain, that crown might have been conferred on Bavaria, or some other power; by which means the inconvenience would have been obviated, without any infraction of the terms of the alliance. But the ill effects of suffering Spain to remain in the House of Bourbon, has been severely felt by England and the Maritime Powers. By reason of the good understanding between those two Crowns, Spain has, contrary to all treaties of commerce respecting the navigation of the West Indies, indulged France in every respect, and suffered her to make unwarrantable establishments, to the prejudice of the commercial states.

Among other omissions, our Historian has slightly passed over the affair of the Catalans, without any particular state of their case, any representation of their distress, or account of the desperate resolution they took to defend themselves, when abandoned by us. This was a subject which would have admitted all the colouring which he is so fond of lavishing upon almost every occasion; but perhaps he thought these particulars would reflect too severely on the conduct of the Tory Ministry, at that time.

In the last year of King William's reign; a reign particularly distinguished by many important events, the following particulars have escaped our Author.

He has taken no notice, I. ꞌOf Whitacre's cafe. II. Of the confinement of Bosseli in the Bastile for attempting King William's life. III. Of the refusal of Portugal to acknowledge the pretended Prince of Wales. IV. Of the Convention signed with Sweden by the Earl of Marlborough, by which a pecuniary compensation was given to the court in lieu of the succours they demanded. V. Of the memorable report of the Board of Trade. VI. Of the proceedings against Fuller, for libelling the last House of Commons. VII.[d] Of the contested election at Malmsboury—with others less remarkable.—Historians above all other Writers, should remember Prior's maxim,

Authors, before they write, should read.[1]

This Writer seems, in many places, to be inconsistent with himself, and to argue against his own principles. At one time he appears the sanguine friend of liberty, and applauds all opposition against the stretches of prerogative; and yet, at another, he censures the resentment which the Parliament expressed against such encroachments. Speaking of the Parliament's refusal to comply with King William's message, by which he desired the Dutch guards to be continued in his service, he observes, 'that such an opposition in an affair of very little consequence, savoured more of clownish obstinacy, than of patriotism.' This observation does not only seem inconsistent with his former reflections, but is in itself extremely unjust. It must be remembered, that King William had ventured to maintain a greater number of troops than had been voted by Parliament, and they resolved to shew their sense of such a violation of the constitution, by sending all foreign troops out of the kingdom, which was so far from being a clownish obstinacy, that, on the contrary, it was a laudable resentment, and truly patriotic. Besides, they obliged him to no more than he promised to do by his own declaration; and it was high time to challenge the performance of his word, when he made such stretches of prerogative against the votes of Parliament: and though the affair might be in itself, of little consequence, yet it was of great moment, when considered as a precedent to posterity.

Sometimes he appears to have fallen into palpable contradictions: he tells us, in his account of the rebellion in 1745, that the Papists and Jacobites gave the court of Versailles to understand, that if the Chevalier de St George, or his eldest son, Charles Edward, should appear at the head of a French army in Great Britain, a revolution would instantly follow in his favour. 'This intimation,' says he, 'was agreeable to Cardinal de Tencin, who had succeeded Fleury as Prime Minister of France. He was of a violent enterprizing temper. He had been warmly recommended to the purple by the Chevalier de St George, and *was* WARMLY *attached to the Steuart family.* His ambition was flattered with a prospect of *giving a King to Great*

Britain, of performing such eminent service to his benefactor, and of *restoring to the throne of their ancestors*, a family connected by the ties of blood with all the greatest Princes in Europe.' And yet a few pages after, he does not scruple to say, that 'the French Ministry were never *hearty* in the Chevalier's cause.'

But we wish he has not been guilty of some wilful mistakes in his narrative of this rebellion. He has lavished all the powers of the Pathos, in laboured descriptions of horror. He tells us, that after the decisive action at Culloden, the Duke of Cumberland advanced into the Highlands, and 'that every house, hutt, or habitation, was plundered and burned without distinction. All the cattle and provision were carried off; the men were either shot upon the mountains, like wild beasts, or put to death in cold blood, without form of trial; the women, after having seen their husbands and fathers murdered, were subjected to brutal violation, and then turned out naked, with their children, to starve on the barren heaths. One whole family was inclosed in a barn, and consumed to ashes. Those ministers of vengeance were so alert in the execution of their office, that in a few days there was neither house, cottage, man, nor beast, to be seen in the compass of fifty miles; all was ruin, silence, and desolation.'

It is not in our power to prove a negative, but we have at least a right to expect the sanction of some authority[e] for such injurious assertions; but the Reader may readily determine the Writer's country, not only from his exaggerated account of the methods used to extinguish this rebellion; but likewise from his relation of the massacre of Glencoe, and from his remarks on the union. On this occasion we cannot but recollect the words of Martial, *Nic malus esticives, nec banus historicus.*[2]

In describing characters, which is supposed to be this Writer's great excellence, he appears to have taken fancy, rather than truth, for his guide. He has made quibbling distinctions, without differences; and amused us with a jingling of words, without any decisive meaning. Of Queen Mary he says.

Mary was in her person tall, and well proportioned, with an oval visage, lively eyes, agreeable features, a mild aspect, and an air of dignity. Her apprehension was clear, her memory tenacious, and her judgment solid. She was a zealous Protestant, scrupulously exact in all the duties of devotion, of an even temper, of a calm and mild conversation. She was ruffled by no passion, and seems to have been a stranger to the emotions of natural affection; for she ascended, without compunction, the throne from which her father had been deposed, and treated her sister as an alien to her blood. In a word, Mary seems to have imbibed the cold disposition and apathy of her husband; and to have centered all her ambition in deserving the epithet of an humble and obedient wife.

It is a most unjust and cruel reflection to affirm, that she was a stranger to the emotions of natural affection; a reflection which is not warranted by any circumstance related in the course of his history. That she felt these emotions, is evident from her great anxiety and solicitude for the fate of her father, at the time of her regency, when she was obliged to make vigorous preparations against him, by the duty which she owed to her husband and to her country. Candor would have taught our Historian, that the wife of such an ambitious and resolute Sovereign as King William, must necessarily act by constraint, and not by choice. Her good sense and prudence, doubtless suggested, that obedience to the will of her husband, was the only expedient to make her life easy; and in her behaviour towards her father and her sister, she may be supposed to have rather followed his dictates than her own inclinations.

His character of William III. he is not less inaccurate and injurious.

[quotes from the *History* the character of William III]

This character is, in many respects, falsified by the circumstances of King William's life, as related by our Historian, and is an assemblage of contrarieties which scarce ever met together but in the Author's imagination.

He allows William to have been religious, generally just, and sincere; and yet (speaking of the partition treaty) he says, 'Lewis knew that William was too much of a politician to be *restricted* by notions of private justice; and that he would make no scruple to infringe the laws of particular countries, or even the rights of a single nation, when the balance of power was at stake. He judged right in this particular: the King of England lent a willing ear to his proposals, and engaged in a plan for dismembering a kingdom, in despite of the natives, and in *violation of every law human or divine.*'

Now by what peculiar sagacity Lewis came to form such an opinion of William's injustice, who was 'generally *just* and *sincere.*'—And how the latter, whom our Author allows to have been *religious*, could consent to a proposal, which, according to him, was a violation of every law, human or *divine*, we must leave our Author himself to reconcile.

Again—with what truth, even from his own history, can he reproach the memory of King William, as one who was dead to all the warm and generous emotions of the human heart, a cold relation, an indifferent husband? He is not warranted by any thing he has set forth in his history, to pronounce this judgment. On the contrary, in page 124, he tells us, that 'Queen Mary expired to the INEXPRESSIBLE grief of the King, who, for some weeks after her death, COULD neither see company, nor attend to the business of state.' How is the sensation of INEXPRESSIBLE grief to be reconciled with the[f] 'cold disposition and apathy,' of King William? Does such violent sorrow correspond with insensibility? Besides, can we suppose a man of an aspiring, ambitious temper, who was at the same time religious, generally just and sincere, to have been dead to all the warm and generous emotions of the human heart? Do not even the vices of his reign contradict this character? Does not his partiality to his countrymen and favourites, and in particular his friendship for, and extraordinary liberality towards, the Lords Portland and Albemarle, shew him to have been susceptible of warm and generous impressions[g]?

In his character of Prince George of Denmark, he says—'He was a Prince rather of an *amiable* than a *shining* character, *brave*, good-natured,' &c. Here it may not be improper to observe, that *bravery* seems rather to fall under the division of *shining*, than of *amiable* qualities.

He is not more accurate in drawing some inferior characters, which he has hastily sketched, just as the present whim guided his pencil. In his narrative of the debates during Sir Robert Walpole's administration, the last speaker is with him always the best orator. In one place, Sir William Wyndham is called the *unrivalled orator*; in another Mr P. stands unequalled, and carries off the prize of eloquence. And in a third, L.C. bears it from them both, nay, even from Cicero himself.

The Writer has taken so little pains to digest his matter, that he has not only fallen into repetitions, but has related many things out of their proper order. The division of his sections is extremely inaccurate, and the transition from one circumstance to another is often sudden and unnatural: by which means, the Reader is frequently surprized with some material incident, without any break to prepare his mind for the reception of it.

Upon the whole, we cannot in justice forbear to acknowledge, that, in our judgment, this compilation, which is called, *a compleat history*, is a hasty, and indigested performance:—too voluminous for an abridgment, and too imperfect for an history. The Author's partiality to the Tory party is manifest in almost every page; and, in stating the arguments which passed on any subject, he generally relates those only which were urged on one side, suppressing what was offered on the other: which, without any other circumstance, unavoidably creates a suspicion of his impartiality. Cicero very justly observes,—*Primaest historial lex, ne quid falsi dicere audeat; deinde, ne quid veri non audeat; ne quasuspicio graties sit in scribendo, ne qua simultatis.*[3]

The great excellence of this work, is the elegance and spirit of the style, which is, in general, nervous, clear, fluent, bold, and florid; and those Readers who are content with acquiring only a general knowlege of our history, cannot be more agreeably instructed: for his manner of writing is so extremely entertaining, that attention seldom sleeps over his pages.—In few words, this Writer's merit is rather that of an ingenious novelist than of an accurate historian. His imagination overpowers his judgment; and we must take the liberty to add, his confidence in his own abilities appears so conspicuous, that in all probability he will never take pains to correct his imperfections.

NOTES

a Our Historian has remarked, in the words of Somers, that the Patriots at the Revolution, were guilty of many omissions, in not sufficiently circumscribing the power of the Crown. He blames them, in particular, for leaving the King full power over Parliaments, over Corporations, over the Militia, &c. as the Reader may see more at large, by turning to the History.

b In the reign of Charles the second, about the 1682, a very sensible treatise was wrote against Hereditary Right, entitled, *The Rights of the Kingdom, or Customs of our Ancestors.* This tract which is extremely scarce, contains some curious observations in antiquity.

c This Whitacre was Solicitor of the Admiralty, and was ordered into custody of the Serjeant of the House of Commons, for taking insufficient bail for one Bolton, who was committed for a confederacy with Kid, and made his escape; and the house ordered a committee to inspect into Whitacre's conduct. The committee, in their report, laid before the House a presentment of the Grand Jury of Southampton against Whitacre, for corruption. Upon the circumstances of the case, the House resolved, that he had been guilty of several breaches of trust; ordered the Attorney General to prosecute him; and resolved, that the office of Solicitor was unnecessary, and ought to be suppressed.

d The circumstances of this contest were very particular. The petitioning burgesses, and Colonel Park, the candidate for that borough, were all taken into custody. This controversy was rendered the more remarkable by the censure which the House passed on the Earl of Peterborough. That Nobleman having fallen under the displeasure of the House, for having interfered in the election in an unwarrantable manner, he desired to be heard in his justification, which was granted. But notwithstanding his endeavours to clear his conduct, it was resolved, that it appeared to the House, that the Earl was guilty of many indirect practices, in endeavouring to procure the said Park to be elected a burgess.

e It is observable, that the Author has not thought proper to produce one single authority for his history from the commencement of his present Majesty's reign; and we think, it is too great a stretch of presumption for a writer in a private station, who has no particular opportunities of information, to expect credit on his own single testimony.

f The Reader will remember, that in his character of Queen Mary, he says, 'She imbibed the cold disposition and apathy of her husband;' so that this must be taken as part of his character.

g It will worth the Reader's while to consult Mr Ralph's character of William III. and he will there see with what superior judgment that able Historian hath treated the subject.

1 From Matthew Prior's poem 'Protogenes and Appelles'. The relevant verse reads:

> Tea, says a Critic big with Laughter,
> Was found some twenty Ages after:
> Authors, before they write, shou'd read:
> 'Tis very true; but We'll proceed.

2 Martial, *Epigrams:* 'He is not a bad citizen but nor is he a good historian.'

3 Cicero, *De Oratore*, II, 62: 'The first law of history is that it should not venture to say anything false. Secondly, it must dare to say anything that is true,. There should be no trace of improper influence or rivalry in writing.'

48. Lady Mary Wortley Montagu, letter

3 October 1758

From a letter to the Countess of Bute, *The Complete Letters of Lady Mary Wortley Montagu*, ed. Robert Halsband, Oxford, 1966, vol. III, pp. 179–80. The reference here is to Smollett's *Complete History of England*, 1757–8.

The story deserves the Pen of my dear Smollet, who I am sorry disgraces his Talent by writing those Stupid Romances commonly call'd History.

49. Dr James Grainger, *A Letter to Tobias Smollett*

1759

From *A Letter to Tobias Smollett, M.D. Occasioned by his Criticism upon a late Translation of Tibullus*, by Dr Grainger, 1759, p. 21. Grainger's translation of Tibullus had been adversely noticed in the *Critical Review*.

Nor does the Severity of the *English* Language only reject some foreign Images, as unfitting to her Manner; but *Decency* likewise, and a *Regard* to the Public, must oblige a translator, sometimes *wholly to omit*, and sometimes to *alter* the Ideas of the Original. *Tibullus* required much of this *weeding*, which however otherwise inclined to favour him, I scrupulously performed. If this has offended you, I rejoice in your Displeasure; and that you are offended on this Score, I cannot doubt, when I reflect on what horrid, I had almost said infernal scenes, one of your Intimates has affronted the Public with in *Peregrine Pickle*.

50. Joseph Reed, *A Sop in the Pan for a Physical Critick*

1759

From Joseph Reed's pamphlet, *A Sop In the Pan for a Physical Critick: in A Letter to Dr SM★LL★T. Occasion'd by A Criticism on a late MOCK-TRAGEDY, call'd MADRIGAL and TRUL-LETTA*, By a HALTER-MAKER, 1759, pp. 1–24.

Reed was stung by *The Critical Review's* treatment of his mock-tragedy. Here he impugns Smollett as reviewer, historian and dramatist, referring particularly to Smollett's play *The Regicide* in a series of derisive footnotes.

A LETTER TO DOCTOR SM★LL★T.

*Dear*TOBY!

It is now seven Months since you did me the Honour of criticising my *Mock-Tragedy*, call'd MADRIGAL and TRULLETTA. From the natural Fondness of an Author to the Children of his Brain, I was almost tempted to give you an immediate Reply; but on a Supposition that so superficial a Criticism would not affect my

Piece, I dropp'd the Design. However, as some Friends have assured me that my *dramatic* Character hath been partly darken'd by the Shade, which you have endeavour'd to throw on that Performance, I am, at their Request, and in Vindication of my own injur'd Production, prevail'd on to examine the Validity of your profound Criticism.

But, before I proceed to such Examination, it may not be amiss to premise, that I shall not use you with the least Snarling, or Scurrility. I should be sorry in the *Author*, to sink the Character of the *Tradesman*: For, tho' Scurrility be so essential a Requisite, to a *Compiler* of a CRITICAL REVIEW, it is altogether inconsistent with the Dignity of a *Halter-maker*.

I would not have you imagine, my learned *Aesculapian*! that I am at all afraid of fighting *you with your own Weapon:* I can assure you I am no despicable Proficient in *vulgar Repartee*, having been almost three Years a constant Attendant at BILLINSGATE; the History of which Place, I shall publish by Subscription, and by way of Appendix to YOUR *History* of *England*.

Here I shall drop the Antagonist, a few Moments, to ask your Advice, as a Friend: Few have dealt more LARGELY in the Press than yourself, and consequently few are more able to advise me than yourself, in such an Undertaking. Don't you think, that a History of this Importance, written in a correct and elegant Style, and adorn'd with upwards of a hundred CUTS of the most remarkable *Scolds*, *Oyster-Boats*, *Cod-Smacks*, &c. engraved by your *Dutch* Artist, would turn out a pretty profitable Undertaking? I am almost convinc'd you do; and by way of giving you, and my most worthy Friend, the Public, a Specimen of my literary Abilities, I shall here annex a short Extract from my said intended History.

In this remarkable Year (1756) this renouned Academy, which, in the Space of a few Years, had produced a greater Number of *Orators* than all the Schools of *Greece* and *Rome*; like other Seminaries of *British* Learning, began to be on the Decline: for, such is the Vicissitude of sublunary Things, that *Oratory*, as well as *Empire*, is subject to Mutability. The Cause of this unhappy Declension in our Academy, is variously accounted for. Some ascribe it wholly to the Number of *Charity-Schools*, in and about this Metropolis, which have, of late, so greatly contributed, to civilize the lower Orders of Mankind: Others to the Growth of *Methodism*; while a different Party, with greater Plausibility indeed, impute it to the Dearness and Scarcity of *Gin*; which is universally allow'd to be a most powerful

Inspirer of *Vociferation*. That all these Opinions were merely conjectural, will evidently appear from the following Incident, which is too well authenticated to be disprov'd, or even disbeliev'd.

In the close of the Year 1755, a certain *Caledonian* Quack, by the Curtesy of *England*, call'd a *Doctor of Physick*, whose real, or assum'd Name was FERDINANDO MAC FATHOMLESS, form'd a Project for initiating and perfecting the Male-Inhabitants of this Island, in the Use and Management of the *linguary Weapon*, by the Erection of a *Scolding Amphitheatre*. For this Purpose, he selected, and engag'd, on weekly Salary, about a Dozen of the most eminent Professors of *Vociferation* in this Academy: but, after he had been at a considerable Expence, the unfortunate *Emperic* could not get his Project licenc'd.

The Doctor was greatly mortified at his unexpected Disappointment, but being resolved that *his own*, and the *Sisterhood's* Talents should not be lost to the World, *he set about publishing a periodical Work, called the Hyper-Critical Review*; in which the *Billingsgate* Oratory is so much exhausted, that, to this Incident only, can be justly imputed the visible Decay of *Vociferation* in this Academy. The fair Orators of *Billingsgate* are now almost as silent, as the Fishes they dispose off: *Wit, Repartee* and *Politeness* have taken up their Residence in *Chancery-Lane!*

However absurd or offensive the Doctor's Project might appear, it would scarce have fail'd of being advantageous to the Community, had it luckily pass'd into Execution. It would have greatly diminished the Clamour of *Scolding Wives*, and thereby contributed to the domestic Tranquility, nay, probably to the Preservation, of the Lives of many of his Majesty's liege Subjects. Poisons are expell'd by Poisons: a Diarrhoea is generally carried off by a Dose of Physic; and, by a Parity of Reason, *Scolding* may be most effectually cured by *Scolding*: for a Woman's Tongue, like a Jack Bowl, is observ'd to run the longest, when it meets with the fewest *Rubs*.

An Institution of this Kind would have likewise been serviceable to many Classes and Degrees of Men among us; particularly to those young Gentlemen, that are design'd for the *long Robe*. A constant Attendance, for two or three Months, at the *Scolding Amphitheatre*, would have been as compleat a Qualification for the *Bar*, as a dozen Years Attendance at some of our Courts of Judicature: for, whoever hath carefully observ'd the Method of our *Law-Proceedings*, must allow, that he is generally esteemed the most learned and successful Council, who is the greatest *Scold*.

This short Extract will, I am persuaded, convince you, that I am as well qualified for an *Historian*, as yourself.

Some Persons, to whom I have shewn this Part of my History, were ready to treat the Fact above-related, as *fictitious*, till I

CHOICE

100 Riverview Center
Middletown, Connecticut 06457
(203) 347-6933

LATE ARRIVAL OF REVIEW BOOKS

To keep our review service current, CHOICE has
scheduled 3 weeks for you to complete a review.
Reviews are due 4 weeks from the time the books
are mailed. If the book is delayed in the
mail, please allow yourself enough time to
write a thorough review, and if your review
will be more than 2 weeks late, please let us
know by letter or phone.

If your review is not received at CHOICE 4
weeks after the original due date we will send
you a query in the form of a late notice.
Please always check and return any query form
so that we may clear or change your review due
date in our computer system.

Your help in letting us know the status of
your review, and an approximate due date so
that we can schedule it for a particular
issue, is greatly appreciated.

prevailed on them to read the said *Review*: but they are now, to a Man, convinc'd of its Truth. Every judicious Reader must be of the same Opinion, if he will be at the pains to peruse that *periodical Work*: For it is evident, even to Demonstration itself, that none but an Assemblage of *Fish-women*, would throw out such a Heap of Dirt and Scurrility, as flows down the Channel of that Production.

If you have any Acquaintance with this *physical* Countryman of yours, it would not be amiss to desire him, at the Conclusion of his next Volume, to publish the following Erratum, viz. *In the Title Page of our preceding Volumes*, for By a Society of Gentlemen, read By a Society of old Women. It may indeed appear a kind of Solecism, as the said *physical Projector* is at the Head of the *learned Sisterhood*; but whoever will carefully examine his Abilities, as a *Critic*, must soon be convinc'd that the *Critic-Doctor*, is as meer an *old Woman*, as ever wore Petticoats.

Having given you thus much by way of Preface. I shall proceed to examine your elaborate *Criticism* on my *Mock-Tragedy*.

In your *Critical Review* for *August* last, you say, 'Parody or Burlesque, tho' ever so well executed, have very little Merit in them; because the highest Degree of Perfection, which they are capable of attaining to, may be acquir'd by a *very moderate Capacity*.'

To this Proposition I have but one Objection, namely *that it is not true*. I could mention a Variety of Pieces of the *Burlesque* kind, written by *Butler, Pope, Swift, Gay*, and Others, which have done great Honour to the *English* Language; but shall confine myself to one, *viz*. The Tragedy of *Tom Thumb the Great*.

Was this Piece (which is not the best I have seen) written by a Man of a *very moderate Capacity*? I answer, No; and the Person, who will publickly assert, that the ingenious *Fielding*, was a Man of a *very moderate Capacity*, must certainly incur the Censure of being a Fool or a Knave.

I know but one Proof of this remarkable Proposition of yours, I mean the *Regicide*; which incomparable Production, is the greatest Burlesque on Nature, that I ever had the *Pleasure* of perusing, and may with great Propriety be said, to have been written by a Man of even scarce a *very moderate Capacity*. I have, indeed, met with some quibbling *Critics*, who will not allow the *Regicide* to be a Burlesque Poem, and have even gone so far as to assert, that the Author design'd it for a serious Tragedy: this I must own I cannot assent to; for if the Doctor intended the Performance for a serious Production

I cannot help thinking him one of the most impudent, self-sufficient Scriblers, that ever defiled Paper, and that he deserves to be flogg'd, like a sawcy School-Boy, before the respective Doors of his several Subscribers, for his Impudence, in sollicating the Favour of the Public in so *extraordinary* a manner.

You proceed by telling us, 'The most necessary Requisite, in a Performance of this Nature, is indeed a *good Memory*; which the Author of the Piece before us, seems *happily possess'd off*; as there is scarce a Passage, in any of what the theatrical World calls *Stock-Plays*, which is not introduced.'

By the Phrase *happily possess'd off*, you certainly, against your Will, pay me a kind of Compliment: for unless, you imagine my Piece to have some Merit, you cannot with Propriety suppose me to be *happy* in the Possession of a good Memory.

Had you honestly examin'd my Tragedy, you would have found that my intended Ridicule is so far from being confin'd to *Stock-Plays*, that the major Part of the borrow'd Passages are taken from plays, that, Meteor–like, have blaz'd a while, and then sunk into Oblivion: nay, some of them from a Play, that was never exhibited at all; witness your *Regicide*: Which I apprehend, your Book-seller, to his Cost, finds to be a *Stock-Play* indeed, rotting in his Warehouse and destin'd for waste Paper.

In short, Doctor, my Design, throughout the whole Performance, was to expose the *Buckram* of the *modern* dramatic Diction; which hath been us'd, as a kind of *Poetical Fig-Leaves*, to cover the *Nakedness* of Sentiment. This will account for the seeming Freedoms I have taken with the venerable *Shakespear*: The Materials I had borrowed from the Moderns, were so dull, heavy, and spiritless, that I was under a Necessity of calling in *Shakespear*, and Others of establish'd Merit, to enliven and qualify the Flatness of the many Passages I had borrow'd from Authors of a *later* Date.—But to go on with your Criticism.

You say, 'All the Humour lies in the Application of them to *Taylors*, *Coblers*, &c., who compose the *Dramatis Personae*.' For once, my learned Emperic, you are in the right; and pray, where is the mighty Absurdity in all this? If you intend this Remark as a Sneer, you have miss'd your Aim; for half the Ridicule in *Hudibras* and the *Beggar's Opera* (which I presume you allow to be Burlesque Productions) would be lost, if the Authors had not plac'd the *Agents*, in these Pieces, in the lowest Life.

You proceed, 'We shall extract one Scene, which we believe our Readers will be as well, if not better, contented with, than the whole Tragedy:' and accordingly you quote the *Second Scene* in the *third Act*. I must here do you the Honour of acknowledging that you have been Conjurer enough, to pick out the dullest Scene in the whole Play: I pronounce it the dullest, on account of the Quantity of *philosophical Matter*, and the Number of Bombastic Expressions contained in it; and render'd still more dull to your Readers, by your Omission of the Notes for its Illustration in the Original. But tho' you might have *private Reasons* for such a disingenuous Extract. I shall here supply the Deficiency, and leave the Quotation, (at my own Risque) to the Masters in Criticism, to judge of the Injustice of your degrading Characteristic.

ACT III. SCENE II.
STRAPADA, BUCKRAMO.

Buck. My Ears deceive me or I heard the Voice
Of dear STRAPADA once; but now alas!
No more my Friend—'tis he—avenging Steel!

(Puts up his Bodkin.)

Rest here unseen—his lab'ring Mind is lock'd
In Contemplation's closest Cell—I'll try
To rouse him from this Trance of Thought—what ho!
STRAPADA!

   Strap Ha!—BUCKRAMO!—Thou wast once
My trustiest Friend: in my Heart's Core I wore thee;
Ay, in my Heart of Hearts[a]

   Buc. Ammonian JOVE![b]   (*kneeling*)
And all ye Gods and Goddesses; peruse
The Folio of my past and present Thoughts
Peruse it Page by Page; or, in the Way
Of modern Connoissieurs videlicet,
Run o'er Contents and Index—if you find
A Wish, unless to have TRULLETTA mine,
Preferr'd to good STRAPADA's dearest Friendship,
Hurl my thrice-thankless Spirit vengeful down
Into th' infernal pitchy Lake, prepar'd
For negro-foul'd Ingratitude.

   Strap. By SATURN![c]
His Mother's in his Face——the dear SCOURELLA——
It is too much to bear—spite of my, Vow

[d]I must, I must relent—there is a way
To reinstate thee in my Love: be virtuous.
The Friends of Virtue are STRAPADA's Friends:
—Forgo the black Design on MADRIGAL,
And be as dear as ever—what incites thee
To seek his Blood?
   Buck. He robs me of my Mistress;
And, in return, I rob him of his Life
The Robber rob and Robbery grows Virtue.[e]
   Strap. The Subtlety of Schools may paint this Maxim;
The Schools, where learned Error stalks abroad[f]
With such gigantick Strides, in Wisdom's Garb;
But Truth, and sound Philosophy, disclaim
The paultry Dawbing—know, blood-thirsty Youth!
Know, thou Death's Orator! dread Advocate[g]
For bowelless Severity! Forgiveness
Is greater, wiser, manlier Bravery
Than wild Revenge.
   Buck. Ha! whither wouldst thou lead me!
   Strap. To Virtue; to Forgiveness—talk no more
Of fell Revenge.
   Buck. Not talk of it, STRAPADA?
I'll talk of it tho' Hell itself should gape[h]
And bid me hold my Peace—not talk of it?
Not of Revenge? the Attribute of th' Gods,[i]
Who stamp'd it on our Natures to impell
Mankind to noblest Darings.
   Strap. Rather call it
The Attribute of Devils, stamp'd on Man,
To draw deluded Mortals to Destruction.
   Buck. No more, no more—tempt me no more in vain:[j]—
My Soul is wrought to the sublimest *Rage*[k]
Of horrible Revenge.
   Strap. And thou art fix'd
On bloody Purpose?
   Buck. Fix'd, as *Cambrian* Mountain
On its own Base, or gaming Lords on Ruin[l]
   Strap. Then all my flattering Hopes of the Reclaim
Are lost, and my shock'd Soul akes at thee—[m] yet
Attend my last Request—defer thy Purpose,
Till the cold Earth, in her parental Bosom,
Receive the venerable Master's Corse.
E'er long the sad Procession will begin:

Then do not with unallow'd Broil prophane
The dread Solemnity of funeral Rites:
But lend thy kind Assistance to support
Thy sorrowing Mistress thro' the mournful Scene.
This thou wilt promise?
   Buke. By yon Silver Lamp,[n]
Which stringless hangs, or hangs by String unseen
In azure Firmament, I will!
   Strap. Till then farewel!"

After the Quotation of this Scene, you begin to wind up your Criticism, and thus definitively to pass Sentence on my poor injur'd Performance, *viz.* 'This is sufficient to give our Readers a proper Idea of this Piece, which the Author has contriv'd to stretch into five Acts; a melancholly Circumstance for the poor Audience, who, we doubt not, were heartily sick of the Performance before the Conclusion of it; for tho' we may here and there meet with something laughable, it must have been a dismal three Hours Entertainment.'

Here endeth the the Criticism of the learned and sagacious Doctor T—— Sm★ll★t, which, considering the Malevolence of his Disposition, and *current Pay* from the Bookseller, join'd to his known Inclination to *degrade* all Writings, but his own, or those he is *interested* in commending, contains not altogether so much Severity, as might naturally be expected from a Man, who will at any time sacrifice Truth and Sincerity to gratify his Spleen and Illnature.

That your sentence may not hang too heavy on my Tragedy, I beg leave to throw out a few Observations on the Injustice of it.

You have certainly acted unfairly in not annexing the Notes, to shew how largely I had *borrow'd*, and what Passages were design'd *to be ridicul'd* in the *Scene*, you have quoted. From which Omission your Readers might naturally conclude that all the *Buckram* and *Bombast*, therein contained were my own. The Reason of such Omission is plain. Had you annexed the Notes; the foregoing *unintelligible Rant* in your REGICIDE must have been exposed to *ridicule*. In short, Doctor! as you have *stifled the Evidence* on one Side, every unprejudiced Reader must pronounce your Sentence partial, extra-judicial and illegal.

Your Remark on the Author's Contrivance to stretch the Piece into *five Acts*, which you, in a sort of critical Jargon, call a *melancholly Circumstance for the poor Audience*, I know not whether to impute to Ignorance or Illnature. If, you had been acquainted with the *usual Length* of an *English* Tragedy, you might have known that my *five Acts* are not quite so long, as *three* in most of our *Stock-Plays*, even as they are *curtailed* in the Representation. My Division of the Matter into *five Acts* was a Means of rendering the Production *more burlesque*, as it was a more exact Model of *English* Tragedy.

I must necessarily acknowledge that the Play was a *dismal Entertainment*, without ascribing any Defect to the Piece. As the Father of *English* Tragedy expresses it, *It was Caviar to the Multitude*, and more adapted to the *Closet*, than the *Stage*.

That the Play was most inhumanly butcher'd in the Representation, none will deny; for if even so compleat a Collection of *theatrical Wretches* was, in any one Play, brought upon the Stage of a *Theatre-Royal*, I will venture to renounce all Pretensions to Common-Sense. But, notwithstanding the Disadvantage of its Representation, the Play was *sav'd*; a Circumstance so contrary to my Expectation, that I gave it up for *damn'd* before the Conclusion of the first Act. If your REGICIDE had been so situated, I am convinced that all its Elegance, Nature, and Simplicity, would not have carried it through the second Act.

Whatever may be your real Sentiments of my Performance, I am not ashamed of espousing the Opinion of some known Judges in *dramatic* Literature, *viz.* 'If the MOCK TRAGEDY had been got up at *Drury-Lane*, with a GARRICK in MADRIGAL and a CLIVE in TRULLETTA, there are few Pieces in the *English* Language, capable of affording a more entertaining Exhibition.'[1]

You see, Doctor! I have run over your Criticism with as much Brevity (and let me add, Good-nature) as possible. I shall now lay before the Public the Sentence of another *Critical Court of Judicature* on my Performance, to shew that even Criticks *themselves* may differ in Opinion in Matters of Criticism.

'Mr REED, it seems, is a Tradesman, a *Rope-maker*. This Circumstance does him Credit as an Author; as many, who are Writers by Profession, are, beyond all Comparison, inferior to him in Merit. He seems to have read the Productions of the *British* Theatre with good Taste; and he has here so humourously parodied, and applied, a Variety of *bombastic Passages*, in the Writings of some of our most eminent Authors, that it is impossible to peruse his *comic* Scenes, without sharing in the Diversion, which this facetious Performance must have afforded its merry Author in the Writing.'

MONTHLY REVIEW for September 1758.

I shall not be at all surprized, if you should throw out some illnatur'd Innuendos, that your Rival REVIEWERS have given this favourable Character of my Piece through *interested* Considerations. To obviate such future Insinuation, I hereby declare, on my poetical and *hempen* Veracity, that I do not personally, or nominally know any one of the Gentlemen, who are the Authors of the *Monthly Review*, and that by no Means direct or indirect, did I sollicit a favourable Character of my Production: nay, that I have even been so remiss in Gratitude, as not to return my verbal, nor epistolary Thanks for the Honour they have done my Performance.

And now I would beg leave to ask that profoundly-sagacious Critick, Doctor T—— SM*LL*T, if he hath not unfairly endeavoured to prepossess his Readers against my MOCK-TRAGEDY, for Reasons entirely *personal*. Guilty or not Guilty, honest TOBY?——Nay, never hesitate, good Doctor! but, for once in your Life, tell the Truth, and shame the Devil.—Perhaps you have too great a Respect for your internal Friend, *the Father of Lies*, to put him to the Blush.—I repeat the Question; and am persuaded, if you speak the Truth, that you will answer in the Affirmative. I don't assert this through Vanity, but have some Grounds to justify my Assertion; and shall therefore proceed to lay before the Public the real or suppos'd Cause of your saying so much against my Performance; or more properly of your saying so *little* against it.

Mark now how plain a Tale shall put you down.[1]

Shak. K.Hen. IV.

My Manager Mr THEOPILUS CIBBER, of *wrong-headed* Memory, about three Weeks before the Exhibition of my Tragedy, told me he had made Mention of that Piece to Dr SM*LL*T, whom he represented as a great Admirer of Performances of the *burlesque* kind, and desired to know if it were agreeable to me that the Play should be read to the Doctor. I told Mr CIBBER I had no Objection. On which he pulled out the Copy, and desired me to strike out, at least to mark, all the Passages I had borrow'd from the REGICIDE, that he might drop them in the Reading: for, added he, tho' the Doctor should ever so highly admire the humourous Ridicule, which you have levelled at his poetical Brotherhood, he would not fail of being greatly enraged at the Freedom you have taken with his REGICIDE. It will, continues my *upright* Manager, be your Interest to make a Friend of the Doctor. As he presides over the poetical Province in the CRITICAL REVIEW, your Piece will, in all Likelyhood, have a favourable Character, if you strike out those Passages, which immediately affect him.

I must own, I was weak enough to listen to CIBBER's Insinuation; and the next Day, (as I had not time, at our Interview, to find out all my Extracts from the REGICIDE) sent him a Letter, in which were contained every Passage I had borrow'd from the Doctor. CIBBER accordingly put the *Stage-Mark* on them: and not one Line of yours was spoken in the Representation. If my Manager and I had not quarrell'd about the rascally Exhibition of the Play, I don't know but those *beautiful Rants*, I had selected from your Tragedy, might have slept in Silence and Oblivion: but after the above Conference, I was determined to publish them, least he should have insinuated to the World, that I had omitted some Passages in your *subscriptionary Drama*; thro' fear of so redoubtable a Critic, as Dr SM★LL★T.

I doubt not but you will be ready to represent this Tale, as an Invention of my own; especially as your Friend with the *unpartition'd Nose* is gone to the Bottom. But, Doctor! though I have no *positive*, I don't want *negative*, Evidence of the Truth of this Story. I told it to many Persons of Credit in CIBBER's Life time; and openly declared, before the Publication of your Criticism, that I expected to be handled by you with the greatest Severity.——Nay, the Marks above-mentioned are in the *Stage-Copy*, which hath been in Mr RICH's Hands ever since the Exhibition of the Piece.

I shall now give a Recital of those Passages I have extracted from your REGICIDE, with their References; that the World may judge whether or no your Resentment to my Piece does not flow from *personal Motives*.

My first Extract from your Tragedy is that admirable Imprecation in page 9.

> *By th' Powers of Hell*
> *I will be drunk with Vengeance!*

To which my learned Friend Dr HUMBUG adds, in Note 25. in the same Page.

'*A Liquor* I never yet heard off.'

I don't pretend to justify this Remark of the Doctor's, nor enter into any Dispute whether or no a Man may really *get drunk with Vengeance*. A small Alteration will silence all Cavils on this Passage of yours; wherefore if the *Regicide* have the good Fortune to hobble into another Impression, I would advise you to make it.

> By th' Powers of Hell
> *I will be drunk with a Vengeance!*

This will render the Passage more intelligible, though not altogether so poetical.

The next Remark on you is occasion'd by *Buckramo's* saying to his Friend *Strapada*;

> *Or thou wilt run me into Madness.*

To which Line Dr HUMBUG Subjoins the following Note, *viz.* 'A very common tragical Expression—nay, I have known many dramatic Heroes uttering such Complaints, when they have been absolutely *mad* from their first Speech in the Play. An Instance of this dramatic Madness may be found in a Tragedy, which was publish'd by Subscription in the present Century.

My Friend HUMBUG would have mention'd the Character of STUART in the *Regicide*, as his Proof of dramatic Madness; but, out of Regard to so great a tragic Genius as Dr *Sm★ll★t*, I prevail'd on him to leave the Publick in the dark, as to that particular.

The next Passage taken from your Play, is that beautiful Imprecation.

> May this Carcase rot,
> A loathsome Banquet *to the Fowls of Heaven;*
> If e'er my Breast admit Thought, to bound
> The Progress of my Rage

To which Dr HUMBUG subjoins in Note 25. Page 10. Our Author in this spirited Image, which is taken from the *Regicide*, hath, in my Opinion, followed the Doctor too closely: for with Submission to so great a Genius, as the Doctor, *loathsome Banquet*, seems to border a little on the *Tipperarian* Idiom.'

The following Image from your *Regicide* passes without any Remark.

> *Thou hast been tender over-much, and mourn'd*
> *Even too profusely.*

These elegant Flourishes had not gone without a Comment, if *tender over-much and mourning even too profusely*, had not been Phrases of such inimitable Excellence, as to require no further Illustration.

This is also another of your Images:

> *My Soul is wrought to the sublimest Rage*
> *Of horrible Revenge.*

But as the Note to this Passage hath been already given, there is no Occasion to repeat it.

Page 25. Note 3.

> *But see, where silent, as the* Noon *of Night,*
> *These Lovers lie!*
> Regicide.

'That ıs I presume when the Moon is in her Meridian, and not as commonly supposed at Midnight.'   Dr Humbug

But here comes the Master-piece of *British* Rant.

> *May Heaven exhaust*
> *Its Thunders on my Head! May Hell Disgorge*
> *Infernal Plagues to blast me, if I cease*
> *To persecute the Caitif, till his Blood*
> *Assuage my parch'd Revenge!*

This Exclamation of yours also passes without a Comment. No human pen, but that of a *Longinus*, could have done it Justice; for *if Heaven exhausting its Thunders, Hell disgorging infernal Plagues; ceasing to persecute the Caitif, and Blood assuaging a parch'd Revenge*, be not, as the fine Lady in *Lethe* calls it, the very *Squintessence* of the Sublime, I may fairly say in Captain *Bobadil's* Phrase, *I have no more Judgment than a Malt-Horse.*

The last Passage, I have drawn from your *admirable* Tragedy, is that beautiful exclamatory Interrogation,

> *How shall Acknowledgement enough reward*
> *Thy Worth unparallell'd?*

If any *dramatic Hero*, since the Days of Euripides, ever utter'd a more pompous and sublime Exclamation, I will be bound to undergo the Punishment of reading over all the Cart-loads of Rubbish, which you palm upon the World, for good Writing.

I believe my Readers are, by this time, convinc'd that your Resentment against my Tragedy is purely *personal*—The foregoing are not *all* the Passages in your REGICIDE, that deserv'd my Notice: the Piece from Beginning to End is a continued Chain of *Sublime Bombast*. There is so little Meaning or Nature in the whole Production, that it may be justly intitled the most compleat and elaborate *Libel* on Tragedy and Common-sense, that was ever foisted upon the Pubic. But, notwithstanding its Defects, it would be the highest Injustice in me to say it is void of Merit: its medicinal Qualities will atone for the Want of poetical ones. Since the Discovery of its physical Virtues, I have bilk'd the Faculty of many a Shilling: for, when a Puke is wanted in my Family, a Perusal of twenty or thirty Lines Seldom fails of the desir'd Effect; double the Number is a Dose for the strongest Constitutions, and with a whole Act I would engage to vomit any Coach-Horse in the three Kingdoms.

My late Mention of the perillous Word *Libel*, induces me to advise you to be more cautious of your future political Writings. Have always in view the Fate of your Brother Doctor,[2] whose Life and Actions seem so near a Counter-part of your own. He was bound an Apprentice to the Faculty, but *extracted* such sublime Notions of LIBERTY, that he most heroically broke through his *Parchment* Bondage: Was not this exactly your Case? After his Enfranchisement, he assum'd the Title of *Doctor of Physic* (no Matter how he came by it) Did not you the same? He started into the *literary* World as a *Novel Writer* with the MARRIAGE ACT, you with RODERIC RANDOM. When the Public was glutted with *Novels*, he turned his Head to *Politics*, and commenced a Retailer of pernicious Principles: Did not you do so likewise? In his Letters to the People of *England*, he libell'd the best of *Kings*: You, in your *History of England*, Spare not the best of *Constitutions*. He hath already been *exalted* for his Labours; and tho' you have not met with *Exaltation*; it is not because you have not deserved as many Favours of the *King's Bench*, as he hath received. For a Proof of this last Assertion, I recommend my Readers to a Perusal of that Part of your *History of England*, which treats of the glorious REVOLUTION in eighty eight.

Now, Doctor! It is almost time to take my leave of you for the present. If you have any Remains of Truth and Honesty in you; you must acknowledge that, in the Course of this Epistle, I have treated you with a *friendly* and *decent Familiarity*: wherefore I hope you will graciously vouchsafe me a Reply. I shall not take the scurrilous Character, which you will probably give of this Epistle in your CRITICAL REVIEW, for an Answer; and therefore desire you will rumage over all the Lumber in your Head for Materials, that I may have something from you, that has a Spice of Wit and Humour in it. Don't give me any of your vamp'd up Translations—I'll take no foreign Coin—Let the Reply be all your own, and then I may reasonably expect it will be *Starling*.

I must farther intreat you to avoid all Quotations, Phrases and Proverbs, either in Prose or Verse, of foreign Extraction: It would be highly ungenerous in you to puzzle me with *Exotics*, as I don't understand any Language, but that of my native Country.

These Premises complied with, I wish you Success in your Reply, with all my Heart: If it be a good one, you cut out a little more Work for me, and I may probably dine my Family a few Days *at your Expence*; if a bad one, I shall take no Notice of it. You see I am willing to do any thing *in an honest Way* to provide for my Babes: I hate a lazy life, and must have my Hands or Head employed. When my *hempen* Calls are brisk, I *am not at Home to the Muses*; but when my Trade grows dull, I am glad to receive their Ladyships. I am afraid your Reply will cut a very indifferent Figure, as you have manifestly exhausted your Vein of Humour in the Composition of RODERICK RANDOM, the best (I was going to add the only tolerable) Piece you have yet published: If you would design to accept of a little Help from an Antagonist, a small Phial of my *Heliconian Liquid Snuff* would enable you to furnish out such a Reply, as would do Honour to your decay'd Genius.

This Snuff is no chymical Preparation, but only the genuine Matter, which descends through that Protuberance of the human Phyz, called the Nose. The Invention of it cost me very little Pains or Study. The old Observation, that *a Snotty Nose is the Sign of a wise Head*, was the sole Hint, that led me to the Discovery. I need not inform a Person of your anatomical Learning and Abilities, that the Nose is Conduit to the Brain, or that the *chrystaline Substance*, flowing down the said Conduit, is the Drainings or Drippings of the Brain.——These Drippings I carefully extract from my Nose, by the Pressure of my fore Finger and Thumb, convey them into a Tin Reservoir, placed in my Coat-pocket, and afterwards pour them into small Phials for the Benefit of *decay'd* or *crude* Authors.

I could give you many Testimonies of the great Efficacy of this Snuff, authenticated under the Hand and Seal of the several Authors, who have received Benefit thereby; but as it would savour too much of the Practice of our modern *Nostrum-Mongers*, I shall be totally silent on the Occasion. In short Doctor, all the *stew'd Prunes* in the World would not do you half so much good, as a single Phial of my admirable Snuff.

Well, dear TOBY! the most intimate Friends must part: I have, in the Language of my Calling, *spun* my *Thread to the Mark;* and now it is time to *wind up*. Permit me to assure you that I am always.

at your Service,

King David's Fort,
March 31. 1759.   A HALTER-MAKER

NOTES

a ———*In my Heart's Core I'll wear him*;
   Ay, in my Heart of Hearts.   Hamlet.
   If we admit the Heart to be form'd like an Onion, I suppose this Phrase
   means the innermost Coat.   Dr HUMBUG.

b As I cannot, with all my Sagacity, as an Editor, Trace any Imitation of
   the following Prayer, I must conclude it to be an Original.
                                                         Dr HUMBUG.

c ———*By Heav'n!*
   His Father's in his Face.   Fair Penitent.

d This Conflict in the Bosom of STRAPADA plainly shews, that our Author
   design'd to draw him a Man, as well as a Philosopher; two characters
   which seldom meet in the same Person; especially in dramatic
   Philosphers. The Struggle is so great, that the Tenderness of the Man
   overcomes the Stiffness of the Sage; and compells him to break that
   Vow, which, a few Minutes ago, he would have *given the Empire of so
   many thousand Worlds* to forswear with Impunity. In the midst of the
   Conflict, we still find him so great a Friend to Virtue, that he only
   pardons his repenting Friend on Condition of his being Virtuous. That
   this Frailty, in regard to his Vow, may not appear a Blemish in the
   Character of our heroic Cobler, I must beg leave to inform my Readers,
   that such Breach of rash Vows, in dramatic Heroes, hath seldom or
   never been counted criminal. I could produce many Instances of such

Frailty: that of *Pierre* in *Venice Preserv'd* may suffice, without quoting further Authorities.

Dr. HUMBUG.

e Our Author seems to have had in View that moral and musical Line *viz.*

    Deceive Deceivers and Deceit grows Virtue.   Merope.

f ————*Faction stalks abroad*

   In such gigantic Strides—   Virginia.

A Sentiment that *stalks* very majestically in the road of black Verse.

Dr HUMBUG.

g *O thou Death's Orator! Dréad Advocate*

  For bowelless Severity!   Brothers.

A Man must have no *Bowels*, who cannot feel the force of these wonderful Metaphors.   Dr HUMBUG.

h *I'll talk of it, tho' Hell itself should gape*

  And bid me hold my Peace.   Hamlet.

i *Revenge the Attributes of Gods; they stamp'd it*

  With their great Image on our Natures.   Venice Preserv'd

j *No, more, no more: tempt me no more in vain.*

Black Prince.

k *My Soul is wrought to the sublimest Rage*

  Of horrible Revenge.   Regicide.

    A very sublime way of telling the World he is in a damn'd Passion. This Image, in my Opinion, would be more proper and intelligible, if the Word *Rage* were alter'd to *Pitch.*   Dr HUMBUG.

l Our Author seems to be led away by the prevailing Opinion of *Gaming,* which paints it as the Effect of Idleness and Prodigality; but I am not yet so much a Slave to vulgar Prejudice, as to suppose that Idleness and Prodigality are the Sources of *Gaming.* Yet should we judge of its Merits, from its Prevalency in the fashionable World, we might rather esteem it to be the Effect of a laudable Desire of acquiring Riches, and a praise-worthy Calling; under which Character the worst of Men insinuate themselves into the Company of Gentlemen and Nobles. And I am of Opinion, that the Philosopher's Stone (notwithstanding all the Labours of the chymical Tribe) will be found, if ever it be found, by *a gaming* Projector.

Dr HUMBUG.

m *And my shock'd Soul akes at him.*   Merope.

See Note 23 of the Second Act————

The Note referr'd to alludes to the following Line in

    And given my very Soul a Fit of the Gripes.

It runs thus.—— 'This Line may possibly admit of a Cavil among some quibbling Criticks; but there are innumerable dramatic Author-

154

ities to justify our Author, and incontestably prove that the Soul is subject to the Disorders of the Body. Among such Authorities is the judicious *Aaron Hill*, Esq; who says in his *Merope*,

And my shock'd Soul akes at him.

Now if the Soul be liable to *Aches*, I would ask these pitiful Carpers, the Criticks, why it may not be as naturally subject to a *Fit of the Gripes*.

Dr HUMBUG.

n Less metaphorically speaking, the *Moon*.
1 The reference is to *I Henry IV*, II, iv, 281 and should read: 'Mark now how a plain tale shall put you down.'
2 Reed here refers to another of Smollett's adversaries, Dr John Shebbeare (see No. 46).

51. Oliver Goldsmith on Smollett

3 November 1759

From *The Bee, being Essays on the Most Interesting Subjects*, V, Saturday 3 November 1759, from the section called *A Resverie*. Reprinted in Oliver Goldsmith, *Collected Works* ed. A. Friedman, 5 vols, Oxford, 1966, vol, 1, pp. 449–50.

My attention was now diverted to a crowd, who were pushing forward a person that seemed more inclined to the *stage coach of riches*; but by their means he was driven forward to the fame machine, which he, however, seemed heartily to despise. Impelled, however, by their sollicitations, he steps up, flourishing a voluminous history, and demanding admittance.[1] 'Sir, I have formerly heard your name mentioned (says the coachman) but never as a historian. Is there no other work upon which you may claim a place?' 'None, replied the other, except a romance,[2] but this is a work of too trifling a nature to claim future attention.' 'You mistake (says the inquisitor) a well-written romance is no such easy task as is generally imagined. I remember formerly to have carried Cervantes and Segrais,[3] and if you think fit, you may enter.' Upon our three literary travellers coming into the same coach, I listened attentively to hear what might be the conversation that passed upon this extraordinary occasion; when, instead of agreeable or entertaining dialogue, I found them grumbling at each other, and each seemed discontented with his companions. Strange! thought I to myself, that they who are thus born to enlighten the world, should still preserve the narrow prejudices of childhood, and, by disagreeing, make even the highest merit ridiculous. Were the learned and the wise to unite against the dunces of society, instead of sometimes siding into opposite parties with them, they might throw a lustre upon each other's reputation, and teach every rank of subordinate merit, if not to admire, at least not to avow dislike.

In the midst of these reflections, I perceived the coachman, unmindful of me, had now mounted the box. Several were approaching to be taken in, whose pretensions I was sensible were very just. I therefore desired him to stop, and take in more passengers; but he replied, as he had now mounted the box, it would be improper to come down; but that he should take them all, one after the other, when he should return. So he drove away, and, for myself, as I could not get in, I mounted behind, in order to hear the conversation on the way.

NOTES

1 The 'voluminous history' is Smollett's *Complete History of England*, which appeared in 1757–8, and was reviewed by Goldsmith in *The Monthly Review*, (see No. 45).

2 The 'romance' alluded to here is probably *Roderick Random*, the novel which established Smollett's reputation. Alternatively, it could be a reference to *Peregrine Pickle*, by which Smollett earned considerable notoriety.

3 Jean Regnauld de Segrais (1624–1701), whose own novels and collaborations were popular in translation in eighteenth-century England.

52. Smollett's Apologue to *Roderick Random*

1760

Taken from the fifth edition of *Roderick Random*, 1760. The Apologue is wanting in the first and some of the later editions.

A young painter indulging a vein of pleasantry, sketched a kind of conversation-piece, representing a bear, an owl, a monkey, and an ass; and to render it more striking, humorous and moral, distinguished every figure by some emblem of human life.

Bruin was exhibited in the garb and attitude of an old, toothless, drunken soldier; the owl, perched upon the handle of a coffee-pot, with spectacle on nose, seemed to contemplate a news-paper; and the ass, ornamented with a huge tye-wig, (which, however, could not conceal his long ears) sat for his picture to the monkey, who appeared with the implements of painting. This whimsical groupe afforded some mirth, and met with general approbation, until some mischievous wag hinted that the whole was a lampoon upon the friends of the performer: an insinuation which was no sooner circulated, than those very people who applauded it before, began to be alarmed, and even to fancy themselves signified by the several figures of the piece.

Among others, a worthy personage in years, who had served in the army with reputation, being incensed at the supposed outrage, repaired to the lodgings of the painter, and finding him at home, 'Heark ye, Mr Monkey, (said he,) I have a good mind to convince you, that though the bear has lost his teeth, he retains his paws, and that he is not so drunk but he can perceive your impertinence—'Sblood! sir, that toothless jaw is a damned scandalous libel—but, don't you imagine me so chopfallen as not to be able to chew the cud of resentment.'—Here he was interrupted by the arrival of a learned physician, who advancing to the culprit with fury in his aspect, exclaimed, 'Suppose the augmentation of the ass's ears should prove the diminution of the baboon's—nay, seek not to prevaricate, for by the beard of Aesculapius! there is not one hair in this periwig that will not stand up in judgment to convict thee of personal abuse—Do you observe, captain, how this pitiful little fellow has copied the very curls—the colour, indeed, is different, but then the form and foretop are quite similar.'—While he thus demonstrated in a strain of vociferation, a venerable senator entered, and waddling up to the delinquent, 'Jackanapes! (cried he), I will now let thee see, I can read something else than a news-paper, and that, without the help of spectacles—here is your own note of hand, sirrah, for money which if I had not advanced, you yourself would have resembled an owl, in not daring to shew your face by day, you ungrateful, slanderous knave.'

In vain the astonished painter declared that he had no intention to give offence, or to characterize particular persons: they affirmed the resemblance was too palpable to be overlooked, they taxed him with insolence, malice, and ingratitude; and their clamours being overheard by the public, the captain was a bear, the doctor an ass, and the senator an owl to his dying day.

Christian reader, I beseech thee, in the bowels of the Lord, remember this example while thou art employed in the perusal of the following sheets; and seek not to appropriate to thyself that which equally belongs to five hundred different people. If thou shouldst meet with a character that reflects thee in some ungracious particular, keep thy own counsel; consider that one feature makes not a face, and that though thou art, perhaps, distinguished by a bottle nose, twenty of thy neighbours may be in the same predicament.

53. Oliver Goldsmith on *Sir Launcelot Greaves*

1760

From *The Public Ledger* (16 February 1760), no. 31, reprinted in *The Works of Oliver Goldsmith*, ed. P. Cunningham, 12 vols, 1900, vol. vi, p. 91. This extract comes from 'the description of a wowwow in the country, in a letter to the author.' A Wow-wow is defined in the essay as a confused heap of people of all denominations, assembled at a public house to read the newspapers, and to hear the tittle-tattle of the day. Goldsmith's modern editor Professor A. Friedman finds this attribution unproven, None the less, Goldsmith contributed three essays to *The British Magazine* in February, March and April 1760, and since this piece is a puff for Smollett's novel and the magazine, it is included here under Goldsmith's name.

We should certainly have had a war at the Wow-wow, had not an Oxford scholar, led there by curiosity, pulled a new magazine out of his pocket, in which he said there were some pieces extremely curious, and that deserved all their attention. He then read the adventures of Sir Launcelot Greaves to the entire satisfaction of the audience, which being finished, he threw the pamphlet on the table: that piece gentlemen, says he, is written in the very spirit and manner of Cervantes, there is a great knowledge of human nature, and evident marks of the master in almost every sentence; and from the plan, the humour, and the execution, I can venture to say that it dropt from the pen of ingenious Dr ———. Everyone was pleased with the performance, and I was particularly gratified in hearing all the sensible part of the company give orders for the *British Magazine*.

54. An anonymous ode in praise of Smollett

1760

From *Lloyd's Evening Post, and British Chronicle*, VI, 20–22 February 1760, 179. This poem was apparently sent anonymously to the editor by 'K', who remains unidentified.

To DR. SMOLLETT
AN ODE

'Tis thine alone. O Smollett, to prepare
   The mental feast, that shall for ages hence
Delight as now, and soothe the sons of Care,
   With sweet repasts, of Science, and of Sense.

Thine is the pow'r, to touch, to rouze the soul;
   To guide each movement of the human heart;
To raise the passions, or their rage controul;
   And rule the bosom by thy magic Art.

Adown my cheek the tender social tear
   Steals unawares, when thy Monimia mourns:
Her sighs I feel, her soft complaints I share,
   As Love now melts, or Jealousy now burns.

But blood-ey'd Fury rends my throbbing breast,
   When faithless Fathom rises to my view;
When flushed with fraud, the villain stands confest,
   And unsuspected, plans his plots anew.

Again I sigh, again soft Pity flows,
   When noble Zelos, Honor's rigid son,
Opprest with grief, and stagg'ring with his woes,
   Recounts the triumph his revenge had won.

Such is thy skill, such is thy pleasing strain,
   Such is thy fancy, such thy Attic fire!
Entranced we read, what Critics can't arraign,
   What Age approves, and what the Fair admire.

But in thy Hist'ry, all thy Genius blooms,
   Old England's battles o'er again we wage,
Tread Cresci's plain, and follow Edward's plumes,
   And glow with Conquest, Liberty, and Rage.

There Truth appears in her transparent charms,
   How lovely she! when stript of Faction's veil,
When, undisguis'd, Kings take her to their arms,
   And rule with equity the Commonweal.

There shines thy Pitt (superior to all praise)
   The great Restorer of the British Name:
Th' historic Muse his dazzling Deeds displays,
   Records his virtues, and reflects his Fame.

Thee, Smollett, thee the sons of Science hail!
   Applaud thy clear, thy comprehensive page,
Nervous as Hyde, and accurate as Boyle,
   Warm as the Poet, sober as the Sage.

And lo! th' exulting Muse expands her wings:
   'Tis hers, to register the men divine,
Who trace the Source of Aganippe's springs;
   Or watch at Wisdom's adamantine shrine.

Ah, radiant Maid! thy raptures all infuse,
   Thy thrilling raptures let my bosom fire.
Be mine—the majesty of ev'ry Muse;
   Be mine—the music of the melting Lyre.

Immortal wreaths shall then my Smollett grace;
   Immortal strains shall charm his pensive mind,
   Such—as when Horace sung th' Augustan Race,
   And changed to Gods those Conq'rors of Mankind.

55. Anonymous pamphlet, *The Battle of the Reviews*

[16 March] 1760

From *The Battle of the Reviews*, 1760. Extracts from an anonymous pamphlet traducing Smollett as novelist and reviewer under the pseudonym Sawney MacSmallhead.

Pages 17–19:

In Consequence of an Axiom, methinks, in Metaphysics, 'That the Effect is of the same Condition with the Cause,' I am induced to form another Analogy between the Mushroom and the Author, which had like to escape me. The Mushroom owes its Being to a Principle of Putrefaction, so also does the Author, as it sufficiently appears from his maggotty Brains. The Mushroom will decay and all its best Juices evaporate, unless almost as soon as gathered, it is converted into *Ketchup*, is made an Ingredient in *Sauces*, or is preserved in some *Pickle*. In like Manner, the Author may, for a little Time, be in Request, but he droops into Oblivion, lies neglected on a Shelf, and cannot afford the Pleasure of a second Reading, unless his Genius can *catch up* Some Sparks of Brightness and Vivacity, can dress his Thoughts with the *Sauce* of Reason, and can preserve them in the *Pickle* of Judgment. Again, Mushrooms being hard of Digestion, being naturally cold, and of Consequence poisonous, the same Qualities will indisputably be inherent to an Author; but as these require an intricate Investigation of their Causes, I shall reserve a Place for them in another Work, and here only shall make a seasonable *Innuendo* to the courteous Reader for complimenting me with his hearty Thanks for bringing to Light this so significant Analogy of the Author and Mushroom, which without any Tergiversation or Evasion, he must declare to be 'noble, new, and never before so much as thought of.'

Insigne, recens, adhuc indictum ore alio.[1]

HOR.

162

Pages 103–17:

Sampson Mac Jackson, and *Sawney Mac Smallhead* are the Names of the two select *Critical Reviewers*. They were both *North Britons*, and both seem to have had the Advantages of a liberal Education, improved by good natural Parts, Reflection and Study. The first, in the twenty-fifth Year of his Age had a strong Inclination to be initiated, among the People of the *Orcades*, in their Mysteries of bloating Bag pipes with Boreal Blasts, whereby they could at Pleasure contract them into a Flow of harmonical Proportions or make them scout about with impetuous Velocity to annoy unknown Ships on their Coasts; but perceiving that these mystical Blasts were neither according to their Promises, nor his Expectations, substantial enough to settle him in the Ease of Life, he removed under the Meridian of *London*, where he professed himself a nice Architect of Words. The second, as *Boileau* says of *Persult*, deserting the infertile Science of *Galen*, which he had studied during the Term of Seven-Years in the Island of *Skie*, living all the Time upon an herbaceous Diet, whereby his Visage became transfused with a greenish Paleness, and his Guts often pinched with a Cholic Forceps, removed also under the Meridian of *London*, where, as Quacks had engrossed the lucrative Branches of Medicine, he sollicited a Partnership with his Countryman, and was admitted to an equal Partition of the Issues and Profits of Word-building. What will not keen Stomachs do? Stomachs! that still retained the Whet of their native Air. Their Superstructures rose apace; clear Heads projected, and tho' their Manner of Execution was somewhat different, each pleased, and each, I must believe, has his Admirers.

Both shew no small Share of Erudition; in *Mac Jackson*, disclosing itself by a competent Knowledge of several Languages, and by having read well the best Books in these Languages: In *Mac Smallhead*, by his Acquaintance with Medicine, and such Parts of Natural Philosophy as are relative to that Science, besides a Taste for History and the Belles Lettres; but all not to that Degree of Perfection as he himself imagines, or would fain persuade others. The Invention of *Mac Jackson* appears not as if it could deduct a constant Supply from its own Fund without being exhausted, and therefore by having Recourse sometimes to the external Helps Memory has suggested from other Logodedalists, by refining upon

their Thoughts, by converting them artfully into its own substance, it may not improperly be compared to a Bee industriously
sipping Honey from every Flower. Nature, though not very
extensive, having the Ascendant in *Mac Smallhead's* Invention,
makes it easy, not much indebted to Art, readily recruited by a little
Attention to the common Occurrences of Life, and more like a
Fountain, sometimes pure, sometimes turbid, than a large River.
Elocution on *Mac Jackson's* Side, may be reputed his Master-piece;
for his Words flow with Smoothness; are just, pure and elegant;
they clothe the Thought with a rich, yet decent Attire; their
Charms are not without Force, and the Warmth they excite begets
a Deal of Pleasure. But methinks a graceless and tiresome
Monotony reigns through the Whole: The same Order, the same
turns, the same junction, the same Transitions, the same Cadence
present themselves almost every where; so that by perusing a Page
or two of his Writings, you may say you have perused ten
thousand, that is, abstracting from the Matter, and considering
only the Elocution. There is one Thing *Mac Jackson* seems
particularly anxious about, which is the ending of a Period, or
where a Stop is necessary, with a Word of two, three or more
Syllables. This, it must be confessed, is a Beauty, completes the
Harmony, and should most commonly be observed, though not
always; because a Monosyllable is often more energic, especially
when the Sense implies any Thing little, quick, hot, rash,
passionate, and precipitate. For this Reason we so justly admire the
exiguus Mus, and *procumbit humi Bos* of *Virgil*, and all the other Falls
either in the Middle or End of Lines, which no other Poet ever used
so judiciously, whose very Words are a lively Picture of the very
Nature of what they describe. A striking Example of a soft and
gentle Fall in the Middle of a Verse, may be seen towards the
Beginning of the seventh Book, where, by the Poet's describing the
ushering in of a Calm, in these Words, *cum venti posuêre*, you
imagine you hear the Winds blowing their last.

Sawney Mac Smallhead's Elocution partakes of both the temperate
and Simple Kinds, sometimes embellished with the gay Flowers of
figurative Thoughts and Expressions, and Sometimes contenting
itself with the Cleanliness of modest and near Apparel; but the
former often degenerates into what the *French* call a *Faux brillant*,
bearing no remote Resemblance to a Coat edged with Tinsel, instead

of Gold or Silver Lace, which, however, may strike at a Distance, but discovers the Cheat when closely examined: The Latter, by too great an Affectation of what the *French* also call *l'heureuse Negligence*, falls into the very Vice of which it seemed the virtue, and like a Woman turned Slattern through mere Love, often loses by being careless of her Person, the Admirer of a former Elegance. *Mac Smallhead* likewise, in a great Measure, expresses himself by Circumlocution, as if the Language he writes in contained but few proper Words, so that if some of his Pieces in this Strain were resolved into simple Propositions, they would dwindle away from their promising gigantic Aspect into that of Pigmies.

Sampson Mac Jackson's Moral, in most of the Subjects he treats of, is found, instructive, and strikes Home: That of *Mac Smallhead* is something too vague and indeterminate, flourishing like a Prize-fighter, now and then giving a Scar, but seldom a Wound. His RANDOMS and PICKLES may stand excusable in the Time they were written: *Sawney*, no Doubt, being then borne down by the Torrent of Ribaldry the late worshipful Justice *Henry Fielding*, Esq; poured upon him and others. But in emulating the Pattern of so instructive, or as the Bucks say, of so destructive a Moral; though in many Respects he had proved himself a worthy Rival, he cannot however claim an Equality with the worshipful Justice; for in Effect he is more harsh and forced; is destitute of a like Vivacity; is too circumstantial in Descriptions often quite unnecessary, makes Nature ridiculous, and not what she is or may be; shews no great Fertility of Invention; and has but few striking Incidents. Notwithstanding as he has been deemed by the polite Readers of the *British* Nation one of the principal adepts in farcical Eloquence, I shall venture to place him next to the worshipful Justice, but next[a], with a great Space lying between; or, as when *Domitius Aser* being asked, what Poet came nearest *Homer*, answered, '*Virgil* is the Second, yet nearer the First than a Third;' so according to this Notion, but by inverting the Proposition, *Sawney* will be nearer a Third than the worshipful Justice.

In another Point of View, Majesty and Dignity fit easy on *Sampson: Sawney* only apes them. *Sampson* has stronger Bones and Sinews: *Sawney* more Flesh. *Sampson* by diversifying his Style may become the most elaborate Writer of his Age: *Sawney* has his Merit, and when exact may be fancied. As a Critic, *Sampson* has always proved himself a just Discerner of the Good and the True in

Writing: *Sawney* is not without sufficient Abilities in that Respect; but his Prejudice and Passion have often made these Abilities, together with his professed Candour, suspected. Yes, this is *Sawney's* Peccadillo; none can deny but that in the Main he deserves well of the Republic of Letters; yet his Merit, such as it is, is quite tarnished by his Vanity; a Vanity, always fulsome and always odious. He himself may boast, but few know with what Pretensions, that he is a Non-pareil, uniting in his Genius the Sublimity of *Homer*, the Majesty and Judgment of *Virgil*, the Force of *Demosthenes*, the Copiousness of *Cicero*, the Correctness of *Caesar*, the Erudition of *Varro*, and the Sagacity of *Lucretius*. Such indeed is a fine Encomium, and *Sawney* in the Humility of his Heart deserves it. Strange Infatuation! But how must his Ostentation be relished, who is always extolling himself, and always depreciating others; or, what Man, unless a base Sicophant will praise him, who lavishes Praises on himself? Does not the human Mind naturally conceive that she is sublime, erect and big with Indignity against a Superior? It is therefore, that we willingly raise those, whose unaspiring Thoughts seem to be sincere: We do so, as imagining ourselves greater, and as often as Emulation foments no Animosities, Humanity of Course succeeds. But he who arrogantly puffs himself up, is believed to depress and despise us, and not to make himself so great, as others less. This is the Vice of those, who are neither willing to yield, nor can contend; they deride superior Merit, and upon such a Monument strive to erect their ignominious Trophies.

I am much afraid, the serious Mood *Sawney Mac Smallhead* had just now put me into, will not be so acceptable to the gentle Reader, who, I believe, would rather have me laugh and tell Truth at the same Time, than form an Attack in earnest upon a Critic, so formidable in repelling it, and now in War Time more particularly, for Fear of a Surprize, so deeply entrenched. What! an Attack in Earnest! It consists but of Words, and Words are but Wind, and I dare say this Wind will not BLOW, neither from him or from me. The Laqueys, who on the *Critical* List, held up his and his Partner *Sampson Mac Jackson's* Tails, enjoyed in fair and legible Letters the Names of *Duncan Mac Croudy*, *Archibald Mac Bonacs*, *Donald Mac Haggess*, and *Paddy Fitzpatrick*; the last, very probably an *Hibernian*, or thence deriving his Origin. Being without Characters as I said, I was apt to surmise that they were Non-entities; or like the

Eccho, Voices and Nothing more; or perhaps a Sort of Eatables their Owners chiefly fed upon, and were fond of; though I hardly believe that; for the last appearing to be something like an *Irishman*, they would not play the Cannibal and eat him; or, in fine, a poor necessitous Crew, never to receive sepulchral Honours after Death, nor to be ferried over any of the infernal Rivers, in *Charon's* flat-bottomed Boat, but to remain as a strolling Company of Players till Doomsday on the Banks of the *Styx*. However, these nominal Beings (call them what you will; for their Genus and Species are quite unknown) were destined to be Aids de Camp to his Typographical Highness, who as Patron of the *Critical Review*, was to be General in Chief of its Army, and to command in Person the Center, *Sampson Mac Jackson* being appointed by him to command the Right Wing, and *Sawney Mac Smallhead* the Left.

Pages 141–5:

The Drift of this Manoeuvre was soon perceived by the *Critical* Leaders. *Sawney Mac Smallhead*, the most forward of them, posted instantly after *Jack* with some light armed Troops of *Blackardism*. The Pursuit was close, and *Jack* saw himself before he was aware of it, cut off from all Comunication with his Brethren, and his Rear-guard beginning to be harassed by a Platoon firing of *bitter Taunts* and *opprobrious Obloquy*. What should poor *Jack* do? How should he save himself from being circumvented by such a Torrent of Abuse and Scurrility? He had no Courage to face about; and if ever he had any, it now all fell into his Heels, suggesting, that it was his best Way to run hard for it. He did so, and setting up his *Ignis fatuus* to lead his wandering Steps, he ordered his chosen Crew, now as much distracted as himself, to follow with him the unerring Guide through Thick and Thin. The Consequence was, when they had crossed *Tottenham-Court* Road, the *Ignis fatuus* rested upon a Soil-pit, or deep Trench full of Mire and Nastiness; and *Jack* confident with himself that this Pit must be a sure Azylum to them, he plunged in without Hesitation and all his Crew after him. Some grave Authors are of Opinion, that there is here a Descent to the *Tartarean* Regions; because, tho' often plumbed by the most curious and diligent Antiquarians with Lines extended *in indefinitum*, no Bottom had ever been found. 'Tis certain, some expert Harponiers had been employed to fish out *Jack* and his Companions; but their Labour being all to no Purpose, the World was at a

Loss to account, with any Shew of Truth, for the Phenomenon, till Monsieur *Maubert de Gouvert* assured them in one of his Political *Mercuries*, of his having received undoubted Intelligence, that they had been condemned by *Rhadamanthus*, one of the Judges in Hell, to undergo the Metamorphosis of Frogs[b], and to be for ever croaking Inhabitants of the River *Lethe*'s dormant Waters.

That *Jack o' the Lanthorn* received some Overthrow, or that his Detachment was routed and dispersed, appeared but too visibly to General *Gruffy*, by *Sawney*'s triumphant Return to the Field of Battle. The *Monthly Reviewers* had now in Reality the worst of it: They were pressed hard on all Sides, and many of their Ranks were thinned, and some entirely mowed down in a desperate Push made by the Enemy to come to close Quarters by staring them point blank in their Faces to reconnoitre their *Inanity*. A Retreat, could they have effected it with any Regularity, might have been of Service to them; but they were so broken and disheartened, that not being able to rally, they followed their General's Example, who was one of the first to run away with as much Speed as his mettlesome Pegasus of the Asinine Species could carry him. However, they made a Stand at the Tabernacle, but it was rather to seek the Protection of the holy Man's Sanctuary by laying Hold of his Horns, than with any Inclination to fight again with Foes who had so roughly handled them, and who now bent upon cutting them off entirely, were pursuing them with their whole collected Force.

Pages 149–51:

Victory does not always smile upon those she has favoured, so as to render in all Respects their Satisfaction complete. *Sawney Mac Smallhead*, who had been a very bustling Hero during the Battle, and who in some Measure might be said to be his General's Right-hand Man, had the Misfortune to be way-laid, whilst he was viewing the Attack on the Tabernacle from a rising Ground, and sending off his Aids de Camp with Directions to make it as hot as possible. It seems Dr *Sh—bb—e*, who bore him an old Grudge for some former Bickerings, having previous Notice of the Battle between the two *Reviews*, obtained a Day-rule from the *King's-Bench* Prison, on Pretence of being only a Spectator of it. He had privately mustered together about a hundred and fifty stout Tars with Admiral *K——s*'s Commission in their Pockets to apprehend

Sawney for high Crimes and Misdemeanors. The Opportunity of
his being thinly guarded and at some Distance from the main Body
of the Army served their Purpose. In short, they carried him off
with little Opposition, and clapped him fast in Durance. *Sawney*
ever since has left off the Trade of Reviewing, thinking, Cobler
like, he should make both Ends meet better by laying up all the
loose Hints that occur to him in a Sort of Repository, which he is
now compiling and digesting in Conjuction with his old Crony
Timothy Crabshaw.

NOTES

a Proximus———sed longo proximus intervallo.
                              VIRG. *Lib.* 5. *Aeneid.*
   [Virgil, *Aeneid*, v, 320. Literally 'next, with a great space lying between' as
   in the text.]
b Ranas in Gurgite nigras.   JUV.
1 Horace, *Odes III*, xxv, 7–8. The meaning is given in the text, i.e. 'noble,
   new, and never before so much as thought of.'

56. Notice in *The Imperial Magazine* on Smollett as historian

1760

From *The Imperial Magazine*, I, October 1760, 519, from the
article, 'On the Present State of Literature in England'.

Dr Smollett is certainly an ingenious writer on some subjects, but
he strangely misapplies his talents when he writes history; his
history of England, which has had so great a run amongst the
vulgar (a set of people whose approbation would give me but an
indifferent opinion of a book before I read it) is an instance of this.
Novel-writing seems much more adapted to his genius; his
flowery style, which disgusts us in history, pleases in *Roderick
Random*; a novel, which though faulty in several respects, has
certainly some merit; and is much superior to the common run of

those works, which reflect so great a disgrace on the polite literature of the nation. I cannot help regretting the unhappy fate of many writers, whose abilities, were they possessed of independant fortunes, would do honour to themselves and country, obliged by want to subject themselves to the imperious dictates of ignorant booksellers. This it is that cramps the fire and genius of authors, and reduces a man of ingenuity to be the dirty writer of a critical review.

57. Horace Walpole on Smollett's libel

1760

From *Memoirs of the Reign of King George the Second*, ed. Lord Holland, 3 vols, 1846 (1822), vol. III, p. 259, covering the year 1760.

In February was tried a criminal of a still different complexion. Dr Smollett was convicted in the King's Bench of publishing scurrilous abuse on Admiral Knollys in the *Critical Review*. Smollett was a worthless man, and only mentioned here because author of a *History of England*, of the errors in which posterity ought to be warned. Smollett was bred a sea-surgeon, and turned author. He wrote a tragedy, and sent it to Lord Lyttelton, with whom he was not acquainted. Lord Lyttelton, not caring to point out its defects, civilly advised him to try comedy. He wrote one, and solicited the same Lord to recommend it to the stage. The latter excused himself, but promised, if it should be acted, to do all the service in his power for the author. Smollett's return was drawing an abusive portrait of Lord Lyttelton in *Roderick Random*, a novel; of which sort he published two or three. His next attempt was on the *History of England*; a work in which he engaged for booksellers, and finished, though four volumes in quarto, in two years; yet an easy task, as being pilfered from other histories. Accordingly, it was little noticed till it came down to the present time: then, though compiled from the libels of the age and the most paltry materials, yet being heightened by personal invectives, strong Jacobitism, and the worst representation of the Duke of Cumberland's conduct in Scotland, the sale was prodigious. Eleven thousand copies of that trash were instantly sold, while at the same time the university of Oxford ventured to print but two thousand of that inimitable work, *Lord Clarendon's Life*! A reflection on the age sad to mention, yet too true to be suppressed! Smollett's work was again printed, and again tasted: it was adorned with wretched prints, except two or three by Strange, who could not refuse his admirable graver to the service of the Jacobite cause.

Smollett then engaged in a monthly magazine, called the *Critical Review*, the scope of which was to decry any work that appeared favourable to the principles of the Revolution. Nor was he single in that measure. The Scotch in the heart of London assumed a dictatorial power of reviling every book that censured the Stuarts, or upheld the Revolution—a provocation they ought to have remembered when the tide rolled back upon them. Smollett, while in prison, undertook a new magazine; and notwithstanding the notoriety of his disaffection, obtained the King's patent for it by the interest of Mr Pitt, to whom he had dedicated his history. In the following reign he was hired to write a scurrilous paper, called the *Briton*, against that very patron, Mr Pitt.

58. Charles Churchill in *The Apology*

May 1761

From Charles Churchill's poem *The Apology*, in *Works*, ed. Douglas Grant, 1956, pp. 41 and 45.

Offended by an anonymous review in *The Critical Review* of his *Rosciad*, Churchill attacked Smollett and others in this *Apology*. He ridicules Smollett as novelist, historian, dramat-

ist and critic, and in lines 166–9 parodies a speech by the
Queen in Smollett's *The Regicide*, III, i.

Lines 144–69:

> Whence could arise this mighty critic spleen,
> The Muse a trifler, and her theme so mean?
> What had I done, that angry HEAVEN should send
> The bitt'rest Foe, where most I wish'd a Friend?
> Oft hath my tongue been wanton at thy name,
> And hail'd the honours of thy matchless fame.
> For me let hoary FIELDING bite the ground
> So nobler PICKLE stand superbly bound.
> From LIVY's temples tear th' historic crown
> Which with more justice blooms upon thine own.
> Compar'd with thee, be all life-writers dumb,
> But he who wrote the Life of TOMMY THUMB.
> Who ever read the REGICIDE but swore
> The author wrote as man ne'er wrote before?
> Others for plots and under-plots may call,
> Here's the right method—have no plot at all.
> Who can so often in his cause engage
> The tiny Pathos of the Grecian stage,
> Whilst horrors rise, and tears spontaneous flow
> At tragic Ha! and no less tragic Oh!?
> His NERVOUS WEAKNESS all to praise agree;
> And then, for sweetness, who so sweet as he?
> Too big for utterance when sorrows swell
> The too big sorrows flowing tears must tell:
> But when those flowing tears shall cease to flow,
> Why,—then the voice must speak again you know.

Lines 298–313:

> Is there a man, in vice and folly bred,
> To sense of honour as to virtue dead;
> Whom ties nor human, nor divine, can bind;
> Alien to GOD, and foe to all mankind;
> Who spares no character; whose ev'ry word,
> Bitter as gall, and sharper than the sword,
> Cuts to the quick; whose thoughts with rancour swell:
> Whose tongue, on earth, performs the work of Hell?
> If there be such a monster, the REVIEWS
> Shall find him holding forth against Abuse.

'Attack Profession!—'tis a deadly breach!
The Christian laws another lesson teach:—
Unto the end should charity endure,
And Candour hide those faults it cannot cure.'
Thus Candour's maxims flow from Rancour's throat,
As devils, to serve their purpose, Scripture quote.

59. Unsigned notice of *Sir Launcelot Greaves*

May 1762

From *The Monthly Review*, May 1762, xxvi, 391. Smollett was an occasional contributor to the *Monthly Review*, which may explain the inclusion of such a brief notice which yet demurs and flatters.

Better than the common Novels, but unworthy the pen of Dr Smollett.

60. Unsigned review of *Sir Launcelot Greaves*

May 1762

From *The Critical Review*, XIII, 1762, 427–9.

Instances of the *vis comica* are so rarely exhibited on the stage, or in the productions of our novelists, that one is almost induced to believe wit and humour have taken their flight with public virtue.

The poets of these days aim at nothing more than interesting the passions by the intricacy of their plots; if a smile be accidentally raised upon the countenance, it rather proceeds from our finding the characters of the drama in some ridiculous or unexpected situation, than from their having said or done anything characteristical. In novels especially, the historian thrusts himself too frequently upon the reader. Take a single chapter and it will appear egregiously dull, because the whole joke consists in untying some knot, or unravelling some mystery, and is generally placed in the epigrammatic fashion, in the tail. It is the suspense merely, with respect to the issue, that engages the reader's attention. Characters are distinguished merely by their opposition to some other characters; remove the contrast, and you annihilate the personages, just as little wits in conversation are reduced to more inanimate figures, when you have taken away the fool who drew forth their talents. How different from this is the ridiculous simplicity of Adams, the absurd vehemence of Western, the boisterous generosity of Bowling, the native humour of Trunnion, and the laughable solemnity of Uncle Toby! Each of these characters singly is complete; without relation to any other object they excite mirth; we dip with the highest delight into a chapter, and enjoy it without reflecting upon the contrivance of the piece, or once casting an eye towards the catastrophe. Every sentence, and every action, diverts by its peculiarity; and hence it is that the novels in which those characters are to be found, will furnish perpetual amusement, while others, which entertain merely from the nature of the incidents, and the conduct of the fable, are for ever laid aside after a single perusal: an engaging story will bear relating but once; a humorous character will bear viewing repreatedly.

The two principal characters, unless we except that of Miss Darnel in this little ingenious piece, seem to be formed on those of the admirable Cervantes, the grave knight of la Mancha, and his facetious Squire. They resemble without imitating, and remind us of what imparted exquisite enjoyment, without diminishing their own novelty. Readers unacquainted with the don and his squire, will be delighted with Sir Launcelot and Crabshaw; those who have attended that mirror of chivalry through the course of his strange adventures, and listened with wonder to the shrewd remarks of Sancho, will be surprised at the possibility of giving originality to characters formed on that model. Nor are these the only portraits on which this author hath lavished the powers of genius; those of Crowe, Ferrit, Oakly, and some others, are truly characteristical, and demonstrative of the genuine humour, satirical talents, and benevolent heart of the writer. That admirable faculty of describing sea characters with propriety, so conspicuous in his other productions, is here displayed with renovated vigour. Captain Crowe is a tar of as extraordinary a cast as either Bowling, Trunnion, Pipes, or Hatchway. His manners and dialect are purely those of the watry element; yet both are perfectly original. It has been said that Shakespeare has drawn a natural character in Caliban, not to be found in nature. We may with equal reason affirm, that Crowe is a true seaman that never existed, who talks in tropes and figures borrowed from his profession, but never used before. In a word, the author has invented a language for this amphibious species, so extremely natural, that nothing can be better adapted to express the character, of which the reader may peruse a specimen in the following address:

'What cheer, brother? You see how the land lies. Here have Tom and I been fast ashore....'

61. Unsigned notice of *Sir Launcelot Greaves*

May 1762

From *The Library, or Moral and Critical Magazine*, by a Society of Gentleman, 1762, II, 262.

Such of our readers as are fond of novels, will receive ample gratification from two which the last month has produced. The first is *Sir Launcelot Greaves*, by Dr Smollett, whose excellent talent at this species of writing hath been fully experienced in some former works, and particularly in his *Roderick Random*. Sir Launcelot Greaves is a kind of English Quixote, and his adventures are conducted with much humour. There are many characters well drawn, many diverting incidents, and many fine strokes of genius, nature, and passion. The author has introduced certain persons too often, and especially Captain Crowe, whose appearance is some-times disgusting, and whose sea jargon is absolutely unintelligible to a land reader; but, on the whole, the performance has considerable merit. The language in general, is such as might be expected from Dr Smollett, who has, perhaps, as much facility and variety of expression as most writers of the age.

The other novel is *Sophia*, by the justly celebrated Mrs Lennox.

62. [William Rider], from *Living Authors of Great Britain*

1762

From *An Historical and Critical Account of the Lives and Writings of the Living Authors of Great-Britain* (1762), pp. 11–12.

Probably the first biographical and critical account of Smollett, in a compilation devoted to the 'Lives and Writings' of living authors. For an introduction and notes to this see O.M. Brack Jr's facsimile edition (Augustan Reprint Society, Publication No. 163, 1974).

Tobias Smollett, M.D. is a Native of *Scotland*. He was a Sea Surgeon at the Time of the Expedition to *Cartbagena*. It does not appear that he had ever much Practice as a Physician. The first Work by which he acquired Reputation in the Republic of Letters, was his Romance of *Roderick Random*, which must be acknowledged to be the best Work of the Kind in our Language, next to those of the late ingenious Mr *Fielding*. He after this published the *Adventures of Peregrine Pickle*, which, tho' it is wrote with some Spirit, has been justly censured, because it in the Incidents bears too strong a

Resemblance to *Roderick Random*; as also, because the Account given in it of the Manners and Customs of the *French* in many Particulars deviates from the Truth. *Count Fathom*, another Romance of the Doctor's seems to be superior to the foregoing. The *History of England*, which is his Master piece, entitles him to a place amongst Authors of the first Rank, as it is but doing Justice to say of it, that it is the best History of *England* that ever was wrote. It is a strong Proof of its Merit, that it has been translated into all the Languages of *Europe*. The Doctor, encouraged by his Success, continues to give a *Continuation* of it; but some have complained, that the *Continuation* falls short of the first Part. No Author has been concerned in a greater Variety of Publications than Dr *Smollett*, as indeed no Author has a greater Variety of Talents. He is not, however, universal, having attempted dramatic Poetry, and failed in it. He wrote a Tragedy called the *Regicide*, which was never acted, and a Farce called the *Tars of Old England*, which was acted at *Drury-Lane* without Success.

63. Richard Smith, a letter to Tobias Smollett

26 February 1763

Richard Smith (1735–1803) was Recorder of Burlington, New Jersey, provincial councillor-at-law for that State, and a member of the Continental Congress, from which he resigned in 1776. A Quaker, he was recognized as a man of wide learning and integrity.

Sir:—You will pardon the Curiosity of a Man distant from you many Thousand Miles—who will however take it as a very particular Favor to have that Curiosity satisfied by a note from you sent at the first Opporty either via Philada or New York.—The

Writer of this Letter as well as many of his Acquaintances has often been delighted with, not to say instructed, by your works and out of mere gratitude he cannot refrain from returning you his hearty Thanks. It is from Truth indeed and not from Adul[ation]—That I must say I look upon you as the First Genius in Britain and the fin [ished]? [mas]ter?—and I should be glad to hear his Majesty has honored you with [recognit]ion at least equal to Johnson's—Of the circumstances of yor Life we know at this Distance [l]ittle—but I sho^d be glad to be informed whether *Roderick Random* or *[Peregrine Pic]kle* contain any Traces of your real adventures—and at what age or under what circumstances they were written. Count Fathom shows a Smollett in every page but it has not all the Graces of my Favorite Pickle—as to Lancelot Greaves many here are pleased to say that you Lent your Name upon that Occasion to a Mercenary Bookseller. The Voyages which go under your Name [Mr Rivington whom I consulted on the matter tells me] are only nominally yours or at least were collected [by your] understrappers. Mr Rivington also gives me such an acco't of the Shortness of Times in which you wrote the *History of England*—as is hardly credible. I should be glad to be truly instructed in that particular and I was Desired by Several to ask you whether the 4th Vol. of the Continuation is to be the last, or whether You will not chuse to continue it to the End of the War—which I hope will be the Case—To this string of Quest's leave me to add the Request of a List of yr Genuine Works and whether you are like soon to Purchasing among the First.

If I ask any Thing impertinent you will punish [my n]eglect—but you can hardly conceive the pleasure I should take [com]municating yo'r answer to my Friends—and in having in Pos[session] a Letter from the Author of the Complete Hist of Engld and Continuation.

> I am You most Obdt
> & very humble sevt.
> Richard Smith.

Atty at law, Recorder
of the City of Burlington.

> Burlington, New Jersey.
> 26 Feb. 1763.

64. Tobias Smollett, a letter to Richard Smith

8 May 1763

From *The Letters of Tobias Smollett*, ed. Lewis M. Knapp, Oxford, 1970, p. 112. A reply to Richard Smith's letter of February 1763. This extract concerns the distinction Smollett makes between his own history and Roderick Random's.

The Curiosity you express with regard to the Particulars of my Life and the variety of situations in which I may have been cannot be gratified within the Compass of a Letter. Besides, there are some Particulars of my Life which it would ill become me to relate. The only Similitude between the Circumstances of my own Fortune and those I have attributed to Roderick Random consists in my being born of a reputable Family in Scotland, in my being bred a Surgeon, and having served as a Surgeon's mate on board a man of war during the Expedition to Carthagene. The low Situations in which I have exhibited Roderick I never experienced in my own Person.

65. Charles Churchill in *The Author*

December 1763

From Charles Churchill's poem *The Author*, in *Works*, ed. Douglas Grant, 1956, pp. 249–50 and 253–4. A further attack by the author of *The Apology* on Smollett as poet, and suggesting that Smollett was in receipt of a State Pension. He was not.

Lines 107–26:

How do I laugh, when PUBLIUS, hoary grown
In zeal for SCOTLAND's welfare, and his own,
By slow degrees, and course of office, drawn
In mood and figure at the helm to yawn,
Too mean (the worst of curses Heav'n can send)
To have a foe, too proud to have a friend,
Erring by form, which Blockheads sacred hold,
Ne'er making new faults, and ne'er mending old,
Rebukes my Spirit, bids the daring Muse
Subjects more equal to her weakness chuse;
Bids her frequent the haunts of humble swains,
Nor dare to traffick in ambitious strains;
Bids her, indulging the poetic whim
In quaint-wrought Ode, or Sonnet pertly trim,
Along the Church-way path complain with GRAY,
Or dance with MASON on the first of May?
'All sacred is the name and pow'r of Kings,
All States and Statemen are those mighty Things
Which, howsoe'er they out of course may roll,
Were never made for Poets to controul.'

Lines 247–62:

Is there an Author, search the Kingdom round,
In whom true worth, and real Spirit's found?
The Slaves of Booksellers, or (doom'd by Fate
To baser chains) vile pensioners of State;
Some, dead to shame, and of those shackles proud
Which Honour scorns, for slav'ry roar aloud,
Others, *half-palsied* only, mutes become,
And what makes SMOLLETT write, makes JOHNSON dumb
Why turns yon villain pale? why bends his eye
Inward, abash'd, when MURPHY passes by?
Dost Thou sage MURPHY for a blockhead take,
Who wages war with vice for Virtue's sake?
No, No—like other *Worldlings*, you will find
He shifts his sails, and catches ev'ry wind.
His soul the shock of int'rest can't endure,
Give him a pension then, and sin secure.

66. Giuseppe Baretti, an Italian's view of Smollett

20 January 1764

From *Giuseppe Baretti and his Friends* by Lacy Collison-Morley, 1909, p. 165.

This extract comes from Baretti's *FRUSTRA LETTER-ARIA* no. 9, of 20 January 1764. (This ran for two years from 1763 to 1765.) Baretti here criticizes *An Essay on The Revolutions of Literature* by Signor Carlo Denina, Professor of Eloquence and Belles-Lettres in the University of Turin arguing the superiority of the Scots historians of the eighteenth century.

Mallet wrote good English, and I remember that Richardson, author of the famous *Pamela*, used to say that Mallet was the only Scotchman who never confused 'shall' and 'will' in the future tense.... Smollet [*sic*], or Smolett, as Signor Denina spells it, the translater of *Don Quixote* and author of *Roderick Random* and some other novels, has been much praised, though I cannot remember whether in the *Monthly* or the *Critical Review*, but has written nothing whatever to bring him real fame.[1] This is the information I can give Signor Denina about contemporary Scotch writers. Let him show it to his English friends, and he will find it rather nearer the truth than what he has given his countrymen in his Essay, on the authority of some Scotchman.

NOTE

1 Denina's remarks on Smollett are in ch. XI, section 11 of his *Essay* where he writes: 'Dr Smollett might have proved an admirable historian, had he preferred, as is the duty of every ingenious man, future glory to present gain.'

67. [John Berkenhout] on Smollett's *Travels*

June 1766

From *The Monthly Review*, June 1766, xxxiv, 419–29. The review is by John Berkenhout (1731?–91), a medical doctor and miscellaneous writer, who wrote mostly on medical and military matters. The following extracts comprise his introductory and concluding remarks; he also gives descriptive accounts of the contents of each letter of the *Travels*, which are here omitted.

Travels, more than any other Species of writing, seem calculated to afford both instruction and entertainment; and yet nothing can be more insipid, tedious and uninteresting than the remarks of the generality of travellers. The English are beyond all doubt the greatest travellers in the world; for in all places on the continent, which are frequented by strangers, we find the number of Englishmen greatly to exceed that of all other nations taken together. Hence it were natural to expect a constant inundation of *written* travels, especially through France and Italy. Nevertheless we have but few books of this kind, in proportion to the number of travellers; and among these few books, very inconsiderable is the number of those which are worth reading. The reason is plain: our travellers are in general young men of fortune, and are led by their tutors; and both of them, from the youth of one and the narrow education of the other, are as incapable of observation as if they were conducted through France and Italy blindfold. For want of that knowledge, steadiness, sagacity, and penetration, which can be only founded on study, and ripened by experience, they traverse the continent in a continued mist, gaping staring, blundering along, and viewing every object in a false light. This however is by no means the case of the Author now before us. He hath not travelled without a previous acquaintance with mankind; and his abilities, as a writer, are universally known.

Dr Smollett's travels appear in the form of letters from different part of the continent, written, or supposed to be written, to his friends in England. The Doctor's motives for undertaking this journey we learn from his first epistle, which is dated *Boulogne sur Mer*, June 23, 1763. 'You knew (says he) and pitied my situation, traduced by malice, persecuted by faction, abandoned by false patrons, and overwhelmed by the sense of a domestic calamity, which it was not in the power of fortune to repair. You know with what eagerness I fled from my country as a scene of illiberal dispute and incredible infatuation, where a few worthless incendiaries had, by dint of perfidious calumnies and atrocious abuse, kindled up a flame which threatened all the horrors of civil dissension.'—'My wife earnestly begged I would convey her from a country where every object served to nourish her grief: I was in hopes that a succession of new scenes would engage her attention, and gradually call off her mind from a series of painful reflections; and I imagined the change of air, and journey of near a thousand miles, would have a happy effect upon my own constitution.' Prompted by these considerations, the Doctor, his lady, two young ladies and a servant, embark at Dover for Boulogne, where, after a rough passage of eight or nine hours, they arrive early in the morning. Having been imposed on by the skipper, the Doctor, for the benefit of future travellers, writes thus: 'When a man hires a packet-boat from Dover to Boulogne, let him remember that the stated price is five guineas; and let him insist upon being carried into the harbour in the ship, without paying the least regard to the representations of the matter, who is generally a little dirty knave.' After remaining three days in a bad inn at Boulogne, our travellers removed into private lodgings in the same place, paying at the rate of three guineas per month for very good accommodations in a house tolerably furnished.

[quotes extensively from the *Travels*]

Letter XLI. Boulogne June 13, 1765. In this epistle, which is the last in the book, the Doctor continues to complain of the inconveniencies of travelling in France, and concludes, that posting is much more convenient and reasonable in England. Our carriages and horses are much better, and our drivers more obliging and alert, owing to the possibility, if we are ill-used at one inn, of being accommodated at another. The Doctor, throughout his whole journey, had very frequent disputes with landlords, postmasters, and postilions, which must certainly have rendered his tour much less agreeable than it otherwise might have been. Of this he seems convinced; for in this letter he is of opinion, that the only method of travelling with any degree of comfort, is to submit to imposition, and to stimulate those who serve you by extraordinary gratifications. We cannot take leave of the Doctor without thanking him for the entertainment we have received in the perusal of his travels; which, as they are the work of a man of genius and learning, cannot fail of being useful and instructive, particularly to those who intend to make the same tour.

68. Unsigned notice of Smollett's *Travels*

1766

From *The London Magazine or Gentleman's Monthly Intelligencer*, XXXV, 1766, 243-9.

We are assured our readers will reap equal satisfaction with ourselves in the perusal of Dr Smollett's travels through France and Italy; on which account we shall give them, now and hereafter, some extracts from that performance, which bespeaks the scholar and the gentleman. Here no affected, pert journalist presents his crude observations; every thing is the product of learning and experience, and that thorough knowledge of mankind which the Dr is well known to have acquired. The whole is wrote in a very familiar and agreeable stile, in the form of letters. This publication may be of infinite service to our country, by giving some check to the follies of our Apes, male and female, of French fashions and politeness, with whom we are over run; and of such beings as the Dr in his twenty-ninth letter thus describes:

[the remainder of the notice consists of extensive quotations of Letters XXIX and VII from the *Travels*]

69. Unsigned review of Smollett's *Travels*

May 1766

From *The Royal Magazine*, XIV, 1766, 233.

From a writer of *Dr Smollett's* genius, judgement, and taste, the reader will naturally expect to meet with a fund of instructive and entertaining particulars in these *Travels*; and we will venture to assure him that he will not be disappointed, as they are replete with new, curious, valuable, and interesting observations on the manners, customs, religion, policy, commerce, arts, and antiquities of every place the ingenious author visited in his tour, conveyed in a familiar style, in a series of letters. Amidst such agreeable variety, it is difficult to select an extract: however, we shall give the Doctor's severe, but just character of the French, as a sufficient specimen of the spirited, agreeable manner in which he has communicated his remarks.

[quotes *Travels*, Letter VI, pp. 48–51]

70. Smollett compared with Marivaux

September 1766

From *The British Magazine*, September 1766, VII, 'A Critical Examination of the Respective Merits of Voltaire, Rousseau, Richardson, Smollett, and Fielding', pp. 460–3.

Page 463:

Such are the modern writers that figure in the higher walks of fiction; (i.e. Voltaire, Fielding, Richardson & Rousseau) but in both countries, there are many others that move in a subordinite station, and though with but half the praise of any of the former, are yet not without just applause. When we mention Marivaux in France, and Smollett in England, we are of opinion, that our readers who understand both languages will find a likeness. In fact, both have written but one novel of any reputation; the *Paysan Parvenue* of France, and *Roderic Random* here, being what has formed their respective fame. Marivaux is natural, so is the other, but with this difference, that the French writer dives more deeply into the human mind, and exhibits its operations with profounder skill. In a word, the writers of both nations, now, have a much greater likeness than in the earlier ages of taste....

71. 'Mercurious Spur' in *The Race*
1766

From Cuthbert Shaw, *The Race* (2nd ed., enlarged, 1766), reprinted in *The Repository: Or, Weekly General Entertainer*, 1790, vol. 2, pp. 242–3 and 266.

Cuthbert Shaw (1738–71), under the pseudonym 'Mercurius Spur', ridicules Smollett in verses in imitation of Pope's *Dunciad*. For Shaw see Eric Partridge, *Poems of Cuthbert Shaw and Thomas Russell*, 1925.

From pp. 242–3:

> Next Smollett came. What author dare resist
> Historian, critic, bard, and novellist?
> 'To reach thy temple, honour'd Fame,' he cried,
> 'Where, where's an avenue I have not tried?
> But since the glorious present of today
> Is meant to grace alone the poet's lay,
> My claim I wave to ev'ry art beside,
> And rest my plea upon the Regicide
> . . . .
> . . . .

But if, to crown the labours of my Muse,
Thou unauspicious, should'st the wreath refuse
Who'er attempts it in this scribbling age,
Shall feel the Scottish pow'rs of Critic rage,
Thus spurn'd, thus disappointed of my aim,
I'll stand a bugbear in the road to Fame;
Each future minion's infant lores undo,
And blast the budding honours of his brow.'
He said—and, grown with future vengeance big,
Grimly he shook his scientific wig.
To clinch the cause, and fuel add to fire,
Behind came Hamilton, his trusty squire.
A while *he* paus'd revolving the disgrace,
And gath'ring all the horrors of his face;
Then rais'd his head, and turning to the sound,
Burst into bellowing, terrible and loud.
'Hear my resolve, and first by G–d swear—
By Smollett, and his gods; who'er shall dare
With him this day for glorious fame to vie,
Sous'd in the bottom of the ditch shall lie;
And know, the world no other shall confess
Whilst I have crab-tree, life, or letter-press.'
Scar'd at the menace, *authors* fearful grew,
Poor Virtue trembled, and e'en Vice look'd *blue*.

From p. 266:

Smollett stood grumbling by the fatal ditch;
Hill call'd the Goddess whore, and Jones a bitch;
Each curs'd the partial judgement of the day,
And, greatly disappointed, sneaked away.

72. Philip Thicknesse on the *Travels*

1766

From Philip Thicknesse, *Observations on the Customs and Manners of the French Nation. In a Series of Letters*, 1766, pp.

90–1. This was reviewed by *The Critical Review* unfavour-
ably, and Thicknesse, blaming Smollett, returned to his
attack on Smollett and *The Critical Review* editors in his *Useful
Hints To Those Who Make a Tour of France*. 1768, (see passim).
In his *A Year's Journey Through France and Part of Spain*, 2 vols,
Dublin, 1777, Thicknesse moderates his criticism of Smollett
(see below, extract 2).

1.

According to Mr Smollett's account of a Nation improved, perhaps
since Lord Bolingbroke resided among them, a man may as well
eat with the dogs of Greenland, or drink urine with the civilized
inhabitants of Kamschatka, as eat an olio of mortified flesh, dirt and
tobacco, with a Parisian of the present age. But I will venture to
say, that either the Doctor has kept very bad company, or his own
ill state of health and want of appetite, or both together, have been
the means of warping his judgement, and corrupting his own
imagination. To read the account given of the King's Bench Prison
in the *History of Sir Launcelot Greaves*, and that of a *Journey Through
France*, a man would be inclined to prefer a twelvemonth's
residence in that University, rather than live the same time among
the Hottentots of Paris or Nice; and yet I believe the author of that
romance is better able to give a just account of the King's College[1]
in the Borough, from three months residence there, than to give a
character of a most extensive kingdom from having resided
eighteen months at Nice.

2.

Could Dr Smollett rise from the dead, and sit down in perfect
health, and good temper, and read his travels through France and
Italy, he would probably find most of his anger turned upon
himself. But, poor man! he was ill; and meeting with, what every
stranger must expect to meet, at most French inns, want of
cleanliness, imposition, and incivility; he was so much disturbed by
those incidents, that to say no more of the writings of an ingenious
and deceased author, his travels into France, and Italy, are the least
entertaining, in my humble opinion, of all his works.

NOTE

1 A reference to Smollett's imprisonment in 1760 for the libel of Admiral Knowles. Thicknesse, like Smollett, had served three months in the King's prison, for libel.

73. Madame Riccoboni on Smollett's *Travels*

14 November 1767

From *The Private Correspondence of David Garrick*, 2 vols, 1831–2, vol. II, p. 524. Garrick's French correspondent here inveighs against nationalist prejudice in Smollett's *Travels Through France and Italy*, 1766. Here translated from the French.

Smollett is a 'charming author'—a low knave who's no better acquainted with the *mores* of his own country than with those of France, and all of whose works are loathsome—I said loathsome.

74. Oliver Goldsmith on Smollett's *Tears of Scotland*

1767

From *The Beauties of English Poesy*, selected by Oliver Goldsmith, 1767. In his critical notes Goldsmith made this comment on Smollett's poem.

This ode, by Dr Smollett, does rather more honour to the author's feelings than his taste. The mechanical part, with regard to numbers and language, is not so perfect as so short a work as this requires; but the pathetic it contains, particularly in the last stanza but one, is exquisitely fine.

75. Laurence Sterne on 'Smelfungus'

1768

From Sterne's *A Sentimental Journey*, 2 vols, 1768, pp. 28–9, the famous passage in which Sterne responds to the splenetic distemper of Smollett's *Travels* (see Sterne's footnote.)

I pity the man who can travel from *Dan* to *Beersheba*, and cry, 'Tis all barren—and so it is; and so is all the world to him who will not cultivate the fruits it offers. I declare, said I, clapping my hands chearily together, that was I in a desert, I would find out wherewith in it to call forth my affections—if I could not do better, I would fasten them upon some sweet myrtle, or seek some melancholy cypress to connect myself to—I would court their shade, and greet them kindly for their protection—I would cut my name upon them, and swear they were the loveliest trees throughout the desert: if their leaves withered, I would teach myself to mourn, and when they rejoiced, I would rejoice along with them.

The learned SMELFUNGUS travelled from Boulogne to Paris—from Paris to Rome—and so on—but he set out with the spleen and jaundice, and every object he passed by was discoloured or distorted—He wrote an account of them, but 'twas nothing but the account of his miserable feelings.

I met Smelfungus in the grand portico of the Pantheon—he was just coming out of it—'*Tis nothing but a huge cock pit*,[a] said he—I wish you had said nothing worse of the Venus of Medicis, replied I—for in passing through Florence, I had heard he had fallen foul upon the goddess, and used her worse than a common strumpet, without the least provocation in nature.

I popped upon Smelfungus again at Turin, in his return home; and a sad tale of sorrowful adventures had he to tell, 'wherein he spoke of moving accidents by flood and field, and of the cannibals which each other eat: the Anthropophagi'—he had been flea'd alive, and bedeviled, and used worse than St Bartholomew, at every stage he had come at—

—I'll tell it, cried Smelfungus, to the world. You had better tell it, said I, to your physician.

Mundungus, with an immense fortune, made the whole tour; going on from Rome to Naples—from Naples to Venice—from Venice to Vienna—to Dresden, to Berlin, without one generous connection or pleasurable anecdote to tell of; but he had travelled straight on, looking neither to his right hand or his left, lest Love or Pity should seduce him out of his road.

Peace be to them! if it is to be found; but heaven itself, was it possible to get there with such tempers, would want objects to give it—every gentle spirit would come flying upon the wings of Love to hail their arrival—Nothing would the souls of Smelfungus and Mundungus hear of, but fresh anthems of joy, fresh raptures of love, and fresh congratulations of their common felicity—I heartily pity them: they have brought up no faculties for this work; and was the happiest mansion in heaven to be allotted to Smelfungus and Mundungus, they would be so far from being happy, that the souls of Smelfungus and Mundungus would do penance there to all eternity.

NOTE

a *Vide* S—'s *Travels.*

76. Unsigned notice of *Adventures of an Atom*

8–11 April 1769

From *The London Chronicle*, 1769, 1922, noticing the anonymously published *Atom*.

This work, which is attributed to the Author of *Roderick Random*, is a satirical political history of the publick transactions, and of the characters and conduct of some great men in a certain kingdom, to which the Author has given the name of Japan, during the late and present reigns.

77. Unsigned review of *Adventures of an Atom*

April 1769

From *The Gentleman's Magazine*, XXXIX, 1769, 200–5.

This work is rather an history and adventures related by an atom than an account of it's own successive progress through various bodies, of which it composed a part.

The supposed editor, Nathaniel Peacock, an haberdasher of St Giles's, declares, that as he was sitting alone in his garret, he heard a shrill small voice, proceeding, as he thought, from a crack in his own pericranium, calling him by his name; that upon his answering to the voice, in the utmost horror and amazement, it proceeded to this effect.

[quotes from *Atom* (as appended to *Sir Launcelot Greaves* in the Shakespeare Head edition), pp. 300–1]

Mr Nathaniel Peacock at the atom's command became amanuensis, and recorded what is contained in this book.

The revolutions of this Atom in the island of Japan are not enumerated, but it's progress from Japan to the pericranium of Nathaniel Peacock, is thus related.

[quotes from *Atom*, pp. 302–3]

The political anecdotes are in substance as follows:

About the middle of the most considerable of three periods, into which Japan is usually divided, called *Foggien*, when that nation was at peace with all her neighbours, Mercury having undertaken to exhibit a mighty nation governed by the meanest intellects that could be found in the ropository of preexisting spirits he infused into the mass destined to sway the sceptre, at the very moment of conception, the spirit which had been expelled from a goose that was killed to regale the mother. The animalcule thus inspired was born, and succeeded to the throne under the name of *Got-hama-baba*. He was in his life and conversation still a goose. He was rapacious, shallow, hot-headed, and perverse; he had an understanding just sufficient to appear in public without a slavering-bib; and he was without sentiment or affection, except a blind attachment to the worship of the White Horse, to whom the Japonese had erected a temple, called *Fakkubasi*. Of all his recreations, that which he most delighted in was the kicking the breech of his prime minister, an exercise which he performed in private every day; it was therefore necessary that a minister should be found to undergo this operation without repining: This circumstance having been foreseen by Mercury, he, a little after the conception of *Got-hama-baba*, impregnated the ovum of a future minister, and implanted in it a soul which had successively passed through the bodies of an ass, a dottrel, an apple-woman, and a cowboy. Tutors were provided for him, but his genius was not capable of cultivation: he was called Faka-kaka, and caressed as the heir of an immense fortune. His character was founded upon nagatives, he had no understanding, no oeconomy, no courage, no industry, no steadiness, no discernment, no vigour, no retention: He was reputed generous, and good humoured, but he was really profuse, chicken-hearted, negligent, fickle, blundering, weak and leaky. All these qualifications were agitated by an eagerness, haste and impatience, that completed the most ludicrous composition which human nature ever produced. He appeared always in hurry and confusion, as if he had lost his wits in the morning, and was in quest of them all day.

Such were *Got-hama-baba*, the emperor of Japan, and *Faka-kaka*, his prime-minister. Among the subordinates to *Faka-kaka*, was *Sti-phi-rum-poo*, who from a lawyer became a lord. *Nin-kom-poo-po*, who from an inferior nation, having taken a rich prize, became commander of the fleet, and *Foksi-Roku*, a man of more sense than all the rest put together, but bold, subtle, interested, insinuating, ambitious, and indefatigable, a latitudinarian in principles, a libertine in morals, without birth, fortune, character or interest: He had risen by sagacity, assurance and perseverance, proof against all disappointment and repulse.

Foksi-Roku hovered between the triumvirate just mentioned, and another knot of competitors for the adminstration, that is in fact, for the empire, headed by *Quamba-cun-dono*, a great *Quo*, or lord, related to the emperor, who bore supreme command in the army, and was called *Fatzman*, by way of eminemce. This accomplished prince had not only the greatest mind, but the largest body of all the subjects in Japan.

With the *Fatzman* was connected *Gotto-mio*, vice-roy of Xicoco, one of the islands of Japan, weak, wealthy, proud, intractable, irrascible, and universally hated.

There was also one *Soo-san-sin-ho*, who was president of a council of twenty-eight, that assisted the emperor: He was a shrewd politician, had great learning, and true taste; but he loved to enjoy the comforts of life, and therefore with more parts than all, was more a cypher than any.

The author proceeds to relate some historical incidents, relating to an attack made by the Chinese upon a foreign territory belonging to Japan, called *Fatsisio*, in which the Japonese were great sufferers.

When the news of these disasters arrived, great commotion arose in the council. The Dairo Got-hama-baba fluttered, and clucked and cackled and hissed like a goose disturbed in the act of incubation. Quamba-cun-dono shed bitter tears: The Cuboy snivelled and sobbed: Sti-phi-rum-poo groaned Gotto-mio swore:

but the sea Sey-seo-gun, Nin-kom-poo-po underwent no alteration. He sat as the emblem of insensibility, fixed as the north star,
and as cold as that luminary, sending forth emanations of frigidity.

The first astonishment of the council was succeeded by critical
remarks and argumentation. The Dairo consoled himself by
observing, that his troops made a very soldierly appearance as they
lay on the field in their new cloathing, smart caps, and clean
buskins; and that the enemy allowed they had never seen beards
and whiskers in better order. He then declared, that should a war
ensure with China, he would go abroad and expose himself for the
glory of Japan. Foksi-roku expressed his surprise, that a general
should march his army through a wood in an unknown country,
without having it first reconnoitered: but the Fatzman assured him,
that was a practice never admitted into the discipline of Japan.
Gotto-mio swore the man was mad to stand with his men, like
oxen in a stall, to be knocked on the head without using any means
of defence. 'Why the devil (said he) did not he either retreat, or
advance to close engagement with the handful of Chinese who
formed the ambuscade?' 'I hope, my dear Quanbuku, (replied the
Fatzman) that the troops of Japan will always stand without
flinching. I should have been mortified beyond measure, had they
retreated without seeing the face of the enemy:——that would
have been a disgrace which never befel any troops formed under
my direction; and as for advancing, the ground would not permit
any manoeuvre of that nature. They were engaged in a *cul de sac*,
where they could not form either in hollow square, front line,
potence, column or platoon.——It was the fortune of war, and
they bore it like men:——we shall be more fortunate on another
occasion.' The president Soo-san-sin-o, took notice, that if there
had been one spaniel in the whole Japonese army, this disaster
would not have happened; as the animal would have beat the
bushes and discovered the ambuscade. He therefore proposed, that
if the war was to be prosecuted in Fatsissio, which is a country
overgrown with wood, a number of blood-hounds might be
provided and sent over, to run upon the foot in the front and on the
flanks of the army, when it should be on its march through such
impediments. Quamba-cum-dono declared, that soldiers had much
better die in the bed of honour, then be saved and victorious, by
such an unmilitary expedient: that such a proposal was so contrary
to the rules of war, and the scheme of enlisting dogs so derogatory

from the dignity of the service, that if ever it should be embraced, he would resign his command, and spend the remainder of his life in retirement. This canine project was equally disliked by the Dairo, who approved of the Fatzman's objection, and sealed his approbation with a pedestrian salute of such moment that the Fatzman could hardly stand under the weight of the compliment. It was agreed that new levies should be made, and a new squadron of Fune equipped with all expedition; and thus the assembly broke up.

After many miscarriages, the administration was at length called to answer for itself before the tribunal of the populace.

At this time, says the author, there was one Taycho, who had raised himself to great consideration in this self-constituted college of the mob. He was distinguished by a loud voice, an unabashed countenance, a fluency of abuse, and an intrepidity of opposition to the measures of the Cuboy, who was far from being a favourite with the plebeians. Orator Taycho's elequence was admirably suited to his audience; he roared, and he brayed, and he bellowed against the m——r: He threw out personal sarcasms against the Dairo himself. He inveighed against his partial attachment to the land of Yesso, which he had more than once manifested to the detriment of Japan: he inflamed the national prejudice against foreigners; and as he professed an inviolable zeal for the commons of Japan, he became the first demagogue of the empire. The truth is, he generally happened to be on the right side. The partiality of the Dairo, the errors, absurdities, and corruption of the ministry, presented such a palpable mark as could not be missed by the arrows of his declamation. This Cerberus had been silenced more than once with a sop; but whether his appetite was not satisfied to the full, or he was still stimulated by the turbulence of his disposition, which would not allow him to rest, be began to shake his chains anew, and open in the old cry; which was a species of musick to the mob, as agreeable as the sound of a bagpipe to a mountaineer of North-Britain, or the strum-strum to the swarthy natives of Angola. It was a strain which had the wonderful effect of effacing from the memory of his hearers, every idea of his former fickleness and apostacy.

Got-hama-baba had a farm among the Tartars of Yesso, which he inherited by lineal descent, and valued more than all his regal possessions in Japan; this farm was now in danger of invasion by the Chinese, and Got-hama-baba was doubtful whether his subjects would willingly enter into a continental war for its defence he sounded them upon the subject, and found them vehemently against it.

[quotes from *Atom*, pp. 353–4]

In the mean time, however, Got-hama-baba's apprehensions for the farm encreased, not only on account of the Chinese, but of one Brut-an-tiffi, a tartarian free-booter, who hovered about it with very threatening appearances. Got-hama-baba now foamed and raved, and cursed and swore; he not only kicked, but cuffed the whole council of twenty-eight, and played at foot-ball with his imperial Fiara. The council, in the midst of the confusion which different opinions produced, were suddenly surprized at the apparition of Taycho's head nodding from a window that overlooked their deliberations. At the sight of this horrid spectacle, the council broke up, and the unfortunate Faka-kaka only, whose fear made him incapable of motion, was left behind. Taycho then bolted in at the window, and accosted him in these words, 'It depends upon the Cuboy, (Minister) whether Taycho continues to oppose his measures, or become his most obsequious servant: look upon the steps by which I have ascended.' Accordingly Faka-kaka looked, and saw a multitude of people who had accompanied their orator into the palace court, and raised for him an occasional stair of various implements. The first step was an old fig-bex, the second a night-man's bucket, the third a cask of hempseed, the fourth a tar barrel, the fifth an empty kilderkin, the sixth a keg, the seventh a bag of soot, the eighth a fishwoman's basket, the ninth a rotten pack-saddle, and the tenth a block of hard wood from Fatsisio; it was supported on one side by a varnished letter-post, and on the other by a crazy hogshead: the artificers who erected this climax, and exulted over it with hideous clamour, were grocers, scavengers, halter-makers, draymen, distillers, chimney-sweepers, oyster-women, ass-drivers, aldermen, and dealers in waste-paper. Faka-kaka having considered this work with astonishment, and heard the populace swear that they would exalt their orator above all competition, was again addressed by Taycho: You see, says he, it will signify nothing to strive against the torrent—admit me to a share of the administration; I will become your slave, and protect the farm at the expence of Japan to the last Oban.

Taycho's offer was accepted, and soon after, to shew his power over the many headed monster, he, without scratching it's long ears or tickling it's nose, or drenching it with gin, or making the least apology for his acting in direct opposition to the principles which he had inculted all his life, crammed down it's throat an obligation to pay a yearly tribute to Brut-an-tiffi, in consideration of his forbearing to seize Got-hama-baba's farm; a tribute which amounted to seven times the value of the lands for the defence of which it was paid, and the beast, far from shewing any signs of breathing, closed its eyes, opened his hideous jaws, and as it swallowed the inglorious bond, wagged its tail, in token of intire satisfaction:

Brut-an-tiffi, was now become the good ally of Got-hama-baba, yet his farm soon after fell into the hands of the Chinese. Taycho, still embarrassed, engaged to recover it, and told the people in plain terms, that they should part with their substance and their senses, their bodies and their souls, to defend and support Brut-an-tiffi. The hydra, rolling itself in the dust, turned up its huge unweildy paunch, wagged its forky tail, licked the feet of Taycho, and through all its hoarse discordant throats began to bray applause, and the sacrifice was immediately made.

Several expeditions to the coast of China were performed by Taycho for the monster's amusement, the issue, indeed, as might be expected, was loss of money, and credit, and life; but though the beast was at first disposed to be unruly, and began to growl, yet Taycho having drenched it with a double dose of Mandragora, it brayed aloud, Taycho for ever! rolled itself up like a lubberly hydra, yawn'd and fell asleep.

Some time after, however, fortune seemed to favour Japan against China, and Taycho therefore determined to secure the honour by taking the whole management of the war upon himself: One day in council, when the Dairo was present, he, instead of giving his opinion, presented a two-penny trumpet to the illustrious Got-hama-baba for his amusement, a sword of ginger-bread, covered with leaf gold: to the Fatzman, and a rattle to Fika-kaka the Cuboy: at the same time without ceremony, he tied, a scarfe round the eyes of his imperial majesty, and producing a number of padlocks, sealed up the lips of every lord in the council, before they could recover from their first astonishment, and the assembly broke up abruptly.

The emperor, was at length reconciled to his hood-winked state, but the farm still lying heavy at his heart, he neglected his sword and his trumpet, and no longer took any pleasure in kicking his Cuboy, and in a short time took to his bed and died.

Taycho immediately mounted the beast Legion, and rode to the habitation of Gio-gio, the successor of Got-hama-baba, whom he found attended by Yak-Strot, a native of the Mountains of Ximo, who had superintended his education, deeply engaged in drawing plans of windmills.

Soon after a peace was proposed: Taycho arrogated to himself the province of settling the articles of treaty, and broke it off because the emperor would not engage to drive some troops that acted against Brut-an-tiffi, from one or two of his villages, of which they had got possession.

Upon breaking off this treaty, the court of China, piqued at the insolence with which it had been treated by Taycho, formed a new alliance with the king of Corca, whom Taycho had also insulted in the person of his ambassador.

Japan having now a new enemy to grapple with, and Brut-an-tiffi being on the brink of ruin, Taycho knowing that if he continued longer in office, he must lose his popularity, contrived a quarrel with the council, as a pretence to throw it up.

He proposed, in presence of the Dairo, to take the ships of Corca, as those of China had been taken before, without any declaration of war; pretending that by this measure, the treasures of Corca would be directly brought into the ports of Japan, though this treasure existed only in his own fiction, and the imagination of those, upon whom he succeeded in his imposition.

The council and Dairo, not immediately and implicitly acquiescing in this project, Taycho bit his thumb at the president, forked out his fingers on his forehead at Gotto-mio; wagged his under jaw at the Cuboy; snapped his fingers at Sti-phi-rum-poo; grinned at Nin-kom-poo-po, made the sign of the gallows at Foksi-roku, and then turning to Yak-Strot, he clapped his thumbs in his ears, and began to bray like an ass; finally, pulling out the badge of his office, he threw it at the Dairo, who, in vain, entreated him to be pacified, and wheeling to the right, stalked away, clapping his hand upon a certain part that shall be nameless.

He then applied to the blatent beast, boasting his merit, and complaining, that this project, which would have ruined Corca, and enriched Japan, had been overruled by the influence of

Yak-Strot; he retired to a cell in the neighbourhood of the city, and employed the common cryer to proclaim it about the streets, that being reduced to the meer necessaries of life, he would sell his ambling mule and furniture, with an ermine robe of his wife's, and the greater part of his kitchen utensils. The mobile, though it was well known that Taycho was worth more than 20,000 obans, cryed shame, that a man that saved the nation, should be reduced to so cruel a distress, and their clamour soon rung in the ears of Gio-gio, and his favourite.

To soothe the monster, and at the same time ruin Taycho's popularity he was offered a pension: he took it, but the monster was not soothed, nor did Taycho become unpopular, he continued to tickle the monster and embroil the state. The negociation for peace was at length renewed, and a treaty concluded, every seperate article of which was stigmatized by Taycho and his instruments, in which they succeeded, though every body knew, that the terms which Taycho himself had prescribed the year before, were in every respectless honourable and advantageous.

Taycho, among other expedients, engaged a profligate Bouze, who had been degraded for his leud life, to write certain metrical incantations to fascinate the beast, and one Jan-ki-dzin, who having been reduced to low circumstances by debauchery, had made advances to Yak-Strot, who rejected them, to throw balls of filth, which he had an excellent art in making, at Yak-Strot, and all who had not abetted Taycho and his measures.

Jan-ki-dzin, arrived at such a pitch of insolence, that he armed some of his balls at the Dairo himself, and one of them taking place between his eyes, defiled his whole visage.

Had the laws of Japan been executed in all their severities, this audacious plebeian, says our author, would have been crucified on the spot; but Gio-gio, being good-natured to a fault, contented himself with ordering some of his attendants to set him in the stocks, after having seized the whole cargo of filth, which he had collected at his habitation for the manufacture of his balls. Legion immediately released him by force, and hoisting him on their shoulders, went in procession through the streets, hollowing, huzzaing, and extolling him, as the palladium of the liberty of Japan. But the monster's officious zeal on this occasion, was far from being agreeable to Mr orator Taycho, who taking umbrage at the exaltation of his dirt thrower, devoted him from that moment to destruction.

The author traces the fortunes of this new favourite of the beast, no farther than his escape into China: but he gives an account of the retreat of Yak-Strot, from his publick station, of whom he gives this character.

[quotes from *Atom*, pp. 484–5]

The author concludes his work by an account of the beast's untractableness, with respect to all who mounted him after Taycho, and some transactions relating to a tax laid upon the inhabitants of Fatsisio.

The folly of the multitude, and the knavery of pretenders to patriotism, are ridiculed in this little work with great spirit and humour; but there is a mixture of indelicacy and indecency, which though it cannot gratify the loosest imagination, can scarce fail to disgust the coarsest.

78. Unsigned review of *Adventures of an Atom*

May 1769

From *The Critical Review*, XXVII, 1769, 362–9.

This satire unites the happy extravagance of Rabelais to the splendid humour of Swift. The reader needs only to peruse a few pages to perceive that it alludes to this present age; though, we will not say, to this country. The author takes advantage of Pythagorism to endue his atom with reason and organs of speech, which he exerts in the brain of Mr Nathaniel Peacock, who died in the parish of Islington, on the 5th day of April last, and lies buried in that church yard, in the north-west corner, where his grave is distinguished by a monumental board, inscribed with the following tristich:

> Hic, haec, hoc,
> Here lies the block
> Of Old Nathaniel Peacock

As we write only from conjecture, we shall not be excessively positive (though we think we are pretty sure) that the Island of Japan, where the chief scene of the atom's adventures lie, is no other than that of Great-Britain; and our opinion is chiefly founded upon the following character which the author draws of the Japonese.

[quotes *Adventures of an Atom*, vol. I, pp. 303–6]

It is possible that a speculative, philosophical reader, who seldom or never enters into the bustle of life, and whose nerves are too delicate for extravagant objects, may think the above character overloaded with satire. A reader who knows life, and who has observed what has passed in this island within the space of two years past, must think that the author's pencil, if it has a fault, errs on the side of delicacy. We will venture, however, to pronounce, that it is more characteristically true than any picture ever drawn of a certain people, and that ridicule and reality are here blended together with inimitable art and originality.

When we carry in our eye, that our author's Cuboy is the first minister of state; that the Fakku-basi, or the temple of the white-horse, denotes a certain electorate, we have an inexhaustible fund of entertainment; and while we disapprove of the severity with which a certain respectable character is drawn, we cannot help being secretly pleased with the justness of certain outlines.

Few readers can be at a loss in recognizing the following character.

[quotes 'Of all his recreations' to 'last of the intestines', vol. I, pp. 309–12]

If we except the forbidding aspect, which was far from being the case, and which our author seems to have called in to aid the deception, the following character is so very descriptive of a deceased noble lawyer who is supposed to be one of the Cuboy's assistants, that it cannot be mistaken.

[quotes 'The most remarkable of these' to 'at certain seasons of the year', vol. I, pp. 320–2]

The character of a first lord of the N——y, likewise deceased, and certain ministers of state, both dead and living, are drawn in the same high style of recognizable caricature; but we have many reasons for avoiding particulars.——Supposing that the land of Yesso signifies G——y, few readers can mistake the following portrait.

[quotes 'There was one Taycho' to 'fickleness and apostacy', vol. I, pp. 349–50]

The character of Brut-an-tiffi, a warlike German potentate, is finished to the highest perfection; but that of the London mob exceeds all description, both for humour and justness.

We are unwilling to be more particular in our account of this truly original piece of humour, for reasons that may be easily guessed: but we must conclude, by saying as Shakespeare does of music, that the man who does not love and relish this performance, has no wit in his own composition.

79. [John Hawkesworth], review of *Adventures of an Atom*

June 1769

From *The Monthly Review*, June 1769, XL, 441–55.

Hawkesworth (1715?–73), one-time editor of *The Gentleman's Magazine*, wrote revised accounts of recent voyages to the South Seas for the Admiralty from 1771.

The history is in substance as follows: The atom, after having passed through several vicissitudes in the island of Japan, was enclosed in a grain of rice, eaten by a Dutch mariner at Ferando, brought as a particle of his body to the Cape of Good Hope, discharged there in a scorbutic dysentery, taken up in a heap of soil to manure a garden, raised to vegetation in a sallad, devoured by an English supercargo, brought to London, amputated with a diseased part of his body, thrown upon a dunghill, gobbled up by a duck, of which one Ephraim Peacock having eaten plentifully at a feast of the cordwainers, it was mixed with his circulating juices, and fixed in the principal part of that animalcule, which in process of time expanded itself into a son of Ephraim called Nathaniel Peacock. Nathaniel became at length a haberdasher in St Giles's: the atom was lodged in his pineal gland; and one night, as he was musing in his garret, called him three times by his name. Nathaniel answered with great fear and astonishment, and the atom, having discovered its nature and situation, told him, that, for the instruction of British ministers, it would communicate some political anecdotes, of which it became conscious in Japan. Nathaniel, having recovered from his fright, became amanuensis to the atom, and the political anecdotes which were thus dictated and recorded, make the substance of this work.

Nothing however, could bear less resemblance to it, than a concise epitome of the events, taken out of the terms in which they are related; our account therefore must of necessity consist chiefly of extracts, which we shall select as judiciously as we can.

The Author's description of the Japonese, whose political history he gives, is in these terms:

[quotes from *Atom*, pp. 303–5]

The Author having characterised the chiefs who disputed the administration, or, in other words, says he, the empire of Japan, proceeds to relate some historical incidents. He gives an account of some encroachments made by the Chinese on the Japonese settlements; of the king's kicking his ministers all round on hearing the news; of the capture of Chinese vessels by the advice of Sti phi-rum-poo, previous to a declaration of war; and of some disadvantages suffered by the Japonese troops that were sent to repress the foreign incroachments of the Chinese.

[quotes from *Atom*, pp. 337–9]

The author proceeds to give an account of an attack made by the Chinese upon an island called Motao, of a fleet sent out under

Admiral Bihn-gho to assist the governor, of the miscarriage of the measure, and the sacrifice that was made of Bihn-gho, who, by the advice of Foksi-roku was made the scape goat of the administration. 'Bhin-gho, says the Author, underwent a public trial, was unanimously found guilty, and unanimously declared innocent; by the same mouths condemned to death, and recommended to mercy; but mercy was incompatible with the designs of the administration.'

Subsequent miscarriages producing yet greater confusion among the people, the conduct of administration was summoned before the venerable tribunal of the populace.

[quotes from *Atom*, p. 349 and following, with extracts to conclusion of novel]

There is much spirit, humour and satire in this piece; but there is also much nastiness and obscenity: of that kind, however, which is disgusting, and consequently not pernicious. There are also some inconsistencies, to which works of fiction are very liable; but which the best writers have been extremely careful to avoid.

In the beginning of the first volume the Atom declares that Fate determined it should exist in the empire of Japan a thousand years ago; that it continued to undergo various vicissitudes there, till a few years before it entered the body of Ephraim Peacock at a city feast, who transmitted it to his son, the supposed recorder of these events: yet in the beginning of the second volume, the same Atom declares that it constituted a part of one of Richard the IIId's yeomen at the battle of Bosworth. There are many inaccuracies of style and expression; but it would be treating a hasty performance of this kind too severely to point them out.

80. Notice of *Adventures of an Atom*

1769

From *The Town and Country Magazine*, 1769, I, 269, from the section 'Accounts of Books and Pamphlets.'

A Sarcastic production in imitation of Rabelais and Swift, meant to lash the m——rs, politics, and parties of a certain island; and is executed with much genuine wit, and original humour.

81. Unsigned review of *Humphry Clinker*

June 1771

From *The London Chronicle*, 15–18 June 1771, 2264, 580.

The chief Characters in this entertaining work are Mr Bramble, a worthy, but capricious, elderly Gentleman: Mrs Tabitha Bramble his Sister, a cross old Maiden; Miss Lydia Melford Mr Bramble's Niece; Mr James Melford his Nephew; both under the guardianship of Bramble; and Humphry Clinker, a distressed Post-Chaise Driver, who is taken into the service of Mr Bramble, &c. all which characters are well drawn, in a series of letters.

Previous to Humphry Clinker's being introduced to the Reader, several letters pass between different persons, from one of which the following passages are taken.

[quotes from *Clinker*, vol. I, pp. 71–7, quoting J. Melford's account of James Quinn in a letter of 30 April from Bath]

82. Unsigned review of *Humphry Clinker*

June 1771

From *The London Magazine*, XL, 1771, 317–19.

Dr Smollett's reputation is so justly established, particularly in the walk of novel-writing, that very little need be said to recommend the present performance to the public. Yet, though we have read it with much satisfaction, we cannot pretend to say it is wholly without imperfections: the title is certainly an improper one, because Humphrey Clinker is one of the least considerable in the whole catalogue of persons; there is besides, no great contrivance in the plan, nor any thing extremely interesting in the incidents. The characters, however, are marked with all that strength of colouring, for which Smollet's pencil is deservedly celebrated; and the reader is either continually entertained with some whimsical relation, or what is still better, instructed with some original remarks upon men and things, that do honour to the good-sense and humanity of the author.

The chief characters of this novel are, Mr Bramble, a Welch old batchellor of great benevolence and extensive understanding: He has a sister, an old maid, the very reverse of himself in the amiable particulars we have mentioned, together with a niece and a nephew both under age, to whom he is guardian. Having a desire for a journey into Scotland, he goes from Bath to London, and thence northwards accompanied by this family and their domestics. Previous to the tour, Miss Melford, his niece, discovers prepossession for a strolling player, which nearly involves her brother in a duel, and excites the displeasure of her uncle and aunt; but promising never more to hold the smallest intercourse with Mr Wilson, the actor, she is forgiven, and our travellers proceed in as much harmony as the irrascibility of Mrs Tabitha Bramble will admit, who is generally miserable herself, or endeavouring to make others miserable. On the road, this virago quarrelling with one of the servants, Humphrey Clinker, a poor country fellow, pickt up in a stable-yard, is engaged through necessity in his room; and though at first strongly disliked by the old maid, becomes a remarkable favourite in consequence of being a very warm methodist. The description of Scarborough, Harrowgate, and the various places through which the family pass in their way to Scotland, as well as in their return, constitutes from this period the chief part of the expedition, and the whole is concluded by a marriage between Miss Melford and Mr Wilson, who turns out a gentlemen of fortune; with another marriage between Mrs Tabitha and one Lismahago, a Scotch lieutenant on half pay, a very extraordinary personage; and a third between Tabitha's woman, Winifred Jenkins, and Humphrey Clinker, who proves in the catastrophe a natural son to Mr Bramble.

From these materials the reader will see, that much of the dreadful dangers, the surprizing escapes, the deep distresses, and the romantic passions which characterize our modern novel-writers, is not to be expected in this performance; in fact, it is something greatly preferable to a novel; it is a pleasing, yet an important lesson on life; and that part of it which describes the Scotch nation, is at once calculated to entertain the most gay, and to give the most serious a very useful fund of information. Having said this, we shall make no apology for laying before our readers a letter (the work is written in the epistolary manner) from Mr Bramble to his friend Dr Lewis in Glamorganshire.

[quotes from *Clinker*, vol. II, pp. 36–42, giving the whole of Bramble's letter Edinburgh, 18 July]

83. Unsigned notice of *Humphry Clinker*

June 1771

From *The Town and Country Magazine*, III, 323. This did not normally review fiction. On p. 317 ff. of this issue, they quoted two letters from *Humphry Clinker* giving 'satirical descriptions of London and Bath'.

The author of this production has so completely established his reputation as a novel writer, that to say this performance is not inferior to any of his former pieces, will be a sufficient recommendation of the work. In this opinion we have laid before our readers two extracts, *page* 317.

84. Unsigned review of *Humphry Clinker*

July 1771

From *The Court and City Magazine*, II 1771, 310–12.

This work is written in a series of letters, the principal personages are, Mr Bramble, worthy misanthropical old gentleman; Mrs Tabitha, his sister, a cross old maid; Miss Lydia Melford, his niece, and Jeremy Melford, a young Oxonian, his Nephew, to both of whom Mr Bramble is guardian; with a Mr Dennison, Miss Melford's lover; and Humphry Clinker, a poor honest post-chaise boy. The scene lies in Gloucester, Bath, London, Edinburgh, Glasgow, etc. The characters are strongly marked in point of spirit and humour, and supported with great propriety. Old Bramble is a curious original, and does honour even to the pen of Dr Smollett. The following satirical description given by this honest cynic of the manner of living in London, after he has expatiated upon the happiness of a country life, will give the reader some idea of his character.

[quotes from *Clinker*, vol. I, pp. 168–172, quoting letter of Bramble, London, 8 June.]

Some farther Extracts from this performance, which, excepting some few *indelicate* passages, appears well calculated for the instruction and entertainment of the reader, will be given in a future Magazine.

85. Unsigned review of *Humphry Clinker*

July 1771

From *Every Man's Magazine, or The Monthly Repository, of Science, Instruction and Amusement*, 1771, I, 33–4.

Three little pocket volumes having lately made their appearance under the title of *The expedition of Humphry Clinker*, ascribed to the pen of the celebrated *Dr Smollett*; the attention of the curious has been attracted to this performance by the literary reputation of the author—the following extract is therefore given, in compliance with the taste of the public for this kind of writing, but we are sorry to say there are many reasons which point out the prudence of the Doctor in not placing his name to the title page. His descriptions are partial, exaggerated, and ill-natured, particularly with respect to the city of London. Of the capital of his native country, the reader will find, he gives a more favourable account, than any that has yet appeared.

[quotes from *Clinker*, vol. II, pp. 36–42, quoting Bramble's letter from Edinburgh, 18 July]

86. Unsigned review of *Humphry Clinker*

July 1771

From *The Gentleman's Magazine*, XLI, 317–21.

This work is by no means a novel or romance, of which Humphry Clinker is the hero; Humphry makes almost as inconsiderable a figure in this work as the dog does in the history of Tobit: nor is it indeed principally a narrative of events, but rather a miscellany containing dissertations on various subjects, exhibitions of character, and descriptions of places. Many of the characters are drawn with a free but a masterly hand; in some particulars perhaps they are exaggerated, but are not therefore the less entertaining or instructive: Some appear to be pictures of particular persons, but others of human nature, represented indeed in individuals peculiarly distinguished, but drawn rather from imagination than life. Some, however, are as extravagant as fancies of Calot, but though they do not less deviate from nature, their irregularities discover the same vivacity and spirit.

In this part of the work consists its principal excellence, and its principal defect is the want of events. The whole story might be told in a few pages, and the author has been so parsimonious of his invention, that he has twice overturned a coach, and twice introduced a fire, to exhibit a scene of ridiculous distress, by setting women on their heads, and making some of his dramatic characters descend from a window by a ladder, as they rose out of bed.

It is by no means deficient in sentiment, and it abounds with satire that is equally sprightly and just. It has, however, blemishes, which would be less regretted where there was less to commend. In the celebrated treatise on the art of sinking in poetry, under the article stile, the incomparable author considers one, which on account of the source whence it is derived, he calls the *prurient*; there is another stile, which with respect to its source, may justly be termed the *stercoraceous*. The stercoraceous stile would certainly have found a place in the art of sinking, if it had been then to be found in any author not wholly contemptible. But it was not then in being; its original author was Swift, the only writer who had ever made nastiness the vehicle of wit: since his time they have frequently been confounded, and by those who could not distinguish better, the nastiness has been mistaken for the wit: Swift therefore has been imitated in this particular by those who could imitate him in nothing else; and others have, under the sanction of Swift, taken the liberty to be filthy, who were under no necessity to seek occasions for wit in an hospital or a jakes.

The stile of this work is frequently *stercoraceous*, and sometimes it is also *prurient*. The *prurient* however is as harmless as the *stercoraceous*, as it tends much more to chill than to inflame every imagination, except perhaps those of the thieves and bunters in Broad St Giles's, to whom the coarsest terms being familiar, they convey sensual ideas without the antidote of disgust.

Among other parts of this work which might have been spared, is the description of several places both in England and Scotland that are well known; but among the pictures of life, which may serve as monitors of the supine and thoughtless, the extravagant and the vain, is the following, which is inserted at once as specimen and recommendation of the work. It is part of a letter from one of the principal characters, a satyrical but benevolent man, between 50 and 60, now on a journey to the north of England, to a friend of his youth in London.

[quotes from *Clinker*, vol. II, pp. 136–42, quoting Bramble's letter of 30 September]

87. John Gray on *Humphry Clinker*

8 July 1771

John Gray in a letter from London to Smollett in Italy. From Lewis Melville, *The Life and Letters of Tobias Smollett (1721–1771)*, 1926, pp. 249–50. Gray was the author of a 12-volume *History of the World* published in 1767, and translations of the *Odes and Epistles of Horace* (1778).

I have read the *Adventures of Humphry Clinker* with great delight, and think it calculated to give a very great run, and to add to the reputation of the author, who has, by the magic of his pen, turned the banks of Loch Lomond into classic ground. If I had seen the MS. I should like to have struck out the episode of Mr Paunceford.[1] The strictures upon Aristarchus are but too just; shallow judges, I find, are not so well satisfied with the performance as the best judges, who are lavish in its praises. Your half-animated sots say they don't see the humour. Cleland gives it the stamp of excellence, with the enthusiastic emphasis of voice and fist; and puts it before anything you ever wrote. With many, I find, it has the effect of exciting inquiries about your other works, which they had not heard of before. I expected to have seen an account of it in both *Reviews*, but it is reserved for next month.

NOTE

1 See *Humphry Clinker*, vol. I, pp. 95–9, quoting Jeremy Melford's letter from Bath, 10 May.

88. Unsigned review of *Humphry Clinker*

August 1771

From *The Monthly Review*, August 1771, XLV, 152.

Some modern wits appear to have entertained a notion that there is but one kind of *indecency* in writing; and that, provided they exhibit nothing of a lascivious nature, they may freely paint with their pencils dipt in the most odious materials that can possibly be raked together for the most filthy and disgusting colouring.—These nasty geniuses seem to follow their great leader, Swift, only in his obscene and dirty walks. The present Writer, nevertheless, has humour and wit, as well as grossness and ill-nature.—But we need not enlarge on his literary character, which is well known to the public. *Roderick Random* and *Peregrine Pickle* have long been numbered with the best of our English romances. His present work, however, is not equal to these; but it is superior to his *Ferdinand Fathom*, and perhaps equal to the *Adventures of an Atom*.

89. Unsigned review of *Humphry Clinker*

August 1771

From *The Critical Review*, XXXII, 1771, 81–8.

Though novels have long since been divested of that extravagance which characterised the earlier productions in Romance, they have, nevertheless, continued, in the hands of meaner writers, to be distinguished by a similarity of fable, which, notwithstanding it is of a different cast, and less unnatural than the former, is still no less unfit for affording agreeable entertainment. From the wild excursions of fancy, invention is brought home to range through the probable occurrences of life; but, however, it may have improved in point of credibility, it is certainly too often deficient with regard to variety of adventure. With many, an adherence to simplicity has produced the effects of dulness; and, with most, too close an imitation of their predecessors has excluded pleasure of novelty.

The celebrated author of this production is one of those few writers who have discovered an original genius. His novels are not more distinguished from the natural management of the fable, and a fertility of interesting incidents, than for a strong, lively, and picturesque description of characters. The same vigour of imagination that animates his other works, is conspicuous in the present, where we are entertained with a variety of scenes and characters almost unanticipated. Thus, in particular, Mr Bramble, Mrs Tabitha Bramble, and lieutenant Lismahago, are painted with the highest touches of discriminating humour and expression. As to Humphry Clinker, he is only to be considered as the nominal hero of the work. The inimitable descriptions of life, which we have already observed to be so remarkable in our author's works, receives, if possible, an additional force from the epistolary manner in which this novel is written; which is farther enhanced by the contrasts that arise from the general alternating insertions of the letters of the several correspondents. The following epistle places the character of Mr Bramble in a light, at once so amiable, so distressful, and so ludicrous, that we shall extract it, for the entertainment of our readers:

[quotes from *Clinker*, vol. I, pp. 29–32, letter of J. Melford, Hot Well, 20 April]

The letters from Mr Bramble, and Mr Melford, his nephew, upon their expedition to North Britain, contain so many interesting observations, that they must not only gratify every reader of curiosity, but also tend to correct many wrong notions concerning that part of the Island. We would willingly give an account of many of the particulars related of Edinburgh and its inhabitants, but as our readers are probably less acquainted with the manners of the people farther North, we shall extract the representation which is given of the oeconomy in the house of a Highland gentleman:

[quotes from vol. II, pp. 72–6, letter of J. Melford, Argyleshire, 3 September]

We should deprive our readers of a prospect of, perhaps, one of the most beautiful rural scenes that exist in nature, did we not produce the account of the waters of Leven, with Dr Smollett's description of it, in a highly poetical Ode. We find, from another passage in the work, that Lough Lomond, from whence the river Leven issues, is a body of pure highland water, unfathomably deep in many places, six or seven miles broad, and four and twenty miles in length. This contains above twenty green islands, covered with wood; some of them cultivated for corn, and many of them stocked with red deer.

[quotes from vol. II, pp. 82–5, letter of Matt. Bramble, Cameron, 28 August]

Instead of visionary scenes and persons, the usual subjects of Romance, we are frequently presented with many uncommon anecdotes, and curious expressions of real life, described in such a manner as to afford a pleasure even superior to what arises from the portraits of fancy. We are every where entertained with the narration or description of something interesting and extraordinary, calculated at once to amuse the imagination, and release the understanding from prejudice. Upon the whole, the various merits of this production might raise to eminence a writer of inferior reputation to that of this celebrated author; and we should have indulged ourselves in extracting more copiously from it, were we not certain that the original must come into the hands of all such as are readers of taste, by whom we may venture to affirm it will be ranked among the most entertaining performances of this kind.

90. Obituary verses on Smollett

October 1771

From *The Royal Magazine*, 25 (misnumbered 24), 1771, 656.

On the Report of the Death of Dr SMOLLETT.

Death's *random* darts too certainly transfix,
And souls unwilling Charon's sure to land 'em;
Ah, take some gloomier soul to gloomy Styx,
And give us back facetious *Roderick Random*.

91. Unsigned review of *Humphry Clinker*

November 1771

From *The Universal Magazine*, XLIX, 1771, 256–7.

The Captain finding Mr Crab in the library reading, according to custom, asked him if he had got any thing new. Yes, says Mr Crab, it is *The Expedition of Humphry Clinker*. And how do you like it, says the Captain? I am sorry to say, replied Mr Crab, that I am greatly disappointed—I expected something better from the author of *Roderick Random*. It seems to me to be exceptionable in every thing but the style and language—Humphry Clinker is a lusus naturae a kind of human animal that never existed but in the brain of the author. Indeed he figures so seldom in the business of the drama, and furnishes so little entertainment to his guest the reader, that the book might as well have been intitled *The Feast of Duke Humphry*. Mr Bramble, who, it must be confessed, has some originality about him, is represented as a man of sense and erudition; and, he is the principle conduit-pipe, through which our author conveys his own real sentiments of men and things.

He makes a tour from Gloucester to Bristol—Bath and London. In these three great cities, so renowned, so celebrated all over Europe for their trade, riches, magnificence, &c. Mr Bramble can find nothing to commend, but much to blame and condemn. Bristol-wells is a stinking dog-hole—A miserable hospital for wretched incurables. The new building at Bath are tasteless, inconvenient, and crouded upon one another, like the houses of cards built by children. Their amusements are irrational—The ill-breeding of such a motly mixture of people insufferable—And the noise, nonsense and knavery, not to be borne by any man of common sense. London, forasmuch as it exceeds the other two cities in size and circumference, excels them in every thing that is eminently pernicious both to body and mind. The air is not fit to breathe, the water to drink, nor the bread to eat. The first becomes noxious by being frequently respired through putrid lungs, or contaminated with the infectious effluvia of old venereal ulcers, &c. The second is an infusion of dead carcasses, human excrement, and the poisonous sweepings of mechanics shops and warehouses. The third is a mixture of chalk, allum, and bone-ashes. The butter is manufactured with candle-grease and kitchen-stuff. But his analysis of London milk comprehends such an assemblage of filth and nastiness, as nothing but the stream down Snow-hill, in Swift's Description of a City Shower, can equal. The provisions in general are sophisticated, and rendered so destructive to health, that a foreigner (from this account) would think it impossible for a human being to survive six months within the bills of mortality.

This most unfaithful portrait of poor Old England does mend a little upon us, when Mr Bramble quits London to travel north-wards, though we find matters queer enough in Northumberland, and even amongst his own relations. For he says, that hospitality, which is constantly in the mouth of every Englishman, is no where so little practiced as in England; and, that if a Frenchman, German, or Italian, should come over to visit a Gentleman in London, whom he had entertained at his house abroad in the genteelest manner, the Islander would carry him to the Saracen's-head or Blue-boar, and make him pay his share of the reckoning.

I was at a loss to guess at the author's drift and design, till Mr Bramble had crossed the Tweed; and then I found that England was sacrificed, and, as it were, thrown into shadow, in order to bring the mother-country forwards, and shew her in a more brilliant light. Every thing between the Tweed and the Orkneys is inchanting—The houses magnificent—The people polite, and their entertainments elegant. When he calls Edinburgh a hot bed of genius, I was inclined to think he meant some sarcasm, alluding to the rich manure that is nightly ejected from every window into the streets of that famous city. But when I saw the respectable names of the two Humes, Robertson, Wilkie, &c. I dropped the thought, and adopted the metaphor. However, it must be acknowledged, that great ingenuity and a most pregnant imagination were necessary, to draw so many beautiful pictures from the contemplation of so barren a subject.

I am the more displeased with this flagrant partiality to Scotland, as I fear it will tend rather to widen than heal the breach that at present subsists betwixt the South and North Britons, whom every lover of his country would wish to see united without distinction or difference.

Setting aside this objection, I think the book abounds in many masterly strokes, and has a great deal of merit; though I hate that Hottentot, Captain Lismahago; and the ridiculous letters of Mrs Tabitha Bramble, and her maid Jenkins, are too childish to amuse the meanest capacity.

92. Richard Brinsley Sheridan on novels and romances

1772

From *The Letters of Richard Brinsley Sheridan*, ed. Cecil Price, Oxford, 1966, vol. I, pp. 61–2, letter of 30 October 1772 to Thomas Grenville. Thomas Grenville (1755–1846) was a book-collector and statesman.

For my own Part when I read for Entertainment, I had much rather view the characters of Life as I would wish they *were* than as they *are*: therefore I hate Novels, and love Romances. The Praise of the best of the former, their being *natural*, as it is called, is to me their greatest Demerit. Thus it is with Fielding's, Smollett's etc. Why should men have a satisfaction in viewing only the mean and distorted figures of Nature? tho', truly speaking not of Nature, but of Vicious and corrupt Society. Whatever merit the Painter may have in his execution, an honest mind is disgusted with the Design.

93. John Hall Stevenson—a pun on Smollett

1772

From John Hall Stevenson, *Makarony Fables*, Dublin, 1772 pp. 75–6. The title is described as *Mock scholastic or hermetic society. The Franciscan Makaronies of Medenham. Satiric poems by one of their members, Cosmo* (i.e. Stevenson). The extract is from the satiric poem 'Queries To The Critical Reviewers'.

Stevenson (1718–85) was a close friend of Sterne and the leader of the so-called 'Demoniacs' who gathered at his house to talk, drink and examine his library.

POSTSCRIPT.

My Compliments to Doctor S.
To whom this Postscript I address.

Physician, Critick, and Reformer,
Expounder both of Dream and Riddle,
Historian and chief Performer
Upon the Caledonian Fiddle!
Master of Dedication Sweet,
Renown'd Translator of Translations—
That like old Cloaths in Monmouth-street
Display their glittering Temptations—
You are so us'd to a Northern Trammel
You cannot enter into Lyric Fable,
One might as well expect to see a Camel
Pass through a Needle's Eye into a Stable:
And therefore I am forc'd to study
To find out something you can understand,
Pleasant and fresh, tho' somewhat muddy;
Just like the Mug of Porter in your Hand.
And yet, when all is said and done,
This something's nothing but a Pun.

A PUN.

You are so very good at Smelling,
For we have often heard you tell it,
I wonder you don't change your Spelling
And write yourself Professor Smellit.

94. A dispute about the ethical qualities of Smollett's novels

1773

From *The Monthly Ledger*, I, 1773, 389 and 461. The first extract is under the signature of 'Nestor' and the rejoinder to it is by 'Caution'.

Many novels are justly censured, as turning the brains of weak readers with idle romantic notions, fitted for some fairy land, but not current in that we inhabit: but these are not what I mean. The novels of Le Sage, Fielding, and Smollett, are not liable to this objection: in them the pencil of nature and dictates of prudence are united.—

Of this number I cannot but reckon what the entertaining author of the 'Scattered remarks' has observed, on the novels of Smollett and Fielding. This ingenious gentleman seems, in this point, to have quite forgotten the *utile*; for neither the 'history nor the ethics' of the first appear to me calculated either 'to enlarge the ideas or refine the mind,' if, by this, real improvement is to be understood. Although he was a man of sense and humour, the moroseness of his temper made him look on the worst side of every thing, and he has represented human nature accordingly. But, though he has painted vice in strong, and even glaring, colours, it does not seem to be done with a view to condemn it; for he no where forms the necessary contrast, by giving us virtuous examples to follow; without which the most entertaining novel cannot improve, and will only serve to familiarize the mind of the reader with folly and vice. If to these considerations be added the excessive profanity of this author's novels, I think we may fairly pronounce them absolutely unfit for the perusal of youth, or even of mature age without the greatest caution.

95. [Ralph Griffiths], review of Smollett's *Ode to Independence*

December 1773

From *The Monthly Review*, December 1773, XLIX, 500. The other poet referred to here is probably William Mason (1725–97).

Men of the most liberal minds are the most smitten by the claims of independency; and no man was ever more sensible of their power, than the late ingenious Dr Smollett;—who adored the goddess with unfeigned devotion and celebrated her praises in the pure dictates of his heart.

Mason's Ode to Independence is elegant, but cold; Smollett's glows with that enthusiams which, it might be imagined, the subject would never fail to kindle.

Independency, however, is not a female deity in Smollett's poem; though a goddess in Mason's performance.

After describing, with great vigour of fancy, and with very poetical colouring, the birth and attributes of the Son of Liberty, the poet proceeds to celebrate the atchievements [*sic*] of this demi-god, in support of the glorious cause of his celestial mother:

[quotes Smollett's *Ode*]

For the authenticities of this piece, we must depend on the credit of the bookseller; exclusive of the internal evidence, which, we believe, will suffice for the satisfaction of those who are acquainted with the peculiar spirit and show of the Doctor's poetical vein.

96. Andrew Henderson, an attack on Smollett

1775

From Andrew Henderson, *A Second Letter to Dr SAMUEL JOHNSON* etc. *With An impartial Character of Doctor Smollet*, 1775, pp. 12–14.

Henderson (1734–75), author and bookseller, published *Letters* in 1775 attacking Samuel Johnson for his *Tour in the Hebrides*.

Tobias Smollett, son to the (goodman) i.e. farmer of Unghern, in the shire of Dumbarton, was a man of very little learning, and always remarkable for perverseness, obstinacy, and revenge. Being an apprentice to a Surgeon at Glasgow, he eloped from his master, went abroad as third mate to a Surgeon in 1739, but soon took to another trade; for returning with a creole to Britain, he commenced Doctor, Man-midwife, Historian, and Romancer at Chealsea, where every Sunday, his assistants criticized the monthly sixpenny pamphlets, heard the decisions of their host, and then retired with horror and ridicule.

In 1753, he was found guilty of a cowardly assault upon an innocent man, Mr Patrick Gordon, the real compiler of *Roderick Random*, and striking the man after he was down; he was afterwards found guilty of writing a libel against Admiral Knowles, fined and confined three months to the prison of the King's Bench for his pains; he was fluctuating in his friendship, and if an enemy his tender mercies were cruel; a sanguine temper appears in all he has done; his characters as of William I. are contrasts to themselves; that of King John the granter of magna charta, contains thirteen epithets, each blacker than another, while that of Mary Queen of Scots is a profusion of encomium. His account of the Duke of Cumberland's conduct in Scotland is shocking; 'for fifty miles round all was silence, horror and desolation'? whereas there was scarce a hut pulled down, a stone displaced, or a person killed who was not actually in arms, even on the day of the battle of Culloden, much less afterwards, nor have I the least reason to alter the account contained in my history of the rebellion, a book which underwent five editions, and was first published by Mr Griffiths Anno 1748, when he invited me to write the history of Scotland.

Smollets disposition was roving and unsettled; nor had he judgment to investigate a matter with sagacity: however, he had some humour, but then it was of a kind ludicrously cruel, and if once prejudiced he would propogate with his utmost dexterity of insinuation, a report hurtful to the innocent, would first condemn anonymous productions, and then ascribe them possitively to people who did not know what size they were of: However it is a kind of honour to his tomb, that it was taken notice of by Doctor Samuel Johnson, the man who could represent an island as an entire square, which in many places is actually indented with Bays.

97. A biographical and critical view

1775

From *The Westminster Magazine, or The Pantheon of Taste*, III, 1775, 225–8. An anonymous memoir of Smollett, with critical comments on the novels. The first extended biographical/critical account, it was reproduced in *The Annual Register* for 1775, and incorporated into what Bouce calls 'the first genuine life of Smollett prefixed to the 1777 edition of his *Plays and Poems*'. The Prefatory material to this latter provides the substance of all subsequent biographical/ critical writing on Smollett until the 1820 edition of Robert Anderson's *Miscellaneous Works of Tobias Smollett*, 6th edn.

It is generally said, that the Lives of Literary Men can be little more than an enumeration and account of their Works. There have been few men of real genius who have written more voluminously than

Dr Smollett; yet the foregoing observation will by no means apply to him. On the contrary, he has himself wrought up the incidents of his own life, at least the earliest part of it, in one of the most entertaining Novels that ever appeared in any language. Everybody knows I must mean *Roderick Random*; a book which still continues to have a most extensive sale, and first established the Doctor's reputation. All the first volume, and the beginning of the second, appears to consist of real incident and character, tho' certainly a good deal heightened and dignified. The Judge, his grandfather; *Crab* and *Potion*, the two apothecaries; and *Squire Gawky*; were characters well known in that part of the kingdom where the scene was laid. Captains *Oakhum* and *Whiffle*, Doctors *Macshave* and *Morgan*, were also said to be real personages; but their names we have either never learnt, or have now forgotten. A Bookbinder and Barber long eagerly contended for being shadowed under the name of *Strap*. The Doctor seems to have enjoyed a peculiar felicity in describing these Characters, particularly the Officers and Sailors of the Navy. His *Trunnion*, *Hatchway*, and *Pipes*, are highly-finished originals: but what exceeds them all, and perhaps equals any character that has yet been painted by the happiest genius of ancient or modern times, is his *Lieutenant Bowling*. This is indeed Nature itself; original, unique and *sui generis*. As well as the ladder of promotion, his very name has long become proverbial for an honest blunt seaman, unacquainted with mankind and the ways of the world.

It is pretty surprising that, notwithstanding Dr Smollett was so very successful in hitting off original characters in narration, he could never succeed in the Drama. Very early in life he wrote a Tragedy, entitled, *The Regicide*, founded on the story of the assassination of James I, of Scotland; which with all his interest and address he never could get represented on the Stage. He afterwards published it by subscription; with what success we cannot now recollect: but we are much mistaken if he has not alluded to some of his own Theatrical occurrences, in the story of *Melopyne*, in *Roderick Random*.

By the publication of that Work the Doctor had acquired so great a reputation, that henceforth a certain degree of success was insured to everything known or suspected to proceed from his hand. In the course of a few years, *The Adventures of Peregrine Pickle* appeared; a Work of great ingenuity and contrivance in the composition, and in

which an uncommon degree of erudition is displayed; particularly
in the description of the entertainment given by the Republican
Doctor, after the manner of the Ancients. Under this personage the
late Dr *Akenside*, author of a famous Poem, entitled, *The Pleasures
of the Imagination*, is supposed to be typified; and it would be
difficult to determine whether profound learning or genuine
humour predominate most in this Episode. Butler and Smollett
seem to be the only two who have united things seemingly so
discordant, happily together; for *Hudibras* is one of the most learned
works in any language; and it requires no common share of
reading, assisted with a good memory, thoroughly to relish and
understand it. Another Episode of the *Adventures of a Lady of
Quality*, likewise inserted in this Work, contributed greatly to its
success, and is indeed admirably well executed. Yet, after giving all
due praise to the merit and invention displayed in *Peregrine Pickle*,
we cannot help thinking it is inferior, in what may be called *naïvete*,
a thing better conceived than expressed, to *Roderick Random*.

These were not the only original compositions of this stamp,
with which the Doctor has favoured the Public. *Ferdinand Count
Fathom* and *Sir Launcelot Greaves* are still in the list of what may be
called *reading Novels*, and have gone through several editions; but
there is no injustice in placing them in a rank far below the former.
No doubt invention, character, composition, and contrivance, are
to be found in both; but then situations are described which are
hardly possible, and characters are painted, which, if not altogether
unexampled, are at least incompatible with modern manners; and
which ought not to be, as the scenes are laid in modern times.

The last Work which we believe the Doctor published, was of
much the same species, but cast into a different form—*The
Expedition of Humphry Clinker*. It consists of a series of letters,
written by different persons to their respective correspondents. He
has here carefully avoided the faults which may be justly charged to
his two former productions. Here are no extravagant characters nor
unnatural situations. On the contrary, an admirable knowledge of
life and manners is displayed; and most useful lessons are given
applicable to interesting, but to very common situations.

We know not that ever the remark has been made, but there is
certainly a very obvious similitude between the characters of the
three heroes of the Doctor's chief productions. *Roderick Random*,
Peregrine Pickle, and *Matthew Bramble*, are all brothers of the same

family. The same satirical, cynical disposition, the same generosity and benevolence, are the distinguishing and characteristical features of all three. But they are far from being servile copies or imitations of each other. They differ as much as the *Ajax*, *Diomed*, and *Achilles* of Homer. This was undoubtedly a great effort of genius, and the Doctor seems to have described his own character at the different stages and situations of his life.

He was bred to Physic, and in the early part of his life served as Surgeon's Mate in the Navy. It appears from *Roderick Random*, that he was at the siege of Carthagena; of which expedition he gives a faithful, tho' no very pleasing account. Soon after his return he must have taken his degree of Doctor of Physic, tho' we have not been able to learn at what time and at what place. It is said, that, before he took a house at Chelsea, he attempted to settle as practitioner of physic at Bath; and with that view, wrote a Treatise on the Waters—but was unsuccessful: chiefly because he could not render himself agreeable to the Women, whose favour is certainly of great consequence to all candidates for eminence, whether in Medicine or Divinity. This, however, was a little extraordinary; for those who remember Dr Smollett at that time, cannot but acknowledge that he was as graceful and handsome a man as any of the age he lived in; besides, there was a certain dignity in his air and manner which could not but inspire respect wherever he appeared. Perhaps he was too soon discouraged; in all probability, had he persevered, a man of his great learning, profound sagacity, and intense application, besides being endued with every other external as well as internal accomplishment, must have at last succeeded, and, had he attained to common old age, been at the head of his profession.

Abandoning Physic altogether as a profession, he fixed his residence at Chelsea, and turned his thoughts entirely to writing. Yet, as an author, he was not near so successful as his happy genius and acknowledged merit certainly deserved. He never acquired a Patron among the Great, who by his favour or beneficence relieved him from the necessity of writing for a subsistence. The truth is, Dr Smollett possessed a loftiness and elevation of sentiment and character which appears to have disqualified him from currying favour among those who were able to confer favours. It would be wrong to call this disposition of his, pride or haughtiness; for to his equals and inferiors he was ever polite, friendly, and generous.

Booksellers may therefore be said to have been his only patrons; and from them he had constant employment in translating, compiling, and reviewing. He translated *Gil Blas* and *Don Quixote* both so happily, that all the former translations of these excellent productions of genius are in a fair way of being superseded by his. His name likewise appears to a translation of Voltaire's Prose Works, but little of it was done by his own hand; he only revised it, and added a few Notes. He was concerned in a great variety of compositions. His *Historie of England* was the principal work of that kind. It has in itself real intrinsic merit; but considering the time and circumstances in which it was written, it is indeed a prodigy of genius, and a great effort of application. It had a most extensive sale, and the Doctor is said to have received 2000 l. for writing it and the Continuation. He was employed, during the last years of his life, in abridging the *Modern Universal History*, great part of which he had originally written himself, particularly the Histories of France, Italy, and Germany. He lived nearly to complete this Work, and it is said it will soon be published.

In the year 1755 he set on foot the *Critical Review*, and continued the principal manager of it, till he went abroad for the first time in the [year] 1763. To speak impartially, he was, perhaps, too acrimonious sometimes in the conduct of that Work, and at the same time too sore, and displayed too much sensibility when any of the unfortunate authors whose Works he had, it may be, justly censured, attempted to retaliate. He had made some very severe strictures on a pamphlet published by Admiral Knowles, as well as on the character of that gentleman, who commenced a prosecution against the Printer, declaring he only wanted to know the Author, that if a gentleman, he might obtain the satisfaction of a gentleman from him. In this affair the Doctor behaved with great spirit. Just as sentence was going to be pronounced against the Printer, he came into Court, avowed himself the Author, and declared himself ready to give the Admiral any satisfaction he chose. The Admiral forgot his declaration, and began a fresh action against the Doctor, who was found guilty, find 100 l. and condemnd to three months imprisonment in the King's-Bench. It is there he is said to have written *The Adventures of Sir Launcelot Greaves*; in which he has described some remarkable characters, then his fellow-prisoners.

When Lord Bute was called to the chief administration of affairs, he was prevailed upon by him to write in defence of his measures;

which he did in a Weekly Paper, called *The Briton*. This gave rise to the famous *North-Briton*; wherein, according to the opinion of the Public, he was rather baffled. The truth is, the Doctor did not seem to possess the talents necessary for political altercation. He wanted temper and coolness. Besides, his patron is supposed to have denied him the necessary information, and to have neglected fulfilling his engagements with him. The Doctor has not forgotten him in his subsequent performances. He is described under the character of *Yak-Strot*, in *The Adventures of an Atom*.

His constitution being at last greatly impaired by a sedentary life, and assiduous application to study, he went abroad for his health in the year 1763. He wrote an account of his travels in a Series of Letters to some friends, which were afterwards published in Two Volumes, Octavo. During all that time he appears to have laboured under a constant fit of chagrin. But the state of his mind will be best learnt from himself. Thus he writes in his first Letter: 'In gratifying your curiosity I shall find some amusement to beguile the tedious hours; which, without some such employment, would be rendered insupportable by distemper and disquiet. You knew and pitied my situation, traduced by malice, persecuted by faction, abandoned by false patrons and overwhelmed by the sense of a domestic calamity, which it was not in the power of fortune to repair.' By this domestic calamity he means the loss of his only child, a daughter, whom he loved with the tenderest affection. The Doctor lived to return to his native country: but his health continuing to decline, and meeting with fresh mortifications and disappointments, he went back to Italy, where he died on October 21, 1771,[1] having been born in the year 1720.

It would be needless to expatiate on the character of a man so well known as Dr Smollett, who has besides given so many strictures of his own character and manner of living in his writings, particularly in *Humphry Clinker*; where he appears under the appellation of Mr *Serle*, and has an interview with Mr *Bramble*; and his manner of living is described in another letter, where *Young Melford* is supposed to dine with him at his house in Chelsea. No doubt he made a great deal of money by his connexions with Booksellers; and had he been a rigid economist, or endued with the gift of retention (an expression of his own), he might have lived and died very independent. However, to do justice to his memory, his difficulties, whatever they were, proceeded not from extravagance or want of economy. He was hospitable, but not ostentatiously so; and his table was plentiful but not extravagant. No doubt he had his failings; but still it would be difficult, to name a man who was so respectable for the qualities of his head, or amiable for the virtues of his heart.

NOTE

1 In fact Smollett died on 17 September 1771.

98. James Beattie on ludicrous compositions

1776

From James Beattie, *Essays*, Edinburgh, 1776. The first extract is from chapter III, 'Incongruity not Ludicrous', section II, sub-section 3, *Pity*, p. 431; the second is from chapter IV, 'An Attempt to Account for the Superiority of the Moderns in Ludicrous Writing', pp. 475–6.

Beattie (1735–1803), distinguished Scots moral philosopher, writer on aesthetics, and friend of Samuel Johnson.

Even pity alone is, for the most part, of powers sufficient to control risibility. To one who could divest himself of that affectation, a wooden leg might perhaps appear ludicrous; from the striking contrast of incongruity and similitude;—and in fact we find that Butler has made both himself and his readers merry with an implement of this sort that pertained to the expert Crowdero; and that Smollett has taken the same freedom, for the same purpose, with his friend Lieutenant Hatchway. But he who forgets humanity so far, as to smile at such a memorial of misfortune in a living person, will be blamed by every good man. We expect, because from experience we know it is natural, that pity should prevail over the ludicrous emotions.

We have a far greater variety of authors to allude to, in the ways of parody and burlesque, than the ancients had; for we have both ancient authors and modern; and to an excessive admiration of the former some late wits have ascribed the origin of a new species of ludicrous character, whereof we have several strong outlines in the travelling physician in *Peregrine Pickle*, and a finished portrait in the *Memoirs of Martinus Scriblerus*. There was indeed, in the days of Horace,[1] a sort of character not unlike this; a set of critics, who, despising the literary productions of their own time, were perpetually extolling the ancient Roman authors, and tracing out divine beauties of style in writings that were become almost unintelligible. But these critics are rather to be ranked with those of our antiquarians who prefer Chaucer and Langland to Dryden and Milton.

NOTE

1 Cites Horace, *Epistola ad Augustam*, 19–27.

99. James Beattie compares *Sir Launcelot Greaves* and *Don Quixote*

1776

From James Beattie, *Essays* (1776), 3rd edn, London, 1779, pp. 323–4, from an 'Essay on Laughter and Ludicrous Composition'.

Sir Launcelot Greaves is of Don Quixote's Kindred, but a different character. Smollett's design was, not to expose him to ridicule; but rather to recommend him to our pity and admiration. He has therefore given him youth, strength, and beauty, as well as courage, and dignity of mind, has mounted him on a generous steed, and arrayed him in an elegant suit of armour. Yet, that the history might have a comic air, he has been careful to contrast and connect Sir Launcelot with a squire and other associates of very dissimilar tempers and circumstances.

100. *The Westminster Magazine* on Smollett's originality

1776

From *The Westminster Magazine*, 1776, IV, 129, from 'An Essay on Novel-Writing', continued in IV, 522.

As *substitutes* for Virtue (almost unanimously neglected by our later Novelists) *Humour* and *Character* appear, who, when led forth by a masterly hand, prove an inexhaustible fund of risibility and entertainment. In these two Dr Smollet particularly excelled: his *Bowling*, *Trunnion*, *Hatchway* and *Pipes*, are truly originals, and real sons of genuine Humour, and will always meet with the plaudits of *Nature* and critical *Discernment*. Nor was he less successful in characters; for it is observable, when men eminent in any station of life were tinctured by strong peculiarities and striking foibles, they were marked by this Author as game, and accordingly introduced to the penetrating eye of a judicious Public. Of this the poetical Dr Akenside[1] remains a melancholy instance, whom Dr Smollet presented to the Public with all the exaggerated colours of invidious caricatura.

The merits of this latter Gentleman as a Novel-Writer, I purpose examining in a future Essay, and comparing him with an Author no less celebrated than himself, namely, Mr Fielding.

Of English Novel-writers, the late Henry Fielding was indisputably the most admirable, and the most natural. All his characters
are from Life, whether humorous or serious; and they are such
correct copies, that we instantly *feel* the resemblance, and either
laugh or weep, think or dissipate, as he thinks proper. Such was the
fidelity and power of his pen, that the original men and women,
with all the events and enterprises that befel them, are immediately
before us; and we are charmed by every stroke, because it is a
transcript from the Volume of Human Nature.

Smollet trod in his steps pretty successfully, deviating from the
path of the common-place Novelists, and giving to his scenes the
recommendation of general similitude to Nature; but his wit is
more elaborate, and his sentiment has less of simplicity, than we
discover in the wit and sentiment of his Master, to whom he must
certainly yield the first place.

I know not if I shall escape censure, were I to allow him to hold
the *second* amongst modern Englishmen. In the opinion of a great
many, Sterne might stand before either. We give him infinite
credit, and infinite tears for his power over our hearts when he
chooses to *melt* them; but surely Fielding and Smollet both know
better how to *tickle* them. Does not Sterne go too far for fun?

NOTE

1 The reference to Akenside is to Smollett's derisive representation of him
(unnamed) in ch. XLVI of *Peregrine Pickle*.

101. On Smollett's *Ode to Independence*

1777

From Tobias Smollett, *Plays and Poems*, 1777, pp. 266–72,
editor unknown. The prefatory *Life of Smollett* and remarks
on the novels are taken from *The Westminster Magazine* article
of 1775 (see No. 97) and in turn provides the substance of

later biographical commentaries. The extract here comments on Smollett's most famous poem.

Lyric poetry imitates violent and ardent passions. It is therefore bold, various, and impetuous. It abounds with animated sentiments, glowing images, and forms of speech often unusual, but commonly nervous and expressive. The composition and arrangement of parts may often appear disordered, and the transitions sudden and obscure; but they are always natural, and are governed by the movements and variations of the imitated passion. The foregoing ode will illustrate these observations.

The Introduction is poetical and abrupt.

> Thy spirit, Independence, let me share!
> Lord of the lion-heart and eagle-eye,
> Thy steps I follow with my bosom bare,
> Nor heed the storm that howls along the sky.

The picture exhibited in these lines is striking, because the circumstances are happily chosen, briefly, and distinctly delineated. It is sublime, because the images are few, and in themselves great and magnificent. The 'lion-heart and eagle-eye' suggest an idea of the high spirit and commanding aspect of Independence: and the poet following with 'bosom bare' denotes, in a picturesque manner, the eagerness and enthusiam of the votary. The last circumstance is peculiarly happy.

> Nor heeds the storm that howls along the sky.

It marks the scene: it is unexpected, and excites surprize: it is great and awful, and exites astonishment. Combined with the preceding circumstance, it conveys a beautiful allegorical meaning; and signifies, that a mind truly independent is superior to adversity, and unmoved by external accidents. We may observe too, in regard to the diction, that the notions of sound and motion communicated by the words 'Howl' and 'along,' contribute, in a peculiar manner, to the sublimity of the description.

> Lord of the lion-heart and eagle-eye,
> Thy steps I follow with my bosom bare,
> Nor heed the storm that howls along the sky.

These lines are written in the true spirit of Lyric poetry. Without preparing the mind by a cool artificial introduction, rising gradually to the impetuosity of passion, they assail the imagination by an abrupt and sudden impulse; they vibrate through the soul, and fire us instantaneously with all the ardour and enthusiasm of the poet. Many of the odes of Horace are composed in the same spirit, and produce similiar effects. Without any previous argument or introduction, in the fulness of passion and imagination, he breaks out in bold, powerful, and impetuous figures.

> Quo me, Bacche, rapis, tui
> Plenum? Quae nemora aut quos agor in specus
> Velox mente nova?————
> Qualem ministrum fulminis alitem————[1]

The poet, full of enthusiasm and admiration, continues his prosopopeia; and, in a strain of poetry exceedingly wild and romantic, gives us the genealogy of Independence.

> A goddess violated brought thee forth,
> Immortal Liberty, whose look sublime
> Hath bleached the tyrant's cheek in every varying clime.

According to the acceptation of our author, Liberty means the security of our lives and possessions, and freedom from external force: Independence is of higher import, and denotes that internal sense and consciousness of freedom which beget magnanimity, fortitude, and that becoming pride which leads us to respect ourselves, and do nothing unworthy of our condition. Liberty therefore is, with perfect propriety, said to be the mother of Independence, and Disdain his father—Disdain arising from indignation against an oppressor, and triumph on having frustrated or escaped his malice. This stern personage is strongly characterized in the following direct description.

> Of ample front the portly chief appear'd:
> The hunted bear supply'd a shaggy vest;
> The drifted snow hung on his yellow beard;
> And his broad shoulders braved the furious blast.

Men may enjoy liberty without independence: they may be secure in their persons and possessions, without feeling any uncommon elevation of mind, or any sense of their freedom. But if their liberty is attacked, they are alarmed, they feel the value of their condition, they are moved with indignation against their oppressor, they exert themselves, and if they are successful, or escape the danger that threatened them, they triumph, they reflect on the happiness and dignity conferred by freedom, they applaud themselves for their exertions, become magnanimous and independent. There is therefore no less propriety in deducing the origin of Independence from Disdain and Liberty, than in fixing the aera of his birth. The Saxons, according to our author, free, simple, and inoffensive, were attacked, escaped the violence of their adversary, reflected on the felicity of their condition, and learned independence.

The education of Independence, and the scene of his nativity, are suited to his illustrious lineage, and to the high achievements for which he was destined.

> The light he saw in Albion's happy plains,
> Where under cover of a flowering thorn,
> While Philomel renewed her warbled strains,
> The auspicious fruit of stol'n embrace was born—
> The mountain Dryads seized with joy,
> The smiling infant to their charge consign'd;
> The Doric muse caressed the favourite boy;
> The hermit Wisdom stored his opening mind.

The imagery in these lines is soft and agreeable, the language smooth, and the versification numerous.

Independence thus descended, and thus divinely instructed and endowed, distinguishes himself accordingly by heroic and beneficent actions.

> Accomplish'd thus, he winged his way,
> And zealous roved from pole to pole,
> The rolls of right eternal to display,
> And warm with patriot thoughts the aspiring soul.

The ode may be divided into three parts. The poet sets out with a brief address to Independence, imploring his protection. He sees, in idea, the high object of his adoration, and, transported by an ardent and irresisible impulse, he rehearses his birth, education, and qualities. He proceeds, in the second place, to celebrate his office and most renowned achievements; and returns, at the end of the third strophe, to acknowledge with gratitude the protection he had requested, and the power of Independence in preserving him untainted by the debasing influences of Grandeur, and the admiration of vain magnificence. Animated with this reflection, and conscious of the dignity annexed to an independent state of mind, he inveighs against those 'Minions of Fortune' who would impose upon mankind by the ostentation of wealth, and the parade of pageantry.

> In Fortune's car behold that minion ride,
> With either India's glittering spoils opprest:
> So moves the sumpter-mule, in harness'd pride,
> That bears the treasure which he cannot taste.
> For him let venal bards disgrace the bay;
> And hireling minstrels wake the tinkling string:
> Her sensual snares let faithless Pleasure lay;
> And all her gingling bells fantastic Folly ring;
> Disquiet, Doubt, and Dread, shall intervene;
> And Nature, still to all her feelings just,
> In vengeance hang a damp on every scene,
> Shook from the baleful pinions of Disgust.

These lines, embellished by fancy, and recommended to the heart by harmony, are the invective of truth and honest indignation.

In the last antistrophe the poet descends from his enthusiasm; he is less impetuous; the illustrious passions that animated and impelled him are exhausted; but they leave his mind full of their genuine and benign influences, not agitated and disordered, as if their tendency had been vicious, but glowing with self-approbation, soft, gentle, and composed.

NOTE

1 Horace, *Odes*, XXV, i, 'Whither, O Bacchus, dost thou hurry me, overflowing with thy power? Into what groves or grottoes am I swiftly driven in fresh inspiration?

102. Unsigned review of Smollett's *Plays and Poems*

July 1777

From *The Monthly Review*, July 1777, LVII, 77, in which the *Regicide* and *Reprisal* are dismissed as 'undramatical' and the poems as 'unequal and incorrect'.

The genius of Dr Smollett was of no inconsiderable character. He was in possession of humour, of a peculiar kind of fancy, of a talent for the description of life and manners, in which he had no contemporary equal, except Henry Fielding.—But he beheld his powers in a light which deceived him. He was capable of delineating the individual object with an happiness, in a secondary degree, his own. But when he aimed at bringing his characters into the business of the stage, and creating a dramatic series of events, his genius, or, at least, his judgment, failed him.

103. William Kenrick reviewing *Plays and Poems*

1777

From *The London Review*, V, 1777, 206–10.

William Kenrick (1725(?)–79), a quarrelsome hack writer who had satirized Smollett in 1752 in his parody *Fun* (see No. 28), here writes more warmly of Smollett.

We have here an elegant edition of Dr Smollett's plays and poems, *The Regicide* a tragedy, *The Reprisal* a comedy, with some satires, elegies, and odes; which serve to shew this ingenious writer to have been no mean versifier, though his modesty did not permit him to boast excellence in that line of his profession. As to the Memoirs of his life, prefixed, they are concise and well enough written: the writer, however, appears to have had chiefly in view, not the character of Doctor Smollett, but that of Mr Garrick; by whom it is more than probable these memoirs were manufactured. At least we conceive no other writer would be so extremely solicitous to exculpate that comedian from the charge, brought against him by Dr S. in regard to his managerial shuffling about the author's tragedy, the Regicide. Whether Mr G. be the writer of the memoirs or not, certain it is that he must have furnished the memorialist with copies of the private letters, here published, admitting them to be genuine copies of the epistolary correspondence between Dr Smollet and Mr Garrick.—The life-writer gives the following account of the origin of the misunderstanding which Dr S. is said to have so sincerely repented.

Very early in life (at the age of eighteen) he wrote a tragedy intitled *The Regicide*, founded on the story of the assassination of James I. of Scotland. In the Preface to the publication of this piece, by subscription in the year 1749, he bitterly exclaimed against false patrons, and the duplicity of theatrical managers. The warmth and impetuosity of his temper hurried him on this occasion into unjust reflections against the late Lord Lyttelton, and Mr David Garrick; the character of the former he satirised in his novel of *Peregrine Pickle*, and he added a burlesque of the monody written by that nobleman on the death of his Lady. Against Mr Garrick he made illiberal illfounded criticisms, and, in his novel of *Roderick Random*, gave a very unfair representation of his treatment of him respecting this tragedy. Of this conduct he afterwards repented and acknowledged his errors, though, in the subsequent editions of the novel, the passages which were the hasty effusions of disappointment are not, as we think they should have been, omitted.

Such omission, indeed, would have been a greater proof of Dr Smollett's conviction of his error than any subsequent encomium on Mr G. in his other works, or any compliment or concession in a private letter to the party traduced. From the known ingenuousness of Dr Smollett's disposition, therefore, it is to be doubted whether his repentance was so sincere as here represented, or that he was so thoroughly convinced his censure had been illiberal or ill-grounded; as in either case we conceive he would have been just enough to have retracted it on the spot. It appears, indeed, that about the time Mr G. brought on our author's comedy, *The Reprisal*; he was put into so good a humour with theatrical managers, as to make a kind of aukward apology for what he had formerly written about them in general, and Mr G. in particular. But the Doctor had, by this time, seen a little more of the world, and been convinced probably of the political expediency of playing the hypocrite with hypocrites, and treating every man in his own way; if, as is also probable, his latter concessions, so inconsistent with the former assertions, were not as much the partial effect of humiliating acknowledgement, as the other of a spirited and just resentment. But Mr G. put out of the question, the life-writer speaks with some judgement and impartiality of Dr S. and his writings: of which he gives us the following particulars:

[quotes here from the preface to *Plays and Poems* on Smollett's novels]

We know not that ever the remark has been made, but there is certainly a very obvious similitude between the three heroes of the Doctor's chief productions. Roderick Random, Peregrine Pickle and Mathew Bramble, are all brothers of the same family. The same satirical, cynical disposition, the same generosity and benevolence, are the distinguishing and characteristical features of all three; but they are far from being servile copies or imitations of each other. They differ as much as the Ajax, Diomed, and Achilles of Homer. This was undoubtedly a great effort of genius; and the Doctor seems to have described his own character at the different stages and situations of his life.

104. [Mrs Anne Grant], a letter on Scotch manners

1778

From *Letters from the Mountains, Being the Real Correspondence of a Lady. Between the Years 1773 and 1807*, by Mrs Anne Grant

(London, 1809), Boston, 1891, vol. I, p. 205. Elsewhere in her letters Mrs Grant refers to a sullen visitor to her region of Scotland whom she calls 'Smelfungus', which was Sterne's name for Smollett in his *Sentimental Journey*. This extract is from letter XXXVIII, to Miss Ewing, Glasgow, from Fort Augustus, 24 November 1778.

Smollett, in *Humphry Clinker*, is the only writer that has given a genuine sketch of Scotch manners; and in what relates to the lower class of Highlanders even he appears allowably ignorant, not knowing their language, and having left the country so young, that he was in a great measure a stranger to the Highlands, though born a borderer on it.

105. Anonymous remarks on Smollett in Scotland

1780

From *The Mirror*, Edinburgh, III, 70–1. This was a periodical paper published during 1779 to 1780, and the extract comes from an account of Scottish literature in no. 83, for Tuesday 22 February 1780.

The *English* excel in comedy; several of their romances are replete with the most humorous representation of life and character, and many of their other works are full of excellent ridicule. But, in *Scotland*, we have hardly any book which aims at humour, and, of the very few which do, still fewer have any degree of merit. Though we have tragedies written by *Scots* authors, we have no comedy, excepting *Ramsay's Gentle Shepherd*;[1] and though we have tender novels, we have none of humour, excepting those of *Smollett*, who, from his long residence in *England*, can hardly be said to have acquired in this country his talent for writing; nor can we, for the same reason, lay a perfect claim to Arbuthnot, who is a still more illustrious exception to my general remark.

NOTE

1 Allan Ramsay (1686–1758), *The Gentle Shepherd; A Scots Pastoral Comedy*, Edinburgh, 1725.

106. Thomas Davies on Garrick and Smollett

1780

From Thomas Davies, *Memoirs of the Life of David Garrick*, 1780, 2 vols, vol. I, pp. 280–7. Davies here records the history of the Smollett-Garrick relationship which turned from one of mutual animosity to mutual respect. This extract includes a letter from Garrick to Smollett of 26 November 1757.

Dr Smollet, before he knew which way his genius would conduct him, had conceived a very early opinion of his talents for writing dramatic poetry. Fired with his notion, he set about a tragedy, (he says himself at the age of eighteen) the story of which he took from the History of Scotland, called the *Regicide*. Unacquainted as he was then with the world, he imagined that he had nothing to do but to shew his work to the manager of a theatre, and it would be instantaneously brought on the stage. But the difficulties he met with gave him an utter dislike to managers and players. Mr Garrick was in such high favour with the public, that the doctor conceived his opinion would fix the fortune of his play. The actor, in reading over a play, has undoubtedly an eye to his own reputation; and if it comprehends a character in which he imagines that he should be distinguished to his advantage, he will be ready to give his voice in favour of it. How far this might, or might not, be the case with respect to the *Regicide*, I cannot tell. It is certain, that Mr Garrick did not warmly espouse that play. I believe he very cautiously and constantly referred him to the manager, with a promise, that if it was to be played, he should have no objection to act a part in it. Mr Quin too was sollicited to patronize the *Regicide*; but, I believe, his answer was more decisive and more offensive than that of Mr Garrick: however, Smollett supposed that the latter had interest to do what he pleased in a theatre, and the weight of his resentment fell chiefly upon him. In his *Roderick Random*, the author told his own story with an unpardonable malignity to Garrick; but the actor was sufficiently revenged by the publication of the *Regicide*; which at once fully justified the neglect of the managers, and the contempt of the players.

Smollett was not satisfied with the many severe strokes of satire which he had bestowed on the governing players, and especially on Mr Garrick, in his *Roderick Random*; but by a very malicious and laboured criticism which he had put into the mouth of his Peregrine Pickle, the hero of a novel of that name, and published about three years after the other, he endeavoured to degrade Mr Garrick and Mr Quin to the lowest class of their profession. The doctor was a man of genius, but he certainly rated it to its full value. He was a man too who abounded in generosity and good-nature; but was at the same time extremely splenetic and resentful; nor did he always consider whether the matter of quarrel was founded in justice, or arose from his unreasonable and too contemptuous opinion of others.

However unsuccessful Smollett was in one part of dramatic poetry, he was resolved to try his abilities in another; he fancied that his talents for humour and character, which he had so happily displayed in his novels, might be easily wrought up into comic scenes. In 1757 he wrote his *Tars of Old England*, a comedy of two acts, which comprehends all the provincial jargon of Ireland, Scotland, and France; and was, indeed, no ill contrivance to secure the success of this farrago.

Mr Garrick was applied to, I suppose, with some doubts of the author, of his farce meeting a favourable reception from a man whom he had so grossly slandered. However the manager approved the piece; and he acted it in the best manner he could. *The Tars of Old England* procured the author a pretty large benefit: and here Mr Garrick had the satisfaction to gratify Smollett by not asking the price, which might in rigour have been exacted by the managers, for the charges of a benefit. Of this Mr Garrick apprized him in the following letter.

TO DR SMOLLET.

Sir,   Nov. 26, 1757

There was a mistake made by our office-keepers to your prejudice, which has given me much uneasiness. Though the expence of our theatre every night amounts to 90l. and upwards, yet we take no more from gentlemen who write for the theatre, and who produce an original performance, than 60 guineas; they who alter only an old play, pay 80 guineas for the expence, as in the instance of *Amphytrion*: this occasioned the mistake which I did not discover till lately. Though it is very reasonable to take fourscore pounds for the expence of the house, yet as we have not yet regulated this matter, I cannot possibly agree that Dr Smollet shall be the first precedent. I have inclosed a draught upon Mr Clutterbuck for the sum due to you. I am, most sincerely,

Your most obedient,
humble Servant,
D. GARRICK.

From this time not only all animosities between the manager and the doctor ceased, but a very warm and reciprocal friendship commenced, which lasted till Smollett's death. He was truly desirous of making amends for his many illiberal and bitter censures of Mr Garrick; and at the close of his history speaks of him not only with justice, but with all the warm colouring of laboured panegyric. In giving a sketch of the Liberal Arts during the reign of George the Second, Smollett expresses himself of Garrick in the following words:

The exhibitions of the stage were improved to the most exquisite entertainment by the talents and management of Garrick, who greatly surpassed all his predecessors of this, and, perhaps, every other nation, in his genius for acting, in the sweetness and variety of his tones, the irresistible magic of his eye, the fire and vivacity of his action, the elegance of attitude, and the whole pathos of expression.

Not content with this public declaration of his sentiments with respect to Mr Garrick, upon the latter's presenting him with his

Winter's Tale, altered from Shakespeare, in acknowledging the receipt of his favour, Smollett tells him with an earnest protestation, 'that in what he had published concerning him, in his account of the Liberal Arts, he had spoken the language of his heart; that he could not, in such a part of his work, forbear doing justice to a genius who had no rival. Besides, he thought it a duty incumbent on him to make a public atonement, in a work of truth, for the wrongs done him in a work of fiction.'

He concluded in expressing a deep regret that his ill health prevented him from a personal cultivation of his good-will, and deprived him of the unspeakable enjoyment he should derive from his private conversation.

107. James Beattie on Smollett

1783

From James Beattie, *Dissertations Moral and Critical*, Dublin, 1783, 2 vols. vol. II, pp. 316–17. This extract comes from the essay 'On Fable and Romance'.

Smollett follows the same historical arrangement in *Roderick Random* and *Peregrine Pickle*: two performances, of which I am sorry to say, that I can hardly allow them any other praise, than that they are humorous and entertaining. He excels, however, in drawing the characters of seamen; with whom in his younger days he had the best opportunities of being acquainted. He seems to have collected a vast number of merry stories; and he tells them with much vivacity and energy of expression. But his style often approaches to bombast; and many of his humourous pictures are exaggerated beyond all bounds of probability. And it does not appear that he knew how to continue a regular fable, by making his events mutually dependent, and all co-operating to one and the same final purpose. On the morality of these novels I cannot compliment him at all. He is often inexcusably licentious. Profligates, bullies, and misanthropes, are among his favourite characters. A duel he seems to have thought one of the highest efforts of human virtue; and playing dextrously at billiards a very genteel accomplishment. Two of his pieces, however, deserve to be mentioned with more respect. *Count Fathom*, though an improbable tale, is pleasing, and upon the whole not immoral, though in some passages very indelicate. And *Sir Launcelot Greaves*, though still more improbable, has great merit; and is truly original in the execution, not-withstanding that the hint is borrowed from *Don Quixote*.

108. *The English Review* in defence of Smollett

1783

From *The English Review*, II, 1783, 92–3. In a review of Blair's *Lectures on Rhetoric and Belles-Lettres*, the reviewer defends Smollett against the censures of Blair and Beattie.

This conduct is not only strange in itself, but exposed to an interpretation that cannot redound to the honour of our Author. Beside the suspicion which it opens against the rectitude of his opinions in general, it is an instance of literary cowardice, for which no apology can be offered. What indeed, renders this behaviour the more reprehensible, is the circumstance, that while he bestows high praise on Dr Johnson, which he does not credit, he is so partial and mean, as not to mention Dr Smollett, but in order to censure him. We are, indeed, sensible that Dr Beattie has fallen into same error; and while we are at a loss to account for this cruelty to the Author of *Roderick Random*, it is natural to believe that it would not have been exercised, if he had been still alive. For in that case he would have been able to have acted in his defence. We are old enough to remember the favour which that unfortunate man was happy to show to his countrymen; and we know, at this moment the celebrity which he enjoys in England. The variety of his ability, his natural discernment, his knowledge of the world, the fertility of his imagination, his wit, and his humour, drew to him an attention, which the more confined capacities of Dr Beattie and Dr Blair can never hope to command. And it is probable, that his name will be remembered with respect and gratitude by the public, at a period when those of his detractors will be utterly forgotten. When men address themselves to the world, they ought as much as possible to divest themselves of their prejudices; and it will be always found that their renown and fame will be constantly in proportion to the honest impartiality with which they exercise their talents.

109. Samuel J. Pratt on Smollett

1785

From Samuel J. Pratt, *Miscellanies*, 1785, 4 vols, vol. III, pp. 124–5. This extract is from Pratt's *Moral Tales*, no. X, *On Novel-Writing, with the story of Varro and Clodio*.

Pratt (1749–1814) was a minor poet and writer of *belles-lettres*, who also published under the name Courtney Melmoth.

Smollett trod in his [Fielding's] steps pretty successfully, deviating from the path of the common-place Novelists, and giving to his scenes the recommendation of general similitude to Nature: but his wit is more studied, his laugh more laboured, and his sentiment less simple. Rousseau is in nature: the heart throbs to his eloquence, but he is too voluptuous. Le Sage appears to unite the excellencies, both serious and comic, of them all.

110. Clara Reeve on Smollett

1785

From Clara Reeve, *The Progress of Romance*, Colchester, 1785, Reprinted Facsimile Text Society, New York, 1930, vol. II, p. 10. One of the early histories of the novel, written in dialogue form using the character names of Hortensus, Sophronia and Euphrasia. This extract is from *Evening IX*. A review of Reeve's book in the *Critical Review*, LX, July 1785, 58, commented 'To Dr Smollett, the fair critic is somewhat more complaisant; but her account of his novels is so very trifling, that we are almost ready to suspect that she has not yet read them.'

Euph. Whenever you recollect any books of this kind that are worthy of our notice, and that are not mentioned in my notes, you will oblige me by reminding me of them.

Hort. I will then put you in mind that Dr *Smollett* was a novel writer.

Euph. Dr *Smollett's* Novels abound with wit, and humour, which some Critics think is carried beyond the limits of probability; all his characters are over charged, and he has exhibited some scenes that are not proper for all readers; but upon the whole, his works are of a moral tendency,—their titles are, *Roderick Random—Peregrine Pickle—Sir Launcelot Greaves—Ferdinand Count Fathom—Adventures of an Atom.*—Many years after these he gave the public another, in no respect inferior, and in some superior to them all, called *Humphrey Clinker.*

Hort. Honest *Humphrey* is an acquaintance of mine, and he is really a pleasant fellow.—But as you say many of the characters are *outrée*.

111. Rev. Vicesimus Knox on Smollett

1785

From an essay on *Novel Reading* in Knox's *Essays Moral and Literary* (9th edn.), 1787, 3 vols, vol. I, p. 132.

Knox (1752–1821), ordained minister and master of Tonbridge School. A belle-lettristic writer whose *Elegant Extracts* (1789) and *Elegant Epistles* (1790) made a significant contribution to the popularization of Sterne's writings.

Smollett undoubtedly possessed great merit. He would, however, have been more generally read among the polite and refined, if his humour had been less coarse. His *Peregrine Pickle* has, I am convinced, done much mischief; as all books must do, in which wicked characters are painted in captivating colours. It is certainly advisable to defer the perusal of his works, till the judgment is mature.

112. Robert Burns on Smollett

1787

From *The Letters of Robert Burns*, ed. J. De Lancey Ferguson, Oxford, 2 vols, 1931, p. 113. From a letter to Dr John Moore, August 1787.

My reading was only increased by two stray volumes of *Pamela*, and one of *Ferdinand Count Fathom*, which gave me some idea of Novels.

113. Robert Burns on Smollett

18 July 1788

From *The Letters of Robert Burns*, ed. J. De Lancey Ferguson, Oxford, 2 vols, 1931, p. 236. From a letter to an Edinburgh bookseller, Mr Peter Hall, 18 July 1788.

I want Smollett's works, for the sake of his incomparable humour.—I have already *Roderick Random* and *Humphrey Clinker.*—*Peregrine Pickle, Launcelot Greaves*, and *Ferdinand Count Fathom*, I shall want; but, as I said, the veriest ordinary copies will serve me.—I am nice only only in the appearance of my Poets.—

114. Two letters from William Cowper on Smollett's *Don Quixote*

1788

Extract (i) is from the *Letters of William Cowper*, ed. J.G. Frazer, 1912, vol. II, p. 159, from a letter to Lady Hesketh dated 7 February 1788. Extract (ii) is from *The Correspondence of William Cowper*, ed. Thomas Wright, 4 vols, 1904, vol. III, p. 242, from a later letter to Lady Hesketh, dated 6 May 1788. Lady Hesketh was Cowper's cousin.

(i)

Don Quixote by any hand must needs be welcome, and by Smollett's especially, because I have never seen it. He had a drollery of his own, which, for aught I know, may suit an English taste as well as that of Cervantes, perhaps better, because to us somewhat more intelligible.

(ii)

My dearest Cousin—You ask me how I like Smollett's *Don Quixote?* I answer, well,—perhaps better than any body's; but having no skill in the original, some diffidence becomes me. That is to say, I do not know whether I *ought* to prefer it or not. Yet there is so little deviation from other versions of it which I have seen, that I do not much hesitate. It has made me laugh I know immoderately, and in such a case *ça suffit.*

115. Robert Burns on Smollett

1790

From *The Works of Robert Burns*, Liverpool, 1800, 4 vols, ed. J. Currie, vol. II, *General Correspondence* etc., pp. 310–12. The letter is to Dr John Moore and is dated 14 July 1790, written upon receipt of Moore's novel *Zelucco*. Burn's 'Comparative view' was never written.

Dumfries, Excise-office, 14th July, 1790.

Sir,

Coming into town this morning, to attend my duty in this office, it being collection-day, I met with a gentleman who tells me he is on his way to London; so I take the opportunity of writing to you, as franking is at present under a temporary death. I shall have some snatches of leisure through the day, amid our horrid business and bustle, and I shall improve them as well as I can; but let my letter be as stupid as ★ ★ ★ ★ ★ ★ ★ ★ ★, as miscellaneous as a news-paper, as short as a hungry grace-before-meat, or as long as a law-paper in the Douglas cause; as ill spelt as country John's billet-doux, or as unsightly a scrawl as Betty Byre-mucker's answer to it; I hope, considering circumstances, you will forgive it; and as it will put you to no expence of postage, I shall have the less reflection about it.

I am sadly ungrateful in not returning you my thanks for your most valuable present, *Zeluco*. In fact, you are in some degree blameable for my neglect. You were pleased to express a wish for my opinion of the work, which so flattered me, that nothing less would serve my over-weening fancy, than a formal criticism on the book. In fact, I have gravely planned a comparative view of you, Fielding, Richardson, and Smollett, in your different qualities and merits as novel-writers. This, I own, betrays my ridiculous vanity, and I may probably never bring the business to bear; but I am fond of the spirit young Elihu shews in the book of Job—'And I said, I will also declare my opinion.' I have quite disfigured my copy of the book with my annotations. I never take it up without at the same time taking my pencil, and marking with asterisms, parenthesis, &c. wherever I meet with an original thought, a nervous remark on life and manners, a remarkably well-turned period, or a character sketched with uncommon precision.

Though I shall hardly think of fairly writing out my 'Comparative view,' I shall certainly trouble you with my remarks, such as they are.

I have just received from my gentleman, that horrid summons in the book of Revelations—'That time shall be no more!'

116. Anonymous remarks on Smollett's art

1791

From *The Critical Review*, II, n.s., 1791, 233. These remarks come in the course of a review of recent fiction.

... after Dr Smollett had introduced a new aera of novel-writing. With all our respect for that eminent writer, and we feel for him a *filial* reverence as our great ancestor, we must own that, in his works, descriptions were exaggerated till every idea was lost in the exuberance of resemblances, and a series of events too often produced by the lucky concurrence of circumstances brought together with little probability to increase the mirth.

117. William Creech on the pernicious effects of reading

1791

From William Creech, *Edinburgh Fugitive Pieces* (Edinburgh) 1791, rev., 1815, pp. 341–3. A collection of miscellaneous writings and local journalism. He writes this letter under the pseudonym of Peregrine Pickle's father, Gamaliel Pickle.

TO THE PRINTER

OF THE

EDINBURGH EVENING COURANT

I have a wife, Sir who has contracted a habit much more pernicious to me than the habit of swearing, which you took notice of in your last paper; I mean the habit of reading and writing. Let me tell you, Sir, frankly, that for all my aversion to snuff and tobacco, I had rather see her with a pipe and box than a book. From morning to night she sits poring over some book or other, which may be very entertaining for aught I know, as I make it a rule to look into none of them. But of what use is all this to me? If I set her down to mend my stockings, she is reading Locke upon the Human Understanding; and if I wish to have dinner an hour sooner than usual, she will not stir a step if she gets into the middle of a play of Shakespeare. The house is dirty as a poet's garret (under favour Sir), and my children are worse clad than parish bastards. Tommy's breeches have hung about his heels all this week, owing to the *Revolution in the Low Countries*; and Johnson's *Lives* have nearly starved my youngest daughter at breast. But what is more extraordinary, she seems to read to no purpose, and with no method; for my friend Hildebrand Huggins, who understands such things, tells me that she reads every kind of books, on any subject whatever; breakfasts on Tillotson, dines on the *Thirty-nine Articles*, drinks tea with *Roderick Random*, and goes to bed with *Humphry Clinker*. She has long had a practice of reading in bed, and while I am sleeping by her side, and dreaming of the pleasures of a gold chain, she is in close contest with some hero or other of romance! As this is the case, you cannot suppose she had any very violent attachment to me; and although her affections are no longer mine, it is very hard that I can have no satisfaction. I cannot challenge Pope's Homer for seduction, nor state damages against Tom Jones; and yet if a man deprive me of my wife's affections, what is it to me whether he be dead or alive? Pray, Sir, say a few good things on this subject; for as my wife reads your paper, who knows but your advice may have a good effect, and work well for,

Sir,
Your's to command,
Gamaliel Pickle.

118. Lord Woodhouselee
on Smollett and Cervantes

1791

From A.F. Tytler (Lord Woodhouselee), *Essay on the Principles of Translation*, 1791, p. 282. From Chapter XII of Woodhouselee's work on the difficulty of translating *Don Quixote*, where the writer compares Motteux and Smollett's translations.

Smollett inherited from nature a strong sense of ridicule, a great fund of original humour, and a happy versatility of talent, by which he could accommodate his style to almost every species of writing. He could adopt alternately the solemn, the lively, the sarcastic, the burlesque, and the vulgar. To these qualifications he joined an inventive genius, and a vigorous imagination. As he possessed talents equal to the composition of original works of the same species with the romance of Cervantes; so it is not perhaps possible to conceive a writer more completely qualified to give a perfect translation of that romance.

119. Mrs Barbauld on Smollett's
Gothicism in *Ferdinand Count Fathom*

1792

From Mrs Barbauld and John Aikin, *Miscellaneous Pieces in Prose*, 1792 (1773), pp. 126-7. This extract is from an essay 'On the Pleasure derived from Objects of Terror'.

Anna Laetitia Barbauld (1743–1825) was the sister of John
Aikin, and the editor of Richardson's *Correspondence*. In 1810
she edited a 50 volume edition of *The British Novelist*, with
biographical and critical prefaces. (see No. 135).

Hence, the more wild, fanciful, and extraordinary are the circumstances of a scene of horror, the more pleasure we receive from it;
and where they are too near common nature, though violently
borne by curiosity through the adventure, we cannot repeat it, or
reflect on it, without an over-balance of pain. In the *Arabian Nights*
are many most striking examples of the terrible, joined with the
marvellous: the story of Aladdin, and the travels of Sinbad, are
particularly excellent. The *Castle of Otranto*[1] is a very spirited
modern attempt upon the same plan of mixed terror, adapted to the
model of Gothic romance. The best conceived, and the most
strongly worked-up scene of mere natural horror that I recollect, is
in Smolett's *Ferdinand Count Fathom*; where the hero, entertained in
a lone house in a forest, finds a corpse just slaughtered in the room
where he is sent to sleep, and the door of which is locked upon
him.[2] It may be amusing for the reader to compare his feelings
upon these, and from thence form his opinion of the justness of my
theory. The following fragment, in which both these manners are
attempted to be in some degree united, is offered to entertain a
solitary winter's evening.

NOTES

1 Horace Walpole's *The Castle of Otranto* was published in 1765.
2 Mrs Barbauld here refers to the opening of chapter 21 of *Ferdinand Count
Fathom*, one of the two 'Gothic' chapters of the novel: the other is
chapter 20.

120. [Francis Garden] on Smollett's genius

1792

From *The Bee, or Literary Weekly Intelligencer*, Edinburgh, 18 vols, VII, 1792, 130–2. The writer is Lord Gardenstone under the pseudonym 'Bombardinion'. He had earlier commented on Smollett as historian, and on the *Travels*. Those comments, together with the extract below, are reprinted in *Miscellanies in Prose and Verse*, Edinburgh, 1792, but apparently not included in the first edition of that collection of 1791.

For the talent of drawing a natural and original character, Dr Smollett, of all English writers, approaches nearest to a resemblance of our inimitable Shakespeare. What can be more chaste, amusing, or interesting, than Random, Trunnion, Hatchway, Lismahago, Pallet, the pindarick physican, Tom Clarke, Farmer Prickle, Strap, Clinker, Pipes, the duke of Newcastle, and Timothy Crabtree? The last is indeed a close imitation of Sancho Pança, as Morgan is partly borrowed from one of Shakespeare's Welshmen; but still both are the imitations of a great master, not the tame copies of a common artist. Matthew Bramble is a most estimable portrait of a country gentleman; and admirably contrasted with his sister Tabby. This novel was written when its author was declining both in health and fortune; yet he displays all the spirit and vivacity of Roderick Random; and in some passages, such as that respecting the Smith's widow, is irresistibly pathetic. All which passes on board the Thunder, is a series of almost unexampled excellence. The night scene in bedlam, in Sir Launcelot Greaves, is drawn with uncommon force of judgement and of fancy. In the same publication, the ruin of captain Clewlin and his family, enforces with astonishing eloquence, the madness and infamy of paternal tyranny, and the delicious raptures of paternal tenderness. In the character of honest Bowling, Smollett, if any where, excels himself: The captain's speech to his crew, when about to engage a

French man of war, is such a master-piece, that, in reading it, we feel a sort of involuntary impulse for a broadside. The phlegm of an old lawyer is happily illustrated in the conduct of Random's grandfather, and forms the most striking contrast imaginable to the ferocious benevolence of the naval veteran. The disappointment of the maiden aunts, on opening the old man's will, is infinitely natural and amusing. The entertainment in the manner of ancients, affords a strang specimen of the learning and abilities of its author. The oration of Sir Launcelot to an election mob, is in the true spirit of Cervantes. The knight elucidates, with exquisite sense, humour and propriety, the miserable farce of representation in parliament; and the insolence of a rabble, incapable and unworthy of a better government, is in harmony with the conviction of every reader. In this age, many gentlemen publish volumes of criticism, and attempt to illustrate the human mind upon metaphysical principles. In their works, it is usual to cite passages from poets, and other writers in the walk of invention; yet it is singular that they have seldom or never quoted Smollett, whose talents reflect honour on his country, and who, next to Buchanan, is by far the greatest literary genius of whom north Britain has to boast. The admiration of the public bestows an ample atonement for the silence of our professed critics. His volumes are in every hand, and his praises on every tongue.

BOMBARDINION

Laurencekirk January 2, 1792.

121. [Jeremiah Whitaker Newman], from *The Lounger*

1792?

From Jeremiah Whitaker Newman, *The Lounger's Common Place Book*, 3rd edn, 3 vols, 1805. Newman published anonymously between 1792 and 1805, and the first edition of this work is dated 1792, in 4 vols. There was a second edition in 1796, with additions. His comments were called upon by Robert Anderson in his *Miscellaneous Works of Tobias Smollett*, 1796, in Anderson's prefatory remarks. This extract comes from pp. 191 ff. of vol. III of the 1805 edition of Newman's *Lounger*. Newman (1759–1839) was a practising surgeon, and a medical and miscellaneous writer.

Smollett, Tobias, a navy surgeon, a physician, and a novel writer, before that species of composition was rendered so common and contemptible, and, I believe, the founder of the *Critical Review*; a work which involved his bookseller in a law-suit with the late Admiral Knowles, who professed, that his only reason for commencing an action was, to know the real author, in order that he might obtain satisfaction. As sentence was about to be pronounced, Smollett gallantly stood forth, avowed himself writer of the strictures in question, and that he was ready to justify his conduct. This generous and heroic naval commander immediately prosecuted the writer, whose spirited conduct, gained him much credit and applause.

In the practice of physic he never was eminent; he despised the low arts of finesse, servility, and cunning. But it is not to record his want of success in a profession where merit cannot always insure good fortune, that he is here introduced; I notice him as a writer of that species of modern romance, which has been denominated a novel, a literary department in which he has been happy, superior, in my opinion, to the moral, the pathetic, but tiresome Richardson, and the ingenious, but diffuse Fielding, with all his knowledge of the human heart.

I am aware, that in this decision many readers will differ from me; but can they with truth declare, that they have not sometimes yawned, and sometimes slept, over the wire-drawn pages of *Grandison* and *Clarissa*, or the common-place introductory discussions, and tedious narratives of *Jones, Joseph Andrews*, and *Amelia*. That Fielding repeatedly displays considerable knowledge of the human heart, and that passages may be pointed out in Richardson, which do credit to his imagination and his understanding, equal to the best efforts of Smollett, I cannot deny; yet, after perusing their works, I never quit them with such reluctance as I feel on closing the pages of our author, who, without introducing so much of what has been called fine writing, possesses, in an eminent degree, the art of rousing our feelings, and fixing the attention of his readers.

The Adventures of Peregrine Pickle, though they have been censured as low, scurrilous, and immoral, (a charge of a serious nature, and which I shall hereafter consider) I have always preferred to the other productions of Smollett: they relate, in language by turns strong, easy, elegant, and pathetic, a succession of events, forming a natural, well-drawn picture of human life, which the thoughtless may peruse with advantage, and the prudent man, with emotions of triumph.

From the wild unlucky boy, teizing his aunt and the commodore, by mischievous pranks, and heading a rebellion at school against his master, we trace the headstrong youth, of pride unbroken, and unbridled appetite, plunging into folly, vice, and dissipation; wasting his substance, injuring the woman of all others he loved, and at last pining in a prison, that severe school, which too tardily teaches us the falsehood and treachery of a base world, fascinating only to plunder, and bewitching, only to destroy. Roused by the voice of friendship, and again restored to affluence, he returns, with a stern reluctance, founded on a sense of his own unworthiness and vicious imprudence, to society and love; convinced that, after all the bustle of pleasure, and glitter of wealth, real happiness is only to be found in moderate enjoyment, domestic tranquility, and social virtue.

A good style has been defined, 'proper words in proper places;' and I have not met with a more just selection of appropriate terms, and descriptive expressions, than in the following short passage of Smollett, though on a trifling subject; it is when Tom Pipes kills the gardener's dog. 'He was that instant assaulted by the mastiff, who fastened on the outside of his thigh. Feeling himself incommoded by this assailant, he quitted the prostrate gardner, turned round to the dog, and grasping the throat of that ferocious animal with both his hands, he squeezed it with such incredible force and perseverance, that the creature quitted his hold: his tongue lolled out of his jaws, the blood started from his eyes, and he swung, a lifeless trunk, in the hands of his vanquisher.'

His feast, after the manner of the ancients, is well managed and replete with rich strokes of humour, and pointed satire, which, in the rancour of toryism, he directed, with engerness, against his whig opponent, Akenside. Yet in this, and other parts of *Peregrine* Smollett has, with some justice, been thought indelicate; but it should be recollected, that in delineations of certain circumstances, and certain characters, it is difficult for the author who draws from nature, and real life, to avoid shocking the fastidious eye of nicety, and scrupulous decorum. The path of humour is pleasant and inviting, but it is a dangerous one, and too often leads us astray into the bye roads of indelicacy, as well as illnature. To say a *good thing*, how ever smutty or malignant, is a temptation equally irresistible to the humourist, the mimic, and the bon-vivant; and, as I have said in another place, we ought to recollect, that it is the nature of all humour to be sometimes gross, and sometimes inelegant.

In this respect, the dialogue between Pipes, and the hedge nymph, his master had accidentally picked up on the road, and afterwards introduced into company as a fine lady, is culpably obscene, though the story is well told, and the irresistible buoyancy of early impression well marked. The behaviour of Pickle to Hornbeck, is also highly unjustifiable; not satisfied with injuring that unfortunate husband, beyond repair, he adds personal violence to insult. Yet, with these, and other faults, I can not but consider it, contrary to the general opinion, as superior to *Roderick Random*, and as a first-rate novel, whose merits far exceed the modern puny productions of frivolous fashion, and feeble sentiment, which load the shelves of our libraries, and teach nonsense and iniquity to our wives and daughters.

Peregrine's transition from mirth, petulance, and gaiety, to anxiety, agitation, confusion, and concern, after first beholding the lovely Emilia Gauntlett, and the progress of the generous passion of love, as long as he restrained himself within the bounds of good sense; also the curious mode of replacing a lost love letter, are well imagined. But when the young man was corrupted by prosperity, and his principles contaminated by excess and the baleful maxims of foreign climes, that aweful veneration, which her presence used to inspire, gradually abated, and he gazed on the lovely, the virtuous Emilia, with impure desire.

After a variety of plans to lull her vigilance and apprehensions, he considers the licentiousness and late hours of a masquerade, (that hot-house of sin and hell) as a fit place for the execution of his purpose. The address of Emilia to her lover, on discovering his treacherous and unprincipled design, deserves to be repeated; it is animated, pointed, and such as her situation would naturally inspire: 'for, what must have been the emotions of a virtuous sensible woman, at this insolent treatment from a man whom she had honored with the most disinterested affection, and genuine esteem? it was not simply horror, grief, or indignation, but the united pangs of them all.'

As soon as her feeling suffered her to speak, she addresses him in the following words.

[quotes *Peregrine Pickle*, chs LXXXII and CXI, and reports the narrative of Peregrine's attempt upon Emilia's virtue, and their ultimate reconciliation at the close of the novel. Cf. vol. III, ch. 76, pp. 29–33]

I was very young when these adventures fell in my way, and perhaps on that account, they made a deeper impression, and appeared in the eyes of a school-boy more worthy of attention, and better written, than they really are; circumstances which I hope will excuse thus serving up to my readers a second-hand hash from the novel shop. I well remember the forlorn situation of Peregrine, his declining every kind of proffered assistance, and the obstinate peculiarity of his conduct, with regard to Emilia, struck me as a noble exertion of manly and philosophical self-denial, not un-worthy the characters of Socrates or Cato. I could not help bestowing on his behaviour warm encomiums, and viewing him with a mixture of envy and admiration, but the *happy* conclusion was not suitable to the enthusiasm of juvenile fancy, dreaming of, and seeking, as objects of meditation, themes far more gratifying, interesting, and affecting, than reason, nature and probability.

'Had I been in such a situation,' (have I often exclaimed in the blissful extacy of fourteen) 'had I written this novel, or had I been in the circumstances of Peregrine, I would have suffered myself or my hero to perish in prison, unassisted; the cup of comfort should have been dashed untasted from my lips; to add to my punishment, my last look should have been cast on the woman I was dying for and adored. Without suffering myself to enjoy a heaven, which was placed within my grasp; after darting my eyes on that bosom, where gods would wish to have revelled, I would have turned them from the delicious, enchanting sight, and sunk into everlasting sleep.

I need not add, that to the pourer forth of such a rhapsody, the performance of Smollett would have been more pleasing, had its termination been in the stile of Spagnolet, less happy.

As a traveller, Smollett was petulant, illiberal, and almost on every occasion lost his temper; but some excuse is to be made for a frame, convulsed by the pangs of disease, and a life embittered by disappointment, and domestic calamity; a spirit wounded by ingratitude, and irritated by the malignant shafts of envy, dullness, and profligacy. He is said to have been a literary retainer to the Earl of Bute, and to have experienced ingratitude from that nobleman, who in many instances was a generous patron to men very inferior in ability to Smollett. Under such impressions perhaps he ought not to have written, but on certain occasions, the pen will be found to afford a similar relief to the dram-bottle, or a round of diversions; and where is the man, who having once found solace in a pursuit, will not naturally seek for comfort and consolation in the same path?

At the age of eighteen, this writer produced the *Regicide*, a Tragedy on the subject of James the First, King of Scotland, animated, nervous, and pathetic. The character of the virtuous, the brave, but the gentle Dunbar, is finely contrasted with the headstrong, fierce, ambitious Stewart, while the amiable Eleanora, esteeming the first, but in spite of herself loving the latter, is distracted between her passion and her duty.

This piece of Smollett's, excels in language, situation, and every other dramatic requisite, most of the wretched things which were presented to the public at that period, but are now forgotten; yet, with all its merits, it was never able to procure admission on the stage. I was tempted to mention it in this place, by the following passage in a Preface prefixed to the play, which I submit, without a comment, to the consideration of Messrs. Harris, Sheridan, and Colman, jun.

'As early as the year 1739, my play was taken into the protection of one of those little fellows, who sometimes fancy themselves great men. After being neglected by him, with the strictest attention to politeness and etiquette, I was introduced to Mr Lacy, of courteous memory, who found means to amuse me for two seasons, by practising on me the various arts of procrastination, occasionally sweetened with compliments and promises. My patience was at last exhausted, and I demanded from him, in warm terms, a final answer, which amounted to a refusal. The gentleman coolly added, that he really saw no great objection to the piece, but feared my interest was not sufficient to support it in the representation, *as no dramatic composition, however perfect, could succeed with an English audience, by its merit only, but must depend in a great measure, on a faction raised in its behalf.'*

122. James Lackington on Smollett's popularity

1793

From James Lackington, *Memoirs of the forty-five first Years of the Life of James Lackington, Bookseller* etc. (1793), 1795 new edn, corr. and enlarged, p. 420.

Before I conclude this letter, I cannot help observing, that the sale of books in general has increased prodigiously within the last twenty years. According to the best estimation I have been able to make, I suppose that more than four times the number of books are sold now than were sold twenty years since. The poorer sort of farmers, and even the poor country people in general, who before that period spent their winter evenings in relating stories of witches, ghosts, hobgoblins, &c. now shorten the winter nights by hearing their sons and daughters read tales, romances, &c. and on entering their houses, you may see *Tom Jones, Roderick Random*, and other entertaining books, stuck up on their bacon racks, &c. If *John* goes to town with a load of hay, he is charged to be sure not to forget to bring home *Peregrine Pickle's Adventures*; and when *Dolly* is sent to market to sell her eggs, she is commissioned to purchase *The History of Pamela Andrews*. It short, all ranks and degrees now READ. But the most rapid increase of the sale of books has been since the termination of the late war.

123. Isaac D'Israeli on Smollett as Petronius

1795

From Isaac D'Israeli, *Essay on the Manners and Genius of the Literary Character*, 1795, pp. 140–1. The extract comes in chapter XI, 'The Characters of Writers not Discoverable in their Writings'. The Bayle referred to is probably Pierre Bayle, the seventeenth-century French writer.

The licentious tales of La Fontaine are well known, but not a single amour has been recorded of the 'bon homme.' Bayle is a remarkable instance; no writer is more ample in his detail of impurity, but he resisted the pollution of the senses as much as Newton. He painted his scenes of lewdness merely as a faithful historian, and an exact compiler. Smollett's character is immaculate, yet what a description has he given of one of his heroes with Lord Straddle. I cannot but observe on such scenes, that their delineation answers no good purpose. Modesty cannot read, and is morality interested? He assumed the character of Petronius Arbiter; we applaud and we censure this mere playfulness of fancy. It is certain, however, by these instances, that licentious writers may be very chaste men.

124. Richard Cumberland on 'fast writing'

1795

In his novel *Henry*, 4 vols, 1795, Richard Cumberland the younger (1732–1811) gives a comic account of the work of

Fielding, Richardson and Smollett. This extract comes from
the 3rd ed of 1798, vol. I, book 2, chapter I, p. 98, bearing the
chapter heading 'Reasons for writing as fast as we can'.

There was third, somewhat posterior in time, not in talents, who
was indeed a rough driver, and rather too severe to his cattle; but in
faith, he carried us on at a merry pace over land or sea; nothing
came amiss to him, for he was up to both elements, and a match for
nature in every shape, character, and degree: he was not very
courteous, it must be owned, for he had a capacity for higher things,
and was above his business: he only wanted a little more suavity
and discretion to have figured with the best.

125. Robert Anderson on Smollett

1796

From *Miscellaneous Works of Tobias Smollett*, ed. Robert
Anderson, 1796, pp. liv-lxi. Anderson (1750–1830), a fellow
Scot and a physician like Smollett, published a *Life* of
Smollett in 1796, and six revised editions of the *Miscellaneous
Works* (as above) between 1796 and 1820. The critical remarks
extracted here represent that part of Anderson's commentary
which is independent of previous biographical/critical commentaries. Anderson made increasingly scholarly attempts to
distinguish between Smollett's own life and that life attributed to him from the fiction (see Mark Longaker, *English
Biography in the Eighteenth Century*, Philadelphia, 1931, pp.
486–91).

As a writer of that species of modern romance which has been
denominated a *novel*, he is entitled to the praise of being one of the
greatest that our nation has produced. He ranks with Defoe,

Richardson, and Fielding, the great masters of prosaic fiction; and though we cannot say that he has surpassed them, he has entered into a noble competition. His novels exhibit a series of odd, extravagant, but natural pictures of life and manners, drawn with the descriptive fidelity of a Hogarth. He has painted the characters, and ridiculed the follies of life, with equal strength, humour and propriety. The style is characterized by a just selection of appropriate terms and descriptive expressions; of 'proper words in proper places.' But he is not without faults. His characters are sometimes overcharged, his humour is often coarse, and he has exhibited some scenes which may corrupt a mind unseasoned by experience. His system of youthful profligacy, as exemplified in some of his libertines, is without excuse. Profligates, bullies, misanthropes, gamblers, and duellists, are among his favourite characters. His writings, however, are of a moral tendency; they have spirit, humour, and morality, and display the beauties of that genius which allures and rewards the attention of the discreet reader. Unguarded as they are in many of their representations, they are highly entertaining, and will always be read with pleasure.

His *Adventures of Roderick Random* is a novel of first rate merit. It is written in such a manner as to please all times and all people. It exhibits a natural, lively, and enteraining representation of the difficulties to which a friendless orphan is exposed, from his own want of experience, as well as from the selfishness, malice and base indifference of mankind. The mean scenes in which he is involved, are described with true humour; and every reader finds entertainment in viewing those parts of life where the manners and passions, are undisguised by affectation, ceremony, or education, and the whimsical peculiarities of disposition appear as nature has implanted them. The base purposes of hypocrisy, cant, selfish plausibility, cunning, and pretended friendship, are exposed in a masterly manner; and the inconsistencies that flow from the motley and repugnant qualities which are often whimsically blended together by the folly of men, are described with infinite humour and sagacity. Many of his characters are drawn from real life. The originals of *Gawkey*, *Strap*, *Crab*, *Potion*, *Oakhum*, *Whiffle*, *Mackshane*, and *Morgan*, were, in his own time, known and pointed out: but short as the time is since the publication of this novel, it at present derives no advantage from that source, and owes its celebrity to its intrinsic merit alone. In describing sea characters, he is peculiarly happy. *Trunnion*, *Hatchway*, and *Pipes*, of *Peregrine Pickle*, are highly finished originals; but *Lieutenant Bowling* exceeds them, and perhaps equals any character that has yet been painted by the happiest genius of ancient or modern times. This is indeed nature itself. As well as the ladder of promotion, his very name has long become proverbial for an honest blunt seaman, unacquainted with mankind, and the ways of the world. The moral tendency of the story none can deny. It is written with the purest intentions of promoting virtue, and correcting the ordinary follies of life. But in the accomplishment of this purpose, it is to be feared that scenes are laid open which it would be safer to conceal from youthful and inexperienced readers. The base purposes of fraud and duplicity are exposed; but a due attention to the common duties of life, decent deportment, purity of manners, and the appearance of morality and seriousness, are brought into discredit and suspicion. Such representations, it is to be feared, may be disadvantageous to early; dear-bought experience having long convinced us, how very narrow the defiles between ridiculed rectitude and flagitious conduct.

[Anderson's discussion of *Peregrine Pickle* is not reproduced here since it is substantially taken from Newman's comments, see No. 141]

The history of *Count Fathom*, though improbable, is pleasing, and, upon the whole, not immoral, though in some place very indelicate. It is professedly written to unfold the mysteries of fraud, to instruct the ignorant, and entertain the vacant; but the characters of that profligate adventurer and his wicked associates, are represented in such horrible features, that humanity is shocked, and the imagination is disgusted. The representation of a virtuous character, in opposition to the adventurer, contributes, indeed, in some degree, to relieve the attention from a succession of flagitious objects, and by contrast, heightens the expression, and gives a *relief* to the moral of the whole. But, the advantage of introducing vicious and profligate characters, into a moral production, by way of exposing them to shame and ridicule, may be reasonably doubted; for a series of crimes and follies may give a mind unseasoned by experience, an insight into vice which the good moral drawn from them may not prevent being put in practice. In many parts of this novel, it must be acknowledged, he has delightfully copied the style and manner of his master Le Sage; and it may be asserted, without hazard of contradiction, that his description of *Fathom's* adventure in Chap. XX. and XXI. is wrought up to a pitch of horror which rivals, if not exceeds, the most terrible touches in the *Castle of Otranto*, surpasses every thing of the kind which we find in *The Romance of the Forest*, or *The Mysteries of Udolpho*. The history of *Sir Launcelot Greaves*, though still more improbable, has great merit, and is truly original in the execution, notwithstanding that the hint is borrowed from Don Quixote. There are many characters well drawn, many diverting incidents, and many fine strokes of genius, nature, and passion. But some of the humorous characters are exaggerated beyond all bounds of probability; and certain persons are too often introduced, particularly *Captain Crowe*, whose appearance is sometimes disgusting. It is written with the same vivacity and energy of expression which characterize his other productions.

His *Adventures of an Atom* belong to the class of compositions in fictitious history, in the form, rather than the substance of the work, which is all true in the main, though the circumstances are occasionally heightened by the decorations of fancy, or tinged by the dark hues of political prejudice. Having characterized the chiefs that disputed the administration of *Japan* (England), he professes to give 'a plain narration of historical incidents, without pretending to philosophize like *Hume*, or dogmatize like *Smollett*.' The characters of the Whig party are, in general, drawn with unwarrantable severity. Political prejudice never appears more justly reprehensible, than when it attempts to cast a veil over distinguished merit, and loads exalted characters with obloquy. Though the work, for ingenuity and contrivance in the composition, is inferior, upon the whole, to his former productions, it is written, for the most part, with his usual energy and felicity of expression. His comparison of the *Council Board* to the allegorical *Table of Cebes*, is well managed; and his digressions on *alchemy*, *magic*, *necromancy*, *sorcery*, or *witchcraft*, display tht peculiar combination of profound learning and genuine humour which forms the basis of ludicrous composition.

In his *Expedition of Humphry Clinker*, he has carefully avoided the faults which may be justly charged to *Count Fathom* and *Sir Launcelot Greaves*. It consists of a series of letters written by different persons to their respective correspondents, in the manner of Richardson. It has no extravagant characters, nor unnatural

269

situations; on the contrary, an admirable knowledge of life and manners is displayed, and most useful lessons are given, applicable and interesting to very common situations. It has all the spirit and vigour of his former works, and is evidently the production of a mind enriched and mellowed by experience, and softened, but not soured by misfortune. In the conduct of the characters of *Lismahago, Tabitha Bramble,* and *Humphry Clinker,* there are many touches which occasion the most exquisite merriment. The whole work, indeed, abounds with situations of the truly comic kind; the incidents and characters are unfolded with fine turns of surprise, and it is among the few works of invention produced by the English writers, which will always continue in request. . . .

Roderick Random, Peregrine Pickle, and *Humphry Clinker,* are undoubtedly efforts of genius and fancy, which rival the masterly productions of the moral, the sublime, the pathetic, but tiresome Richardson, with all his profound and accurate knowledge of the various workings of the human heart, and the ingenious, the humorous, but diffuse Fielding, with all his wit, learning, and knowledge of mankind. That Fielding repeatedly displays a thorough acquaintance with nature, and that innumerable passages may be pointed out in Richardson, which do equal credit to the goodness of his heart and the depth of his understanding, cannot be denied; yet, after perusing the wire-drawn pages of *Pamela,* Clarissa, and *Grandison,* or the common-place introductory discussion and diffuse narrative of *Joseph Andrews, Tom Jones,* and *Amelia,* we never quit them with so much reluctance, as we feel in closing the pages of Smollett, who, with less regularity of fable, and without introducing so much of what may be called fine writing, possesses, in an eminent degree, the art of rousing our feelings, and fixing the attention of his readers.

126. Dr John Moore on Smollett

1797

From *The Works of Tobias Smollett, with Memoirs of his Life*, etc, including *A View of the Commencement and Progress of Romance*, by Dr John Moore, 8 vols, 1797, vol. I. Moore, a relation and familiar friend of Smollett, composed a *Life* of Smollett published with the above edition in 1797, and this was later used by Robert Anderson, together with Moore's comments on the novels, both in the making of Anderson's various editions of Smollett's *Works*, and in his edition of Moore's *Works* (1820). The following two extracts—later conjoined by Anderson—come from *A View of the Commencement and Progress of Romance*, pp. xci–xciii, and *The Life of T. Smollett, M.D.*, pp. clxxix–clxxxi.

From *A View...of Romance:*

Dr Smollett, in the *Continuation of his History of England*, observes, that towards the end of the reign of George II. and about the beginning of that of his present majesty, 'genius in writing spontaneously arose; and though neglected by the great, flourished under the culture of a public which had pretensions to taste, and piqued itself on encouraging literary merit.' He proceeds to enumerate the most distinguished writers in the various branches of literature at that period, and gives his suffrage to the great talents of one who pursued the same line with himself, in the following words: 'The genius of Cervantes was transfused into the novels of Fielding, who painted the characters and ridiculed the follies of life with equal strength, humour, and propriety.'

The success of Richardson, Fielding, and Smollett, in this species of writing, produced, what great success generally does produce, a prodigious number of imitators: but by far the greater part of them, like Hamlet's players, imitated abominably; and instead of representing the manners of the age, exhibited men and women, neither having the manners of Christians nor Pagans, and who seemed to have been made by the least expert of Nature's journeymen.

There were, for a considerable time, so many novels written of this description, and with so few exceptions, that the very words Romance or Novel conveyed the idea of a frivolous or pernicious book. Even this, however, did not diminish the number, though it made many people at pains to declare, that for their part they never read novels; a declaration sometimes made by persons of both sexes, who never read any thing else. This is being by much too cautious. They might, with equal prudence, declare, that they never would read any book, because many books are silly or pernicious. The truth is, that the best romances always have been, and always will be, read with delight by men of genius; and with the more delight, the more taste and genius the reader happens to have. Nothing can be so interesting to men as man. The modern romances are or ought to be a representation of life and manners in the country where the scene is placed. Had works of this nature existed in the flourishing ages of the Greek and Roman republics, and had some of the best of them been preserved, how infinitely would they be relished at present! as they would give a much more minute and satisfactory picture of private and domestic life than is found in history, which dwells chiefly on war and affairs of state. This species of writing may also be made most subservient to the purposes of instruction; but even those which afford amusement only, provided they contain nothing immoral, are not without utility, and deserve by no means to be spoken of with that contempt which they sometimes are, by their most intimate acquaintance. These gentlemen ought to recollect in what manner they usually employ that portion of their time which they do not pass in reading what they so much affect to despise: they ought to recollect how many languid intervals there are in their journey through life; how often they fill them up in a more pernicious way; and if a novel or romance should now and then help them to jog along with more innocence and less yawning, they ought to be a little more grateful.

From *The Life of T. Smollett, M.D.*:

The romances of Dr Smollett are not so much distinguished for the invention of the story, as for strong masculine humour, just observations on life, and a great variety of original characters. In *Humphry Clinker* he hardly attempts any story; it is a mere vehicle for characters and remarks on life and manners. The characters of the different correspondents are supported throughout with the utmost propriety, and the peculiar style suitable to each writer is maintained with more precision than in any romance in the epistolary form with which I am acquainted.

The similitude among the characters of Random, Pickle, and Bramble has been repeatedly remarked. The two former display the same fondness for practical jokes which was observed in Smollett when a boy, the same spirit in exposing presumptuous ignorance, stigmatising hypocrisy, repelling pride, and applauding merit, that he displayed in his meridian; and in the letters of Mathew Bramble, the same peevishness appears that Smollett himself betrays in his *Travels*, with that sensibility, benevolence, and generosity of disposition which he possessed from the beginning to the end of his life.

If we except the character of Lismahago, some features of which, though highly comic, are extravagantly stretched, Dr Smollett has avoided the marvellous, and adhered more closely to nature and to familiar life in *Humphry Clinker* than in any of his other romances. It is justly observed by Dr Anderson, in his *Life of Smollett*, that this performance has all the spirit of his former works, and is the production of a mind mellowed by experience, and softened, not soured, by misfortune: it is peculiarly entertaining to observe his address and attention to nature, in the different representations of the same places and people, and transactions by the different characters.

Many useful lessons are given for the conduct of life, particularly in the story of Mr Baynard, who is brought to the brink of ruin by the vanity of his wife and the good-natured facility of his temper. The whole of Bramble's account of the Temple of Cold Reception is admirably taken from nature.

The letters of Tabitha Bramble and Winifred Jenkins are pleasingly characteristic, and capable of surprising the most solemn of mankind into laughter, if their features be not kept steady by stupidity as well as pride.

From the assemblies of high-life Dr Smollett thought that humour was banished by ceremony, affectation, and cards; *that nature being castigated almost to still-life, mirth never appeared but in an insipid grain.* His extreme fondness for humour therefore led him to seek it where it was to be found, namely, in the inferior societies of life, which, in despite of the acuteness with which he seized and described it, has exposed him to the censure of the fastidious.

The excellence of the few Poems left by Dr Smollett, proves that he possessed the true genius of a Poet. His Tragedy, his two Satires, and the *Tears of Scotland*, have been already mentioned. The last is exquisitely pathetic.

The Ode to Leven Water is accurately as well as poetically descriptive, and at once simple and sentimental.

The Love Elegy, in imitation of Tibullus, is harmonious, solemn, and affecting. It would have been better without the last stanza, the thought in which has been often used.

In the Ode to Independence, Smollett seems to have collected all the energy and enthusiasm of his poetical towers, describing with judgment and fertility of fancy, the lineage, education, and achievements of Independence, and concluding with sentiments of gratitude for the influence of that power on his own mind, which had preserved him from servility, and enabled him to look with contempt on folly and presumption, though clothed in ermine and lodged in those sculptured halls.

> Where Title his ill-woven chaplet wears,
> Full often wreath'd around the miscreant's brow,...

127. A letter on familiar narrative

1797

From *The Monthly Magazine or British Register*, 1797, IV, 180–1. The signatory of this letter to the editor, 'M.H.' here disputes Samuel Johnson's argument in *Rambler* no. 4 (1750) on the purpose and moral effect of fiction (No. 8).

Sir,

I was led into a train of reflections, a few days since, from perusing a paper in Dr Johnson's *Rambler*, respecting works of fiction, in which he sanctions an opinion, which appears to have been generally received: that in narratives where historical veracity has no place, the most perfect models of virtue ought only to be exhibited. The arguments adduced in support of this notion, are those which regard the prevalence of example, the respect due to the innocence of youth, and the moral advantages which may be expected to result from engaging the affections on the side of virtue.

Notwithstanding the authority of so respected a moralist, I am, I confess, inclined to suspect this reasoning to be fallacious. The greater proportion of modern novelists, from the incomparable Richardson, down to the humble purveyors of the circulating libraries, appear to have aimed at proceeding upon this principle: to calculate the effects produced by their labours upon the morals and manners of the age, might, perhaps, be an unpleasant and an invidious task.

The business of familiar narrative should be to describe life and manners in real or probable situations, to delineate the human mind in its endless varieties, to develop the heart, to paint the passions, to trace the springs of action, to interest the imagination, exercise the affections, and awaken the powers of the mind. A good novel ought to be subservient to the purposes of truth and philosophy: such are the novels of Fielding and Smollett.

The beauty of romance consists principally in the display of a picturesque fancy, and the creative powers of a fertile and inventive genius. The excellence of a novel is of a distinct nature, and must be the result of an attentive observance of mankind, acute discernment, exquisite moral sensibility, and an intimate acquaintance with human passions and powers. A luxuriant and poetic style of composition accords with the legends of romance. The language of his novelist should be simple, unaffected, perspicuous, yet energetic, touching, and impressive. It is not necessary that we should be able to deduce from a novel, a formal and didactic moral; it is sufficient if it has a tendency to raise the mind by elevated sentiments, to warm the heart with generous affections, to enlarge our views, or to increase our stock of useful knowledge. A more effectual lesson might perhaps be deduced from tracing the pernicious consequences of an erroneous judgment, a wrong step, an imprudent action, an indulged and intemperate affection, a bad habit, in a character in other respects amiable and virtuous, than in painting chimerical perfection and visionary excellence, which rarely, if ever, existed.

Fictitious histories, in the hands of persons of talents and observation, might be made productive of incalculable benefit; by interesting curiosity, and addressing the common sympathies of our nature, they pervade all ranks; and, judiciously conducted, would become a powerful and effective engine of truth and reform.

M.H.

128. William Godwin on Smollett's style

1797

From William Godwin, *The Enquirer: Reflections on Education, Manners, and Literature*, 1797, pp. 467–70. This extract, is from part II, essay XII, 'Of English Style'. Godwin (1756–1836), philosopher and novelist; author of *Political Justice*; his daugher Mary was Shelley's second wife.

From the examination of Fielding we proceed to that of Smollett.

The effort of the first of these writers, in the novel of *Tom Jones*, in the character of Parson Adams, and a few other instances, are exquisitely meritorius. But, when Fielding delights us, he appears to go out of himself. The general character of his genius, will probably he found to be jejune and puerile. For the truth of this remark, we may appeal, in particular, to his comedies.

Every thing that is the reverse of this may be affirmed of Smollett. He has published more volumes, upon more subjects, than perhaps any other author of modern date; and, in all, he has left marks of his genius. The greater part of his novels are peculiarly excellent. He is nevertheless a hasty writer; when he affects us most, we are aware that he might have done more. In all his works of invention, we find the stamp of a mighty mind. In his lightest sketches, there is nothing frivolous, trifling and effeminate. In his most glowing portraits, we acknowledge a mind at ease, rather essaying its powers, than tasking them. We applaud his works; but it is with a profounder sentiment that we mediate his capacity.

The style of Smollett has never been greatly admired; and it is brought forward here merely to show in what manner men of the highest talents, and of great eminence in the *belles lettres*, could write forty or fifty years ago.

His most considerable production is *Roderick Random*. Let the reader take as a specimen of his style, the story of Mrs Sagely, in the beginning of the second volume, as related by herself.

[quotes *Roderick Random*, vol. II, ch. XXXVIII, pp. 11–12]

It is unnecessary to transcribe the remainder of the passage. Suffice it to say that it is in vain that, in any part of it, we should search for the scholar, the man of education, or the man of taste. The composer of the fictitious writing indeed, sometimes lowers his style to suit the meanness or absurdity of his personages. But this ought never to be done, except where it is attended with comic effect. It is the office of the poet and the novelist to adorn the style of their characters, and to give to real life the most impressive form. We do not suppose the real Hamlet always to have spoken with that felicity or that energy of diction which Shakespeare has bestowed on him. Mrs Sagely's narrative might have been written with simplicity; but it should have been written with elegance. On the contrary we find little in it above the style of a servant-maid over her winter fire.

129. Charles Lamb to Wordsworth
1801

From a letter to Wordsworth of 1801, reprinted in Charles
and Mary Lamb, *Works*, ed. E.V. Lucas, 7 vols, 1903, vol VI,
p. 209.

An intelligent reader finds a sort of insult in being told, I will teach
you how to think upon this subject. This fault, if I am right, is in a
ten-thousandth worse degree to be found in Sterne and many other
novelists & modern poets, who continually put a sign post up to
shew where you are to feel. They set out with assuming their
readers to be stupid. Very different from *Robinson Crusoe*, the *Vicar
of Wakefield*, *Roderick Random*, and other beautiful bare narratives.

130. An American letter on Smollett
1802

From *The Port Folio*, Philadelphia, vol. II, no. 24, 19 June
1802, 185–6. A letter to 'The American Lounger, Samuel
Saunter, Esq.'. *The Port Folio* was founded and edited from
1801 to 1812 by Joseph Dennie under the pseudonym 'Oliver
Oldschool, Esq.' Its volumes contain various references to
Smollett including in the first volume a letter to Smollett
from James Boswell dated 14 March 1768.

SIR,

In reading your 22d number, my attention was taken by some
remarks on novels, under the signature of J.D. I read his letter to

Samuel Saunter more than once, as the subject has always had some interest with me, but am sorry to confess, that I do not very clearly comprehend his meaning. It seems, however, to be his purpose to decry the writings of Richardson, and to show, that Le Sage, Smollett, and Fielding are much better teachers of morality than he. For this end, he tells us, that the former exhibits improbable scences, characters too perfect for imitation, and exalts the brilliant and heroic qualities, generosity, benevolence, and compassion, on the ruins of the humble and unostentatious, but more solid and useful virtues, of prudence, economy, justice. The latter, on the contrary, exhibit manners and characters, *whose prototype is in nature*; they place their personages in scenes, that may actually occur in real life; by shewing the errors into which passion may betray us, they tend to render virtue amiable, and vice odious. This appears to be the meaning of your correspondent: yet I state this meaning with diffidence. I suspect *myself* of misapprehension, not only because the style of J.D. is not remarkably clear, but because these sentiments are very strange in one, who has read either of the works of any of the authors mentioned.

As to Smollett, he is far inferior to the other, in every thing but wit. His characters, for the most parts, are *caricatures*, whose greatest merit lies in their power to make us laugh at their humour and extravagance. It would be difficult to point out a more profligate and hurtful book than *Peregrine Pickle*. *Roderick Random* is a tissue of low adventures; the history of a man without steadiness or principle, and who can be, by turns, a gambler, heiress-hunter, sharper, sailor, and soldier, and I know not what, and who, at last, becomes sober and rich, in a way from which the reader can derive no useful instruction. In *Count Fathom*, there is still prevailing the same spirit of low adventure and chicane. The count is a mere cheat and ruffian. *Sir Launcelot Greaves*, with abundance of coarse, vulgar, and otherwise exceptionable scenes, is the most moral and instructive of all Smollett's works. It is, however, a very lame imitation of Cervantes.

As to the *usefulness* of these several performances, we must consider, that the tendency of a book of this kind does not consist so much in the good or bad, the prosperous or adverse nature, the loftiness or lowness of the incidents and characters, but in the light in which the author places all these; the inferences which his contrivance and arrangement naturally suggest. How differently will the same story be told by a *pure* and a *profligate* narrator? How will the same event inculcate opposite lessons, according to the light in which different hands exhibit it? Without entering into metaphysical inquiries into the 'why' and the 'wherefore,' it is evident, that the tendency of fictitious narrations, and, truth, of narratives of all kinds, depends upon the judgment, the taste, and the views of the narrator.

Smollett's wit and genius were considerable, but his moral discernment was far from being unexceptionable, and his taste far from being pure. He apparently delights in vulgar and profligate company, and of simple and sublime virtue he knows nothing. 'The impulses of sentiment,' 'A thoughtless generosity,' seem to be the height of his ken. The plain, sober, uniform excellence of reason or religion, are not to be looked for in his volumes.

Fielding is coarse, vulgar, and indelicate; recruiting officers, courtezans, sharpers, and adventurers, are too much the company to his liking. An ale-house kitchen, the humours of a landlady and chambermaid, are the scenes most congenial to his experience and taste. The pure and the sound mind will extract wisdom from every thing, and Fielding and Smollett will ever be valued by judicious readers, for their wit, their strong and vivid portraits of human characters, and the testimony which their ingenious narrations, with more or less energy, afford to the beauty and the usefulness of virtue: but the approbation which, with regard to them, will be qualified and moderate, with soar into something like rapture, at the pathetic and varied eloquence, the moral grandeur and sublimity of Richardson.

131. Hugh Murray on the morality of Smollett's fiction

1805

From Hugh Murray, *Morality of Fiction*, Edinburgh, 1805, pp. 106–8.

Smollett is still coarser than Fielding, and does not possess the same intimate knowledge of the human heart. As a painter of manners, however, he is little if at all, inferior. He excels particularly in those of seamen, chiefly, no doubt, from having been once engaged in that profession himself. But his most striking talent seems to be humour, the exhibition of odd and eccentric characters. Of these he has assembled, in *Humphery Clinker*, the most ludicrous and amusing collection that is anywhere to be found.

In a moral view, Smollett is inferior to Fielding. The vices of his heroes are at least as great, without the same good qualities to counterbalance them. We meet nothing of that refined generosity, and those just sentiments, at least, of moral conduct which Fielding's heroes discover. Indeed, Smollett, in regard to his, seems to make hardly any distinction between their best and their worst actions; both are related in the same animated and approving manner.

Roderick Random is generally supposed to contain only an embellished narrative of his own adventures. The character of the hero, therefore, is naturally supposed to resemble his own; high spirited, irritable, and vindictive; not devoid of a certain rough generosity and good humour, but destitute of any fixed principles, and readily yielding to every temptation which chance throws in his way. There is more real life and business in this novel than are commonly to be met with. It does not, indeed, always present these under the most favourable aspect, but is deeply tinged with those irritable and satirical habits which appear to have strongly predominated in the mind of the writer.

Peregrine Pickle presents us with nearly the same features, only that the humour is broader, and the manners still coarser and more licentious.

Humphrey Clinker contains less incident, and is therefore not quite so attractive to the bulk of readers. But it possesses, perhaps, more genuine merit, as being that in which Smollett has most completely displayed his talent for the ludicrous delineation of character. Bramble is supposed to be a picture of himself in more advanced life, after his spirit was lowered, and his temper soused by age and infirmity. He discovers, however, a view of worth and benevolence, which did not appear in his youthful predecessors. In Tabitha malignity and ill-temper are very properly represented under a ridiculous and disgusting aspect. The tendency of the whole is nearly unexceptionable.

132. Lord Woodhouselee on Smollett's humour

1807

From *Memoirs of the Life and Writing of Henry Home of Kames*, 2 vols, Edinburgh, 1807, ed. A.F. Tytler, Lord Woodhouselee, vol. I, bk II, p. 316. Woodhouselee here takes issue with Kames's theories on 'Humour' in his *Elements of Criticism*.

The same is the case with *Tom Bowling*, and the Welshman *Morgan*, in *Roderick Random*. In these characters, humour is associated with a degree of dignity, which is absolutely exclusive of the emotions of contempt. It is no doubt true, that humour may occasionally be conjoined with meanness; as in the characters of *Falstaff, Bardolph, Captain Bobadil*; and in the latter instances, our contempt is excited along with our ludicrous emotions: but the preceding examples shew to demonstration, that this union is not, as has been supposed, essential: on the contrary, the displeasing ingredient of meanness in the latter characters, seems to lessen, and derogate from, the purer pleasure we receive from the equally ludicrous characters in which it has no place.

133. [Lady Anne Hamilton] on Smollett's prostitute pen

1807

In a footnote to the verses by Lady Anne Hamilton, *The Epics of the Ton*, 1807, p. 6. Lady Hamilton (1766–1846) was a lady-in-waiting to Queen Caroline. Her *Secret History of the Court* (1832) was published in her name but without her permission.

Or with poor Smollett, fain for gold to tickle,
Wrought up with liquorish gust the feasts of Pickle.

Note
Poor Smollett! It is lamentable to recollect that the author of *Roderick Random* and of *Humphry Clinker* should have prostituted his pen to delineate the debaucheries of *Peregrine Pickle*. Does the latter display genius? so much the worse. The prostitute, who haunts the way-side in rags, only disgusts the loathing eye: it is she, whose voluptuous limbs shine through the transparent muslin, that lures us to our ruin. *Peregrine Pickle* adorns many a toilet whose Aristotle's *Master-piece* would be thought to carry indelible pollution. It is said that my Lord ——, on entering her ladyship's apartment one morning, perceived the third volume of *Peregrine Pickle* under her pillow. As she was asleep, he gently withdrew it, and substituted in its room a Common Prayer Book. One may imagine her ladyship's surprise, when, on awaking, and resorting to her dear morning's treat, she found the amours of Lady —— converted by magic art into the Litany.

134. Smollett's naval novels

1808

From Edward Mangin, *An Essay on Light Reading*, 1808, pp. 121–40. Mangin (1772–1852), a prebend ordained in the Irish Church, was a miscellaneous writer. His is the most sustained critique of Smollett's 'naval' characters, in a section of the essay called 'Strictures on Smollett'.

Of the few productions which have come under the title of 'Naval Novels,' Smollett has been said to be the originator; and, chronologically speaking, he is so. We cannot, however, agree in the dictum which attributes to him the highest excellence in nautical fiction; and we shall endeavour to show why it is that we differ from the verdict of the majority of critics who have estimated the genius of Smollett as a Naval Novelist. In other respect, no eulogy which has ever yet been paid by the warmest admirers of this great writer can, for one instant, be deemed extravagant. Our present business with Smollett is confined to those parts of his works which tend to exhibit to landsmen the nature of the *goings-on* at sea. Critics in all times have done more to mislead than to guide the multitude; never has the perverseness of the honourable craft been so triumphant as in the false impression regarding sea-stories produced by them on the public mind. This is the more remarkable, as happening in a maritime nation which transcends all others in the power and extent of its navy, and wherein it might consequently be imagined that almost every landsman would have some knowledge of marine affairs. The reverse of this, however, is the fact. No people in the world know less of the matter. Englishmen, indeed, are fond of the subject, but they take no pains to qualify themselves to apply the test of truth to such 'Tales of the Sea' as come before them: and yet we were told by Lord Halifax, one hundred and twenty-nine years ago, that 'the first article of an Englishman's political creed must be, that he believeth in the sea.'

Smollett, being the first writer (at least of novels) who attempted to delineate nautical life, critics and readers have been induced to take every thing uttered by him for gospel; and most unquestionably to him are the public indebted for many scenes afloat, which, being stamped by the hand of genius, are not likely soon to fade. Still it is not safe to rely implicitly on Smollett's representations; for though occasionally these are founded in a deep knowledge of the human heart, seconded by great skill in portraiture, his humour, generally speaking, is not so much that of a painter of real life as of a caricaturist; and the propensity to add the *outré* to what is in itself extravagant, though seen here and there through all his writings, is no where more obvious than in his naval scenes. Upon his exaggeration of naval character and incident, and upon the forced and inconsistent phraseology put into the mouths of his seamen, the critic has erected his standard of excellence in this line of fiction; but critics are, for the most part, 'Gentlemen of England who live at home,' though *not* at ease. [We are sorry to vitiate the quotation.] Now before a man can write like a seaman, he must learn to *think* like a seaman; and while we join in the general testimony as to the surpassing genius of Smollett, we may be allowed to add that vagueness of delineation no less than extravagance is a defect in his naval sketches. For example, we do not discern in his writings those nice distinctions of character which mark the different grades of the profession. Trunnion the commodore, Oakum the captain, Bowling and Hatchway the lieutenants, Jack Ratlin and Tom Pipes the foremast-men, speak alike in the same strain of extravagant metaphor, which is not only misplaced in itself, but, in nine cases out of ten, is broken by the most violent incongruities[a].

In the 73rd chapter of *Peregrine Pickle* we find the following passage in the dying speech of Commodore Trunnion: 'This cursed hiccough makes such a *rippling* in the current of my speech, that mayhap you don't understand what I say. Now, while the sucker of my *wind-pump* will go, I would willingly mention a few things, which I hope you will set down in the log-book of your remembrance, when I am stiff, d'ye see. There's your aunt sitting whimpering by the fire. I desire you will keep her tight, warm, and easy in her old age; she's an honest heart in her own way; and thof she goes a little *crank* and humorsome, by being often *overstowed* with Nantz and religion, yet she has been a faithful *shipmate* to me,' &c. &c.

In the foregoing passage, Smollett might, had he been living, have sheltered himself from our weak assault respecting the application of the phrase 'crank,' under the great authority of Shakespeare, who says that in drunkenness 'the brain is the heavier for being too light.' Be this as it may, we are certain that such a strain of discourse is at once improbable as occurring on a *death-bed*, and perfectly senseless as nautical metaphor. To be 'crank' is to want ballast, not to be 'overstowed;' and if the rippling of the current of a man's speech will prevent his being understood, surely a wind-pump ought not to be called into play to increase the rippling; though, up to the present hour, His Majesty's navy has been unaided by the operations of such an instrument as a *wind*-pump.

In making the above remarks, we fear that we may be considering the great novelist too closely, especially as his works are rather exhibitions or caricatures of life in general, than of that small portion of it which is confined to a ship. Smollett's sea-scenes are only *incidental* to his stories; they do not constitute the staple of *Roderick Random*; while the locality of *Peregrine Pickle*, though some of the principal characters are seamen, is altogether on shore. One of the great difficulties common to naval novelists is unceremoniously got rid of by our Scotch writer;—we allude to the non-introduction of his heroines afloat. They are confined to the shore, a circumstance which confers no very enviable benefit on the landsmen with whom they must associate, inasmuch as Smollett's virtuous women, of whom of course his heroines are formed, are any thing but attractive. It is hardly necessary to say that virtuous women are the best of women; but certain it is that Smollett had not the talent to invest purity with interest. His mind, we fear, was essentially gross, and (not to affect a paradox) his best women are his worst.

The most perfect of Smollett's naval delineations are to be found in his incidents in the cockpit, in which place, as a surgeon's mate, he would necessarily have been domiciliated; and this is not only evident in such parts of *Roderick Random* as are descriptive of scenes at the amputating table, but is also shown in the manner in which he so minutely depicts such cable-tier tricks as 'cutting down', 'reefing sheets,' 'turning the turtle,' 'blowing the grampus,' and similar manual jokes peculiar to the lower regions of the orlop. In descriptions of this nature Smollett seems to revel; but it is worthy of remark, that although he had poetical faculties of no mean order, as manifested not only in his metrical productions but in his prose fictions, (witness the ghastly scene with the robbers in the forest, in *Count Fathom*,) yet he seems incompetent to delineate with minuteness and fidelity the grand aspect of nature on the deep. He endeavours indeed frequently to do this; but his descriptions resemble more the style of a writer labouring in his study, than that of a man whose imagination had been excited by the sublime influences of the scene. His 'tempests' and 'battles' are not exhibited for the grandeur inherent in themselves, but are made subservient to a display of incidents connected with his own individual profession; for example, what he terms the hurricane in *Roderick Random*, is briefly despatched in order that 'Poor Jack Rattlin,' who had fallen from the main-yard arm, at the expense of a broken leg, should be brought below to the surgeon for an operation. All the circumstances contingent upon this accident are described with minute detail, and are unquestionably very interesting. Again, in his 'battles' the reader's attention is not so much engaged by the impending fate of the hostile ships, as by the display of knives, bandages, tourniquets, and all the paraphernalia of marine surgery,—'a terrible show.' This proves that even a great man (and Smollett is truly such) may occasionally smell of the shop.

We have already spoken of the Doctor's tendency to exaggeration[b]; and, that we may not be thought to accuse him rashly, let us cite one of the scenes wherein this tendency will be readily apparent. It is from *Roderick Random*.—We must premise that Captain Oakum has tyrannically commanded the 'sick' of his ship to be reviewed on the quarter-deck.

[quotes *Roderick Random*, vol. I, ch. XXVII, pp. 221–3 from 'This inhuman order shocked us extremely,...' to 'and then departed without any ceremony.']

That for too long a period it had been a practice prevalent in the navy to muster the sick on deck, we readily admit; but we unhesitatingly assert, that at no time of the service, even in the most tyrannical days, (and there is no denying that those of Smollett were certainly the worst,) could such a series of cool atrocities by any possibility have been perpetrated; the officers would have remonstrated, or the crew would have mutinied: flesh and blood, in short, could not have borne it, but would indignantly have asserted the rights of humanity, and forced the cowardly despot to 'walk the plank'. There are times and sufferings under the pressure of which it is difficult to wait the tardy retribution of the law. But a mere violation of probability did not deter Smollett from indulging a desire to satirise the 'Service,' which it has been often said he detested. The wilfulness of purpose breaks out indeed in all his works.[c] Whatever he seems inclined to say, he says plainly and recklessly. There are passages in all his novels, especially in Roderick Random, which no other than himself, not even Fielding, would have dared to put forth. Talk of a 'Family Shakespeare' indeed!—we wish good Mr Bowdler had directed his purifying operations to the works of our physician; for we know, and so does every one else, that no books are more freely put into the hands of youth, by well-meaning persons too, than the works of the novelists.

With reference to his propensity to caricature, it may not be superfluous to allude to the extravagant dress in which Smollett has thought proper to attire Captain Whiffle upon the occasion of his going on board to supersede Oakum in the command of his ship:—'A *white* hat, garnished with a *red* feather, adorned his head, from whence his hair flowed upon his shoulders in ringlets, tied behind with a ribbon. His coat, consisting of *pink*-coloured *silk*, lined with white, by the elegance of the cut retired backward, as it were, to discover a white satin waistcoat, embroidered with gold, unbuttoned at the upper part to display a brooch set with garnets, that glittered in the breast of his shirt, which was of the finest cambric, edged with right Mechlin: the knees of his *crimson velvet breeches* scarce descended so low as to meet his silk stockings, which rose without spot or wrinkle on his meagre legs from shoes of *blue* maroquin, studded with diamond buckles that flamed forth rivals to the sun! A steel-hilted sword, inlaid with gold, and decked with a knot of ribbon which fell down in rich tassel, equipped his side; and an amber-headed cane hung dangling from his wrist. But the most remarkable parts of his furniture were, a *mask* on his *face*, and white gloves on his hands, which did not seem to be put on with an intention to be pulled off occasionally, but were fixed with a curious *ring* on the *little finger* of each hand.' So that it was not, as the Frenchman says in the song, 'on his ring he wore a *fingere*,' but on his glove he wore a ring; or, as Jack would say, he wore a ring '*over all.*'

This is a dress which Smollett might indeed have seen among the fancy characters at a Ranelagh masquerade, but which could not by any possibility have been exhibited on the quarter-deck of a man-of-war, however ridiculous and contemptible the character of the wearer.

It is true that in the days of Smollett, *Jack* himself was rather 'rumly rigged.' A little low cocked-hat, a 'pea-jacket' (a sort of cumbrous Dutch-cut coat), a pair of 'petticoat trowsers' not much unlike a highland kilt, tight stockings with pinchbeck buckles in his shoes, constituted his amphibious 'fit-out;' he had no tail; but, excepting this useful deprivation, no costume could be less adapted for a seaman's work. Fancy a man in this attire at the mast-hand sending down a to '-gallant-yard, or hauling-out a weather-earing in a close-reef topsail breeze.—The tar of Trafalgar was another guess sort of fellow—his jacket was short and succinct, and though his tail, half-mast down his back, brought him up now and then with a round-turn, he had no useless coat-skirts to be caught in the sheeve of a block,—an accident by which his predecessor in the days of Benbow not unfrequently lost what he called his 'precious limbs.' Let him only be taut about the stern, and our Trafalgarian (for Jack, out of a horror of any thing military, despises suspenders) cares not how loose his trowsers may be from fork to foot.

We have spoken freely of what has struck us to be defects in the naval portion of Smollett's comic romances. We must not omit however to allude to the very masterly sketch of Commodore Trunnion. Having ventured to object to certain passages as unworthy of the general skill of the writer, let us specify some of those which manifest his genuine vein of comedy. In this way nothing can be better than the out-bursting of Trunnion's feelings on hearing that one of his juniors had been made a peer of the realm. The speech is too *good* for quotation; but it is perfect in its way, whether considered as manifestation of professional pique, or as illustrative of the weakness of the human heart. By the way it is worthy of notice, that when the scene is afloat, as in *Roderick Random*, Smollett's style and feelings seem to partake of the uncomfortable state of things inseparable we fear from a life at sea, especially as regards the junior officers, among whom the doctor's experience was gained. His pen therefore seems to have been dipped in gall and bilge-water. Nothing short of satirising and abusing the Service will content him; but when his naval heroes are settled comfortably in shore-retirement, as in *Peregrine Pickle*, the spleen of the writer vanishes; all is jocose and kindly on his part, and, for the life of him, he cannot delineate any worse traits in his seaman than those which may be safely said to come under the head of amiable eccentricities.

NOTES

a Innumerable passages similar to the following might be cited in support of this assertion:—'A third, seeing my hair clotted together with blood, as if were, into distinct cords, took notice that my *bows* were *manned* with red ropes instead of my side.'—How either the bows or side of a ship could be '*manned* with *ropes*' we, knowing something of man as well as of nauticals, are quite at a loss to conceive. A seaman would have said 'Red ropes are *shipped* to your bows,' instead of to your side.

b 'It is remarkable,' says a contemporary critic, 'that Sir Walter Scott, in his *Biographical Memoirs* of British Novelists, should have selected for eulogy a circumstance which every seaman must ridicule.'—'Fielding,' says Sir Walter, 'has no passage which approaches in sublimity to the robber scene in *Count Fathom*, or the terrible description of a sea engagement, in which *Roderick Random sits chained and exposed on the poop*, without the power of motion, or exertion, *during the carnage* of a tremendous engagement.' Vol. III, p. 198.

'Every seaman well knows that nothing more unlikely could have occurred before a battle than deliberately to incapacitate and expose to danger one of the two men on whose surgical assistance the lives of so many of the crew, including that the captain himself, would depend.'

c Again in *Roderick Random*.

135. Mrs Barbauld on Smollett

1810

From *The British Novelists*, edited with biographical and critical introductions by Mrs Anna Laetitia Barbauld, vol. XXX, 1810, pp. v. ff.

In 1748 Smollett began his career of a novel-writer by publishing *The Life and Adventures of Roderick Random*, a work replete with humour and character, for a long time universally read by novel-readers, and still a favourite, as are all Smollett's, with those who can overlook their grossness, vugarity, and licentious morals. Smollett seems to have taken Le Sage in his *Gil Blas*, and Scarron in his *Roman Comique*, for his models.

Roderick Random, like *Gil Blas*, has little or nothing of regular plot, and no interest is excited for the hero, whose name serves to string together a number of adventures. This work is in a great measure the history of the author's own life. The novel opens with the story of a young couple turned our of doors by their father on account of an imprudent match, and their consequent distress. It is natural and affecting. The cool selfish character of the parent, the scene of the female relations besieging his death-bed, the opening of the will, and the disappoinment of the gaping cousins, are all admirably drawn, and probably contain much of the author's own story on the death of his grandfather. The character of a British tar is portrayed in that of Tom Bowling, uncle to the hero of the piece. It has been the original of most sailor characters which have been since exhibited. He is drawn brave, blunt, generous, enthusiastically fond of his profession, and with a mixture of surliness in the expression of his kindest affections. There is an admirable stroke of nature in his behaviour, when, after attending the opening of the will, he walks away with his nephew, indignant that nothing had been left him. Full of vexation, he quickens his pace and walks so fast that the poor lad cannot keep up with him; upon which he calls out to him with a cross tone, "What! must I bring to every moment for you, you lazy dog?" his anger thus venting itself on the very person on whose account that anger was excited. Into this novel the author has introduced an account of the expedition to Carthagena, and has given a strong and disgusting picture of the manner of living on board a man of war. It must give pleasure to the reader of the present day to consider how much the attention to health, cleanliness, and accommodation, in respect to our navy, has increased since that account was written. Still, it is probable, nothing can present a more horrible sight than the deck of a man of war after a battle. Many of the characters in these volumes are said to be portraits. Strap the barber, schoolfellow and humble friend of Random, was one Hugh Hewson, whose death was lately announced in the papers. Captain Whiffle was a particular nobleman. Much of the work is filled up with low jokes, and laughable stories, such as, one may suppose, had been circulated in a club over a bottle. Some incidental particulars mark the state of accommodations at that time. Roderick Random comes to London with the *pack-horses*, there being then no stage waggon, and the inventory of his goods and linen was very probably Smollett's own.

Towards the hero of this tale the reader feels little interest; but after he has been led through a variety of adventures, in which he exhibits as little of the amiable qualities as of the more respectable ones, the author, according to the laudable custom of novel-writers, leaves him in possession of a beautiful wife and a good estate.

In the summer of 1750 Dr Smollett took a trip to Paris, and laid in a fund or a new display of character in his *Peregrine Pickle*. This is a work even more faulty than the former in its violation of decency and good morals. It has two or three characters of sailors not devoid of humour, though inferior to his first sketch of Tom Bowling. Commodore Trunnion is so rough and bearish, as scarcely to be like any thing human. He is the Caliban of Smollett. The wife is still more overcharged. Peregrine himself is a proud, disagreeable, ungrateful boy; vicious, as soon as he could know what vice was, and who had deserved to be hanged long before the end of the first volume. The most entertaining and original part of *Peregrine* is the account of a classical feast, supposed to have been held by a learned physician and other gentlemen, after the manner of the ancients. In this there is humour, and a display of learning, though in the former it is inferior to Scriblerus. Dr Akenside was meant to be marked out by the physician, and a painter whom he met at Paris furnished the character of Pallet.

The author has in this work shown his predilection for the party of the Stuarts, by introducing in a touching manner some Scottish gentlemen under exile for having engaged in the rebellion of 1745, whom Peregrine is supposed to meet at Boulogne and who go every day to the sea-side to gaze with fond affection on the white cliffs of Britain, which they were never more to behold but at a distance. This Dr Moore mentions as a real incident he was himself witness to, being with Smollett at the time. Many strictures on the government and manners of France are introduced into this work;

some of them just, but tinged with that prejudice against French manners which he had deeply imbibed, and which showed itself afterwards in his travels.

The Memoirs of a Lady of Pleasure, Lady Vane, written by herself, are introduced into this work. They excited interest at the time, the lady being then much talked of, but can only now raise astonishment at the assurance which could give such a life without compunction.

It is probable that Smollett had been struck with the objections which must have been made to these two novels, that no poetical justice is exercised on the characters; for in his next piece, *Count Fathom*, he has exhibited, as the hero of his piece, a vicious character, who, after going through many scenes of triumphant villany, is detected and punished: but the narration is far from pleasing; knavery is not dignified enough to interest us by its fall. There are more serious characters in this piece, and he has attempted scenes of tenderness and exalted feeling, but with little success. Strong humour he possessed, but grace and delicacy were foreign to his pencil. He could not draw an interesting female character. But in his own way, the picture of Count Fathom's mother, the follower of a camp, is very striking. It is impossible to contemplate her going about, stripping the dying and the dead, with all the coolness of a mind long hardend by scenes of misery, without a thrill of horror. Count Fathom's adventure in the wood, where he is benighted, and narrowly escapes being murdered by ruffians, is exceedingly well told, and a man must have strong nerves to read it without shuddering. There is less of humour in this than in his two former works; but the study of the sharper, who introduces himself to a gaming-table as a boisterous, ignorant country squire, and takes in the knowing ones, is very amusing....

About this time he published another novel, *The Adventures of Sir Launcelot Greaves*. It is an imitation of *Don Quixote*, and is but a flat performance....

Smollett's temper was not well calculated for calmness in such altercations, and the virulence with which he wrote *The Adventures of an Atom*, a political satire describing public characters that figured upon the stage at the end of the last reign and beginning of the present, lost him many of his best friends.

As a novel-writer the characteristics of Smollett are strong masculine humour, a knowledge of the world, particularly of the vicious part of it; and great force in drawing his characters; but of grace and amenity he had no idea. Neither had he any finesse. He does not know how, like Fielding, to insinuate an idea under the mask of a grave irony. He had largely conversed with the world, and travelled, so that his delineations of character and adventures are as different as possible from the effusions of the sentimental theorist. He had certainly vigour of genius, as well as rapidity of execution, but he had none of the finer feelings. To the tender and delicate sensibilities of love he seems to have been a stranger, and he fails whenever he attempts serious and interesting characters. He has little of plot, but deals much in stories of broad mirth, such such as that of the man who got at all the secrets of the town by pretending deafness; and his works would afford much pleasant amusement, if it were not for the coarseness and vicious manners which pervade them all.

His mind, either from the vulgar scenes of his early life, or the society of the crew of a man-of-war, seems to have received an indelible taint of vice and impurity. Vice in his works cannot be said to be seductive; for an air of misanthropy pervades all his compositions, and he has scarcely in any of them given us one character to love. It has been said of Fielding, that he could not draw a thoroughly virtuous character; but Smollett could not draw an amiable one. It must be remembered, however, that vice may pollute the mind, and coarseness vitiate the taste, even when presented in the least attractive form; and it is therefore to the praise of the present generation that this author's novels are much less read now than they were formerly. The least exceptionable of them is *Humphrey Clinker*, which, that a name of so much celebrity might not be entirely passed over, makes a part of this Selection. It was written at a time when the author's mind was mellowed by age, and cultured society had somewhat softened the coarseness of his painting without destroying his vein of humour. It is the only one of his productions in this line which has not a vicious tendency; but though the *moral sense* is not offended in it, the same cannot be said of all the other senses. There is very little of plot in *Humphrey Clinker*. It is carried on in letters, and is rather a frame for remarks on Bath, London, &c. than a regular story. There is a great deal of humour, especially in the first volume: the latter part might be entitled with more propriety A Tour into Scotland, and not an unentertaining one, though the nationality of the author is very apparent. The character of Matthew Bramble, Smollett seems to intend for his own. He is represented as a humourist and a misanthrope, with good sense and a feeling heart under his rough husk. His letters are filled with the most caustic strictures upon every thing he sees and hears; the London markets, the rooms and company at Bath and Bristol, the accommodations in travelling; and, in short, every thing he meets with is disgusting till be comes to Scotland—when the scene is changed. He has introduced a whimsical character, Lismahago, into whose mouth he artfully puts an apology for his countrymen more partial than he would have chosen to take upon himself. The letters of Bramble are amusingly contrasted with those of his niece, who sees every thing with the youthful eyes of admiration, and is pleased and happy every where; by which means the author has in a sprightly manner exhibited both sides of the canvass. The reader is often put in mind of *The Bath Guide*, which has suggested several of his remarks and descriptions, and which may also be traced in the humour of the characters. The letters of Tabitha Bramble are very diverting. Winifred is another Slip-slop; but her bad spelling grows rather tiresome towards the end. It must be observed that the style of the different personages, all appropriate, is admirably kept up during the whole work. *Humphrey Clinker* is the only one of the author's pieces that has no sailor in it. It may perhaps be a greater curiosity or that reason, as the connoisseurs value a Wouverman without a horse.

. 136. Alexander Chalmers on Smollett

1810

From Alexander Chalmers, *Works of the English Poets*, 21 vols, 1810, vol. xv, pp. 543–54, 548, 549, 550, 551–2. Like Smollett, Chalmers was a Scotsman, a medical doctor, and a writer. His work on the English poets is an updating of Johnson's *Lives of the English Poets*, with additional lives by Chalmers. Among his contributions to Smollett scholarship is his claim to identify numerous characters in the novels with people known to Smollett in his life. His critical commentary on Smollett's novels is dependent upon his predecessors such as Anderson (No. 125) and Moore (No. 126) and is here excerpted to avoid repetition.

From pp. 543–4:

As he had upon his marriage, hired a genteel house, and lived in a more hospitable style than the possession of the whole of his wife's fortune could have supported, he was again obliged to have recourse to his pen, and produced, in 1748, *The Adventures of Roderick Random*, in two volumes, 12mo. This was the most successful of all his writings, and perhaps the most popular novel of the age, This it owed, partly to the notion that it was in many respects a history of his own life, and partly to its intrinsic merit, as a delineation of real life, manners and characters, given with a force of humour to which the public had not been accustomed. If, indeed, we consider its moral tendency, there are few productions more unfit for perusal; yet such were his opinions of public decency that he seriously fancied he was writing to humour the taste, and correct the morals of the age. That it contains a history of his own life was probably a surmise artfully circulated to excite curiosity, but that real characters are depicted was much more obvious, independent of those whom he introduced out of revenge, as Lacy and Garrick for rejecting his tragedy, there are traits of many other persons more or less disguised, in the introduction of which he was incited merely by the recollection of foibles which deserved to be exposed. Every man who draws characters, whether to complete the fable of a novel, or to illustrate an essay, will be insensibly attracted by what he has seen in real life, and real life was Smollett's object in all his novels. His only monster is Count Fathom, but he deals in none of those perfect beings who are the heroes of the more modern novels....

His stay here was not long, for in 1751 he published his second most popular novel, *Peregrine Pickle*, in four volumes, 12mo, which was received with great avidity. In the second edition, which was called for within a few months, he speaks, with more craft than truth, of certain booksellers and others who misrepresented the work and calumniated the author. He could not, however, conceal, and his biographers have told the shameless tale for him, that, 'he received a handsome reward' for inserting the profligate memoirs of lady Vane. It is only wonderful that after this he could 'flatter himself that he had expunged every adventure, phrase, and insinuation, that could be construed, by the most delicate readers, into a trespass upon the rules of decorum.' In this work, as in *Roderick Random*, he indulged his unhappy propensity to personal satire and revenge by introducing living characters. He again endeavoured to degrade those of Garrick and Quin, who, it is said, had expressed a more unfavourable opinion of the Regicide than even Garrick, and was yet more unpardonable in holding up Dr Akenside to ridicule....

His first publication, in this retirement, if it may be so called, was the *Adventures of Ferdinand Count Fathom*, in 1753. This novel, in the popular opinion, has been reckoned greatly inferior to his former productions, but merely, as I conceive, because it is unlike them. There is such a perpetual flow of sentiment and expression in this production, as must give a very high idea of the fertility of his mind; but in the delineation of characters he departs too much from real life, and many of his incidents are highly improbable. Mr Cumberland, in the *Memoirs* of his own Life, lately published, takes credit to himself for the character of Abraham Adams, and of Sheva in his comedy of the Jew, which are, however, correct transcripts of Smollett's Jew. It would not have greatly lessened the merit of his benevolent views towards that depressed nation, had Mr Cumberland frankly made this acknowledgement....

From p. 548:

During his confinement in King's Bench for the libel on admiral Knowles, he amused himself in writing the *Adventures of Sir Launcelot Greaves*, a sort of English *Quixote*. This he gave in detached parts in the *British Magazine*, one of those periodical works in which he was induced to engage by the consideration of a regular supply. This novel was afterwards published in two volumes, 12mo, but had not the popularity of his former works of that kind, and as a composition, whether in point of fable, character, or humour, is indeed far inferior to any of them....

From p. 549:

His next production, which appeared in 1769, proved that he had not forgotten the neglect with which he was treated by that ministry, in whose favour he wrote the Briton. This was entitled the *Adventures of an Atom*. Under fictitious names, of Japanese structure, he reviews the conduct of the eminent politicians who had conducted or opposed the measures of government from the year 1754, and retracts the opinion he had given of some of these statesmen in his history, particularly of the earl of Chatham and lord Bute. His biographer allows that many of the characters are grossly misrepresented, for which no other reason can be assigned than his own disappointment. The whole proves, what has often been seen since his time, that the measures which are right and proper when a reward is in view, are wrong and abominable when that reward is withheld....

From p. 550:

He set out, however, for Italy early in 1770, with debilitated body, and a mind probably irritated by his recent disappointment, but not without much of the ease which argues firmness, since during this journey he could so pleasantly divert his sorrows by writing *The Expedition of Humphrey Clinker*. This novel, if it may be so called, for it has no regular fable, in point of genuine humour, knowledge of life and manners, and delineation of character, is inferior only to his *Roderick Random* and *Peregrine Pickle*. It has already been noticed that Matthew Bramble, the principal character, displays the cynical temper and humane feelings of the author on his tour on the continent; and it may now be added that he has given another sketch of himself in the character of Serle in the first volume. This account of the ingratitude of Paunceford to Smollett is strictly true; and as his biographers seem unacquainted with the circumstances, the following may not be uninteresting, which was related to me by the late intimate friend of Smollett, Mr Hamilton, the printer and proprietor of the *Critical Review*.

'Paunceford was a John C——l, who was fed by Smollett when he had not bread to eat, nor clothes to cover him. He was taken out to India as private secretary to a celebrated governor-general, and as essayist; and after only three years absence, returned with forty thousand ponds. From India he sent several letters to Smollett, professing that he was coming over to lay his fortune at the feet of his benefactor. But on his arrival, he treated Smollett, Hamilton, and others, who had befriended him with the most ungrateful contempt. The person who taught him the art of essaying became reduced in circumstances, and is now (1792) or lately was collector of the toll on carts at Holborn Bars. C——l never paid him, or any person to whom he was indebted. He died in two or three years after at his house near Hounslow, universally despised. At the request of Smollett, Mr Hamilton employed him to write in the *Critical Review*, which, with Smollett's charity, was all his support, previously to his departure for India.'

From pp. 551–2:

As an author, Dr Smollett is universally allowed the praise of original genius displayed with an ease and variety which are rarely found. Yet this character belongs chiefly to his novels. In correct delineation of life and manners, and in drawing characters of the humorous class, he has few equals. But when this praise is bestowed, every critic who values what is more important than genius itself, the interest of morals and decency, must surely stop. It can be of no use to analyze each individual scene, incident, or character in works which, after all, must be pronounced unfit to be read.

But if the morals of the reader were in no danger, his taste can hardly escape being insulted or perverted. Smollett's humour is of so low a cast, and his practical jokes so frequently end in what is vulgar, mean, and filthy, that it would be impossible to acquire a relish for them, without injury done to the chaster feelings, and to the just respect due to genuine wit. No novel writer seems to take more delight in assembling images and incidents that are gross and disgusting: not has he scrupled to introduce with more than slight notice, those vices which are not fit even to be named. If this be a just representation of his most famous novels, it is in vain to oppose it by pointing out passages which do credit to his genius, and more vain to attempt to prove that virtue and taste are not directly injured by such productions.

137. William Mudford on Smollett

1810

From William Mudford, *The British Novelists, comprising every work of acknowledged merit which is usually classed under the denomination of Novels*, 5 vols, 1810–16, extracts from vols I and II, passim. Mudford (1782–1848) was a miscellaneous writer, novelist and journalist. Mudford's critical comments are both characteristic of the ethical temper of his time, and refreshingly original in their literary content.

CRITICAL OBSERVATIONS ON *RODERICK RANDOM*

There are few things more difficult of performance than to ascertain which, among the productions of an author, is entitled to be considered as *the best*. Perhaps, indeed, it is impossible to pronounce this decision with such unerring rectitude as shall place it beyond the power of dispute. Each man judges for himself, and no two judge alike. They may agree in particulars, but they differ in general results. Every one, however, is partial to his own opinion, and though he may assent, from courtesy, to that of another, he rarely acquiesces from conviction.

Nor is this obstruction to the definitive estimate of a writer's productions to be attributed solely to the diversity of the notions of mankind when directed towards a single object. There is another cause equally powerful. In the works of every man of genius there will be infused a large portion of those qualities of mind by which he is distinguished. Whether he be sublime or witty, humourous or moral, gay or grave, his writings, collectively considered, will bear the general impression of these attributes separately or together, accordingly as they exist in himself. The only objection (and that is but an apparent one) which can be urged against this position is, when an author attempts a species of composition for which he is unfitted either by natural or acquired talents; as when Racine wrote a comedy, Milton Sonnets, and Pope a Pindaric ode. These are to be regarded rather as the vanity of great minds than as their legitimate exertions, and whatever difficulty there may be in pronouncing which is the *best* of those writers, there can be none in deciding these things to be the *worst*. But, when we consider what may be termed the *genuine* efforts of a superior intellect, and would endeavour, from a patient and accurate comparison of their respective merits, to ascertain which is *the best*, it is then that we feel how hazardous, perhaps how impossible, it is to make the choice. Genius, like that mysterious connexion between the will and every part of the human body, diffuses itself through whatever it attempts; in some undertakings it is stronger and in some weaker; but it seldom so totally prevails, or is so totally absent, as to leave no room for comparison. The task is of course easier where an author has written only two or three works; but, when his productions are numerous and extensive, it is a doubtful enterprise to establish their relative excellence, and from that to deduce the absolute superiority of a particular production. Perhaps, therefore, when I pronounce the present works to be superior to any other of the novels of Smollett, many will dissent from my opinion, and though I may give my reasons why I have formed such a judgment, they may be prepared with other reasons in support of their own notions, equally powerful and equally conclusive. Without conjec-turing, however, what others think, I shall proceed to tell what I think myself.

Though *Roderick Random* is not free from a reproach which may be made to all the novels of Smollett, that they have no regular plot, no series of events skilfully concatenated so as to produce the catastrophe by an easy, natural, and obvious co-operation, yet it is finished with more art than any of the rest. All the personages about whom the reader has been much interested in the progress of the story are brought forward at the conclusion, and disposed of in such a manner as leaves the mind satisfied. The means by which they are assembled together are not, indeed, very probable, but the effect of their union is the entire contentment of the reader. The hero and the heroine are happily married; Strap is comfortably settled, though not with much attention to moral justice; the father is found, and the uncle returns to the element of his own enjoyments.

This, however, does not compensate for the want of that delight which a well-connected narrative would produce. The adventures in which *Roderick* is engaged have very little influence upon the catastrophe; they are, for the most part, as much disjoined from each other as a collection of tales, each of which has its own beginning, middle, and end. It may be replied, perhaps, that the author's purpose was to exhibit different modes of life, and different shades of character; that he seized upon these as they arose to his mind, and embodied them with his work; that each event is intended to display human nature under some distinguishing circumstances; and that as his topics were multifarious, it was less easy to connect them together in such a manner as should shew a regular coherency of part and a simultaneous tendency of the whole, to produce one general effect. But these are arguments which are derived rather from the practice itself than from the necessity of it; they are no justification of a method which the common judgment of critics has condemned. He who wishes to be sensible of the difference between a series of adventures thus loosely thrown together, and a fable artfully contrived, and skilfully pursued, may read novel of Smollett's after having perused the *Tom Jones* of Fielding.

The character of the hero is such as Smollett delighted to depict. He is gay, thoughtless, and immoral; the dupe of artifice, the slave of passion, and the victim of misfortune: a compound of the scholar, the gentleman, and the swaggerer; arrogant in prosperity, and mean in adversity; proud, without the proper foundation of pride, which is virtue; generous without discrimination, and as willing to accept favours as to bestow them. He is easily elated, and easily depressed. He sometimes acts with a high sense of honour and dignity, and sometimes descends to servility and fawning. Though not scrupulous in his means of acquiring wealth, he is eager to display it when he has it, and rejoices in confounding his associates by the splendour of his apparel and the profusion of his expenses. The companion of the great and of the vulgar, of the virtuous and of the profligate, he is represented as indifferent to which he lends his presence. He is quick in offence, and not easily placable; for when, after a lapse of many years, he returns to the town where he was educated, and *Mr* and *Mrs Potion* send up their compliments to him at the inn, he returns them an answer by *Strap*, that 'he desired to have no connexion with such low-minded wretches as they were.' A reply not to be recommended either for its dignity or its propriety.

It is obvious that such a character is not natural. The qualities which compose it are essentially hostile to each other. Smollett was perhaps aware of this, but chose rather to violate probability than to lose an opportunity of conducting his hero into all those various scenes of high and of low life which might give him an occasion of exercising his satirical powers. This might be more easily pardoned if he had always been attentive to preserve him from unnecessary contamination; but he is not very anxious to secure him in the estimation of the reader. There is no one, I suppose, who does not condemn his conduct towards *Strap*. Living upon his property at one time, yet treating him with all the insolence and contumely of a master: reckless of his feelings on every occasion, and expressing no generous sense of that steady and unalterable devotion to his welfare and interest which so eminently distinguishes him; availing himself of his aid on all emergencies, but haughtily indifferent to him when he no longer needs his assistance; and meanly justifying his consent to his departure (see Chap. XX.) by the degrading assertion 'that ingratitude is so natural to the heart of man, that I began to be tired of his acquaintance.' It is true that he is represented as providing for him at last; but the reader may justly suspect that to be an act of profusion rather than of kindness; arising from a superfluity of wealth, not from an inborn sentiment of generosity.

Nor is ingratitude towards his benefactor the only blemish in the character of this various hero. His morals hang loosely about him; his low intrigues, his petty artifices, and his willingness to sacrifice his principles upon the shrine of wealth (as in the pursuit of *Miss Snapper*), all tend to alienate from him the good will of the reader. It is impossible, indeed, not to wish that the author had given him more virtue, that we might have pitied his calamities and rejoiced in his ultimate prosperity, without much violation of moral rectitude.

Strap is a character which I have always considered with great pleasure. Honest, faithful and unsuspecting, his integrity nothing can corrupt, his fidelity no misfortunes can shake, and his simplicity no experience can correct. His errors are from his head, not from his heart, and the estimation of the reader follows him to the last. He is delineated throughout with much consistency; and the lines which Dryden wrote for Shadwell will well apply to him:

> *Strap* alone is he
> Who stands confirm'd in full stupidity:
> Others to some faint meaning make pretence,
> But *Strap* never deviates into sense.

Smollett, however, deserves some of that praise which has been bestowed upon Cervantes: he has contrived, with great dexterity, to make him ridiculous but never contemptible. His virtues are never obliterated by his actions. Under all circumstances, the same good qualities of heart are discernible, and however much their intentions may be perverted by the weakness of his understanding, it is impossible not to esteem the honest sincerity of his views. Many have contended for the honour of being the *original Strap*; but it is doubtful whether Smollett had any particular individual in view.

In adverting to the sentiments and language of *Roderick Random*, I wish I could approve of their general tendency. What Johnson says of Swift may be justly applied to Smollett—that he delighted in ideas which are 'physically impure.' For this strange perversion of the human mind it is not easy to account; and it may justly excite wonder that a man capable of other pleasures should find any in the contemplation of objects from which most persons shrink back with disgust. Nor is this the only charge that may be preferred against him. He is often inexcusably indelicate. The history of *Miss Williams* is needlessly licentious; or, if any excuse can be urged in its defence, it is that it represents a life of prostitution in a manner so loathsome and so offensive, that it will surely excite disgust where disgust may be made to assist the cause of virtue. I am afraid, however, that it was from no conviction of this kind that Smollett wrote it. The discourse also with *Lord Strutwell* upon *Petronius Arbiter* is highly improper, as it tends to lead the mind of youth to a consideration of topics of which, the longer it is kept ignorant the better. The indignant reprehension which *Roderick* is made to utter, in the lines beginning, 'Eternal infamy,' &c. is from his own satire of the *Advice*. Smollett, indeed, seemed fond of bringing himself into notice, in his own works, whenever an occasion offered.

His language is often more colloquial than is required even by the familiar romance; nor is he always careful to make his characters talk with a suitable attention to themselves and their subject. But this is a defect which cannot be attributed to him in the discourse of the officer who is in the stage-coach that conveys *Roderick* and *Miss*

Snapper to Bath. There he is sufficiently natural. Unmeaning oaths, idle blasphemy, and pointless obscenity, are the common qualities of a soldier. In his subsequent productions, however, he paid more attention to this necessary conformity between the diction of his personages and the character he had assigned them.

It were needless to praise the happy skill with which he has pourtrayed the features of *Lieutenant Bowling*. Before he wrote, we had no successful delineation of the naval character. Congreve's *Ben* is compounded merely of such qualities as could be gathered from books and conversation, or from casual inspection; but Smollett had lived among them, and drew from actual observation. He may be regarded as the parent of this species of comic exhibition in England; and from him have been derived all those dull repetitions on the stage which are still repeated, because a nation that has risen to greatness by her navy, is naturally pleased to see its supporters popular. *Lieutenant Bowling* is not indeed much before the reader, and therefore he commands less of his attention than *Trunnion, Hatchway*, and *Pipes*: but from him might justly be anticipated the fuller delineations which ensued.

I have already remarked that Smollett had no power of describing the passion of love. What I have have hitherto said, however, has been simple assertion: but I will now support my opinion by proof. When *Roderick Random* dines with *Narcissa* at her brother's and is left alone with her, after the repast, how does he act? Does he unfold his sentiments by those unutterable looks, by those tender and respectful expressions, by that silent sympathy of feeling which speaks in the gentle pressure of the hand, by those kind attentions which a lover's heart is ever impelled to offer, and by that fearful timidity which dreads the displeasure of the object it adores? Does he act with all that chastened enthusiasm of generosity which love kindles in the heart, with all that vigilance of activity which waits upon the looks of a mistress, and with all that modest reserve which no man ever is without who truly loves? Does he employ all this instinctive 'artillery of love?' to use the words of Cowley. Is he a St Preux, or a Grandison? No. After a few moment's awkward confusion, he clasps his mistress, and exclaims, with frigid hyperbole, 'Why are you so exquisitely fair? Why are you so enchantingly good? Why has nature dignified you with charms so much above the standard of women?' &c. This is not the language of passion, but of gallantry: they are not the expressions of love, but of affectation; and the lady very properly hides her face behind her fan, and says nothing. In the letter, also, which *Roderick* writes to *Narcissa*, we are amused with a sufficient collection of 'glowing hopes' and 'chilling fears.' The whole epistle indeed seems to have furnished the model for that which the school-master writes to *Emilia* in *Peregrine Pickle*.

The plain matter is, that Smollett fails in all attempts to describe the violence of pathetic emotion. Foaming at the mouth, kicking chairs about, light forsaking the eyes, and swearing 'horrible oaths,' are the usual concomitants of passion in his heroes upon the most ordinary occasions. But all this is mere exaggeration: it is the operation of the fancy, not of the judgment. In this particular, he copied nature from books, as she is represented by inferior writers of romance and tragedy.

It is probable, indeed, that had he observed her in her undisguised workings, he would have been unable to transplant them to his pages. The heart to feel and the head to conceive may be given, without the ability to express. On different men different powers are bestowed. If Rousseau could draw a *Julia*, he could not have represented a *Commodore Trunnion*. Smollett has very conspicuous merit of another description. His works will always be read and always be relished, as long as mankind have any delight in what is humourous, gay, and animated. Comic incidents are what he narrates with the greatest effect, as every reader of *Roderick Random* is convinced: but to excite merriment is not his only power: in his later productions he often rises to the dignity of a moral teacher, though his precepts are sometimes delivered with a cynical severity which can be attributed only to the morbid irritability of his character.

It has been said, and with some truth, that he has given an adumbration of his own early life in the adventures of *Roderick Random*. It is certain that he was at the siege of Carthagena, for his ironical account of that ill-conducted business could have been written only by one who had witnessed it; and there died, a few weeks since, at Queensferry, in Scotland, a person of the name of *M'Cullum*, in the ninety-first year of his age, who had served with Smollett upon upon that expedition, as an assistant surgeon, and who always spoke of him with much tenderness and esteem. If indeed he suffered on shipboard what he represents *Roderick* as suffering, he might have exclaimed, with the hero of Virgil,

Quaeque ipse miserrima vidi,
Et quorum pars magna fui.[1]

CRITICAL OBSERVATIONS ON *PEREGRINE PICKLE*

The incidents in *Peregrine Pickle* are not wrought up with the same
skill as in *Roderick Random*. The connexion of events is not always
artfully preserved. Of the characters which are introduced, at the
commencement of the work, more is said than seems necessary,
from the insignificant station which some of them hold in the
progress of the narrative. Smollett appears to have written without
any preconceived notion of his own plan; and finding, afterwards,
that *Peregrime* was to be the hero, he removes his other personages
too suddenly into obscurity.

The verisimilitude of character is, also, sometimes violated. The
letter of *Gamaliel Pickle* to *Miss Appleby* is unnatural. If it be not so,
why, it may be asked, was not the same technical absurdity
maintained in his conversation, and in his letter to *Commodore
Trunnion?* Similar objections may be made to other parts.

I cannot but think that Smollett is eminently unsuccessful in his
love descriptions. The gallantry of his heroes is cold and
unmeaning; and the coquetry of his ladies forced and unamiable.
He was not capable of imparting any warmth to situations and
feelings which have interested every heart in the pages of Rousseau,
and of writers of less eminence in our own country. Why he has
failed, it is not easy to determine. It was not necessary that he
should have been, himself, the victim of love, to describe its
potency. Pope, whom no one will suspect of being amorous, has
left the finest delineation of the tender passion that was ever drawn
by the pen of man, in his Eloisa to Abelard. The fact is, certain, that
no reader is much interested about the success or disappointment of
Smollett's heroes with their mistresses: and, I believe, a lady would
suspect his knowledge of the human heart, when he makes *Peregrine*
carry on various intrigues in Paris, while absent from his *Emilia*.
This is what no man ever yet did, or even could do, who was truly
in love.

Yet, with all these deductions, (and where is the work of man
that is perfect?) *Peregrine Pickle* will always command attention and
excite delight. The character of *Commodore Trunnion* is faultless. It

is drawn from the living volume of nature; and so powerful are its colours, that even they who have had no opportunity of corroborating its accuracy, by their inspection of real life, yet feel that it is *Natural*. Smollett seems to have known that he excelled in depicting naval characters, for he has seldom missed an opportunity of introducing them into his works.

The hero of the tale preserves the goodwill of the reader even in the midst of all his excess, which is no mean praise of the author's skill. He has tempered his virtues with the errors of humanity. He has not exhibited a 'faultless monster,' but a being compounded of human passions and partaking of human frailties. From the consequences of these frailties he extricates him by no improbable circumstances; and there is more merit in a writer than may be commonly supposed, who, when his imagination is confessedly employed, subjects it to the sober probabilities of existence.

One great merit of Smollett, in this work, is the variety of characters which he has introduced, and the art with which he has discriminated them. Even the *Commodore, Hatchway*, and *Pipes*, though all of one genus, yet differ from each other specifically; and *Peregrine, Mr Jolter*, and the loquacious publican, have each their peculiar manner.

In his language, though it is often coarse, he adapts himself skilfully to the speaker; and his expressions are sometimes eminently humourous, from their unexpected application. Perhaps no writer but Smollett could have given dramatic force to *Trunnion* and *Pipes*.

It may be interesting to the general reader to learn, that the republican doctor, in the following work, is meant as a satire upon Akenside, whose love of whatever was ancient is ridiculed, with uncommon learning and vivacity, by his giving an entertainment after the manner of the ancients.

CRITICAL OBSERVATIONS ON *FERDINAND COUNT FATHOM*

In every work of fiction which aspires to please permanently, there should be preserved a certain character of probability, by which the judgment of the reader may be propitiated while his fancy is amused. In the rude ages of literature, indeed, when the human mind was just emerging from the long night of superstition and ignorance which followed the declension and final extinction of the Roman Empire, this qualification was not so necessary. Every invention, however wild, and every tale, however impossible, was then willingly read and willingly believed. The voice of reason was rarely heard in the cloistered silence of monasteries and convents, which, in those times, were the only asylums of neglected learning. All the stores of ancient philosophy and genius were forgotten or unknown; while the fantastic fictions of wizards and demons, of giants and magicians, of sorcery and incantations, were spread by the early writers of romance, and perused with avidity by their unenlightened contemporaries. Nor is it easy to resist the soothing influence of such productions, even while we acknowledge their futility. To deliver our understanding as a captive to the magic potency of fictions that are founded upon events which we know to be ridiculous, is a temporary sacrifice which we sometimes willingly perform: but, as it is a sacrifice, so it is transitory, and we return, with increased alacrity, to the dominion of reason and sense. We are passive, because we know we have the power to shake off the trammels when they become irksome. There is something, too, in custom, which we are neither prepared nor disposed to resist. We endure, in that which can plead the authority of age, what we should reject in a modern composition. It has been justly observed, that were Shakspeare now living, and to produce his dramas as they are now acted, it is highly probable that the audience would be disgusted with those incongruities which are now not only tolerated but admired, and that they would hiss them from the stage.

It is the business of an author, therefore, to consider the age in which he writes, and not the age in which others have written. The *Arcadia* of Sydney was once popular; but would such a romance be now read? New modes of thinking arise, as the human mind unfolds itself in its progress from rudeness to refinement, and it is not unlikely that a period may come the when the prose of Addison, Johnson, Hume, and Gibbon, will be obsolete, and Pope, and Dryden, and Milton, require a glossary, as Chaucer and Spenser do now. Such is the mutability of all that is human. The wit, the humour, the eloquence, the learning which pleased our ancestors, and which continue to please us, will be disrelished by our posterity; and though these mutations may be mortifying to the pride of man, they are consonant to his nature. The present only is our own; that we possess: the past we may reason upon, and about the future we may conjecture; but we are not much affected by what is remote; we are the creatures of present habits and present opinions, and as they are for ever fluctuating, there is, of course, a constant succession of new impressions produced.

The reader has, doubtless, conjectured that the object of these introductory observations is to fix a censure upon Smollett for not having sufficiently preserved credibility in the present work. It is so: *Count Fathom* is the production of a vigorous mind, but it wants that verisimilitude by which alone its moral purposes can be attained. This is a consideration which has been too much neglected by those who have sought to improve mankind through the medium of fiction. Their incidents do not often 'come home to men's business and bosoms,' to use the oft-quoted words of Bacon. And yet, in no other way can we be beneficially affected by fictitious narratives. They should consist of such events as may, in the common course of things, happen to all; we must feel that we stand within the level of similar circumstances, and may, therefore, expect to find similiar results if we engage in them. We must behold ourselves in the conduct of the personages introduced, and be able to exclaim, with Horace, in reference to the simple probabilities of life,

Mutato nomine, de te fabula narratur.[2]

But we cannot find all this in *Count Fathom*; and one of the purposes for which the author professes to have written the work, that of terrifying those from the career of villainy who are hesitating on its confines, will, therefore, remain unanswered. The other end, indeed, may be attained, for it discloses scenes of perfidy by which the unwary may be advantageously instructed.

This combination of villainy however, centered as it is in the person of *Fathom*, constitutes that improbability which I now censure. He has no apparent, no adequate motive to the systematic iniquity which he perpetrates. If we believe it at all, we must believe it to be instinctive, innate, inborn; and that is a supposition which violates all our notions of God and man. He is represented as ripe in treachery even from his cradle, as an infant scoundrel whose only birthright was the gallows. Other human beings sin from vice, but he sins from nature. He is a compound of mere depravity, unvisited by one single virtue. His wickedness proceeds from no disgust of society, from no rankling recollection of injuries, from no misanthropic hatred of mankind, from no bitterness of revenge, nor, indeed, from any of the avowed incentives of human conduct. His cool, malignant, subtle, systematic, unrelenting villainy, appears like a curse pronounced against him by his Creator at the moment of his birth. But I am willing to hope that such enormous turpitude, such aggravated atrocity, never yet blackened the soul of any human being. Knaves there are and have been, whose numerous misdeeds excite the indignant abhorrence of honour and virtue, but still they were sometimes susceptible of emotions that approached to rectitude. The assassin sometimes spares his victim, and the robber will sometimes forego his booty; the gambler is not always rapacious, nor the sharper perfidious; still less then can the same man be uniformly, all those characters as occasion for them presents itself. I know that all the frauds, that all the treachery which *Fathom* commits, have been, and will be again, committed by the various professors of knavery; but never by a single individual. It is this violation of all probability which I condemn; and yet more do I condemn that total absence of motive to villainy in the very outset of his career. '*Nemo repente turpissimus.*'[3] There must be a gradation; there must be a progress from vice to vice: and, in the first instance, there must be an exciting cause. *Fathom*, as far as I can discover, wants this; and the utility of the work is, consequently, greatly impaired. No man fears that he shall become vicious without some pretext, and no man, therefore, will be alarmed at the course of Smollett's hero. Such instinctive degeneracy, such innate depravity, as belong to *Fathom*, will never be believed by the most credulous. Had Smollett exhibited some adequate reason for his original deviation from the common track of integrity and virtue, and had he afterwards contrived incitements commensurate to his actions, the mind of the reader would have been better satisfied. But this he has done only in the single circumstance of his salacity, by which, indeed, his attacks on female chastity are sufficiently accounted for, though his success in those attacks suggests an unfavourable, and I am willing to hope, unjust opinion of the other sex.

I know not, however, what good purpose can be answered by the narration of a series of villainous transactions however skillfully managed. Man needs not to be mentally familiarized with crimes.

It is a knowledge which the intercourse of society will force upon him soon enough; and I am not inclined to rely much upon the moral efficacy of displaying vice as a preventive, though sanctioned by the stern ethics of the Lacedemonians, and enforced by a polite sensualist of the last century. Smollett, however, seems to have thought otherwise, for he has missed no opportunity of representing it under all its aspects. It is justly observed, by the late Dr Beattie, speaking of Smollett's novels, that 'he is often inexcusably licentious; profligates, bullies, and misanthropes, are among his favourite characters. A duel he seems to have thought one of the highest efforts of human virtue; and playing dexterously at billiards a very genteel accomplishment.'—(*Dissert. on Fable and Romance.*) This is certainly true: he usually conducts his hero, or some of his associates, to prison, that he may have an opportunity of unfolding all the misery, and blasphemy, and vice, which generally prevail in those receptacles of debauchery, misfortune, and indiscretion. The scenes, indeed, which he exhibits may be natural: but nature is not always to be displayed; and to those who would vindicate Smollett upon this plea, I would recall the lively reply of Voltaire to a gentleman who was defending the licentiousness of his writings, because, however licentious, they were still natural. '*Avec permission, monsieur,*' said he, '*mon cu est bien natural, et cependant je porte des culottes.*'[4]

While, however, we condemn the improbability of *Fathom's* character, we must allow that it is consistently drawn. By no one action does he belie his principles. His qualifications are multifarious, for they are bestowed upon him at the will of the author, and in their variety he may rival the admirable *Crichton*, with this difference, however, that *Crichton* is reported to have really possessed his numerous accomplishments, while *Fathom* has only the counterfeit of some of his. They were necessary, however, to the success of his schemes.

There is one topic of satire which Smollett seldom omits in his works, and that is the practising physicians at Bath, Tunbridge, Bristol, and other places of similar resort. He is always anxious to render them ridiculous in some way or other. He had early and unsuccessfully tried to establish himself at Bath as a physician, though he wrote a treatise on the medical properties of its waters; and there was, therefore, something of resentment, perhaps, in his acrimony towards those who had succeeded where he had failed.

The texture of his fable, in *Count Fathom*, is more skilfully wrought than in any of his other novels. The catastrophe is produced by a regular series of events; and no character of any importance in the course of the narrative is forgotten at the conclusion. The reader is pleasingly surprised to find, in *Don Diego de Zelos*, the father of *Monimia*, and in *Renaldo* the drawing-master of *Serafina*; though the meeting between *Don Diego* and the *Count de Melville* partakes too much of that sublime disregard of probability by which a writer of romance produces those events that may serve to heighten the admiration of the reader. We are left, however, to conjecture as we can, by what means *Fathom* became acquainted with the consanguinity of *Monimia* and *Don Diego*, how he knew that she was *Serafina*, or that she was alive. That he does know all this, is proved in the letter which he wrote in the apprehension of approaching dissolution; and Smollett should have satisfied the reader's mind by disclosing the means. These may seem minute objections; but, let it be recollected, that one of the ends of writing is to please, and we are not pleased with what we do not understand.

The style of Smollett in this, as well as in his other works, is not remarkable for the purity of its construction. His sentences are harshly involved, and sometimes too abruptly terminated. He heaps clause upon clause, without being sufficiently careful to connect them with ease or elegance. He does not seem to have been capable of writing with dignity or energy; nor is there any thing in his style which can be called eloquent, though he frequently has situations where he might have been so, had he possessed the power. He is sometimes licentious, also, in his use of particular words, employing them either in a sense not English, or in one that is obsolete. Thus, I have noticed, in *Count Fathom*, *elapse* used as a substantive; *puerility* for boyhood, instead of the qualities attendant upon that state; *absconded* for hidden, a sense which is purely Latin; *intendered* for intenerated; *resent*, in its French signification of being sensible of favours or benefits, with many others. But these innovations, by which a language is needlessly encumbered, require to be strongly censured. If every writer is to have the liberty of affixing arbitrary significations to the words which he employs, our dictionaries must be annually composed.

I have had frequent occasion to condemn the unsuccessful efforts of Smollett to depict the pathetic; and I believe my readers will concur with me in opinion, that he fails as often as he attempts it. It is not, indeed, easy to perceive the difference between the ironical declaration of love which *Fathom* makes to *Wilhelmina*, and the serious protestations which are uttered by *Renaldo*. They neither of them use the language of nature. But there is a scene in this work in which there was ample scope for the powerful eloquence of passion; I mean the interview between *Renaldo* and *Monimia* in the church. Let us for a moment (forgetting the improbability of the whole incident) picture to ourselves the reality of such an event, and then judge of the manner in which Smollett has pourtrayed it.

A lover, a warm, an enthusiastic, an adoring lover, believes that the object of his affections has fallen a sacrifice to the unkindness which the artifices of a villain prompted him to shew towards her. Full of this persuasion, his heart is torn with incurable anguish; all the happiness of life is gone, nor does he even wish to recall it; his sighs, his tears, his prayers, are the propitiatory sacrifices which he offers to her injured memory; and he resolves to pass the midnight hours of silence and repose on the grave that holds her mouldering form. He does so: he throws himself on the earth that covers his beloved, and is resigned to all the impetuosity of grief. He calls upon her name, and implores her forgiveness; all is hushed as death: darkness encompasses him, and a solemn awe prevails. Suddenly, gentle music is heard, lights appear, and he beholds before him the apparition of his departed mistress! In such a moment, what would be the feelings of any man? Would they not be absorbed in terror? Would he not be dumb with horror? Would he not gaze upon the vision with all the silent ecstacy of awe and amazement? Or, if he attempted to speak, would not his emotions find vent in disjointed sentences, in broken phrases, in half-suppressed words? Would he (as *Renaldo* does) deliver a regular oration, of some two dozen lines, containing many very pertinent inductions, and some very solid reasoning? Certainly not. But Smollett consulted his head and not his heart. He had invention to plan the incident, but he wanted genius to support it. So, likewise, when *Renaldo* finds that it is no apparition, but his mistress, the unexpected discovery excites no other language than this: 'Where hast thou lived? Where borrowed this perfection? Whence art thou now descended? Thou wilt not leave me? No; we must not part again: by this warm kiss, a thousand times more sweet than all the fragrance of the East–' After perusing such cold and artificial questions, the reader is apt to exclaim, with *Monimia*, 'Indeed this is too much!'

Smollett, however, was certainly not aware of his incapacity, for he is, in all his novels, sufficiently liberal of situations which demand the highest efforts of pathetic delineation. But it is no uncommon reproach to literary men that they mistake their own powers.

I ought not to conclude these observations without allowing to Smollett a part of that praise which he claims in his ironical introductory address to himself, that he has 'carefully avoided every hint or expression which could give umbrage to the most delicate reader.' He is certainly much more decorous in this work, than was his usual custom, and I believe it may be asserted that it contains no 'expression' which is offensive to modesty; but I cannot say as much of 'hints;' and still less can I say so of incidents. It has, indeed, too many of such as a chaste mind can never contemplate with pleasure; and when I consider how many sources of rational delight there are, into which nothing impure need intrude, I cannot but regret that any writer should neglect them, to indulge in the meanest of all wit, and in which they may always expect to be eclipsed by the lowest wretches of society.

CRITICAL OBSERVATIONS ON *SIR LAUNCELOT GREAVES*

If *Roderick Random* be the best of Smollett's novels, this is certainly the worst. It is radically defective in design, and poorly filled with incidents. There is no display of character (if, perhaps, that of *Ferret* be excepted) which at all towers beyond the common delineations of a common writer: and the attempts at humour are so generally abortive, that we with difficulty believe them to be the attempts of Smollett.

By what perversity of judgment he was tempted to adopt so wild and improbable a subject as modern knight-errantry in England, it is impossible to conjecture. We relish the chivalrous adventures of *Don Quixote* and his trusty *Panza*, because the times in which the author wrote gave a sanction, by their practice, to the inimitable satire, and we know that we are reading about things which, as a principle, actually existed. But a knight-errant of the eighteenth century, roaming through the provinces of England, clad in armour, bearing his lance, and attended by his squire, is so ridiculous, that the mind is, at the very first, disgusted, and by no skill of the author's could it possibly be propitiated. We are sure that such a thing could not be, for a man so acting would be lodged in a gaol twenty-four hours after the commencement of his wild career.

In choosing such a plan, Smollett limited himself to a very scanty series of incidents. His knight could perform none of those achievements for which there were numerous opportunities in that rude state of society when chivalry was the call of glory, and every noble youth longed to approve himself in its duties; those duties which tended so powerfully to generate the loftiest feelings of honour, the most refined generosity, the most ardent enthusiasm of courage, the most acute sense of injuries, the most impassioned gallantry, the most fervid devotion, and the most glowing indignation against tyranny and oppression. But, of these virtues some could be excited only by their opposite vices, and the laws of a country must be deplorably inefficient in which individuals are compelled to associate for the maintenance of order and for the security of virtue. Yet, such was every nation of Europe once, and in every nation the feudal institution of chivalry existed in a greater or less degree. But, as civilisation increased, checks upon licentiousness were provided, and that tacit compact by which every member of society resigns the congizance of crimes to a supreme and distinct power, became gradually more and more efficacious, as means were gradually adopted to punish every kind of offence. Accordingly, there soon ceased to exist any necessity for that individual assumption of privileges by which persons and property were protected while protection was inadequately or not at all afforded by legislative provisions: and hence, the decay of chivalry, the grace and virtue of a rude age, but the blemish and imperfection of a polished one.

To ridicule the abuse and the excess of this profession was the object of Cervantes, and it was a just one; for, in his country and age that abuse and that excess had risen to an alarming height. He employed ridicule, a weapon which few can withstand when skillfully directed. His work was the mirror of the times in which he lived, and its wide diffusion produced the effect which its author intended[a]. The choice of his subject was, therefore, as appropriate as the *Lutrin* of Boileau, the *Dunciad* of Pope, or the *Dispensary* of Garth: it was founded upon local and existing manners, and was sure to excite that attention which an ingenious and lively delineation of present customs, modes, and objects, never fails to produce. The genius of Cervantes also was such that he gave to a topic which was national and temporary, that fascination and that excellence by which it still delights all readers of all countries.

But Smollett could not hope for such success, and it was indeed a bold attempt to place himself in avowed competition with Cervantes. His hero is a modern gentleman, signalising his prowess in a country which, of all others, affords the fewest opportunities for the interposition of a knight-errant. Liberty is too well defined, too well felt, and too practically enjoyed in England, to admit to any of those violations of social rights which it was the business of chivalry to avenge or redress. It is wonderful, indeed, that Smollett did not perceive this inherent defect, by which he was, in fact, prevented from representing what it was his obvious intention to represent. *Sir Launcelot* sets forth upon his expedition and performs nothing, because nothing could be performed. He rides about the country to the terror of some, to the admiration of others, and to the astonishment of all: he encounters a highwayman and drives him from his booty: he fights a mock combat with a rival who is half a fool: and when he is taken up as a disturber of the peace, he compels an ignorant and oppressive magistrate to relinquish his post, and performs, himself, some actions of justice and humanity.

Such are the whole, or nearly the whole, of *Sir Launcelot's* exploits; and few as they are, we know that they never could have happened. This consciousness is a sensible diminution of the reader's pleasure. He cannot participate in the situations and feelings of the hero; and without that participation no narrative can be perused with much delight.

The character of *Sir Launcelot*, however, is drawn with every moral grace which can attract. His virtue is conspicuous on all occasions, and his good sense on most. He is personally brave, without being ferocious, and he is courteous and gentle, without meanness or imbecility. The dignity of his mind never forsakes him; and the vigour of his judgment displays itself, sometimes, to great effect. His invective against party scribblers, those men whose venal pages the largest bounty can command, who write without knowledge, and who seek only to inflame the passions of mankind by falsehood and exaggeration, is just and spirited. They are the scourge of society; they contribute nothing to its welfare, but detract largely from its mutual confidence and general harmony. Their existence proclaims, in the loudest manner, that liberty the loss of which they affect to deplore: and their turbulent opposition to whatever *is*, proves that freedom is a blessing which only the good and the wise can truly enjoy. Against such political disturbers the manly censures of Smollett could never be better directed. Nor can I omit to praise the dignified and energetic speech which *Sir Launcelot* makes to *Gobble*, in whose humiliation every reader must rejoice.

The character of *Crabshaw* is a compound of *Panza* and *Ralph*, but vastly inferior to both. He has neither their humour, their wit, nor their dexterity. His misfortunes excite neither mirth nor pity: he is partly a knave and partly a fool: and his ridiculous fondness for *Gilbert* is but a weak and injudicious imitation of *Sancho's* affection for *Dapple*. He is not drawn consistently. In the tenth chapter he suddenly surprises us with a series of musty adages, uttered upon a single occasion: but neither before nor after do we find in him the same propensity to proverbial wisdom. A similar inconsistency may be noted in his use of the provincial idiom. Sometimes he talks in pure English, sometimes in a strange unintelligible jargon: and not unfrequently one half of his speech is in correct phraseology, and the other half in a barbarous northern dialect. For this negligence there seems to be no excuse.

Captain Crowe is well pourtrayed. Here was Smollett's strength, and he knew it. The account of his novitiate is humourous; and his own description of his first essay in the paths of chivalry is irresistibly ludicrous, from its being delivered in sea terms. The author, however, appears to have exhausted the fertility of his invention in *Trunnion*, *Pipes*, and *Hatchway*: they remain unimitated and unimitable. *Lieutenant Bowling* was the day-spring of that invention, and *Captain Crowe* its night, to which no second dawn will follow. The pencil of Smollett has been transmitted to no successor; nor is it likely that another will equal him in that path, for the meed of originality is no longer to be gained.

Ferret is one of those misanthropes which Smollett delighted to draw. To make him contemptible, he has made him a furious opposer of government; and he could not have employed means more effectual. The coarse and vulgar manner in which he declaims against the administration of affairs is just in the style of a modern patriot, who believes invective to be argument, and general reprobation the height of political wisdom. I am inclined to think that Smollett intended some particular person in the character of *Ferret*: it is discriminated by too many individual qualities to be produced merely by the imagination.

This work was originally published, in detached portions, in the *British Magazine*, and the composition bear some marks of this desultory mode of production. The retrospective narrative of *Lawyer Clarke* is too long, too artificial, and too improbable. A man may relate general facts without having witnessed them, but he cannot retail conversations which he never heard. This, however, is done by *Mr Clarke*. Smollett might have obviated such a defect by commencing his narration at an earlier period, and suffering that to be acted which is now very unskilfully told. It is highly probable, however, that he knew not his own intentions, but sat down to each chapter as it was called for; and many errors thus escaped him which a matured plan and careful revisal would have prevented. Consistency is violated also in the person of *Mr Clarke*. He who would use such phrases as *gemmen* and *this here*, would be totally incapable of delivering so long and so connected a recital, with such perspicuity of language, and such pertinency of observation.

To describe the inhabitants of a prison is one of those things which Smollett has never omitted except in *Humphry Clinker*: accordingly, *Sir Launcelot* visits the King's Bench, and a description follows of the mode of life pursued by its tenants. It may be observed, also, that in this work he has embraced a second opportunity of mentioning Garrick with honour. He seems to have been ashamed of the indignity with which he had treated him; and there was more magnanimity in the shame than criminality in the offence.

I am weary of insisting upon Smollett's ludicrous attempts at pathos. In this work, indeed, he has fewer of those attempts than in any other. Yet, he could not let them wholly escape. In the account of *Captain Clewline*, his grief at the expected death of his infant son is expressed, as usual, with 'hideous groans,' 'piteous lamenta-tions,' and 'throwing himself on the floor.' But what shall exceed the tender address of the dying child to its mother, who had incautiously mentioned the word *death* in its hearing?—'Tommy won't leave you, my dear mamma: if death comes to take Tommy, papa shall drive him away with his sword.'—The reader hardly anticipates that this affecting speech occasions the mother to shriek, tear her hair, and be carried out of the room in a state of distraction.

Once more, and I have done. The following is the description of *Sir Launcelot* and *Aurelia*, when meeting each other after a long and disastrous separation. 'The lovers were seated: he looked and languished: she flushed and faltered: all was doubt and delirium, fondness and flutter.'

I will quarrel with no man who tells me that this is natural or serious: but I may be allowed to form an humble opinion of his judgment and taste.

It may be observed, in conclusion, that the work is very abruptly terminated. *Anthony Darnel* dies (or is presumed to die, for we are told only of his approaching death) just at the necessary and convenient moment when *Sir Launcelot* is eager to espouse *Aurelia*; the union between *Mr Clarke* and *Dolly*, though expected, is not gradually produced by any process of courtship; and the marriage of *Captain Crowe* with the knight's housekeeper is contrived with such precipitation as leaves the mind in a state of tranquil incredulity.

CRITICAL OBSERVATIONS ON *HUMPHRY CLINKER*

There is, perhaps, more knowledge of man displayed in this work than in any other of Smollett's novels. In his former productions he delighted to delineate the human character as modified by single and peculiar causes, which could operate only in a particular manner, and which would produce results nearly analogous. He selected an individual, and exhibited him under various aspects, proceeding from these causes; and though there is great merit in a faithful display of character thus engrafted upon local habits, there is yet a much greater merit in that wide and comprehensive exhibition of human nature, which is derived from no profession, from no province, nor from any country, but which embraces the imperishable qualities of civilized man, and which he will be found to possess on all great occasions, where-ever placed and however influenced. It is this excellence which distinguishes Shakespeare from all other dramatists, who, while they pourtrayed man as the growth of their own age, and shewed him as he had been externally modified by the accidental power of laws, customs, and manners; while they forsook the broad and boundless theatre of nature, to descend into her devious and minute wanderings; while they merely sought.

> To catch the manners living as they rose,[5]

Shakespeare flew at nobler game, and penetrating, at once, those hidden but permanent springs of action which are enclosed within every breast, he unfolded a volume to the world which no length of time can rob of its power to instruct and delight. Other dramatic writers have sunk into oblivion, or live only in the estimation of the curious; but the name of Shakespeare is borne along with still accumulating honours.

I do not wish to depreciate the merit of depicting existing manners: to do it successfully requires qualifications that are not often found; but, however successfully done, it must always be inferior to the display of what may be termed characters of nature. Shakspeare, Dryden, and Pope, excelled in both.

Neither would I wish to be considered as comparing Smollett to Shakspeare: I introduced the illustration as something which might better elucidate my meaning than mere precept; and to shew that Smollett had evinced, in this work, a power of intellect of much larger scope than in any of his preceding productions.

It has been said that in *Mathew Bramble* the author intended to give a sketch of his own character. It is known, indeed, that Smollett was sufficiently querulous: he had a peevish irritability of mind, which disposed him to view every occurrence of life with melancholy and discontent. These are certainly unenviable qualities; nor are they less pernicious than unenviable. They rob us of the power of happiness without giving us the means of contentment. They disturb and pervert our faculties, and leave us exposed to the inroads of helpless wretchedness, a burden to ourselves, and an incumbrance upon society. The captious and splenetic disposition of *Mathew Bramble*, however, is softened and relieved by other qualities which win upon the esteem of the reader. He is benevolent, social, friendly, and humane: liberal, upon reflection; intelligent and discriminating: though testy, yet kind; and though resentful, yet placable.

> He is gracious, if he be observ'd;
> He hath a tear for pity, and a hand
> Open as day for melting charity:

As humorous as winter, and as sudden
As flaws congeal'd in the spring of day.[6]

SHAKSPEARE

His virtues are made to preponderate over his failings, and in such a character a morbid irritability of feeling may well be forgiven.

Of his sister, *Mrs Tabitha*, and of her maid, *Mrs Winifred Jenkins*, much cannot be said in commendation. Their letters are tedious, not from their length, but from their contents. Their corrupt orthography is unskilfully managed; and their misapplication of terms is often puerile and too often licentious. To such attempts at exciting merriment much praise cannot be given, even when happily executed. Of language thus debased by ignorance and affectation, the first instance in our country is, I believe, to be found in Shakspeare's comedy of *Much Ado about Nothing*, where the sagacious and eloquent *Dogberry* discourses wth a most profound knowledge of that mode of speech which rhetoricians denominate catachresis. But neither *Mrs Tabitha* nor *Mrs Winifred* have any of that apparently artless propensity to blunder which belongs to their great prototype.

The nephew, *Melford*, is undistinguished by any peculiarities of manner or opinion. He serves, as a faithful chronicler of events, and he is made to tell them pleasingly: but he acquires no place in the reader's mind: we part from him at the end of each letter without caring to meet him again; and we meet him again without much consciousness that we have seen him before. He helps to fill up the picture without adding to its effect. It was certainly in the author's power to have given him more importance, if he wished to do it; and it is to be regretted that he did not. The want of variety in character is very sensibly felt in this work; and *Melford* might have concurred to relieve that want.

The same objections may be made to *Lydia* and to *Wilson*. The former is not consistently drawn. She is first represented as writing with all the insipidity and idle prattle of a girl; and suddenly she reasons upon men and manners with a solidity which, if it really existed, would have forbade her to descant so idly and unprofitably upon her own passion for *Wilson*. Her letters seem to have been introduced merely to break the continuity of her uncle and brother's correspondence. The mystery of *Wilson* is aukwardly unravelled. It is too improbable to please. *Incredulus odi.*[7] Neither is he sufficiently presented before the reader, to excite any interest respecting him. His letter to *Lydia* is another proof of what I have asserted in the prefatory observations on *Peregrine Pickle*, that Smollett was totally disqualified for depicting the passion of love. What ideas he has upon that topic, he has as evidently received by transmission, as a pastoral writer, in the Strand, receives his ideas of kine and tedded grass, of hawthorns, rosy milkmaids, and nightingales. Smollett's genius consisted rather in the power of humourous delineation, of satire, and sometimes of skilful argument: he knew nothing of the emotions of the human heart, when governed by the omnipotent passion of love.

Lismahago is a sketch which betrays a master's hand. Why was it not filled up in all its parts? Smollett knew his countrymen well, and in the disputatious character of *Lismahago* he had developed a quality which Franklin has asserted to be peculiar to them. That pertinacity of contention which converts conversation into a trial of skill, and which is founded in an arrogance of mind that deserves to be humbled where-ever it exists, is, indeed, the common reproach of Scotsmen, and especially of those who, as Dr Johnson sarcastically remarked, have got only a 'mouthful of learning, but not a bellyful.' Why it has become national in them, it were, perhaps, vain to inquire: but it may be generally observed that they who know most are usually least tenacious of their own opinions: I mean that contumelious tenacity which sets itself in opposition to all the ideas of other men. A man whose mind is expanded by knowledge learns to respect the opinions of others, from an intimate consciousness that error roots itself in the rank soil of self-confidence; but a man of scanty information, and being arrogant in mind, or eager for pre-eminence, is anxious to hide his poverty by his presumption, and to gain by insolence what he cannot win by merit. I know not whether Smollett intended to display this almost invariable feature of a contentious disputant; but the reader may perceive that *Lismahago's* arguments are often no less weak than their intrusion is insolent.

What the author's views were with regard to *Humphry Clinker* himself, from whom he has derived the title of his book, cannot easily be conjectured. He seems to have intended a satire on the Methodists in *Humphry's* piety; but he has given virtues to him that are incompatible with hypocrisy: he has made him too respectable to be contemptible. His illegitimate connexion with *Matthew*

Bramble is not well conceived, whom it has a tendency to lower in
the estimation of the reader, because no adequate information is
given how his offspring came to be deserted.

I cannot omit to observe that Smollett's eager vanity to
commemorate himself has led him to introduce not only his
cousin's residence on the banks of the Leven, but his own *Ode* to
that water, a composition which reflects very little credit upon his
talents as a writer. It is evident, also, that the character of S——,
who keeps an open house for the resort of needy authors, is meant
for himself, though I have never head that such was actually his
practice. But he delighted in any opportunity of rendering the
humbler labourers in literature ridiculous and despicable: an
undertaking, however, which confers very little credit upon him
who attempts it. Smollett himself was once a drudge to booksellers; but if his poverty never betrayed him into a mean action it
could be no disgrace that he had laboured obscurely for honest
maintenance. He had, perhaps forgotten, or was unwilling to
remember, his own career; for

> Lowliness is young ambition's ladder,
> Whereto the climber—upward turns his face:
> But, when he once attains the upmost round,
> He then unto the ladder turns his back,
> Looks in the clouds, scorning the base degrees
> By which he did ascend.[8]

But the readiness with which literary men have ever been willing
to persecute their less successful brethren, deserves to be discounte-
nanced, and reprobated as an unjust, a wanton, and a degenerate
hostility. Mere harmless imbecility may surely hope for lenity; if it
neither instructs nor delights, it is at least free from the reproach of
having corrupted. Can as much always be said of their opponents?

NOTES

a Gilbert Stewart denies that knight-errantry received its death-blow (as
  some authors have hastily concluded) from Cervantes. He attributes its
  extinction to a gradual and necessary decay.
1 Virgil, *Aeneid*, II, 5–6: 'The dreadful things I have seen and in which I
  played a major part.'
2 Horace, *Satires*, I, 1, 70: 'With the name changed, the story tells about
  you', or, 'There, but for the grace of God, go I.'

3 Juvenal, *Satires* II, 83: 'No-one is completely vicious immediately.'
4 'Pardon me, sir, my backside is certainly natural, but nevertheless I wear trousers.'
5 Pope, *An Essay on Man*, 14; the couplet actually reads:

> Eye Nature's walks, shoot Folly as it flies,
> And catch the Manners living as they rise;

6 Shakespeare, II *Henry IV*, IV, 4, 30–5.
7 Horace, *Art of Poetry*, 188: 'I disbelieve and hate it.'
8 Shakespeare, *Julius Caesar*, II, 1, 22–7.

138. *The Port Folio* on Smollett

1811

From *The Port Folio*, Philadelphia, vol. VI, November 1811, no. 5, 420–5. An unsigned critique of Smollett's fiction in an essay on 'Critical Comments on Sterne, Smollett, and Fielding.' The biographical portion of this extract has been omitted.

We will next solicit the attention of the reader to the example of Dr Smollett, as a proof, in opposition to the assertion of Dr Johnson, that an author's character may not be known from his page. In doing this, we shall also avail ourselves of the license we have before taken, and mingle some strictures on the style of his writings. Having in the outset of his literary career given Don Quixotte an English dress, he caught the humour of Cervantes. This trait is discernible in all his subsequent productions. Peregrine Pickle is attended by Pipes; Roderic Random by Strap; Mathew Bramble by Humphrey Clinker; Sir Launcelot Greaves by Cranshaw; and they are all but modernized copies of the knight of La Mancha and his squire Sancho Panza.

The first peculiarity we discover in the page of this author in his appetite for mischief. All his favourite characters are perpetually disturbing the king's peace; constantly exciting uproar, and as constantly eluding the researches of justice. He contrives stratagems and expedients for this purpose, always ingenious, but sometimes not very honourable to the favourite character he portrays. We may add to this another trait, if it does not more properly make a part of the foregoing, that the Dr's favourite characters are all fighting men, and at all times ready for a duel, or a riot. His page is further distinguished by an abhorrence of the faculty to which he belonged; nor does his imagination run to more excess, than when he describes the scurvy arts and mean devices which some of his profession employ to obtain popularity and fortune. This is not restricted satire, levelled at an occasional offence; but it constitutes the burden of his page.

His favourite heroes have on all occasions a loftiness of port, a high sense of honour, and demand a vindictive atonement for personal insult. Amidst all their mischievous qualities a greatness of soul is conspicuous, and when they assume their proper port they command involuntarily our respect. Nor are physicians exclusively annoyed by his satirical shafts. Lawyers and military officers are lashed likewise with unmerciful severity. There is in all this not the careless composure of an author who looks at a work of his own creation, and smiles to see how precise and exact his character is drawn: there is not the gay good nature of the wild and eccentric Sterne, who forgets his hero in the laugh he excites, and flies to something else for entertainment. No: there is something more hearty in the sarcasm of Smollett; something more of spleen and vengeance; for, while his victim is writhing under his wound, he regrets only that the wound was not deeper, and the pain more acute.

For the nautical character, if we view his composition in mass, we shall find that he entertains respect. Particular instances of meanness and tyranny in this department he notices; but they are particular instances only. However, when we set in opposition to this his examples of consummate fidelity and invincible attachment, in every trying vicissitude of fortune, all borrowed from nautical life, we may venture the conclusion we have drawn.

His favourite characters abstain from mean actions from a principle of pride; the obligations of religion are no where enforced. Although Smollett, with more prudence than is usual with him, was reserved and guarded on this subject, infidelity occasionally steals from his pen, and betrays him in spite of himself. Without entering more minutely into the consideration of the features his favourite characters present, we are warranted in making the conclusion, that the Dr indulged ideas of this kind: that the wild and irregular excesses of his youth are of little moment, and are very venial, if accompanied by no evidence of actions intrinsically mean—that we must at all times cherish a principle of self-respect as our surest guarantee of enforcing the respect of other men—that prudence, foresight, and discretion are virtues in themselves, but of small amount; that they are more than recompensed, if actions noble and heroic are our objects of pursuit; that they are amongst youth generally, the charactersitics of a mean insipidity of spirit.

Thus far do the life and writings of this eminent author coalesce. It now remains to take some notice of his style. The most obtrusive trait will be found to be his singular anxiety to run the character of the object of his satire down to the lowest point of degradation before he quits the vindictive pursuit. While a solitary shadow of respect lingers on the mind, Smollett considers his task unfinished, and renews his attack with renovated vengeance. He scorns to hold up a character for our diversion merely; if it is not perfectly despicable, it will not answer the expectations of Smollett. This fear of not doing enough, prompts him onwards to do too much, and his characters are, of course, overloaded. They partake of the nature of caricatures, and are more laughed at for their distortions, than admired for just and correct delineations of manners.

Smollett here followed the footsteps of his master Cervantes too tamely. Such excessive colouring is allowed to the don, for his insanity afforded a wider space to expatiate; whereas Smollett's heroes have all the extavaganza of the knight of La Mancha, without his insanity. Dr Akenside, for instance, in an evil hour reproached Scotland for her penury of genius, which Dr Smollett, a true son of Caledonia, deemed himself in honour bound to resent. He has therefore drawn the character of his opponent in such exaggerated colours, in the person of the learned physician, that if such a person should exist and set out upon his travels, Bedlam would be the starting-point of his departure.

Another singular trait in his style is the happy facility he possessed of burlesquing a man in the terms of his art. A memorable instance of this kind maybe found in Peregrine Pickle.

There was a controversy between a mechanic and a naturalist. 'The artist then proceeded to a practical illustration of the power of mechanism: he tilted his arm forward, like a lever, embraced the naturalist's nose, like a wedge, and turned it round with the momentum of a screw.' In this manner does Smollett render the terms of a man's art or profession subservient to his own disgrace. An attorney is felled by an unconscionable blow from commodore Trunnion, and loses his senses. As soon as he recovers them the first idea that seizes his brain is an action of assault and battery. The next paragraph is a still further illustration of this: the commodore seizing roasted turkey would have applied it, sauce and all, by way of poultice to the wound. A violent blow is thus described: 'Pipes bestowed such a stomacher on the officious intermeddler as made him discharge the interjection Ah! with demonstrations of great violence and agony.' The pleasure we derive from such reading results from the novelty of such combinations. Where we can trace no analogy ourselves, nothing diverts us more than to discover one traced by another; provided, as in the instances we have cited, there is no appearance of force in the application. Another feature in Smollett is the ludicrous and cynical asperity of his page. When he falls into one of his pouting fits he is pleased with nothing about him. He quarrels with every thing within his reach, and takes a wonderful satisfaction in diffusing his own discontent. A smiling good-humour would be high treason against the majesty of his spleen, and be banished indignantly from his presence. Directly the opposite of Sterne, whose writings are recommended for the cure of the spleen, Smollett would serve to prolong its influence by convincing us that all our morbid and melancholy ideas of men and manners were well founded.

While our eyes course along his pages in this manner, his spleen itself seems to wear away by such indulgence. We are transported at last into the assemblage of great and noble qualities. The clouds of discontent that loured so long and so heavily on our minds, are dissipated by the beams of orient joy, until the whole intellectual horizon becomes lucid, cheerful, and serene. We venture, therefore, a conjecture, that the splenetic mind of Dr Smollett found relief by indulgence.

Tenderness does not seem to be his forte or what he delighted in; but to make amends, he occasionally surprises his reader by bursts of sensibility so artless and affecting that they find a response in every heart.

We are sorry that the only resemblance between this writer and Sterne consists in the obscenity and the impiety of their pages. Writers of such genius, when they once give a-loose to such effusions, produce incalculable mischief. They are none of that vulgar class, whose genius is incapable of conferring dignity on the subjects they handle; whose very recommendations only serve to add new disgusts, and are, if possible, more loathing than the vice. These writings are, (beyond the intention of their authors,) *benefits*, real, substantial *benefits*. They shew us what sottish conceptions an indulgence in such vices as they recommend will engender. Sterne and Smollett seem by their writings to palliate, apologise for, and almost to consecrate, by their genius, the vices which their pages record. To place them in the neighbourhood of great and glorious qualities, such as irresistibly command our admiration and love, is the artifice which such writers adopt. The lustre obscures from the view the intervening cloud; but feeble indeed is the apology that nature does in some of her freaks present the same appearances. Those writers knew full well that such spectacles are rare, and, therefore, on their own ground, they should find no place in their novels. We should feel more charity if these defects were marked with more pointed reprobation; but, as it happens, those very vices seem introduced more to be imitated and admired than abhorred.

139. Sir James Mackintosh on Smollett

1811

From Sir James Mackintosh, *Memoirs*, ed. Robert James Mackintosh, 2 vols, 1835, vol. II, pp. 104–5, an entry dated 21 June 1811, in response to a reading of Mrs Barbauld's 'Notices' to her *British Novelists*.

The knavery of Count Fathom is not dignified enough to interest us by its fall! Is it true, as Mrs Barbauld says, that the coarseness of Smollett makes him less read now than he was formerly? *Humphrey Clinker* is the only one of the author's pieces that has no sailor. It may, perhaps, be a greater curiosity for that reason, as connoisseurs value a Wouvermans without a horse.[1]

NOTE

1 Philips Wouverman (1619–68), a Dutch painter from Haarlem, possibly a pupil of Frans Hals. His pictures commonly depicted hilly country scenes with horses, usually including a white horse.

140. Isaac D'Israeli on Smollett

1812

From Isaac D'Israeli, *Calamities and Quarrels of Authors*, 1812, pp. 18–23.

Who has displayed a more fruitful genius, and exercised more intense industry, with a loftier sense of his independence, than SMOLLETT? But look into his life and enter into his feelings, and you will be shocked at the disparity of his situation with the genius of the man. His life was a succession of struggles—vexations and disappointments, yet of success in his writings. SMOLLETT, who is a great poet though he has written little in verse, and whose rich genius had composed the most original pictures of human life, was compelled by his wants to debase his name by selling it to Voyages and Translations, which he never could have read. When he had worn himself down in the service of the public, or the booksellers, there remained not, of all his slender remunerations, in the last stage of life, sufficient to convey him to a cheap country and a restorative air, on the continent—the Father may have thought himself fortunate, that the daughter whom he loved with more than common affection was no more to share in his wants; but the Husband had by his side the faithful companion of his life, left without a wreck of fortune. SMOLLETT gradually perishing in a foreign land, neglected by an admiring public, and without fresh resources from the booksellers, who were receiving the income of his works—threw out his injured feelings in the character of *Bramble*; the warm generosity of his temper, but not his genius, seemed fleeting with his breath. Yet when SMOLLETT died, and his widow in a foreign land was raising a plain monument over his dust, her love and her piety but 'made the little less.' She perished in friendless solitude! Yet SMOLLETT dead—soon an ornamented column is raised at the place of his birth, while the grave of the Author seemed to multiply the editions of his works. There are indeed grateful feelings in the public at large for a favourite author; but the awful testimony of those feelings by its gradual progress, must appear beyond the grave! They visit the column consecrated by his name, and his features are most loved, most venerated, in the bust.

SMOLLETT himself shall be the historian of his own heart; this most successful 'Author by Profession,' who, for his subsistence, composed master-works of genius, and drudged in the toils of slavery, shall himself tell us what happened, and describe that state between life and death, partaking of both, which obscured his faculties and sickened his lofty spirit.

'Had some of those who were pleased to call themselves my friends been at any pains to deserve the character, and told me ingenuously what I had to expect in *the capacity of an Author, when I first professed myself of that venerable fraternity*, I should in all probability have spared myself the *incredible labour and chagrin I have since undergone.*'

As a relief from literary labour, SMOLLETT once went to re-visit his family, and to embrace the mother he loved—but such was the irritation of his mind and the infirmity of his health, exhausted by the hard labours of authorship, that he never passed a more weary summer, nor ever found himself so incapable of indulging the warmest emotions of his heart. On his return, in a letter, he gave this melancholy narrative of himself.——— 'Between friends I am now convinced that *my brain was in some measure affected*; for I had a kind of *Coma Vigil* upon me from April to November without intermission. In consideration of this circumstance I know you will forgive all my peevishness and discontent—tell Mrs Moore that with regard to me she has as yet seen nothing but the wrong side of the tapestry.' Thus it happens in the life of Authors, that they whose comic genius diffuses cheerfulness, create a pleasure which they cannot themselves participate.

The remarkable expression of a *Coma Vigil*, difficult to explain, may be described by a verse of Shakespeare in his antithetical account of love, a passion made up of contrarieties. Thus the *Coma Vigil* was

> Still-waking sleep! that is not what it is![1]

Of praise and censure, says SMOLLETT in a letter to Dr Moore,—'Indeed I am sick of both, and wish to God my circumstances would allow me to consign my pen to oblivion.' A wish, as fervently repeated by many 'Authors by Profession,' who are not so fully entitled as was SMOLLETT to write when he chose, or to have lived in quiet for what he had written.

An Author's life is therefore too often deprived of all social comfort, whether he be the writer for a minister, or a bookseller— but their case requires to be stated.

NOTE

1 Shakespeare, *Romeo and Juliet*, I, i, 179.

141. Smollett and Maria Edgeworth compared

1812

From *The Quarterly Review*, vol. VII, no. XIV, June 1812, 331–2. A review of Maria Edgeworth's *Tales of Fashionable Life* (1812).

Among the novelists, (whose duties, though of an inferior rank, are of a similar kind,) we cannot immediately recollect one who has this merit. In *Tom Jones, Peregrine Pickle*, and *Amelia*, we have a most accurate and vivid picture of real life; but it is, if we may venture to say so, *too* real. A novel, which is not in some degree a lesson either of morals or conduct, is, we think, a production which the world might be quite as well without, and, it must be admitted, that the personages of the (otherwise) excellent works which we have mentioned, are brought together, without any such leading object in the association—without reference to any particular principle, and without inculcating any specific system of moral duty. Towards the close, indeed, of the last volume of this class there is usually some attempt at 'Moralizing the tale,' and executing a lame and tardy justice on the prominent offenders; but this produces little beneficial effect on the mind: there is generally no kind of relation between the punishment inflicted and the crimes of those upon whom it is visited, and the errors of the heroes and heroines have as little to do with the annoyance which they suffer, as their virtues with the happiness to which they are ultimately, and for the most part, undeservedly dismissed. This, we admit, is no more than occurs in the great book of the world; but the more accurately that book is copied, the less inclined we should be to recommend to young and ardent minds the perusal of the transcript. We doubt whether the ridicule of Thwackum and Trulliber, or the exposure of Squire Gam and Blifil, have ever stifled the seeds of brutality of vice in any mind; but we are convinced that the gay immoralities, the criminal levities, and the rewarded dissipation of *Tom Jones* and *Peregrime Pickle* have contributed to inflame, and we will venture to add, to debauch many a youthful imagination.

142. Leigh Hunt on Smollett

1813, 1819, c. 1820

From Leigh Hunt, *Correspondence*, ed. his eldest son, 2 vols, 1862, and *Table Talk*, 1851.

From a letter to a Mr Ives, 17 March 1813:

There is a vein in Smollett—a Scotch vein—which is always disgusting to people of delicacy; but it is enough to say of him in this work,[*The Travels*] that he is an invalid with whom even moralists cannot sympathise—one has no patience with his want of patience.

From a letter to Shelley, 20 September 1819:

There were some things about his writings very unpleasant, but he was an honest man, and an independant one, and is understood to have done immense good to the poor wounded sailors in naval fights, by those pictures of pitiless surgery and amputation in *Roderick Random*.

From *Table Talk*, 1851, pp. 41–2:

Though Smollett sometimes vexes us with the malicious boy's-play of his heroes, and sometimes disgusts with his coarseness, he is still the Smollett whom now, as in one's boyhood, it is impossible not to heartily laugh with. He is an accomplished writer, and a masterly observer, and may be called the finest of caricaturists. His caricatures are always substantially true: it is only the complexional vehemence of his gusto that leads him to toss them up as he does, and tumble them on our plates. Then as to the objections against his morality, nobody will be hurt by it. The delicate and sentimental will look on the whole matter as a joke; the accessories of the characters will deter *them*: while readers of a coarser taste, for whom their friends might fear most because they are most likely to be conversant with the scenes described, are, in our opinion, to be seriously benefited by the perusal; for it will show them, that heroes of their description are expected to have virtues as well as faults, and that they seldom get anything by being positively disagreeable or bad. Our author's lovers, it must be owned are not of the most sentimental or flattering description. One of their common modes of paying their court, even to those they best love and esteem, is by writing lampoons on other women! Smollett had a strong spice of pride and malice in him (greatly owing, we doubt not, to some scene of unjust treatment he witnessed in early youth), which he imparts to his heroes; all of whom, probably, are caricatures of himself, as Fielding's brawny, good-natured, idle fellows are of *him*. There is no serious evil intention, however. It is all out of resentment of some evil, real or imaginary, or is made up of pure animal spirit and the love of venting a complexional sense of power. It is energy, humour, and movement, not particularly amiable, but clever, entertaining, and interesting, and without an atom of hypocrisy in it. No man will learn to be shabby by reading Smollett's writings.

143. Hazlitt on Smollett

1814

From *The Edinburgh Review*, Edinburgh, 1814, vol. XXIV, 329–30. Hazlitt's commentary on Smollett in his 'Standard Novels' series in the periodical, later published in 1819 (Lecture VI, 'On The English Novelists') from *Lectures on the English Comic Writers*; see *The Complete Works of William Hazlitt*, ed. P.P. Howe, 21 vols, 1933, vol. 6, pp. 115–17.

Smollett's first novel, *Roderick Random*, which is also his best appeared about the same time as Fielding's *Tom Jones*; and yet it has a much more modern air with it: But this may be accounted for, from the circumstance that Smollett was quite a young man at the time, whereas Fielding's manner must have been formed long before. The style of *Roderick Random*, though more scholastic and elaborate, is stronger and more pointed than that of *Tom Jones*; the incidents follow one another more rapidly, (though it must be confessed they never come in such a throng, or are brought out with the same dramatic facility); the humour is broader, and as effectual; and there is very nearly, if not quite, an equal interest excited by the story. What then is it that gives the superiority to Fielding? It is the superior insight into the springs of human character, and the constant development of that character through every change of circumstance. Smollett's humour often arises from the situation of the persons, or the peculiarity of their external appearance, as, from Roderick Random's carrotty locks, which hung down over his shoulders like a pound of candles, or Strap's ignorance of London, and the blunders that follow from it. There is a tone of vulgarity about all his productions. The incidents frequently resemble detached anecdotes taken from a newspaper or magazine; and, like those in *Gil Blas*, might happen to a hundred other characters. He exhibits only the external accidents and reverses to which human life is liable—not 'the stuff' of which it is composed. He seldom probes to the quick, or penetrates beyond the surface of his characters: and therefore he leaves no stings in the minds of his readers, and in this respect is far less interesting than Fielding. His novels always enliven, and never tire us: we take them up with pleasure, and lay them down without any strong feeling of regret. We look on and laugh, as spectators of an amusing though inelegant scene, without closing in with the combatants, or being made parties in the event. We read *Roderick Random* as an entertaining story; for the particular accidents and modes of life which it describes, have ceased to exist: But we regard *Tom Jones* as a real history; because the author never stops short of those essential principles which lie at the bottom of all our actions, and in which we feel an immediate interest;—*intus et in cute.*—Smollett excels most as the lively caricaturist: Fielding as the exact painter and profound metaphysician. We are far from maintaining, that this account applies uniformly to the productions of these two writers; but we think that, as far as they essentially differ, what we have stated is the general distinction between them. *Roderick Random* is the purest of Smollett's novels; we mean in point of style and description. Most of the incidents and characters are supposed to have been taken from the events of his own life; and are therefore truer to nature. There is a rude conception of generosity in some of his characters, of which Fielding seems to have been incapable; his amiable persons being merely good-natured. It is owing to this, we think, that Strap is superior to Partridge; and there is a heartiness and warmth of feeling in some of the scenes between Lieutenant Bowling and his nephew, which is beyond Fielding's power of impassioned writing. The whole of the scene on ship-board is a most admirable and striking picture, and, we imagine, very little, if at all exaggerated, though the interest it excites is of a very unpleasant kind. The picture of the little profligate French friar, who was Roderick's travelling companion, and of whom he always kept to the windward, is one of Smollett's most masterly sketches. *Peregrine Pickle* is no great favourite of ours, and *Launcelot Greaves* was not worthy of the genius of the author.

Humphry Clinker and *Count Fathom* are both equally admirable in their way. Perhaps the former is the most pleasant gossipping novel that ever was written—that which gives the most pleasure with the least effort to the reader. It is quite as amusing as going the journey could have been, and we have just as good an idea of what happened on the road, as if we had been of the party. Humphry Clinker himself is exquisite; and his sweetheart, Winifred Jenkins, nearly as good. Matthew Bramble, though not altogether original, is excellently supported, and seems to have been the prototype of Sir Anthony Absolute in the Rivals. But Lismahago is the flower of the flock. His tenaciousness in argument is not so delightful as the relaxation of his logical severity, when he finds his fortune mellowing with the wintry smiles of Mrs Tabitha Bramble. This is the best preserved, and most original of all Smollett's characters. The resemblance of *Don Quixote* is only just enough to make it interesting to the critical reader, without giving offence to any body else. The indecency and filth in this novel, are what must be allowed to all Smollett's writings. The subject and characters in *Count Fathom* are, in general, exceedingly disgusting: the story is also spun out to a degree of tediousness in the serious and sentimental parts; but there is more power of writing occasionally shown in it than in any of his works. We need only refer to the fine and bitter irony of the Count's address to the country of his ancestors on landing in England; to the robber-scene in the forest, which has never been surpassed; to the Parisian swindler, who personates a raw English country squire, (Western is tame in the comparison); and to the story of the seduction in the west of England. We should have some difficulty to point out, in any author, passages written with more force and nature than these.

It is not, in our opinion, a very difficult attempt to class Fielding or Smollett;—the one as an observer of the characters of human life, the other as a describer of its various eccentricities: But it is by no means so easy to dispose of Richardson, who was neither an observer of the one, nor a describer of the other; but who seemed to spin his materials entirely out of his own brain, as if there had been nothing existing in the world beyond the little shop in which he sat writing.

144. Lockhart on Smollett

29 December 1814

From *Life and Letters of John Gibson Lockhart*, ed. Andrew Lang, 2 vols, 1897, vol. I, pp. 172–3. From a letter to Archibald Constable, the publisher.

It is to me wonderful how the Scotch character has been neglected. I suppose the Kirk stood low in Smollett's early days, and he had imbibed a disgust for it. He has given us, you see, only a few little sketches, nothing full or rich, like his seamen. Now I think there is just as great a fund of originality and humour in the Scotch character, modified as it is, in the various ranks of life, as in the English or Spanish, or any of those of which so much has been made.

145. Smollett's Scottish humour

1815

From *The Edinburgh Review*, Edinburgh, XXV, Article 4, October 1815, 486–7, commenting on Smollett's humour in a review of William Godwin's *Lives of Milton's Nephews*.

It is impossible, in a Scottish journal, to omit Smollett, even if there had not been much better reasons for the mention of his name, than for the sake of observing, that he and Arbuthnot are sufficient to rescue Scotland from the imputation of wanting talent for pleasantry; though, it must be owned, that we are a grave people, happily educated under an austere system of morals; possessing, perhaps, some humour, in our peculiar dialect, but fearful of taking the liberty of jesting in a foreign language like the English; prone to abstruse speculation, to vehement dispute, to eagerness in the pursuits of business and ambition, and to all those intent occupations of mind which rather indispose it to unbend in easy playfulness.

146. On history in Smollett's fiction

1815

From *The Critical Review*, 5th series, vol. II, 1815, 104. In a review of Mrs West's *Alicia De Lacy: an Historical Romance*.

The delineation of knight errantry continued many centuries; but Cervantes, in his incomparable burlesque romance of *Don Quixote*, eradicated the cankering root of this fictitious bombast; and Le Sage, in his *Gil Blas*, introduced legitimate novel writing. Our countryman, Fielding rivalled him in his *Tom Jones*; while his contemporaries, Smollett, Richardson, Mackenzie, and a few others, fixed the standard of novel writing; but none of them introduced history into their fascinating tales. It would have hurt, rather than assisted, the effect; and, though Smollett was one of the best historians of our own country, we do not find a single historical fact[1] interwoven with his novels.

NOTE

1 The writer has overlooked Smollett's representation of his experience in the unsuccessful attack on Carthagena in 1741 in volume I of *Roderick Random*.

147. John Dunlop on Smollett

1816

From John Dunlop, *The History of Fiction*..., Edinburgh, 1816 (1814), vol. II, pp. 407–8. Dunlop (d. 1842) was an historian of classical literature and history.

Of the writings of Smollett, by far the most original is *Humphry Clinker*. In this novel the author most successfully executes, what had scarcely ever been before attempted—a representation of the different effects which the same scenes, and persons, and transactions, have on different dispositions and tempers. He exhibits through the whole work a most lively and humorous delineation, confirming strongly the great moral truth, that happiness and all our feelings are the result, less of external circumstances, than the constitution of the mind. In his other writings, the sailors of Smollett are most admirably delineated—their mixture of rudeness and tenderness—their narrow prejudices—thoughtless extravagance—dauntless valour—and warm generosity. In his *Peregrine Pickle*, Smollett's sea characters are a little caricatured, but

the character of Tom Bowling, in *Roderick Random*, has something
even sublime, and will be regarded in all ages as a happy exhibition
of those naval heroes, to whom Britain is indebted for so much of
her happiness and glory.

148. Hazlitt on Smollett

1823

Extract from *The Liberal*, no. 11, January 1823, reprinted in
The Complete Works of William Hazlitt, ed. P.P. Howe, 21
vols, 1933, vol. 17, pp. 100–1, from 'Essay X' of 'Uncol-
lected Essays', 'On the Scotch Character'.

The Scotch nation are a body-corporate. They hang together like a
swarm of bees. I do not know how it may be among themselves,
but with us they are all united as one man. They are not straggling
individuals, but embodied, formidable abstractions—determined
personifications of the land they come from. A Scotchman gets on
in the world, because he is not one, but many. He moves in himself
a host, drawn up in battle-array, and armed at all points against all
impugners. He is a double existence—he stands for himself and his
country. Every Scotchman is bond and surety for every other
Scotchman—he thinks nothing Scotch foreign to him. If you see a
Scotchman in the street, you may be almost sure it is another
Scotchman he is arm in arm with; and what is more, you may be
sure they are talking of Scotchmen. Begin at the Arctic Circle, and
they take Scotland in their way back. Plant the foot of the
compasses in the meridian, and they turn it by degrees to 'Edina's
darling seat'—true as the needle to the Pole. If you happen to say it
is a high wind, they say there are high winds in Edinburgh. Should
you mention Hampstead or Highgate, they smile at this as a local
prejudice, and remind you of the Calton Hill. The conversation
wanders and is impertinent, unless it hangs by this loop. It 'runs the

great mile, and is still at home.' You would think there was no other place in the world but Scotland, but that they strive to convince you at every turn of its superiority to all other places. Nothing goes down but Scotch Magazines and Reviews, Scotch airs, Scotch bravery, Scotch hospitality, Scotch novels, and Scotch logic. Some one the other day at a literary dinner in Scotland apologised for alluding to the name of Shakespeare so often, because he was not a Scotchman. What a blessing that the Duke of Wellington was not a Scotchman, or we should never have heard the last of him! Even Sir Walter Scott, I understand, talks of the Scotch novels in all companies; and by waving the title of the author, is at liberty to repeat the subject *ad infinitum*.

Lismahago in Smollett is a striking and laughable picture of this national propensity. He maintained with good discretion and method that oat-cakes were better than wheaten bread, and that the air of the old town of Edinburgh was sweet and salubrious. He was a favourable specimen of the class—acute though pertinacious, pleasant but wrong.[1] In general, his countrymen only plod on with the national character fastened behind them, looking round with wary eye and warning voice to those who would pick out a single article of their precious charge; and are as drawling and trouble-some as if they were hired by the hour to disclaim and exemplify all the vices of which they stand accused. Is this repulsive egotism peculiar to them merely in their travelling capacity, when they have to make their way amongst strangers, and are jealous of the honour of the parent-country, on which they have ungraciously turned their backs? So Lord Erskine, after an absence of fifty years, made an appropriate eulogy on the place of his birth, and having traced the feeling of patriotism in himself to its source in that habitual attachment which all wandering tribes have to their places of fixed residence, turned his horses' heads towards England—and farewell sentiment!

NOTE

[1] Hazlitt's footnote here reads: 'Some persons have asserted that the Scotch have no humour. It is in vain to set up this plea, since Smollett was a Scotchman.'

149. Thomas Carlyle on reading Smollett's novels

From *Thomas Carlyle* by Moncure D. Conway, New York, 1881, pp. 31–2.

Carlyle despised Smollett's work as an historian, but as can be seen from this extract held the novels in extraordinary esteem.

I remember few happier days than those in which I ran off into the fields to read *Roderick Random*, and how inconsolable I was that I could not get the second volume. To this day I know of few writers equal to Smollett. *Humphry Clinker* is precious to me now as he was in those years. Nothing by Dante or any one else surpasses in pathos the scene where Humphry goes into the smithy made for him in the old house, and whilst he is heating the iron, the poor woman who has lost her husband, and is deranged, comes and talks to him as to her husband. 'John, they told me you were dead. How glad I am you have come!' And Humphry's tears fall down and bubble on the hot iron.

150. John Keats on Smollett

5 January 1818

From *The Complete Works of John Keats*, ed. H. Buxton Forman, 5 vols, Glasgow, 1901, vol. IV, pp. 53–4. From a letter to his brothers.

You ask me what degrees there are between Scott's novels and those of Smollett. They appear to me to be quite distinct in every particular, more especially in their aim. Scott endeavours to throw so interesting and romantic a colouring into common and low characters as to give them a touch of the sublime. Smollett, on the contrary, pulls down and levels what with other men would continue romance. The grand parts of Scott are within the reach of more minds than the finest humours in *Humphrey Clinker*. I forget whether that fine thing of the Sargeant is Fielding's or Smollett's,[1] but it gives me more pleasure than the whole novel of *The Antiquary*. You must remember what I mean. Some one says to the sargeant: 'That's a non-sequiter!' 'If you come to that, replies the Sargeant, 'You're another!'

NOTE

1 In fact it comes in Fielding's *Tom Jones*, book IX, ch. 6.

151. Maturin on Smollett

1818

From *The British Review and London Critical Journal*, XI, 1818, 40–2. The novelist Charles Robert Maturin, author of *Melmoth the Wanderer* (1820), and other novels, in a review of Maria Edgeworth's *Harrington and Ormond, Tales* (1817).

Smollett possessed more varied knowledge of the human character, and more extensive experience of human life; was more conversant with its characters and vicissitudes; he was himself an αοηζ πολυτροπος[1]—he knew much, and has told all he knew. The great defect of his works is that his heroes, from Roderick Random down to Matthew Bramble, are all portraits of the same character in various costumes. The same Quixotic gallantry in love and courage, the same high sentiment of honour struggling with depravity of habit and virulence of temper, the same morbid and morose sensibility, the same supercilious courtesy, and misanthropic benevolence. Smollett is said to have sat to himself for the portraits of his own heroes: if so, Smollett, with all the advantages of talent, experience, and spirit was as unhappy as he was unamiable.

These writers seem to have graduated the scale of impurity among them.—Richardson's writings are impure neither from wantonness or depravity, neither because his own imagination was polluted, nor because he sought wilfully to pollute the imagination of others; but merely from that self-sufficiency which filled his imagination with the importance of every detail that related to his fictitious personages, and probably made him believe those details to be of as much importance to his readers. Smollett is often indelicate; sometimes from the licentiousness of humour, which had not then been taught the restraints imposed by modern decorum; and sometimes from the very nature of his subjects, which led him to paint life in all the varieties he had himself experienced, and in the range of which the tavern and the brothel were probably often included. It may be said 'impurity lay in his way, and he found it,' but Fielding seems to have sought it with insatiable, fulsome, gloating avidity.

NOTE

1 'A man of many parts'.

152. Coleridge on Smollett

1818

From Coleridge's lecture on 'Wit and Humour' delivered at the room of the Philosophical Society in Fetter Lane, 24 February 1818, Lecture IX of the 1818 series, reprinted in *Coleridge's Miscellaneous Criticism*, ed. Thomas Middleton Raysor, 1936, p. 108.

Thus again, (to take an instance from the different works of the same writer), in Smollett's Strap, his Lieutenant Bowling, his Morgan the honest Welshman, and his Matthew Bramble, we have exquisite humour,—while in his Peregrine Pickle we find an abundance of drollery, which too often degenerates into mere oddity; in short, we feel that a number of things are put together to counterfeit humour, but that there is no growth from within. And this indeed is the origin of the word, derived from the humoral pathology, and excellently described by Ben Jonson:

> So in every human body,
> The choler, melancholy, phlegm, and blood,
> By reason that they flow continually
> In some one part, and are not continent,
> Receive the name of humours. Now thus far
> It may, by metaphor, apply itself
> Unto the general disposition:
> As when some one peculiar quality
> Doth so possess a man, that it doth draw
> All his effects, his spirits, and his powers,
> In their confluctions, all to run one way,
> This may be truly said to be a humour.[1]

Hence we may explain the congeniality of humour with pathos, so exquisite in Sterne and Smollett, and hence also the tender feeling which we always have for, and associate with, the humours or hobby-horses of a man. First, we respect a humourist, because absence of interested motive is the ground-work of the character, although the imagination of an interest may exist in the individual himself, as if a remarkably simple-hearted man should pride himself on his knowledge of the world, and how well he can manage it:—and secondly, there always is in a genuine humour an acknowledgment of the hollowness and farce of the world, and its disproportion to the godlike within us.

NOTE

1 The reference is to Ben Jonson, *Every Man Out of His Humour*, 'After the Second Sounding', 98–109, cf. Herford and Simpson *Works of Ben Jonson*, vol. III, pp. 431–2.

153. Nathan Drake: Smollett and natural terror

1820

From Nathan Drake, *Literary Hours* (1798), 4th edn, 1820, 3 vols, vol. I, p. 274. Nathan Drake was a medical doctor and miscellaneous writer.

Smollett, too, notwithstanding his peculiar propensity for burlesque and broad humour, has, in his *Ferdinand Count Fathom*, painted a scene of natural terror with astonishing effect; with such vigour of imagination indeed, and minuteness of detail, that the blood runs cold, and the hair stands erect from the impression. The whole turns upon the Count, who is admitted, during a tremendous storm, into a solitary cottage in a forest, discovering a body just murdered in the room where he is going to sleep, and the door of which, on endeavouring to escape, he finds fastened upon him.

154. Sir Thomas Noon Talfourd on Smollett

1821

From 'On British Novels and Romances' in *The New Monthly Magazine*, vol. XIII, pt I, no. 73, February 1821, 207., reprinted in *Critical and Miscellaneous Writings of T. Noon Talfourd*, 3rd American ed., Boston, 1856, p. 109.

Talfourd (1795–1854) was a judge, Member of Parliament and essayist and a friend of many of the early Romantic writers.

Smollett seems to have had more touch of romance than Fielding, but not so profound and intuitive a knowledge of humanity's hidden treasures. There is nothing in his works comparable to a Parson Adams; but then, on the other hand, Fielding has not any thing of the kind equal to Strap. Partridge is dry, and hard, compared with this poor barber boy, with his generous overflowings of affection. *Roderick Random*, indeed, with its varied delineation of life, is almost a romance. Its hero is worthy of his name. He is the sport of fortune rolled about through the 'Many ways of wretchedness' almost without resistance, but ever catching those tastes of joy which are everywhere to be relished by those who are willing to receive them. We seem to roll on with him, and get delectably giddy in his company.

155. Smollett and Defoe compared

1821

An unsigned review in *The Retrospective Review*, vol. 3, pt 2, 1821, 362.

We shall perhaps illustrate our meaning by an actual comparison, in one or two instances, between De Foe and the writers to whom we have alluded. Both he and Smollett have given us successful representations of a sailor's life, but in a very different style, and with very different effect. De Foe's sailor is of the ordinary description of men, one out of a thousand, with nothing very striking or characteristic about him; the sailor in Smollett is altogether an extraordinary being, whose every action is uncouth, and every expression ludicrous. The one has the usual marks of a sailor, but has every thing else in common with the rest of mankind; the other seems to belong to a different species; and a creature formed and bred at sea, having a set of ideas, and modes of speaking and acting perfectly distinct from those possessed by the men who live on shore. The one has merely the technical phrase and vices, the homeliness and simplicity, peculiar to his profession; the other is not so much an individual character, as an abstract of the humour of the whole British navy. The one is an every-day kind of person, whom we have seen a hundred times; the other is a most amusing but imaginary being, whom we have never met with but in the inimitable pages of his creator.

156. Charles Lamb on Smollett

1821

From *The Works of Charles Lamb*, ed. W. MacDonald, 12 vols, 1903, vol. I, p. 120. Reprinted from *The London Magazine* of August 1821 in *The Essays of Elia*, in 'Imperfect Sympathies'.

But I have always found that a true Scot resents your admiration of his compatriot, even more than he would your contempt of him. The later he imputes to your 'imperfect acquaintance with many of the words which he uses;' and the same objection makes it a presumption in you to suppose you can admire him.—Thomson they seem to have forgotten. Smollett they have neither forgotten nor forgiven for his delineation of Rory and his companion, upon their first introduction to our metropolis.—Speak of Smollett as a great genius, and they will retort upon you Hume's *History* compared with *his* Continuation of it. What if the historian had continued *Humphry Clinker*?

157. Sir Walter Scott on Smollett

1821

From Sir Walter Scott, *Lives of the Novelists*, prefixed to Ballantyne's Novelists' Library, Edinburgh 4 vols, 1821–4, vol. I, 1821, pp. i-xlii, Scott's prefaces to the Ballantyne edition of Smollett's novels.

Necessity is the mother of invention in literature as well as in the arts, and the necessity of Smollett brought him forth in his pre-eminent character of a Novelist. *Roderick Random* may be considered as an imitation of Le Sage, as the hero flits through almost every scene of public and private life, recording, as he paints his own adventures, the manners of the times, with all their various shades and diversities of colouring; but forming no connected plot or story, the several parts of which hold connection with, or bear proportion to, each other. It was the second example of the minor romance, or English novel. Fielding had shortly before set the example in his *Tom Jones*, and a rival of almost equal eminence, in 1748, brought forth the *Adventures of Roderick Random*, a work which was eagerly received by the public, and brought both reputation and profit to the author.

It was generally believed that Smollett painted some of his own early adventures under the veil of fiction; but the public carried the spirit of applying the characters of a work of fiction to living personages much farther perhaps than the author intended. Gawkey, Crabbe, and Potion, were assigned to individuals in the West of Scotland; Mrs Smollett was supposed to be Narcissa; the author himself represented Roderick Random; (of which there can be little doubt,) a book-binder and barber, the early acquaintances of Dr Smollett, contended for the character of the attached, amiable, simple-hearted Strap; and the two naval officers, under whom Smollett had served, were stigmatized under the names of Oakum and Whiffle. Certain it is, that the contempt with which his unfortunate play had been treated forms the basis of Mr Melopoyn's story, in which Garrick and Lyttleton are roughly treated

350

under the characters of Marmozet and Sheerwit. The public did not taste less keenly the real merits of this interesting and humorous work, because they conceived it to possess the zest arising from personal allusion; and the sale of the work exceeded greatly the expectations of all concerned....

Peregrine Pickle is supposed to have been written in Paris, and appeared in 1751. It was received by the public with uncommon avidity, and a large impression dispersed, notwithstanding the efforts of certain booksellers and others whom Smollett accuses of attempts to obstruct the sale, the book being published on account of the author himself. His irritable temper induced him to run hastily before the public with complaints, which, howsoever well or ill grounded, the public has been at all times accustomed to hear with great indifference. Many professional authors, philosophers, and other public characters of the time were also satirized with little restraint.

The splendid merit of the work itself was a much greater victory over the author's enemies, if he really had such, than any which he could gain by personal altercation with unworthy opponents. Yet by many his second novel was not thought quite equal to his first. In truth, there occurs betwixt *Roderick Random* and *Peregrine Pickle* a difference, which is often observed betwixt the first and second efforts of authors who have been successful in this line. *Peregrine Pickle* is more finished, more sedulously laboured into excellence, exhibits scenes of more accumulated interest, and presents a richer variety of character and adventure than *Roderick Random*; but yet there is an ease and simplicity in the first novel which is not quite attained in the second, where the author has substituted splendour of colouring for simplicity of outline. Thus, of the inimitable sea-characters Trunnion, Pipes, and even Hatchway, border upon caricature; but Lieutenant Bowling and Jack Rattlin are truth and nature itself. The reason seems to be, that when an author brings forth his first representation of any class of characters, he seizes on the leading and striking outlines, and therefore, in the second attempt of the same kind, he is forced to make some distinction and either to invest his personage with less obvious and ordinary traits of character, or to place him in a new and less natural light. Hence, it would seem, the difference in opinion which sometimes occurs betwixt the author and the reader, respecting the comparative value of early and of subsequent publications. The author naturally prefers that upon which he is conscious much more labour has been bestowed, while the public often remain constant to their first love, and prefer the facility and truth of the earlier work to the more elaborate execution displayed in those which follow it. But though the simplicity of its predecessor was not, and could not be, repeated in Smollett's second novel, his powers are so far from evincing any falling off, that in *Peregrine Pickle* there is a much wider range of character and incidents, than is exhibited in *Roderick Random*, as well as more rich and brilliant display of the talents and humour of the distinguished author.

Peregine Pickle did not, however, owe its success entirely to its intrinsic merit. The Memoirs of a Lady of Quality, a separate tale, thrust into the work, with which it has no sort of connexion, in the manner introduced by Cervantes, and followed by Le Sage and Fielding, added considerably to its immediate popularity. These Memoirs, which are now regarded as a tiresome and unnecessary excrescence upon the main story, contain the history of Lady Vane, renowned at that time for her beauty, and her intrigues. The lady not only furnished Smollett with the materials for recording her own infamy; but it is said, rewarded him handsomely for the insertion of her story. Mr MacKercher, a character of a different description, was also introduced. He was remarkable for the benevolent Quixotry with which he supported the pretensions of the unfortunate Mr Annesley, a claimant of the title and property of Anglesea. The public took the interest in the frailities of Lady Vane, and the benevolence of Mr MacKercher, which they always take in the history of living and remarkable characters; and the anecdotes respecting the demirep and the man of charity, greatly promoted the instant popularity of *Peregrine Pickle*.

The extreme license of some of the scenes described in this novel, gave just offence to the thinking part of the public; and the work, in conformity to their just complaints, was much altered in the second edition. The preliminary advertisement has these words:—'It was the author's duty, as well as his interest, to oblige the public with this edition which he has endeavoured to render less unworthy of their acceptance, by retrenching the superfluities of the first, reforming its manners, and correcting its expression. Divers uninteresting incidents are wholly suppressed; some humorous scenes he has endeavoured to heighten; and he flatters that he has expunged every adventure, phrase, and insinuation, that could be construed by the most delicate reader into a trespass upon the rules of decorum.

He owns with contrition, that, in one or two instances, he gave way too much to the suggestions of personal resentment, and represented characters, as they appeared to him at the time, through the exaggerated medium of prejudice. But he has in this impression endeavoured to make atonement for these extravagancies. Howsoever he may have erred in point of judgment or discretion, he defies the whole world to prove that he was ever guilty of one act of malice, ingratitude, or dishonour. This declaration he may be permitted to make without incurring the imputation of vanity or presumption, considering the numerous shafts of envy, rancour, and revenge, that have lately, both in public and private, been levelled at his reputation.'

In reference to this palinode, we may barely observe, that the passages retrenched in the second edition are, generally speaking, the detail of those frolics in which the author has permitted his turn for humour greatly to outrun his sense of decency and propriety; and, in this respect, notwithstanding what he himself says in the passage just quoted, the work would have been much improved by a more unsparing application of the pruning knife. Several personal reflections were also omitted, particularly those on Lyttleton and Fielding, whom he had upbraided for his dependence on that statesman's patronage....

In the year 1753, Dr Smollett published *The Adventures of Ferdinand Count Fathom*, one of those works which seem to have been written for the purpose of shewing how far humour and genius can go, in painting a complete picture of human depravity. Smollett has made his own defence for the loathsome task which he has undertaken. 'Let me not,' says he, in the dedication to Dr ————, (we are unable to supply the blank,) 'be condemned for having chosen my principal character from the purlieus of treachery and fraud, when I declare my purpose is to set him up as a beacon for the benefit of the inexperienced and unwary, who, from the perusal of these memoirs, may learn to avoid the manifold snares with which they are continually surrounded in the paths of life, while those who hesitate on the brink of iniquity may be terrified from plunging into that irremediable gulf, by surveying the deplorable fate of

Ferdinand Count Fathom.' But, while we do justice to the author's motives, we are obliged to deny the validity of his reasoning. To a reader of a good disposition and well regulated mind, the picture of moral depravity presented in the character of Count Fathom is a disgusting pollution of the imagination. To those, on the other hand, who hesitate on the brink of meditated iniquity, it is not safe to detail the arts by which the ingenuity of villainy has triumphed in former instances; and it is well known that publication of the real account of uncommon crimes, although attended by the public and infamous punishment of the perpetrators, has often had the effect of stimulating others to similar actions. To some unhappy minds it may occur as a sort of extenuation of the crime which they meditate, that even if they carry their purpose into execution, their guilt will fall far short of what the author has ascribed to his fictitious character; and there are other imaginations so ill regulated, that they catch infection from stories of wickedness, and feel an insane impulse to emulate and to realize the pictures of villainy which are embodied in such narratives as those of Zeluco or Count Fathom.

Condemning, however, the scope and tendency of the work, it is impossible to deny our applause to the wonderful knowledge of life and manners, which is evinced in the tale of *Count Fathom*, as much as in any of Smollett's works. The horrible adventure in the hut of the robbers, is a tale of natural terror which rises into the sublime; and, though often imitated, has never yet been surpassed, or perhaps equalled. In *Count Fathom* also is to be found the first candid attempt to do justice to a calumniated race. The benevolent Jew of Cumberland had his prototype in the worthy Israelite whom Smollett has introduced into the history of Fathom. . . .[1]

In the course of 1760, and 1761, *The Adventures of Sir Lancelot Greaves* appeared, in detached portions, in various numbers of the *British Magazine*, or *Monthly Repository*. Smollett appears to have executed his task with very little premeditation. During a part of the time he was residing at Paxton, in Berwickshire, on a visit to the late George Home, Esq., and when post-time drew near, he used to retire for half an hour, to prepare the necessary quantity of copy, as it is technically called in the printing-house, which he never gave himself the trouble to correct, or even to read over. *Sir Lancelot Greaves* was published separately, in 1762.

The idea of this work was probably suggested to our author during his labours upon *Don Quixote*, and the plan forms a sort of corollary to the celebrated romance of *Don Quixote*. The leading imperfection is the great extravagance of the story, as applicable to England, and to the period when it is supposed to have happened. In Spain, ere the ideas of chivalry were extinct amongst that nation of romantic Hidalgoes the turn of Don Quixote's frenzy seems not altogether extravagant, and the armour which he assumed was still the ordinary garb of battle. But in England, and in modern times, that a young, amiable, and otherwise sensible man, acquainted also with the romance of Cervantes, should have adopted a similar whim, gives good foundation for the obvious remark of Ferret: 'What! you set up for a modern Don Quixote! The scheme is too stale and extravagant; what was an humorous and well-timed satire in Spain near two hundred years ago, will make but a sorry jest, when really acted from affectation, at this time of day in England.' To this Sir Lancelot replies, by a tirade which does not remove the objection so shrewdly stated by the misanthrope, affirming that he only warred against the foes of virtue and decorum; or, in his own words, 'had assumed the armour of his forefathers, to remedy evils which the law cannot reach, to detect fraud and treason, abase insolence, mortify pride, discourage slander, disgrace immodesty, and stigmatize ingratitude.' The degree of sanity which the amiable enthusiast possesses ought to have shewn him, that the generous career he had undertaken would be much better accomplished without his armour, than with that superfluous and ridiculous appendage; and that for all the purposes of reformation to be effected in England, his pocket-book, filled with bank notes, would be a better auxiliary than either sword or lance. In short, it becomes clear to the reader that Sir Lancelot wears panoply only that his youthful elegance and address, his bright armour and generous courser, may make him the more exact counterpart to the Knight of La Mancha.

If it be unnatural that Sir Lancelot should become a knight-errant, the whim of Crowe, the captain of a merchant vessel, adopting, at second-hand, the same folly, is, on the same grounds, still more exceptionable. There is nothing in the honest seaman's life or profession which renders it at all possible that he should have caught contagion from the insanity of Sir Lancelot. But, granting the author's premises, and surely we often make large concessions with less advantage in prospect, the quantity of comic humour which Smollett has extracted out of Crowe and Crabshaw, has as much hearty mirth in it as can be found even in his more finished compositions. The inferior characters are all sketched with the same bold, free, and peculiar touch that distinguishes this powerful writer; and, besides these we have named, Ferret and Clarke, the kind-hearted attorney's clerk, with several subordinate personages, have all the vivacity of Smollett's strong pencil. Aurelia Darnel is by far the most feminine, and, at the same time, lady-like person, to whom the author has introduced us. There is also some novelty of situation and incident, and Smollett's recent imprisonment in the King's Bench, for the attack on Admiral Knowles, enabled him to enrich his romance with a portrait of the unfortunate Theodore, King of Corsica, and other companions in his captivity, whose misfortunes or frolics had conducted them to that place of imprisonment....

Finding himself at liberty to resume his literary labours, Smollett published, in 1760, the political satire, called *The Adventures of an Atom*, in which are satirized the several leaders of political parties, from 1751 till the dissolution of Lord Chatham's administration. His inefficient patron, Lord Bute, is not spared in this work; and Chatham is severely treated under the name of Jowler. The inconsistency of this great minister, in encouraging the German war, seems to have altered Smollett's opinion of his patriotism; and he does his acknowledged talents far less than justice, endeavouring by every means to undervalue the successes of his brilliant administration, or to impute them to causes independent of his measures. The chief purpose of the work, (besides that of giving the author the opportunity to raise his hand like that of Ishmael, against every man,) is to inspire a horror of continental connections.

Shortly after the publication of the *The Adventures of an Atom*, disease again assailed Smollett with redoubled violence. Attempts being vainly made to obtain for him the office of Consul, in some port of the Mediterranean, he was compelled to seek a warmer climate, without better means of provision than his own precarious finances could afford. The kindness of his distinguished friend and countryman, Dr Armstrong, (then abroad) procured for Dr and Mrs Smollett a house at Monte Novo, a village situated on the side of a mountain overlooking the sea, in the neighbourhood of Leghorn, a romantic and salutary abode, where he prepared for the press the last, and, like music, 'sweetest in the close,' the most pleasing of his compositions, *The Expedition of Humphry Clinker*. This delightful work was published in 1771, in three volumes, 12mo, and very favourably received by the public.

The very ingenious scheme of describing the various effects produced upon different members of the same family by the same objects, was not original, though it has been supposed to be so. Anstey, the facetious author of the *New Bath Guide*, had employed it six or seven years before *Humphry Clinker* appeared. But Anstey's diverting satire was but a light sketch, compared to the finished and elaborate manner in which Smollett has, in the first place, identified his characters, and then fitted them with language, sentiments, and powers of observation, in exact correspondence with their talents, temper, conditions, and disposition. The portrait of Matthew Bramble, in which Smollett described his own peculiarities, using towards himself the same rigid anatomy which he exercised upon others, is unequalled in the line of fictitious composition. It is peculiarly striking to observe, how often, in admiring the shrewed and sound sense, active benevolence, and honourable sentiments combined in Matthew, we lose sight of the humorous peculiarities of his character, and with what effect they are suddenly recalled to our remembrance, just at the time and in the manner when we least expect them. All shrewish old maids, and simple waiting-women, which shall hereafter be drawn, must be contented with the praise of approaching in merit to Mrs Tabitha Bramble, and Winifred Jenkins. The peculiarities of the hot-headed young Oxonian, and the girlish romance of his sister, are admirably contrasted with the sense, and pettish half-playful misanthropy of their uncle; and Humphry Clinker (who by the way resembles Strap, supposing that excellent person to have a turn towards methodism) is, as far as he goes, equally delightful. Captain Lismahago was probably no violent caricature, allowing for the manners of the time. We can remember a good and gallant officer who was said to have been his prototype, but believe the opinion was only entertained from the striking resemblance which he bore in externals to the doughty captain.

When *Humphry Clinker* appeared in London, the popular odium against the Scotch nation, which Wilkes and Churchill had excited, was not yet appeased, and Smollett had enemies amongst the periodical critics, who failed not to charge him with undue partiality to his own country. They observed, maliciously, but not untruly, that the cynicism of Matthew Bramble becomes gradually softened as he journies northward, and that he who equally detested Bath and London, becomes wonderfully reconciled to walled cities and the hum of men, when he finds himself an inhabitant of the northern metropolis. It is not worth defending so excellent a work against so weak an objection. The author was a dying man, and his thoughts were turned towards the scenes of youthful gaiety and the abode of early friends, with a fond partiality, which, had they been even less deserving of his attachment, would have been not only pardonable, but praise-worthy.

Moritur, et moriens dulces reminiscitur Argos.[2]

Smollett failed not, as he usually did, to introduce himself, with the various causes which he had to complain of the world, into the pages of this delightful romance. He appears as Mr Serle, and more boldly under his own name, and in describing his own mode of living, he satirizes without mercy the book-makers of the day, who had experienced his kindness without repaying him by gratitude. It does not, however, seem perfectly fair to make them atone for their ungracious return to his hospitality by serving up their characters as a banquet to the public; and, in fact, it too much resembles the design of which Pallet accuses the Physician, of converting his guests into patients, in order to make him amends for the expence of the entertainment....

In leaving Smollett's personal for his literary character, it is impossible not to consider the latter as contrasted with that of his eminent contemporary, Fielding. It is true, that such comparisons, though recommended by the example of Plutarch, are not in general the best mode of estimating individual merit. But in the present case, the history, accomplishment, talents, pursuits, and, unfortunately, the fates of these two great authors, are so closely allied, that it is scarce possible to name the one without exciting recollections of the other. Fielding and Smollett were both born in the highest rank of society, both educated to learned professions, yet both obliged to follow miscellaneous literature as the means of subsistence. Both were confined, during their lives, by the narrowness of their circumstances,—both united a humorous cynicism with generosity and good nature,—both died of the diseases incident to sedentary life, and to literary labour,—and both drew their last breath in a foreign land, to which they retreated under the adverse circumstances of a decayed constitution, and an exhausted fortune.

Their studies were no less similar than their lives. They both wrote for the stage, and neither of them successfully. They both meddled in politics; they both wrote travels, in which they shewed that their good humour was wasted under the sufferings of their disease; and, to conclude, they were both so eminently successful as novelists, that no other English author of that class has a right to be mentioned in the same breath with Fielding and Smollett.

If we compare the works of these two great masters yet more, closely, we may assign to Fielding, with little hesitation, the praise of a higher and a purer taste than was shewn by his rival; more elegance of composition and expression; a nearer approach to the grave irony of Swift and Cervantes; a great deal more address or felicity in the conduct of his story; and, finally, a power of describing amiable and virtuous characters, and of placing before us heroes, and especially heroines, of a much higher as well as pleasing character than Smollett was able to present.

Thus the art and felicity with which the story of *Tom Jones* evolves itself, is no where found in Smollett's novels, where the heroes pass from one situation in life, and from one stage of society, to another totally unconnected, except that, as in ordinary life, the adventures recorded, though not bearing upon each other, or on the catastrophe, befal the same personage. Characters are introduced and dropped without scruple, and, at the end of the work, the hero is found surrounded by a very different set of associates from those with whom his fortune seemed at first indissolubly connected. Neither are the characters which Smollett designed should be interesting, half so amiable as his readers could desire. The lowminded Roderick Random, who borrows Strap's money, wears his clothes, and, rescued from starving by the attachment of that simple and kind-hearted adherent, rewards him by squandering his substance, receiving his attendance as a servant, and beating him when the dice ran against him, is not to be named in one day with the open-hearted, good-humoured, and noble-minded Tom Jones, whose libertinism (one particular omitted) is perhaps rendered but too amiable by his good qualities. We believe there are few readers who are not disgusted with the miserable reward assigned to Strap in the closing chapter of the novel. Five hundred pounds, (scarce the value of the goods he had presented to his master,) and the hand of a reclaimed street-walker, even when added to a Highland farm, seem but a poor recompense for his faithful and disinterested attachment. We should do Jones equal injustice by weighing him in the balance with the savage and ferocious Pickle, who,—besides his gross and base brutality towards Emilia, besides his ingratitude to his uncle, and the savage propensity which he shews, in the pleasure he takes to torment others by practical jokes resembling those of a fiend in glee,— exhibits a low and ungentleman-like tone of thinking, only one degree higher than that of Roderick Random. The blackguard frolic of introducing a prostitute, in a false character, to his sister, is a sufficient instance of that want of taste and feeling which Smollett's admirers are compelled to acknowledge, may be detected in his writings. It is yet more impossible to compare Sophia or Amelia to the females of Smollett, who (excepting Aurelia Darnel) are drawn as the objects rather of appetite than of affection, and excite no higher or more noble interest than might be created by the houris of the Mahomedan paradise.

It follows from this superiority on the side of Fielding, that his novels exhibit, more frequently than those of Smollett, scenes of distress, which excite the sympathy and pity of the reader. No one can refuse his compassion to Jones, when, by a train of practices upon his generous and open charater, he is expelled from his benefactor's house under the foulest and most heart-rending accusations; but we certainly sympathize very little in the distress of Pickle, brought on by his own profligate profusion, and enhanced by his insolent misanthropy. We are only surprised that his predominating arrogance does not weary out the benevolence of Hatchway and Pipes, and scarce think the ruined spendthrift deserves their persevering and faithful attachment.

But the deep and fertile genius of Smollett afforded resources sufficient to balance these deficiencies; and when the full weight has been allowed to Fielding's superiority of taste and expression, his northern contemporary will still be found fit to balance the scale with his great rival. If Fielding had superior taste, the palm of more brilliancy of genius, more inexhaustible richness of invention, must in justice be awarded to Smollett. In comparison with his sphere, that in which Fielding walked was limited; and, compared with the wealthy profusion of varied character and incident which Smollett has scattered through his works, there is a poverty of composition about his rival. Fielding's fame rests on a single *Chef d'oeuvre*; and the art and industry which produced *Tom Jones*, was unable to rise to equal excellence in *Amelia*. Though, therefore, we may justly prefer *Tom Jones* as the most masterly example of an artful and well told novel, to any individual work of Smollett; yet *Roderick Random*, *Peregrine Pickle*, and *Humphry Clinker*, do each of them far excel *Joseph Andrews* or *Amelia*; and to descend still lower, *Jonathan Wild*, or *The Journey to the Next World*, cannot be put into momentary comparison with *Sir Lancelot Greaves*, or *Ferdinand Count Fathom*.

Every successful novelist must be more or less a poet, even although he may never have written a line of verse. The quality of imagination is absolutely indispensible to him: his accurate power of examining and embodying human character and human passion, as well as the external face of nature, is not less essential; and the talent of describing well what he feels with acuteness, added to the above requisites, goes far to complete the poetic character. Smollett was, even in the ordinary sense, which limits the name to those who write verses, a poet of distinction; and, in this particular, superior to Fielding, who seldom aims at more than a slight translation from the classics. Accordingly, if he is surpassed by Fielding in moving pity, the northern novelist soars far above him in his powers of exciting terror. Fielding has no passages which approach in sublimity to the robber-scene in *Count Fathom*; or to the terrible description of a sea-engagement, in which Roderick Random sits chained and exposed upon the poop, without the power of motion or exertion, during the carnage of a tremendous engagement. Upon many other occasions, Smollett's descriptions ascend to the sublime; and, in general, there is an air of romance in his writings, which raise his narratives above the level and easy course of ordinary life. He was, like a pre-eminent poet of our own day, a searcher of dark bosoms, and loved to paint characters under the strong agitation of fierce and stormy passions. Hence, misanthropes, gamblers, and duellists, are as common in his works, as robbers in those of Salvator Rosa, and are drawn, in most cases, with the same terrible truth and effect. To compare *Ferdinand Count Fathom* to the *Jonathan Wild* of Fielding, would be perhaps unfair to the latter author; yet, the works being composed on the same plan, (a very bad one, as we think,) we cannot help placing them by the side of each other, when it becomes at once obvious that the detestable Fathom is a living and existing miscreant, at whom we shrink as from the presence of an incarnate fiend, while the villain of Fielding seems rather a cold personification of the abstract principle of evil, so far from being terrible, that notwithstanding the knowledge of the world argued in many passages of his adventures, we are compelled to acknowledge him absolutely tiresome.

It is, however, chiefly in his profusion, which amounts almost to prodigality, that we recognize the superior richness of Smollett's fancy. He never shews the least desire to make the most either of a character, or a situation, or an adventure, but throws them together with a carelessness which argues unlimited confidence in his own powers. Fielding pauses to explain the principles of his art, and to congratulate himself and his readers on the felicity with which he constructs his narrative, or makes his characters evolve themselves in the progress. These appeals to the reader's judgment, admirable as they are, have sometimes the fault of being diffuse, and always the great disadvantages, that they remind us we are perusing a work of fiction; and that the beings with whom we have been conversant during the perusal, are but a set of evanescent phantoms, conjured up by a magician for our amusement. Smollett seldom holds communication with his readers in his own person. He manages his delightful puppet-show without thrusting his head beyond the curtain, like Gines de Passamonte, to explain what he is doing; and hence, besides that our attention to the story remains unbroken, we are sure that the author, fully confident in the abundance of his materials, has no occasion to eke them out with extrinsic matter.

Smollett's sea characters have been deservedly considered as inimitable; and the power with which he has diversified them, in so many instances, distinguishing the individual features of each honest tar, while each possesses a full proportion of professional manners and habits of thinking, is a most absolute proof of the richness of fancy with which the author was gifted, and which we have noticed as his chief advantage over Fielding. Bowling, Trunnion, Hatchway, Pipes, and Crowe, and all men of the same class, habits, and tone of thinking, yet so completely differenced by their separate and individual characters, that we at once acknowledge them as distinct persons, while we see and allow that every one of them belongs to the old English navy. These striking portraits have now the merit which is cherished by antiquaries—they preserve the memory of the school of Benbow and Boscawen, whose manners are now banished from the quarter-deck to the fore-castle. The naval officers of the present day, the splendour of whose actions has thrown into shadow the exploits of a thousand years, do not now affect the manners of a fore-mast-man, and have shewn how admirably well their duty can be discharged without any particular attachment to tobacco or flip, or the decided preference of a check shirt over a linen one.

In the comic part of their writings, we have already said, Fielding is pre-eminent in grave irony, a Cervantic species of pleasantry, in which Smollett is not equally successful. On the other hand, the Scotchman, (notwithstanding the general opinion denies that quality to his countrymen,) excels in broad and ludicrous humour. His fancy seems to run riot in accumulating ridiculous circumstances one upon another, to the utter destruction of all power of gravity; and perhaps no books ever written have excited such peals of inextinguishable laughter as those of Smollett. The descriptions which affect us thus powerfully, border sometimes upon what is called farce or caricature; but if it be the highest praise of pathetic composition that it draws forth tears, why should it not be esteemed the greatest excellence of the ludicrous that it compels laughter? The one tribute is at least as genuine an expression of natural feeling as the other; and he who can read the calamities of Trunnion and Hatchway, when run away with by their mettled steeds, or the inimitable absurdities of the feast of the ancients, without a good hearty burst of honest laughter, must be well qualified to look sad and gentleman-like with Lord Chesterfield or Master Stephen.

Upon the whole, the genius of Smollett may be said to resemble that of Rubens. His pictures are often deficient in grace; sometimes coarse, and even vulgar in conception; deficient too in keeping, and in the due subordination of parts to each other; and intimating too much carelessness on the part of the artist. But these faults are redeemed by such richness and brilliancy of colours; such a profusion of imagination—now bodying forth the grand and terrible—now the natural, the easy, and the ludicrous; there is so much of life, action, and bustle, in every group he has painted; so much force and individuality of character, that we readily grant to Smollett an equal rank with his great rival Fielding, while we place both far above any of their successors in the same line of fictitious composition.

NOTES

1 The reference here is to Richard Cumberland (1732–1811) and his play *The Jew* (1794).
2 Virgil, *Aeneid*, X, 782: 'He is dying, and as he dies he remembers the sweetness of Argos.'

158. Sir Walter Scott on the rules of narrative

1822

From the 'Introductory Epistle' to Scott's *The Fortunes of Nigel*, Edinburgh, 1822, pp. xiv–xv.

He [Fielding] challenges a comparison between the Novel and the Epic. Smollett, Le Sage, and others, emancipating themselves from the strictness of the rules he has laid down, have written rather a history of the miscellaneous adventures which befall an individual in the course of life, than the plot of a regular and connected epopeia, whose every step brings us a point nearer to the final catastrophe. These great masters have been satisfied if they amused the reader upon the road, though the conclusion only arrived because the tale must have an end, just as the traveller alights at the inn because it is evening.

159. Lockhart on the Scottish dialect

1828

From John Gibson Lockhart, *The Life of Robert Burns*, (Edinburgh and London, 1828), the extract taken from the Everyman edn, ch. VIII, pp. 351–2, and ch. IX, pp. 430–1.

In almost all these productions—certainly in all that deserve to be placed in the first rank of his compositions—Burns made use of his native dialect. He did so, too, in opposition to the advice of almost all the lettered correspondents he had—more especially of Dr Moore, who, in his own novels, never ventured on more than a few casual specimens of Scottish colloquy—following therein the example of his illustrious predecessor Smollett; and not foreseeing that a triumph over English prejudice, which Smollett might have achieved, had he pleased to make the effort, was destined to be the prize of Burns's perseverance in obeying the dictates of native taste and judgment. ...

It has already been remarked, how even Smollett, who began with a national tragedy, and one of the noblest of national lyrics, never dared to make use of the dialect of his own country; and how Moore, another most enthusiastic Scotsman, followed in this respect, as in others, the example of Smollett, and over and over again counselled Burns to do the like. But a still more striking sign of the times is to be found in the style adopted by both of these novelists, especially the great master of the art, in their representations of the manners and characters of their own countrymen. In *Humphry Clinker*, the last and best of Smollett's tales, there are some traits of a better kind—but, taking his works as a whole, the impression it conveys is certainly a painful, a disgusting one. The Scotsmen of these authors, are the Jockeys and Archies of farce—

> Time out of mind the Southrons' mirthmakers—

the best of them grotesque combinations of simplicity and hypocrisy, pride and meanness. When such men, high-spirited

365

Scottish gentlemen, possessed of learning and talents, and one of them at least, of splendid genius, felt, or fancied, the necessity of making such submissions to the prejudices of the dominant nation, and did so without exciting a murmur among their own countrymen, we may form some notion of the boldness of Burns's experiment; and on contrasting the state of things then with what is before us now, it will cost no effort to appreciate the nature and consequences of the victory in which our poet led the way, by achievements never in their kind to be surpassed.

160. Charles Dickens on Smollett

1847 and 1854

From the 'Autobiographical Fragment' in John Forster, *The Life of Charles Dickens*, 1872–4, book I, chapter I, pp. 37–8. The substance of this extract from the 'Autobiographical Fragment' features in the fiction in Chapter VII of *David Copperfield*. The subsequent extract is from *The Letters of Charles Dickens*, 2 vols, 1880, vol. I, p. 356.

My father had left a small collection of books in a little room upstairs to which I had access (for it adjoined my own), and which nobody else in our house ever troubled. From that blessed little room, *Roderick Random*, *Peregrine Pickle*, *Humphry Clinker*, *Tom Jones*, *The Vicar of Wakefield*, *Don Quixote*, *Gil Blas* and *Robinson Crusoe* came out, a glorious host, to keep me company. They kept alive my fancy, and my hope of something beyond that place and time—they, and the *Arabian Nights*, and the *Tales of the Genii*—and did me no harm; for, whatever harm was in some of them, was not there for me; *I* knew nothing of it. It is astonishing to me now, how I found time, in the midst of my porings and blunderings over heavier themes, to read those books as I did. It is curious to me how I could ever have consoled myself under my small troubles (which were great troubles to me), by impersonating my favourite characters in them. . . . I have been Tom Jones (a child's Tom Jones, a harmless creature) for a week together. I have sustained my own idea of Roderick Random for a month at a stretch, I verily believe. I had a greedy relish for a few volumes of voyages and travels—I forget what, now—that were on those shelves; and for days and days I can remember to have gone about my region of our house, armed with the centre-piece out of an old set of boot-trees: the perfect realization of Captain Somebody, of the Royal British Navy, in danger of being beset by savages, and resolved to sell his life at a great price. . . . When I think of it, the picture always rises in my mind, of a summer evening, the boys at play in the churchyard, and I sitting on my bed reading as if for life. Every barn in the neighbourhood, every stone in the church, and every foot of the churchyard, had some association of its own, in my mind, connected with these books, and stood for some locality made famous in them. I have seen Tom Pipes go climbing up the church steeple; I have watched Strap, with the knapsack on his back, stopping to rest himself upon the wicket-gate; and I *know* that Commodore Trunnion held that club with Mr Pickle in the parlour of our little village alehouse. . . .

From a letter to Mr Frank Stone, 30 May 1854:

P.S. *Humphry Clinker* is certainly Smollett's best. I am rather divided between *Peregrine Pickle* and *Roderick Random*, both extraordinarily good in their way, which is a way without tenderness, but you will have to read them both, and I send the first volume of *Peregrine* as the richer of the two.

Appendix 1
Quotations from *Peregrine Pickle*

The Shakespeare Head edition of *Peregrine Pickle* is taken from the 3rd edition, 1765, and the 4th edition, 1769. James L. Clifford's edition in the Oxford English Novels series, 1964, and that most commonly cited now, is taken from the 1st edition of *Peregrine Pickle* of 1751. The following table correlates the quotations from *Peregrine Pickle* referred to in the text to these two editions.

No. 13	Shakespeare Head:	ch. XXII	pp. 155–7
	Clifford:	ch. XXV	pp. 117–19
	Shakespeare Head:	ch. XIII	pp. 89–91
	Clifford:	ch. XIV	pp. 65–6
	Shakespeare Head:	ch. LXXXI	p. 63.
	Clifford:	ch. LXXXVIII	pp. 432–3
	Shakespeare Head:	ch. LXXXI	p. 212
	Clifford:	ch. LXXXVIII	p. 532
No. 14	Shakespeare Head:	ch. LI	pp. 120–2
	Clifford:	ch. LV	pp. 272–5
No. 121	Shakespeare Head:	ch. LXXVI	pp. 29–33
	Clifford:	ch. LXXXII	pp. 407–9

Appendix 2
A Key to *The Adventures of an Atom*

A[bercromb]y *see* Abra-moria

Abra-moria (Major-General James Abercromby) defeated (at Ticonderoga, 1758)

Ab-ren-thi (John Abernethy, Irish dissenter, 1680–1740)

A[dministratio]n

Akousti (the King of Poland) *see* Polhassan-akousti

Amazonian Princess (Maria Theresa) *see* Ostrog, Princess of

Apothecary (perhaps 'Sir' John

Hill, 1716?–1775 see also Physician)

Asia (Europe, Asia)

Astrog (Austria)

Banyan merchant, see Thum-Khummqua

B[arringto]n, Lord, see Nob-o-di

Bha-kakh (Sir George Pocock, admiral, 1706–1792)

Bihn-go (Admiral the Hon. John Byng, 1704–1757)

Bonzas (clergy)

Bonzas, one of the gravest doctors of the (Archbishop of Canterbury)

Bron-xi-tic (Ferdinand, Duke of Brunswick)

Brut-an-tiffi (Frederick the Great, King of Prussia, 1712–1786)

Bupo (George I, 1660–1727)

Cambadoxi (Cambridge)

Cambodia (Sardinia)

C[ambridge]

Cell near London (Hayes)

Cham, the Great (the Emperor of Germany)

China, Chinese (France, French)

Chinese pilot (Thierry, defender of Rochefort)

Conservator of the Signet (William Pitt, lord privy seal)

Corea (Spain)

Cuboy, a former (Charles Montagu, first Earl of Halifax, 1661–1715)

Cuboy (prime minister), see also Fika-kaka, Yak-strot

Dairo (King) see Bupo, Got-hama-baba, Gio-gio

Day (nobleman)

Desolate island (ile d'Aix)

Fakku-basi (House of Hanover and the Protestant Succession)

Fan-yah (Havanna)

Fas-khan (Hon. Edward Boscawen, admiral, 1711–1761)

Fatsissian tax (the Stamp Act)

Fatsissio, Fatsissian (America, American)

Fatsissio, General-in-Chief in (William Shirley, Governor of Massachussetts, 1694–1771)

Fatzman, the (commander-in-chief), see Quamba-cun-dono

Fi-de-ta-da (William, Viscount Blakeney, defender of Minorca, 1672–1761)

Fika-kaka (Thomas Pelham-Holles, first Duke of Newcastle, statesman, 1693–1768)

Fishery, defenceless (Newfoundland)

Fla-sao (Plassey)

Fo, religion of (the Roman Catholic Church)

Foggien (eighteenth century)

Foksi-roku (Henry Fox, first Baron Holland, 1705–1774)

Foutao (Gibraltar)

Fortress, strong Chinese (Louisburg)

Frenoxena (Oxford)

Fumma (Portugal)

Fune (navy)

General, a celebrated (Count Daun)

General recall'd (John Campbell, 4th Earl of Loudoun, General, 1705–1782)

Gio-gio (George III, 1738–1820)

Got-hama-baba (George II, 1683–1760, succeeded 1727)

Gotto-mio (John Russell, 4th Duke of Bedford, 1710–1771)

Gowry, Earl of (William Ruthven, 1st earl, 1541?–1584)

Grandmother of Gio-gio (Augusta of Saxe-Gotha, Princess of Wales, mother of George III)

Hag, old rich (Sarah, Duchess of Marl-borough, 1660–1744)

Hel-y-otte (John Elliot, admiral, d. 1808)

He-Rhumn (Admiral Sir John Moore, 1st bart., 1718–1779)

Hob-nob (Major-General Peregrine Hopson)

H[um]e (David Hume, 1711–1776)

Hydra, the (the British people)

Hylib-bib (Lieut.-General Thomas Bligh, 1685–1775 expedition against Cherbourg, 1758)

Ian-on-i (Sir William Johson, 1st bart., 1771–1774)

Jacko (?John Potter, archbishop of Canterbury, 1674?–1747)

Jan-ki-dtzin (John Wilkes, politician, 1727–1779)

Japan, Japonese (Great Britain, British)

Jeddo (Germany)

Jonkh (man-of-war)

Ka-frit-o (Cape Breton island)

Ka-liff (Robert Clive, baron, 1725–1774)

Kamschatka (?India)

Kempfer (Engelbertus Kaempfer)

Kep-marl (George Keppel, 3rd Earl of Albemarle, general, 1724–1772)

Kha-fell (Augustus Viscount Keppel, admiral, 1725–1786)

Khan, the Great (Emperor of Germany), *see also* Cham

Kho-rhé (Goree)

Khutt-whang (Sir Eyre Coote, 1726–1783, general)

Koan general, (Edward Braddock, 1695–1755, ambushed at Fort Duquesne, 1755)

Kobot (George I)

Kow-kin (Richard Rigby, politician, 1722–1788)

Kunt-than (Count Daun, commander of the Austrian army)

Kurd (Prussians)

Legion (the people)

Le-yaw-ter (James O'Hara, Baron Kilmaine and 2nd Baron Tyrawley, fieldmarshal and diplomat, 1690–1773)

Librarian who could not read (probably Sir Frederick Augusta Barnard, king's librarian)

Lley-nah (Robert Henley, 1st Earl of Northlington, lord chancellor, 1708?–1772)

Liha-dahn (General Landohn)

Lli-nam (Manilla)

Llur-cher (Charles Churchill, satirist, 1731–1764)

Lob-kob (Richard Grenville-Temple, Earl Temple, 1711–1779)

Mantchoux empress (Elizabeth, empress of Russia, 1709–1762)

Mantchoux tartars (Russians)

Meaco (London)

Meckado (William the Conqueror)

M[inistr]y

Mobile (the people)

Moria-tanti (Sir John Mordaunt, general, 1697–1780)

Motao (Minorca)

Mura-clami (William Murray, 1st Earl of Mansfield, 1705–1793)

Myn-than (Minden), battle of

Nem-buds-ju (Jews)

Nin-kom-poo-po (George, Baron

Anson, 1697–1762)

Niphon (England), *see* Japan

Nob-o-di (William Wildman, 2nd Viscount Barrington, 1717–1793)

Or-nbos (Henry Osborn, or Osborne, admiral, 1698?–1771)

Osaca bay (Thames' estuary)

Ostrog (Hungary, the Hungarians)

Ostrog, princess of (Maria Theresa, Archduchess of Austria, Queen of Hungary and Bohemia, 1717–1780)

O[xford]

Pekin (Versailles)

Pensions given to 'a secularised Bonza from Ximo' (John Home, 1772–1808); 'a malcontent poet from Niphon' (Samuel Johnson, 1709–1784); 'a reformed comedian of Xicoco' (Thomas Sheridan, 1719–1788); 'an empiric who had out-lived his practice' (Dr. Thompson, king's physician); 'a decayed apothecary' (Henry Pemberton, 1694–1771); Taycho (William Pitt)

Phal-khan (Edward, 1st Baron Hawke, admiral, 1705–1781)

Phipps, Sir William (governor of Massachussetts, 1651–1695)

Phyl-Kholl (Alexander, 8th Baron Colville, vice-admiral, d. 1770)

Physician, a learned (?'Sir' John Hill, a fashionable quack, 1716?–1775)

Pol-hassan-akousti (Augustus III, Elector of Saxony, King of Poland)

Praff-part-phog (Sir Charles Pratt, 1st Earl Camden, 1714–1794, lord chancellor)

Qua-chu (Guadalupe)

Quamba-cun-dono (H.R.H. William Augustus, Duke of Cumberland)

Quan-bu-ku (duke)

Quib-quab (Quebec)

Quintus Curtius (Voltaire)

Quo (nobleman)

Raskalander (?Voltaire's *Pierre le grand*)

Relations, one of [Yak-Strot's] nearest (James Mackenzie)

Rha-rin-tumm (General John Barrington)

Rhum-kikh (William Beckford, Lord Mayor of London, 1709–1770)

Sab-oi (King of Sardinia)

Sa-rouf (Rochefort)

Scribe, the (secretary of the navy)

Sel-uon (Sir Charles Knowles, 1st bart., admiral, d. 1777)

Serednee Tartars (the Swedes)

Sey-seo-gun (admiral), *see* Ninkom-poo-po

Sey-seo-gun-sialty (admiralty)

She-it-kums-hi-til (Whigs)

Shi-tilk-ums-heit (Tories)

S[molle]tt (Tobias George, 1721–1771)

Soo-san-sin-o (John Carteret, Earl Granville, 1690–1763)

Sti-phi-rum-poo (Philip Yorke, 1st Earl of Hardwicke, 1690–1764)

Syko (Queen Anne, 1665–1714)

Taliessin (Taliesin, *c.* 550)

Tartarian Ocean (German Ocean)

Tartary (Germany)

Tartary (India)

Tartar princess (Charlotte Sophie, queen of George III, 1744–1818)

Tartar princess of the house of

Ostrog (Maria Theresa), *see* Ostrog, princess of

Taycho (William Pitt, 1st Earl of Chatham, 1708–1778)

Tensio-dai-sin (King Alfred, 849–901)

Terra Australis (Africa)

Terra Australis Incognita (Australia?)

Thin-quo (Martinique)

Thum-Khumm-qua (Thomas Cumming, Quaker merchant, d. 1774)

T[iconderog]a, unsuccessful attack on (1758)

Tickets of bamboo (bank-bills)

Tohn-syn (George, 4th Viscount Townshend, 1724–1807)

Toks (John Horne Tooke, politician, 1736–1812)

Topsy-turvy (Rockingham ministry, 1765–1766)

Tra-rep (Sir William Draper, lieut.-general, 1721–1787)

Treaty (of Utrecht, 1713); (of Paris, 1763)

Twitz-er (George Grenville, statesman, 1712–1770)

Tzin-khall (Senegal)

White Horse, temple of (House of Hanover, or Protestant succession), *see* Fakku-basi

Woodward, Dr. (?John, geologist and physician, 1665–1728)

Xicoco (Ireland)

Ximian (Scotch)

Ximo (Scotland)

Yaf-frai (Jeffrey Baron Amherst, field-marshal, 1717–1797)

Yak-strot (John Stuart, 3rd Earl of Bute, 1713–1792)

Ya-loff (James Wolfe, major-general, 1727–1759)

Yam-a-kheit (James, Marshal Keith, 1696–1758)

Yan-oni (Sir William Johnson, 1st bart., 1715–1774)

Yesso, farm of (Hanover)

Yesso, Tartars of (Hanoverian troops)

Zan-ti-fic (John Montagu, 4th Earl of Sandwich, 1718–1792)

Select Bibliography

I have not included a bibliography of Smollett's works because this is widely available elsewhere: see, for example, *The New Cambridge Bibliography of English Literature*, ed. George Watson, vol. 2: 1660–1800 (Cambridge, 1971), and *The English Novel*, ed. A.E. Dyson (1974), both of which contain bibliographical sections on Smollett by Lewis M. Knapp. For bibliographies of Smollett criticism see Francesco Cordasco, *Smollett Criticism, 1770–1924: a Bibliography Enumerative and Annotative* (Long Island, 1948), and his *Smollett Criticism, 1925–1945, A compilation* (Long Island, 1974), and Donald M. Korte, *An Annotated Bibliography of Smollett Scholarship, 1946–1968* (Ontario, 1969). For corrections and additions to the above see Boucé (below), pp. 392 ff.) The definitive modern biography of Smollett is that by Lewis M. Knapp, *Tobias Smollett, Doctor of Men and Manners* (Princeton, NJ, 1949), as is the definitive edition of Smollett's letters, *The Letters of Tobias Smollett* (Oxford, 1970).

Modern studies of Smollett

BOEGE, FRED W., *Smollett's Reputation as a Novelist* (Princeton, NJ 1947).

BOUCÉ, P.-G., *Les Romans de Smollett: étude critique* (Paris, 1971), translated in an abridged version as *The Novels of Tobias Smollett* (1976).

BRANDER, L., *Tobias Smollett* (British Council, 1951).

BRUCE, D., *Radical Doctor Smollett* (1964).

BUCK, H.S., *A Study in Smollett, Chiefly 'Peregrine Pickle'* (New Haven, Conn., 1925).

BUCK, H.S., *Smollett as Poet* (New Haven, 1927).

GIDDINGS, R., *The Tradition of Smollett* (1967).

GOLDBERG, M.A., *Smollett and the Scottish School* (Albuquerque, NM, 1959).

GRANT, D., *Tobias Smollett, A Study in Style* (Manchester, 1977).

JOLIAT, E., *Smollett et la France* (Paris, 1935).

JONES, C.E., *Smollett Studies* (Los Angels, 1942).

KAHRL, G.M., *Tobias Smollett Traveler-Novelist* (Chicago, 1945).

MARTZ, L.L., *The Later Career of Tobias Smollett* (New Haven, Conn., 1942).

ROUSSEAU G.S. and BOUCÉ P.-G. (eds), *Tobias Smollett: Essays Presented to Lewis M. Knapp* (New York, 1971).

ROUSSEAU, G.S., *Tobias Smollett: Essays of Two Decades* (Edinburgh, 1982).

SPECTOR, R.D., *Tobias Smollett* (New York, 1968).

WHITRIDGE, A., *Tobias Smollett: a Study of his Miscellaneous Works* (1925).

WIERSTRA, F.W. *Smollett and Dickens* (Dan Helder, 1928).

See also

ALTER, R., *Rouge's Progress* (Cambridge, Mass., 1964).

BROOKS, D., *Number and Pattern in the Eighteenth-century Novel* (1973).

DONOVAN, R.A., *The Shaping Vision* (Ithaca, N.Y., 1966).

MCKILLOP, A.D., *The Early Masters of English Fiction* (Lawrence, 1956).

MELCHIORI, G., *The Tightrope Walkers* (1956).

PAULSON, R., *Satire and the Novel in Eighteenth-century England* (New Haven, Conn., 1967).

PRESTON, T.R., *Not In Timon's Manner: Feeling, Misanthropy and Satire in Eighteenth Century England* (Alabama, 1975).

ROGERS, P., *The Augustan Vision* (1974).

Index

The index is divided into five parts: I Authors and anonymous works quoted from or cited; II Periodicals and journals; III Writers, books and painters to whom Smollett is compared explicitly or implicitly; IV Individual works by Smollett; V Selected topics of Smollett criticism.

I AUTHORS AND ANONYMOUS WORKS QUOTED FROM OR CITED

II PERIODICALS AND JOURNALS

III WRITERS, BOOKS AND PAINTERS TO WHOM SMOLLETT IS COMPARED EXPLICITLY OR IMPLICITLY

INDEX

IV INDIVIDUAL WORKS BY SMOLLETT

V SELECTED TOPICS OF SMOLLETT CRITICISM